Unorthodox Lawmaking

New Legislative Processes in the U.S. Congress

Third Edition

Barbara Sinclair
University of California, Los Angeles

CQ PRESS

A Division of Congressional Quarterly Inc.
Washington, D.C.

CQ Press
1255 22nd Street, NW, Suite 400
Washington, DC 20037

Phone: 202-729-1900; toll-free, 1-866-4CQ-PRESS (1-866-427-7737)

Web: www.cqpress.com

Cover design: Jeffrey Everett

∞ The paper used in this publication exceeds the requirements of the American National Standard for Information Sciences—Permanence of Paper for Printed Library Materials, ANSI Z39.48-1992.

Printed and bound in the United States of America

11   10   09   08   07   1   2   3   4   5

Library of Congress Cataloging-in-Publication Data

Sinclair, Barbara
    Unorthodox lawmaking: new legislative processes in the U.S. congress /
Barbara Sinclair. — 3rd ed.
        p.   cm.
    Includes bibliographical references and index.
    ISBN 978-0-87289-306-1 (alk. paper)
    1. Legislation—United States.   2. United States—Politics and
government—2001–   I. Title.

KF4945.S58 2007
328.73'077—dc22   2007007716

To
Dick Fenno,
teacher, mentor, friend

Contents

Preface   viii

c h a p t e r 1

Clean Air: An Introduction to How the Legislative Process Has Changed   1

A Note on Data   8

c h a p t e r 2

Multiple Paths: The Legislative Process in the House of Representatives   10

Bill Introduction   11

Bill Referral   11

Postcommittee Adjustments   20

Suspension of the Rules   23

Special Rules   25

On the Floor   35

Unorthodox Lawmaking in the House   42

c h a p t e r 3

Routes and Obstacles: The Legislative Process in the Senate   43

Bill Introduction   43

Bill Referral   44

Postcommittee Adjustments   49

Scheduling Legislation for the Floor   51

The Senate Floor   61

Unorthodox Lawmaking in the Senate   72

c h a p t e r   4

Getting One Bill: Reconciling House-Senate Differences

Getting One Bill: Reconciling House-Senate
Differences   73
   Nonconference Reconciliation Procedures   73
   Conference Committees   76
   The Final Step   89
   Reconciling Differences: How Much Change?   90

c h a p t e r   5

Omnibus Legislation, the Budget Process,
and Summits   91
   Omnibus Legislation and the Budget Process   92
   Congress, the President, and Summitry   102
   What Is the Regular Process?   105

c h a p t e r   6

Why and How the Legislative Process Changed   108
   From Decentralization to Individualism in the Senate   108
   Reform and Its Legacy in the House   110
   Budget Reform   112
   A Hostile Political Climate as a Force
      for Innovation: The 1980s and Early 1990s   113
   How Internal Reform and a Hostile Climate Spawned
      Unorthodox Lawmaking   116
   Unorthodox Lawmaking in the Republican
      Congress   131

c h a p t e r   7

The 2005 Energy Bill: About as Orthodox as
It Gets   139
   House Committee Action   141
   Preparing the Bill for the Floor   144
   House Floor Action   146
   Senate Committee Action   147

Senate Floor Consideration   148
The Conference   153
About as Orthodox as It Gets: Enacting Energy
    Legislation in 2005   156

c h a p t e r 8

Medicare/Prescription Drug Legislation: Making Sweeping Policy Change in a Highly Partisan Environment

Medicare/Prescription Drug Legislation:
Making Sweeping Policy Change in a
Highly Partisan Environment   161

The Bush Proposal and the Congressional
    Response   162
Pre-Floor Action in the Senate   164
House Committee Action   166
Senate Floor Consideration   167
House Pre-Floor Decisions   170
House Floor Consideration   171
Reconciling the House and Senate Bills   173
Passing the Conference Report   177
Aftermath   180
Making Sweeping Policy Change in a Highly
    Partisan Environment   181

c h a p t e r 9

Medical Malpractice Caps: Senate Rules and
Unorthodox Lawmaking—or Not   186

House Action   187
Senate Stalemate   190
The Impact of Senate Rules   193

c h a p t e r 1 0

The Budget Process as an Instrument for
Policy Change: Clinton's Economic Program   196

Budget Policy Making and Politics:
    The Context in 1993   197
Committing to the Clinton Plan: Crafting and
    Passing the Budget Resolution   198

Delivering on Promised Policy Change:
Reconciliation   200
Unified Government, Procedural Control,
and Policy Success   210

c h a p t e r 1 1

Republican Majorities, Divided Government, and Budget Politics   215

The Republican Revolution and the Budget Process,
1995–1996   215
Balancing the Budget, 1997   235
Budget Politics after the Balanced Budget Deal,
1998–2000   243

c h a p t e r 1 2

The Republican Tax-Cutting Agenda and the Budget Process: The Bush Tax Cuts of 2001 and 2003   248

Delivering: Cutting Taxes in 2001   249
Once More with Feeling: The 2003 Tax Cut   259
Cutting Taxes via Unorthodox Lawmaking   263
Budget Policy and Politics since the Early 1990s:
A Final Word   264

c h a p t e r 1 3

The Consequences of Unorthodox Lawmaking   268

Lawmaking in the Contemporary Congress   268
Unorthodox Lawmaking and Legislative Outcomes   271
Other Costs and Benefits   276
Assessing Unorthodox Lawmaking   283

References   289
Useful Web Sites for Congress Watchers   293
Abbreviations of Commonly Used In-text
Citations   294
Index   295

Preface

DURING MY FIRST TWENTY YEARS of doing research on Congress and teaching courses about the institution, the gap between the legislative process that I observed and still see on Capitol Hill and the legislative process described in U.S. government textbooks became a chasm. Like most teachers, I tried to give my students a sense of the contemporary legislative process in all its variety while still presenting the "textbook" model as the standard. That approach, I came to believe, was no longer adequate or accurate.

The reception that earlier editions of this book received from my colleagues persuaded me that most share my perception; thus another edition.

This book describes how the legislative process in the U.S. Congress really works today. In it I show how the process has changed, explore the reasons for the change, and examine its consequences. Although based on original research, the book is written with the nonspecialist in mind. No extensive knowledge of Congress is presupposed. I believe that it will help prepare readers to pursue further studies of Congress if they so choose, but my primary aim is to enable them to make sense of congressional politics and to judge claims about congressional performance.

I refer to the contemporary legislative process as "unorthodox lawmaking" to distinguish frequently employed contemporary procedures and practices from what is still often presented in textbooks as the standard process. The term emphasizes the extent of change and gives me a handy way of referring to a set of procedures and practices that are either new or much more frequently employed than they used to be. In fact, the process for major legislation is now less likely to conform to the textbook model than it is to unorthodox lawmaking.

This new edition is similar to the previous ones in intent, organization, and mostly in argument. Wherever possible, I have updated all the data series through the end of the 108th Congress (2003–2004), have substituted more current examples for many of the older ones, and have replaced most of the case studies with new ones. I have also brought the examination of changes and trends up to date, especially through a discussion of heightened partisanship and its consequences. I retained several of the budget case studies and some of the examples from the first and second editions because I believe they help to illuminate how unorthodox lawmaking works in a variety of political contexts.

I chose to describe the contemporary legislative process early in the book, in Chapters 2–5, followed by a chapter that analyzes the trajectory of change and the reasons for it. For those who prefer their history first, the order of those chapters can be reversed, with Chapter 6 read before Chapters 2–5. Chapters 7–9, the case studies of nonbudget legislation, could easily be read after Chapters 2–4 and before Chapter 5, which deals with the budget process.

In addition to the quantitative analysis of the process on major legislation described in Chapter 1, this book is based on my observations and experiences as an American Political Science Association congressional fellow in the office of the House majority leader from 1978 until 1979 and in the office of the Speaker from 1987 until 1988 on an informal basis, as well as interviews with members of Congress, their staffs, and informed observers over the course of more years than I am now willing to admit. I owe Jim Wright, Speaker of the House from 1987 to 1989, and his staff an enormous debt for giving me the opportunity to observe the legislative process from the inside. I am also grateful to all of those very busy people who made time to talk to me over the years and from whom I learned so much. All unattributed quotations are from interviews I conducted.

I would especially like to thank Peter Robinson, formerly of the House Parliamentarian's Office and of Speaker Wright's staff; Stanley Bach, Richard Beth, and Walter Oleszek of the Congressional Research Service (CRS); and Robert Dove, formerly Senate parliamentarian. All are incredibly knowledgeable and extremely generous in sharing their expertise. Elizabeth Rybicki, also of CRS, is fast moving into the same august company in terms of expertise and has always been at the same level in terms of generosity and helpfulness. Stan Bach, Michael Kraft, and Sandy Maisel read the first-edition manuscript and gave me invaluable comments and advice. I want them to know how much I appreciate their detailed and thoughtful reviews; they significantly improved the manuscript. Robin Kolodny, Bruce Oppenheimer, and Steve Smith, who read the proposal and much of an early draft, provided perceptive and helpful advice. Cary R. Covington, Rebekah Herrick, and David Menefee-Libey reviewed the first edition and provided me with many useful suggestions for improving the second.

Stan Bach of the CRS read the new case studies for the second edition and the entire third edition with his discerning eye and commented on them with his combination of great knowledge and common sense. I am truly grateful. Bruce Oppenheimer at Vanderbilt University and Allen Schick at the University of Maryland also reviewed the third edition and gave me useful suggestions. David Jones, Gregory Koger, and Alan Rozzi provided superb research assistance. Much of the quantitative material has been presented in papers at professional meetings; I thank the many colleagues who commented on those papers. I continue to learn from my colleagues in the congressional scholarly community; there are too many to list here, but I thank them all. Of course, none of these people is responsible for any remaining errors. Finally, thanks to Brenda Carter, Charisse Kiino, Allison McKay, and Lorna Notsch of CQ Press. They have been great to work with.

Clean Air: An Introduction to How the Legislative Process Has Changed

In 1970 CONGRESS PASSED A PATH-BREAKING Clean Air Act, legislation Congressional Quarterly called "the most comprehensive air pollution control bill in U.S. history" (*Congressional Quarterly Almanac* 1970, 472).

Reported by the House Interstate and Foreign Commerce Committee, the bill was considered on the House floor under an open rule allowing all germane amendments. Of the nine amendments offered, eight were defeated, most on voice votes; only one technical amendment was accepted. The bill passed the House 375–1.

In the Senate the Public Works Committee reported a bill stronger than the House legislation or the administration's draft. After two days of floor debate, during which ten amendments were accepted by voice vote and two rejected by roll calls, the Senate voted 73–0 to pass the strong bill. The conference committee, consisting of five members of the House committee and nine senators, came to an agreement on a bill much closer to the Senate's stringent version than to the House's milder bill, and both chambers approved the conferees' version by voice vote.

Although the bill was far stronger than the legislation he had initially proposed, President Richard Nixon signed the Clean Air Act, "one of the most far-reaching laws ever passed by Congress to regulate the domestic economy," in the words of a prominent journalist. The act set auto emission standards so stringent that it forced the development of new technology, and it directed the Environmental Protection Agency to establish national air quality standards (Cohen 1992, 13).

* * *

By 1989, when the 101st Congress began work on a major revision of the Clean Air Act, the political and institutional environment had changed, and the path the legislation traversed to enactment was very different from that of its 1970 predecessor. In the Senate the slightly renamed Public Works and Environment Committee again reported a strong bill. The bill was considered on the Senate floor for six days, but the majority leader, George Mitchell, D-Maine, could not muster the sixty votes needed to overcome a threatened filibuster. To construct a bill that could pass the chamber, the majority leader began negotiations with the administration and with a large and shifting group of senators. Members of the Environment Committee participated on a continuous basis, but many other senators with an interest in specific issues also took part. After a month of talks, an agreement was reached. To guard against any unraveling of the compromise, Mitchell and President George H. W. Bush pledged to oppose floor amendments, even those that reflected their policy preferences.

Mitchell offered the compromise worked out in the talks as a substitute amendment to the bill the Environment Committee had reported. He negotiated a complex unanimous consent agreement (UCA) for considering the bill on the floor. That UCA did not limit either debate or amendments; it simply required senators to put the amendments they wished to offer on a list. This provided a modicum of order to floor consideration of the bill. After ten days' debate over a month's time, the Senate passed the bill 89–11. Of about 250 amendments on the list, 25 were offered and pushed to a roll call vote; nine of these passed. None was a "deal breaker."

In the House the legislation was referred to three committees, rather than just one as the 1970 bill had been. The Energy and Commerce Committee, successor to the Interstate and Foreign Commerce Committee, was the lead committee, and after protracted internal negotiations it reported legislation that represented a compromise among its factions. One key issue, however, had been decided by extremely close votes in both the subcommittee and the full committee, and Speaker Tom Foley, D-Wash., was concerned that the issue might well lead to a bitter party-splitting battle on the floor. He thus instructed the lead representatives of the two Democratic factions, Henry Waxman of California, chair of the subcommittee, and John Dingell of Michigan, chair of the full committee, to work out a compromise. In order to pressure them to act expeditiously, Foley set a deadline for floor action on the legislation. The Speaker and his aides then worked with Waxman and Dingell to help them come to an agreement. The other committees, also under Speaker-imposed deadlines, reported their legislative language.

Unlike its 1970 predecessor, the 1990 clean air legislation went to the floor under a rule that restricted amendments to the nineteen listed in the Rules Committee report and that carefully structured how these amendments would be considered. The crucial Waxman-Dingell deal was offered as an amendment on the floor and approved 405–15. In all, six amendments were pushed to a roll call vote and five passed; none of these threatened the key compromises. The House then approved the bill 401–21.

Speaker Foley chose 130 conferees to represent the 7 committees with some jurisdiction over the bill's subject matter. Nine members from two committees represented the Senate. Protracted negotiations produced a bill that passed both chambers easily. A dramatic expansion of the Clean Air Act, the 1990 bill for the first time set up a program for controlling acid rain, established a stringent new program to control emissions of toxic air pollutants, and set new standards and timetables for improving urban air quality (*Congress and the Nation* 1993, 469, 473–474). Although it was considerably stronger than the draft he had proposed, President Bush signed the legislation.

* * *

These examples illustrate how greatly the legislative process on major legislation has changed since the early 1970s.[1] The legislative process on the 1970 Clean Air Act perfectly fits the bill-becomes-a-law diagram that is still a staple of American politics and legislative process textbooks (see Table 1.1). The 1970 bill was considered by a single committee in each chamber. It came to the House floor as drafted and approved by the committee, and it was considered there under an open rule allowing all germane amendments. The Senate also considered the bill as drafted by its committee; no senator mounted a filibuster, and no amending marathon occurred. After both chambers had passed the bill, a small group of senior members of the two committees got together in conference and worked out a compromise between the House and Senate versions.

The process on the 1990 bill, by contrast, was much more complex and not amenable to a nice, neat diagram. The legislation was considered by several committees in the House, and in both chambers compromises arrived at through informal processes altered the bills after the committees reported their legislation. Floor procedures were complex and tailored to the specific bill at issue. In the Senate the real possibility of a filibuster shaped the process, making it necessary for Majority Leader Mitchell to build through negotiations an oversized coalition. The final conference agreement was worked out by a much larger and more diverse group of members than in 1970.

---

1. These accounts are based largely on primary documents, interviews (in the case of the 1990 act), and the following secondary sources: Congressional Quarterly's accounts, Cohen (1992), and Smith (1995, chap. 12).

TABLE 1.1   The 1970 Clean Air Act as an Example of the Textbook Legislative
            Process

Action	House	Senate
Committee	HR17255 referred to the Committee on Interstate and Foreign Commerce. Hearings held March 16–21 and April 14, 1970. Bill marked up. Bill reported June 3, 1970. Rules Committee grants open rule.	S4358 referred to the Senate Public Works Committee. Hearings held March 16–20, March 23–26, and April 17, 1970. Bill marked up. Bill reported September 17, 1970.
Floor	Considered in Committee of the Whole and passed by the House June 10, 1970.	Debated on the floor September 21–22 and passed September 22, 1970.
Conference	Conferees appointed. Conference meets. Conference agreement reached. Conferees file report December 17, 1970.	
Floor	House approves conference report December 18, 1970.	Senate approves conference report December 18, 1970.
Presidential	Sent to the president. President signs December 31, 1970.	

In the contemporary Congress the textbook diagram describes the legislative process for fewer and fewer major bills. The seemingly unorthodox legislative process on the 1990 Clean Air Act is actually more characteristic of contemporary major legislation than the supposedly standard textbook process that the 1970 Clean Air Act went through. To be sure, even during the textbook era not all legislation followed the relatively simple, straightforward process depicted by Table 1.1; there always have been alternative paths. Their use, however, was extraordinary, not ordinary; most major legislation followed the textbook process.[2]

Today the bill that, like the 1970 Clean Air Act, is reported by a single committee and considered on the floor under a simple open rule still exists,

---

2. Shortcut processes to handle noncontroversial legislation did and have continued to exist.

but it is not likely to be major legislation and, even so, it is increasingly rare. In fact, the legislative process is now bifurcated to a considerable extent. Most bills are passed through short-cut procedures—suspension of the rules in the House (see Chapter 2) and unanimous consent during the end-of-the-day "wrap-up" in the Senate (see Chapter 3). These, however, are not major bills; they are neither controversial nor far-reaching in impact. In contrast, the legislative process on major legislation is now regularly characterized by a variety of what were once unorthodox practices and procedures.

Rather than being sent to one committee in each chamber, many measures are considered by several committees, especially in the House, while some measures bypass committee altogether. Not infrequently, after a bill has been reported—but before it reaches the floor—major substantive changes are worked out via informal processes. Omnibus measures of great scope are a regular part of the legislative scene, and formal executive-congressional summits to work out deals on legislation are no longer considered extraordinary. On the House floor most major measures are considered under complex and usually restrictive rules often tailored to deal with problems specific to the bill at issue. In the Senate bills are regularly subject to large numbers of floor amendments that are not necessarily germane; filibuster threats are an everyday fact of life, affecting all aspects of the legislative process and making cloture votes a routine part of the process. This book explores how and why the legislative process in the U.S. Congress has changed since the 1970s and examines the consequences of those changes.

Although the changes in the legislative process in the past several decades that I focus on here were preceded by a long period of stability, they are by no means unique. The Constitution does not specify how Congress is to carry out its core task of lawmaking; beyond a few basic requirements, it allows each house to determine its own rules and procedures. During its history of more than two hundred years, the Congress has altered its legislative process a number of times.

In the very early years the legislative process in both the House and Senate emphasized the full membership's responsibility for lawmaking. The full membership debated a subject on the floor, decided whether legislation was warranted, and, if it was, laid out substantive guidelines. Then a special or select committee was appointed to draft legislation according to those guidelines (Cooper and Young 1989; Risjord 1994).

Even in the early decades not all business could be given so much time and attention; minor business was sent first to small committees. The House then began to create standing—that is, permanent—committees to handle recurrent complex issues, and the Senate began to send to a particular select committee all matters relating to the subject for which the committee had been initially created. During the second decade of the

1800s in the House and not much later in the Senate, standing committees became predominant. The committees did the initial work on legislation; only after they were finished did the rest of the membership have their say.

Floor procedure, too, has changed over time. In the early years both chambers' floor proceedings were relatively fluid and unstructured; even the House placed few limits on members' debate time (Binder 1996). Considering bills in the order they were introduced, the House was able to dispose of all of its business. Soon, however, House floor procedures became problematic. In 1811 the House adopted its first significant restrictions on floor debate, and throughout the nineteenth century the chamber struggled to develop a fair and efficient way of setting and ordering its floor agenda. Not until the 1880s and 1890s did the House develop its premier device for floor scheduling of major legislation: special rules from the Rules Committee (Oppenheimer 1994). Special rules, which required a simple majority of the House membership for approval, allowed legislation to be taken up out of order; this innovation made it possible for the majority party and its leaders, if they controlled the Rules Committee in fact as well as in form, to control the House schedule.

Senate floor procedure changed in much less basic ways over the course of its history (Bach 1994). The chamber's lack of limits on debate, initially the result of no considered decision, became over time a revered defining characteristic (Binder 1997). In the early years the Senate's small size made it unnecessary to limit the time members could debate an issue. Eventually, however, senators' extended debate prerogative became a problem. By then, the prerogative was well entrenched; the formidable barrier the rules themselves erected against change was fortified by the widely accepted myth that extended debate reflected the framers' intent (Binder and Smith 1997). Under extraordinary pressure from the president and the public, the Senate in 1917 for the first time changed its rules in such a way as to make cutting off debate possible. The resulting cloture procedure, however, was cumbersome and required a two-thirds vote for success.

Why has the legislative process changed over time? The long evolution of the legislative process is far too complex to review here, and scholars do not agree about just why things happened as they did (Cooper 1981; Gamm and Shepsle 1989). Certainly increases in workload, alterations in the political and social environment, and the strategic behavior of parties and of members as individuals were important determinants. For example, increases in the congressional workload and in the size of its own membership put pressure on the House to modify procedures that had adequately served a smaller, less busy legislature. Majorities, especially partisan majorities, found their legislative goals stymied by chamber rules that facilitated minority obstructionism. These majorities were able to change such rules in the House but were largely blocked in the Senate. On a more abstract, theoretical level, changes in the legislative process can be seen as the responses of members to the problems and opportunities the institutional structure and the political environment present to members as they pursue, as individuals or collectively, their goals of reelection, influence in the chamber, and good public policy (Fenno 1973; Sinclair 1995).

The alterations in the legislative process since the 1970s are the latest installment in an ongoing story. Examining them sheds light not only on the contemporary legislative process (what is happening on Capitol Hill today) but also on the broader political process. The study also provides insight into how democratic institutions like the Congress evolve and adapt.

Chapters 2 through 5 describe the procedures and practices that make up the new legislative process and document their frequency. Chapter 2 begins with the introduction of a bill and proceeds step by step through the process in the House, examining and illustrating frequently used procedures at each stage. Chapter 3 traces the path a bill takes through the Senate. Before 1970 one could speak of a standard legislative process that most major legislation traversed, but as these chapters show there are now many routes from introduction to enactment. Once the House and Senate have passed legislation, the two different versions must be reconciled, as I explain in Chapter 4. Chapter 5 addresses omnibus legislation, the budget process, and legislative-executive summits.

In Chapter 6 the historical origins of contemporary lawmaking are explored and the change in frequency of particular practices over time is documented. Chapters 7 through 12 use case studies to analyze unorthodox lawmaking. The accounts of the 2005 energy bill, the 2003 Medicare/prescription drug bill and the struggle over medical malpractice reform illustrate the range and variability of the contemporary legislative process. The process on the 2005 energy bill was about as close to the old standard process as one is likely to see now on major, controversial legislation; even so, it included unorthodox elements and the process on the failed energy bills in the preceding two Congresses was much less orthodox. The legislative process on the Medicare/prescription drug bill shows few similarities to the textbook process; a few years ago it would have been considered radically unorthodox but, in fact, shows a number of characteristics in common with what is emerging as typical on top priority, controversial legislation. The battles over medical malpractice reform illustrate what an important role the Senate's special rules—especially extended debate—now play in the legislative process.

The next three chapters focus on the budget process and policymaking through the budget process. They show how the process works and how important it has become in contemporary policymaking. The enactment of President Bill Clinton's economic program in 1993, the subject of Chapter 10, and of President George W. Bush's tax cuts in 2001 and 2003, discussed in Chapter 12, illustrate the use of the budget process as an instrument of comprehensive policy change. Budget politics under divided control—including the Republicans' attempt in 1995 to pass a balanced budget that included a restructuring of Medicare, Medicaid, welfare, and a number of other major programs and the 1997 balanced budget deal between Clinton and Congress—is the focus of Chapter 11. In addition to demonstrating how the contemporary legislative process works, all of the case study chapters are intended to illustrate how the political environment influences that process.

Chapter 13 examines the impact that the new procedures and practices have on legislative outcomes and on how Congress functions. Congress is the least-liked branch of the national government; only a fraction of the American people expresses confidence in the Congress. Americans are not happy with the congressional process or often with the policy produced (Hibbing and Theiss-Morse 1995). Is unorthodox lawmaking, in part, responsible, either directly or indirectly? Does it enhance or inhibit the likelihood of a bill becoming law? What other effects does the change in process have on how Congress functions? Does it foster or discourage deliberation, the development and bringing to bear of expertise, the inclusion of a broad range of interests, and informed and timely decision making?

Americans expect a lot from Congress. Congress should represent the people and pass laws that both reflect the will of the people and that work. That is, citizens expect members of Congress to bring into the legislative process the views, needs, and interests of the people they are elected to represent, and they expect Congress to pass laws that are responsive to popular majorities and that deal promptly and effectively with pressing national problems. Has unorthodox lawmaking made Congress more or less capable of carrying out the formidable tasks with which it is charged?

A Note on Data

I argue here that the legislative process on major legislation has changed. To show this is so, I need to define major legislation and then document change over time. Major measures are defined by the list of major legislation in the *CQ Weekly* (before 1998 *Congressional Quarterly Weekly Report*), augmented by those measures on which key votes occurred (again according to the *CQ Weekly*). This provides a list of about forty to fifty bills (and some other measures such as budget resolutions and constitutional amendments) for each Congress that close contemporary observers considered major. I then examine the course these major measures traversed in selected Congresses. I supplement my data by drawing where possible on the work of other scholars.

The Congresses selected are the 87th (1961–1962), the 89th (1965–1966), and the 91st (1969–1970), all prereform Congresses;[3] the 94th (1975–1976), the first reformed Congress; the 95th (1977–1978), the first Congress of the Carter presidency; the 97th (1981–1982), the first Congress of the Reagan presidency; the 100th (1987–1988) and the 101st (1989–1990), the last Reagan and first George H. W. Bush Congresses; the 103rd (1993–1994), the first Clinton Congress; the 104th (1995–1996), the first Congress in forty years with Republican control of both houses; the 105th (1997–1998); and the 107th (2001–2002) and 108th (2003–2004), the first two Congresses of the George W. Bush presidency. Democrats enjoyed unified control of the presidency and both houses of the Congress in the 87th, 89th, 95th, and 103rd Congresses. Republicans controlled the presidency and the Senate in the 97th; the presidency and both chambers during the 108th Congress and during the first half of 2001, when, with the switch of Jim Jeffords to caucusing with the Democrats, control of the Senate switched to the Democrats. The other selected Congresses saw divided control, with Democrats the majority party until the 104th and the Republicans in the 104th through the 108th. (The Republicans controlled both chambers in the 109th and some data on that Congress are available and included; the Democrats won both chambers in the 2006 elections and so organized both chambers for the 110th Congress [2007–2008]).

---

3. The 89th was also the "Great Society" Congress in which an enormous amount of highly significant legislation was passed—e.g. the Voting Rights Act, Medicare. See Chapter 6 for a discussion of the reforms of the 1970s.

Multiple Paths: The Legislative Process in the House of Representatives

THE LEGISLATIVE PROCESS IN THE CONTEMPORARY Congress is varied and complex. The old textbook process depicted in Table 1.1 was predictable and linear, with one stage following another in an unvarying sequence. At many stages there is now no single, normal route but rather a number of different paths that legislation may follow. The best way to understand the contemporary legislative process is to begin with the introduction of a bill and proceed step by step through the process in each chamber, examining frequently used options at each stage. That is what this and the following three chapters do.

This is not a book on parliamentary procedure; procedures that are obscure and seldom employed are of no interest here. Rather, my aim is to make understandable the procedures and practices that occur on the major legislation considered during any contemporary Congress.[1]

For convenience, I begin the journey in the House of Representatives. Most legislation and other measures—budget resolutions and constitutional amendments—may begin in either chamber. The Constitution requires that tax legislation originate in the House, the people's chamber, and by custom the House also acts first on appropriations—that is, spending—bills. The Senate, however, is fully coequal as a policy initiator. Even in the tax area, the Senate can initiate policy change by amending a minor House-passed tax bill. Yet because the House tends to act before the Sen-

---

1. I have relied heavily on Tiefer (1989), Gold et al. (1992), Oleszek (2004), and Gold (2004) for the fine points of procedure. The people at the Congressional Research Service, especially Stanley Bach, Richard Beth, and Walter Oleszek, were invaluable sources of information. Peter Robinson was also extremely helpful.

ate (Strom and Rundquist 1977), I start with action in that chamber. Although action on the same *issue* may take place simultaneously in the two chambers, formal action on legislation is a sequential process: the House and the Senate cannot act on the same *bill* at the same time.

Bill Introduction

To introduce a bill, a member of the House simply drops it into the "hopper," a wooden box at the front of the chamber, when the House is in session.[2] Bill introduction has not changed in recent years. Only members of the House may introduce bills or resolutions in the House, and a member may introduce as many measures as he or she wishes. Thus even the president needs to find a member of the House to introduce legislation, although doing so is seldom a problem.

In fact, the legislation members introduce has many different origins. Some bills are introduced at the behest of interest groups or even individual constituents, some come from federal government agencies and departments, and some represent a member's own personal policy priorities. The legislative process in Congress is open and permeable. Although only members of Congress can perform official acts like introducing bills and voting, members' behavior is influenced by the president, interest groups, constituents, the media, and public opinion. That makes all of them significant actors in the legislative process.

Bill Referral

Once introduced, the bill is referred to the committee or committees of jurisdiction. Because committees are the primary shapers of legislation and because they differ in membership and perspective, which committee receives the bill can make a difference to the legislative outcome. The

---

2. The term *bill* is here used for bills, which are designated by the prefixes HR (for House of Representatives) and S (for Senate), and for joint resolutions, designated H.J.Res. and S.J.Res. There is no practical difference between the two in process and in effect; both become law. I try to use the term *measure* to indicate a broader class of legislative entities, including not only bills but also concurrent resolutions (H.Con.Res. or S.Con.Res.), which do not become law, and constitutional amendments. In process terms the difference between bills and joint resolutions, on the one hand, and concurrent resolutions and constitutional amendments, on the other, is that the last two do not require the president's signature. Resolutions, designated H.Res. or S.Res., deal with matters entirely within the purview of one body and do not require action by the other.

parliamentarian, a professional, nonpartisan employee of the House, handles referrals under the supervision of the Speaker, whose prerogative it is to make this decision. Referrals are governed by the rules of the House, specifically Rule X, which specifies what subject matters fall within the purview of each committee, and by precedents. Thus, referral decisions are usually fairly routine, but there may be some discretion, especially when new issues arise (King 1994).

Multiple Referral

In 1975 the House changed its rules and permitted the referral of legislation to more than one committee. The prominent issues had changed: many had become more complex, and they no longer fit neatly into the jurisdiction of a single committee. Since that rules change, multiple referral has become increasingly common, especially on major legislation. From the Congresses of the late 1980s (1987–1990) to the present, about 20 percent of all measures have been referred to more than one committee. When only major legislation is considered, the likelihood of multiple referral is even higher. In most Congresses since the late 1980s about three out of ten major measures were multiply referred.[3]

Most multiply referred measures—two-thirds to three-quarters—are sent to two committees. Again, major legislation is different; in the Congresses of the late 1980s and early 1990s (100th, 101st, 103rd), more than half of multiply referred legislation went to three or more committees and, in some cases, to many more. President Bill Clinton's reinventing government legislation (the Government Reform and Savings Act of 1993), for example, went to seventeen House committees; his health care bill was referred to ten. The big trade bill passed by the 100th Congress (1987–1988) was referred to six committees, and five other committees wrote trade-related legislation that was incorporated into the omnibus trade bill. In 1989 a bill to provide aid to Poland and Hungary was sent to seven committees.

Since the Republicans gained control of the House in the 1994 elections, the percentage of major bills referred to more than two committees has been declining—from 29 percent in the 104th Congress to only 7 percent in the 108th. However, in every Congress, there continue to be bills sent to many committees. So, in the 104th, the bill to abolish the Department of Commerce was referred to eleven committees and immigration reform to seven. In the 108th, the bill to overhaul government intelligence operations was sent to thirteen committees.

---

3. Tables with the complete data series for this and most of the other "unorthodox processes" discussed in this chapter can be found in Chapter 6.

It is easy to understand why many committees had jurisdiction over the bill to reinvent government; the bill concerned many federal agencies, each one under the purview of a different committee. But why was the trade bill referred to many committees? Even more curious, why was legislation to aid two countries in eastern Europe multiply referred? The trade bill not only concerned unfair trade practices and authority to negotiate trade agreements, it also contained provisions on the retraining of workers displaced by plant closings and on grants to schools and colleges to improve the teaching of math, science, and foreign languages. The trade bill mandated negotiations with foreign governments to establish a competitive exchange rate for the dollar and to create an independent agency to buy loans owed by developing countries at a discount, required the identification of foreign owners of U.S. businesses and real estate, and prohibited government agencies from buying from companies in foreign countries whose governments restrict purchases from U.S. businesses (*Congressional Quarterly Weekly Report,* May 2, 1987, 813). On the Poland-Hungary bill, the Foreign Affairs Committee, which has jurisdiction over foreign aid, played the lead role, but Ways and Means was involved because of its jurisdiction over granting special trade benefits to foreign countries; programs for scholarships for Polish students, for technical training for Polish farmers and businesspeople, and for the promotion of U.S. exports to Poland and Hungary involved still other committees.

The original 1975 multiple referral rule instructed the Speaker to refer a bill to all committees with jurisdiction. Before 1995 the Speaker had three types of multiple referral available (Davidson and Oleszek 1992). The most frequent type was a joint referral: a bill was sent to two or more committees simultaneously. Or a bill could be divided up and various sections and titles sent to different committees. Such split referrals have been relatively rare; dividing up complex legislation can be difficult. More common were sequential referrals: a measure was assigned to two or more committees in sequence. Typically, the first committee had the most jurisdiction and consequently the largest legislative role.

The Speaker also could combine types of referrals. Thus, legislation might be sent initially to the two or more committees with the most jurisdiction under a joint referral and then sequentially to other committees with lesser jurisdictional interests. As amended in 1977, the multiple referral rule allowed the Speaker to set a reporting deadline for committees under any sort of referral.[4]

---

4. By custom, time limits were set on sequential but not on joint or split referrals. Since the Speaker could decide the type of referral to use, he or she exercised discretion as to time limits.

The 1995 rule, the aim of which was to streamline the process, abolished the old form of joint referral and instructed the Speaker to designate a primary committee (Evans and Oleszek 1995). As interpreted, the rule actually allows for several primary committees under a split referral. During the first one hundred days of the 104th Congress, split referrals were frequently used. The welfare reform bill, for example, was split among the Ways and Means Committee, the Economic and Educational Opportunities Committee, and the Agriculture Committee. Joint referrals and, to an extent, sequential referrals have been replaced by the referral of legislation to a primary committee (based on "the weight of the bill") and *additional initial referral* to one or more other committees.

Committees that receive legislation on additional initial referral may consider it immediately; they need not wait for the primary committee to report before beginning their work. In that sense the new process is similar to the old joint referral procedure. However, when the primary committee reports, the other committees are subject to time limits at the Speaker's discretion; if time limits are imposed, a committee must report within the specified time or be automatically discharged, that is, have the legislation taken away from it. The usual form of such a referral reads, "referred to the [primary] committee, and in addition to the [secondary] committees, for a period to be subsequently determined by the Speaker, in each case for consideration of such provisions as fall within the jurisdiction of the committee concerned."

Once the primary committee reported, Republican Speakers imposed time limits on the other committees if they had not yet reported. Those time limits often were short, in some cases one day. After Republicans took control of the House, turf fights between committees seemed to decline in frequency, although they by no means became extinct. The extent to which the new rule was responsible is unclear. Certainly, when the Republicans first took the majority, committee chairs were under intense pressure from the party leadership and the membership to not allow turf fights to interfere with passing bills on the Republican agenda. And the Republican leadership continued to exert significant control over committee decision making.

Committees given additional initial referral do not always report legislation. Quite frequently the record will indicate that the committee was discharged. In the 108th Congress, for example, the bankruptcy bill was referred to the Judiciary Committee and, in addition to the Financial Services Committee. Judiciary reported but Financial Services was discharged.

The fact that a secondary committee was discharged does not necessarily mean it was not substantively involved in the legislation. In some cases, to be sure, the matter under its jurisdiction may have been so minor that the committee did not see any point in bothering to participate. Fetal protection legislation that made it a separate crime to injure or kill a fetus in vitro was referred to the Judiciary Committee and in addition to the Armed Services Committee because of its jurisdiction over military personnel, including crimes committed by members of the armed forces. It is likely that Armed Services let itself be discharged because of its relatively minimal jurisdictional interest. Alternatively, a committee that allows itself to be discharged may have had its concerns met by the lead committee informally; it may have been promised a floor amendment or, if the bill amended existing legislation (as is often the case), the committee may have been satisfied by the text of the bill on matters under its jurisdiction and so it saw no need to change it. By not reporting, a committee does not give up any claim to jurisdiction. The committee often will receive representation on the conference committee, as Chapter 4 discusses. When the party leadership is ready to take a bill to the floor, it may ask secondary committees to forgo marking up the bill so as to speed up the process.

What does multiple referral mean for how committees work and for how legislation is processed? Clearly, on much of the most important legislation of a Congress, committees must work together if they are to legislate successfully. Some committees—ones that frequently share jurisdiction—have developed standard operating procedures for working together. However, if the committees involved have substantially different and noncongruent perspectives, the relationship can be difficult and may make getting any legislation to the floor harder. In 1990, for example, the Ways and Means Committee and the Education and Labor Committee preferred distinctly different approaches to child care legislation; during months of negotiation, neither side was willing to budge. Only after the Speaker intervened and forced closure was an agreement finally reached.

Some participants and knowledgeable observers contend that the multiple referral rule, especially as it functioned under Democratic control before 1995, encouraged committees to be even more turf conscious and to make even more, often tenuous, claims for jurisdiction than they otherwise would. Certainly in the House, members maintain their influence in the legislative process by aggressively asserting their committees' jurisdictional claims to legislation. Whether multiple referral markedly exacerbated this tendency we cannot know; but without it there would still be turf fights and no method of handling them.

On the plus side, when legislation is referred to a number of committees, multiple perspectives are brought to bear on complex problems. More interests have a voice and a more diverse group of members a say at the committee stage, where it counts most. Given the complexity of today's problems, this is certainly a benefit even if some delay is the cost.

For the Speaker, who is responsible for referral decisions, the high frequency with which major legislation is multiply referred presents both problems and opportunities. When legislation is referred to several committees, the number of people who must come to agreement is multiplied, complicating and often slowing down the legislative process. Multiply referred legislation can present a variety of procedural problems on the floor. Frequently, multiple referral forces the role of jurisdictional and substantive mediator on the Speaker. That role, however, brings with it influence as well as headaches—today, leadership staff routinely oversee the bargaining process through which a bill reported by several committees is prepared for the floor. And, of course, multiple referral also gives the Speaker the opportunity to set time limits for the reporting out of legislation, a power now frequently employed for secondary committees.

Committee Decision Making

According to the textbook story, the legislative process starts in earnest in a congressional committee. That is still usually true—although less than it used to be and, as discussed earlier, more than one committee may be involved. What happens in committee often differs significantly from what was common in the past. Perhaps the greatest change in House committee decision making since the early 1970s is in the extent to which partisanship now drives the process. Most committees used to strive to avoid or at least restrain partisanship; they attempted to reach decisions through a process of bipartisan accommodation, if not consensus (Fenno 1973). They did so because it greatly enhanced the committee's chances for success on the House floor; when a committee reported a bill unanimously, other House members were likely to conclude that the bill was uncontroversial or at least that all the problems had been worked out and so they were inclined to follow the committee's lead. Since members' influence in the chamber depended largely on their committee's success, it made sense for them to work hard to build oversized coalitions at the committee stage. To be sure, there were always committees on which ideological differences among members made consensus decision making impossible. Throughout the 1950s and 1960s, the House Education and Labor Committee was notorious for its knock-down, drag-out battles within committee and also for its dismal record of floor success. Yet, even a committee with as potentially divisive a jurisdiction as the tax-writing Ways and Means Committee tried hard to restrain internal conflicts and go to the floor with a broadly-supported package.

Committees are now much more likely to make decisions on a partisan basis. As the political parties have become more like-minded internally and moved further apart from each other in their policy preferences, bipartisan coalitions have been harder to achieve and less necessary for floor success (see Chapter 6). Since the early 1990s, the committee process on just over half of major measures has been partisan in the House, about double that of the earlier selected Congresses.[5] Despite this, not all bills are the products of partisan committee processes. Committees that deal with nonideological, constituency-benefit legislation—Transportation, for example—do try for unity and bipartisanship. And most committees consider a fair amount of reasonably important but largely noncontroversial legislation. For example, Ways and Means, now a highly partisan committee, in 2003 approved consensually a bill cracking down on Medicare fraud and another giving members of the armed services tax benefits. On the biggest and most consequential bills, however, committees tend to split along partisan lines.

Partisan polarization affects far more than the final vote in committee. With Democrats and Republicans so distant from each other on many policy issues, the Republican majority often excluded the minority from the decision making process altogether. Committee mark-ups were often not true decision making sessions; the real decisions had been made in informal behind-the-scenes bargaining among majority party members of the committee, sometimes with party leadership involvement, or in majority party committee caucuses. The public mark-ups with minority party members present were simply a formality. The rules allow the minority to offer amendments but consideration was perfunctory and all were voted down, with the majority voting in lockstep. The new Democratic majority elected in 2006 promised to allow more minority participation in committee.

Bypassing Committee

Although legislation is now frequently considered by more than one committee, sometimes bills bypass committee consideration altogether. In the late 1980s almost one of five major measures was not considered by a committee in the House. The frequency dropped to an average of about one in ten in the Congresses of the 1990s, but then increased again to an average of more than one in five in the first two Congresses of the 2000s. Furthermore, as we shall see, the lower rate in the 1990s is somewhat deceiving.

The circumstances under which the committee of jurisdiction is bypassed in the House are varied. A majority of the House membership can bypass an unresponsive committee by the discharge procedure: any member may file a discharge petition calling for a measure to be brought out of committee and to the floor; when half the House members—218—

---

5. The figure for the early 1990s forward is based on the 103rd to 105th and the 107th and 108th Congresses and is the mean percentage across these Congresses.

have signed the petition, the measure is taken away from the committee and considered on the floor.[6] In the 97th Congress (1981–1982), in the 102nd (1991–1992), and again in the 103rd (1993–1994), a constitutional amendment to require a balanced federal budget was brought to the floor through the discharge procedure. In all three cases the committee of jurisdiction—the House Judiciary Committee—opposed the measure and had refused to consider or report it.

A House rules change in 1993 may have increased the chances that the discharge procedure succeeds—at least on high-visibility issues. Previously, names on a discharge petition—and thus the names of those who had not signed—were kept confidential until 218 signatures were reached. The rules change specified that the list of who had signed would be public from the first signature, making it easier to pressure members to sign on hot-button issues. Still, the discharge procedure is seldom successful (Beth 1994).

The threat of a discharge petition can pressure a committee and the majority party leadership to bring measures to the floor they would rather not consider. During the 106th Congress (1999–2000), supporters of campaign finance reform and of managed heath care regulation used discharge petitions to convince the Republican leadership to bring these issues to the floor. Although neither petition received the required number of signatures, when the number got close the majority leadership capitulated. If a discharge petition does get 218 signatures, its proponents—and not the majority leadership—control the floor. In 2002, when Speaker Dennis Hastert, R.-Ill., refused to bring up the campaign finance reform bill, supporters did succeed in discharging it and, in a rare occurrence, passed it over the majority leadership's opposition.

When a committee is successfully bypassed, the decision to do so is usually made by the majority party leadership.[7] The rationale for doing so varies widely. Extreme time pressure created by an emergency may dictate bypassing a committee so as to enact a bill quickly. Congress responded to the attacks on the United States on September 11, 2001, by passing on September 14 a resolution authorizing the president to use force in response to the attacks (this was the resolution that authorized attacking Afghanistan) and a bill appropriating funds for this action. In neither case was there time for committee consideration. Other legislation enacted to deal with the aftermath of 9/11, specifically a bill to assist the struggling air-

---

6. Actually, for technical reasons, discharge petitions usually seek to discharge the supporters' rule for the bill rather than the bill itself.

7. The most frequent means the leadership uses is extraction by the Rules Committee—that is, by the Rules Committee making the bill in order even though it has not been reported by committee (Tiefer 1989, 268–269).

lines and another to beef up airline security, also were brought to the floor without committee considerations to expedite the process.

Hurricane Katrina's devastating landfall in late August 2005 prompted the leadership to quickly bring an aid bill for New Orleans and the Gulf Coast region to the floor. Not only had the bill not been considered by committee, Congress had been in recess and almost all members of Congress were still in their home districts, so the bill was passed by unanimous consent without a recorded vote, which would have revealed the lack of a quorum. Occasionally, the emergency that creates the time pressure is purely political. When a federal court ruled that the Federal Trade Commission had gone beyond the scope of existing law in setting up a national do-not-call-list, the Commerce Committee chair, with the full support of the leadership, immediately and without committee consideration brought a bill to the floor that explicitly gave the FTC that power and so reversed the court decision. Speed was deemed necessary to avoid disappointing the fifty million likely voters who had signed on to the list.

Most often, when committees are bypassed, some sort of political strategic consideration plays an important role. In 1988 the Democratic Party leadership took the Senate's version of the Civil Rights Restoration Act directly to the floor because time for action was getting short, and the leaders wanted to pass the bill without change to avoid a conference. The leadership feared delay in the Senate if further Senate action were required. Most supporters were convinced that a bill more to their liking than the Senate version could never overcome a Senate filibuster or a presidential veto.

In 2002, the Republican leadership brought a bill raising the debt limit to the floor without committee action first. Even though it is essential to maintaining the good credit of the United States, House members hate voting for raising the debt limit because it can easily be misrepresented as a vote for budget busting and to no good cause. Republicans, who for years harassed the majority Democrats about their debt ceiling votes, especially detest casting such a vote. Figuring that their best chance of passing the bill was to keep its visibility as low as possible, Republican leaders (with almost no warning) offered an amendment to the rule for another bill that would permit the House to consider the Senate debt limit bill and allow only an hour of debate. The bill passed 215–214. The leadership took the constitutional amendment to ban gay marriage directly to the floor in 2004; the committee chair had declined to hold a mark-up and, in any case, the leadership preferred to control the language of the amendment.

In January 2007, the leadership of the new Democratic majority brought a number of bills to the floor without first offering them for committee consideration. During the campaign, Democrats had promised to pass a specific list of bills during the first one hundred hours that they controlled the House, and delivering on this promise required bypassing committee.

Although most items in the Contract with America, the House Republicans' legislative agenda in the 104th Congress, went through the formal committee process, committee deliberation was largely pro forma. The unfunded mandates bill, for example, was referred to four committees on January 4, 1995, the first day of the session. The Government Reform and Oversight Committee ordered it reported on January 10, having spent only one meeting marking up the bill; Rules followed suit two days later; on January 19 floor consideration began. In fact, the bills in the Contract were actually drafted before the Congress began (the Contract was put together in the summer of 1994), and the Republican leadership was unwilling to brook changes of any magnitude (Owens 1996). During the 1994 campaign, the leaders had promised action on all the items in the first one hundred days, an extremely ambitious schedule that allowed for little real deliberation in committee, and they feared being accused of not keeping their promises if significant changes were made.

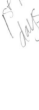

The Republican leadership often used task forces to work out legislation in the 104th but in most cases did not formally bypass committee deliberation. For example, a "design team" led by Speaker Newt Gingrich, R-Ga., worked out the contours of the Medicare reform bill. Immigration policy also was crafted by a task force; according to a participant, about 80 percent of the task force's recommendations were incorporated in the bill reported by the Immigration Subcommittee of the Judiciary Committee. The membership of the task forces and of the key committees of jurisdiction often overlapped. The task force device allowed the leadership to involve other interested members in the process and put pressure on committees to act expeditiously and with sensitivity to the sentiments of the party majority.

Because the issue is substantively, procedurally, and politically complex, Speaker Gingrich set up a task force headed by Chief Deputy Whip Dennis Hastert to draft managed care reform legislation in the 105th Congress and brought that legislation directly to the floor, bypassing the committees of jurisdiction. When Hastert became Speaker in the next Congress, he promised to follow regular order and not bypass committees. Yet the same constellation of problems eventually forced Hastert to turn to unorthodox processes in drafting managed care legislation, and he too effectively began bypassing the committees. (See Chapter 8 of Sinclair 2000 for the full story.)

Postcommittee Adjustments

After a bill has been reported from committee, supporters often make substantive adjustments. The practice has become almost routine, with an average of nearly a third of major legislation subject to such postcommittee adjustments in the post-1980 Congresses for which I have data. Almost half of major legislation in the 104th Congress was subject to some such alteration after committee action. Rarely will legislation be taken back to committee for formal revision. Much more frequently, changes will be negotiated and then incorporated into a substitute bill or an amendment—often called a manager's amendment because it will be offered by the floor manager. The substitute may supersede the committee bill and become the version (called the base bill) taken to the House floor, or it may be incorporated into the committee bill by the rule; alternatively, the substitute or the amendment may be offered by supporters on the floor.

Such postcommittee adjustments are made to enhance the legislation's chances of passage. Almost always both committee and party leaders are involved, with the majority party leadership often taking the lead. Major legislation that involves difficult political, substantive, or procedural problems is most likely to require such alterations. The committee leaders have, in most cases, done in committee what they were willing and able to do to ensure passage; and the majority party leaders are ultimately held responsible for passing the legislation their party members and the House as an institution need and want.

Multiple referral has drawn the majority party leaders into the substantive side of the legislative process; when the committees to which major legislation has been jointly referred cannot come to an agreement among themselves, the party leadership may have to take over the job of negotiating enough of an agreement to avoid a bloody battle on the House floor. A 1987 bill to restructure the farm credit system provides a good example. The House Agriculture Committee reported legislation that included a provision setting up a secondary market in farm mortgages. Securities issues were then in the jurisdiction of the Banking and Commerce committees, and the legislation was sequentially referred to both. The leaders of these two committees and of the Agriculture Committee were, however, far apart substantively; it took strong leadership intervention to get an agreement. The majority whip brokered the deal that was taken to the floor as an amendment. The amendment and the bill passed easily. Similarly, on the child care legislation mentioned earlier, the two committees with major jurisdiction took very different approaches to the problem and could not come to an agreement; the party leadership had to intervene to break the stalemate, and that intervention involved making substantive adjustments to the legislation. In 1995 the House Republican leadership produced the party's welfare reform bill by combining bills passed by three committees and, in the process, altered some controversial provisions. Controversy and saliency often prompt the need for postcommittee adjustments.

Supporters may find that their bill as it emerged from committee does not command enough votes to pass. In 2005, the Armed Services Committee included language in the annual defense authorization bill that would have further restricted women soldiers' proximity to combat—and so also their advancement opportunities in the military. Evidently the committee chair who advocated the change simply did not expect the firestorm of criticism that followed. The party leadership persuaded him to agree to remove the offensive language in a manager's amendment he would offer as soon as the bill went to the floor.

With his thin partisan majorities in the late 1990s and early 2000s, Speaker Hastert often found postcommittee adjustments necessary to pass important bills. Moderate Republicans threatened to vote against the Ways and Means Committee's 1999 tax bill because, they claimed, it concerned itself too little with deficit reduction. They were brought back on board with language that made the tax rate cut dependent on a declining national debt (*CQW* 1999, 1783–1785). In the 107th Congress, the welfare reauthorization bill that the committee reported was too conservative for the small but crucial moderate Republican contingent; to pick up sufficient support to pass the bill, the leadership had to make changes.

Similarly, in the 108th Congress, a bill rewriting the Head Start program required postcommittee adjustments to get enough votes from moderate Republicans to prevail. A bill entitled the "Gasoline for America's Security Act" that Republicans attempted to pass in the wake of Hurricanes Katrina and Rita in fall 2005 was strongly opposed by environmentalists; supporters were forced to delete language that would have made it easier for utilities to expand without installing new antipollution equipment, "a provision that Republican leaders acknowledged would have doomed the bill," as the *New York Times* reported.[8]

Legislation that involves many issues is likely to be both highly consequential and controversial and, as such, not infrequently requires postcommittee fine-tuning. The broad scope of such omnibus measures, which are discussed more in Chapter 5, means that most members have a keen interest in at least some provisions. Putting together a version that is satisfactory to most members of the majority party and to a majority of the House may be difficult for the reporting committee or committees. Budget resolutions that lay out a blueprint for federal spending in the following year—how much will be spent, for what, whether there will be a tax increase, and what the deficit will be—and reconciliation bills that bring law into accord with the budget blueprint (and thus may include changes in a multitude of programs as well as tax increases) are the sort of omnibus

---

8. October 8, 2005.

measures that frequently require postcommittee adjustments orchestrated by the majority party leadership.

In 2005, Republicans struggled to pass a reconciliation bill that would cut $50 billion from entitlement spending as the budget resolution had required. Whip counts showed that the package that emerged from the Budget Committee simply would not pass. Over the course of several weeks, the leadership negotiated with various party factions; the key, according to Speaker Hastert, was finding a balanced package that satisfied the moderates, the conservatives, and those members focused on energy policy, specifically on opening the Arctic National Wildlife Refuge to oil drilling (*Roll Call*, November 18, 2005). After a first compromise proved to be insufficient—planned floor consideration had to be postponed—the leadership put together a package of changes that allowed the bill to squeak through 217–215. The case studies in Chapters 10, 11, and 12 of the 1993 reconciliation bill, which in essence contained President Clinton's economic program; of the even more ambitious 1995 reconciliation bill incorporating congressional Republicans' balanced budget plan; of the 1997 balanced budget deal; and of the 2001 and 2003 Bush tax cuts provide a number of further examples.

When the president is a copartisan, majority party leaders now usually work closely with him and see passing his programs as important to the success of the party as a whole (see Sinclair 2006). That too may motivate postcommittee adjustments. In the wake of 9/11 the House Judiciary Committee reported a bipartisan version of what became the USA PATRIOT Act. The Bush administration believed that bill too weak, so the Republican leadership substituted a tougher administration-backed version for the committee-reported bill and took that to the floor.

Suspension of the Rules

In the House the majority party leadership schedules legislation for floor debate. When a committee reports a bill, it is placed at the bottom of one of the House calendars, the Union Calendar if major legislation. Considering legislation in the order it is listed on the calendar would make little sense, since optimal floor scheduling dictates attention to a host of policy and political factors. The House has developed ways of getting legislation to the floor that provide the needed flexibility. The primary ways of bringing legislation to the floor are through suspension of the rules and through special rules from the Rules Committee, both procedures that the majority party leadership controls.

Noncontroversial legislation is usually considered under suspension of the rules. The motion to suspend the rules is in order on Mondays and

Tuesdays and, since 2003, Wednesdays as well. Legislation brought up under this procedure is debated for a maximum of forty minutes. No amendments are allowed, and a two-thirds vote is required for passage.

During the Congresses from 1989 through 1996, on average 55 percent of all bills that passed the House did so by way of the suspension procedure; from 1997 through 2002, that number was 73 percent on average (Wolfensberger 2002, 11 and later updates). Much of the legislation considered under suspension is narrow in impact or minor in importance. The eight bills considered under suspension on May 16, 2005, were 1) Linda White-Epps Post Office Designation Act (HR627); 2) Robert M. La Follette, Sr. Post Office Building Designation Act (HR1760); 3) Supporting the goals and ideals of Peace Officers Memorial Day (H.Res.266); 4) To authorize the Secretary of the Interior to contract with the city of Cheyenne, Wyoming, for the storage of the city's water in the Kendrick Project, Wyoming (HR1046); 5) Potash Royalty Reduction Act of 2005 (HR485); 6) National Law Enforcement Officers Memorial Maintenance Fund Act of 2005 (HR2107); 7) Newlands Project Headquarters and Maintenance Yard Facility Transfer Act (HR540); and 8) Upper Housatonic Valley National Heritage Area Act (HR938).

Legislation of more far-reaching significance also may be considered under suspension of the rules. This happens if the bill is so broadly supported that using much floor time is unwarranted. On October 6, 2005, the House approved under the suspension procedure the Ava Gardner Post Office Building Designation Act (HR3439) and Con.Res.161—Authorizing the use of the Capitol Grounds for an event to commemorate the 10th Anniversary of the Million Man March. It also approved S1786—A bill to authorize the Secretary of Transportation to make emergency airport improvement project grants-in-aid under title 49, United States Code, for repairs and costs related to damage from Hurricanes Katrina and Rita and HR3895—Rural Housing Hurricane Relief Act of 2005.

The Speaker has complete discretion over what legislation is considered under suspension. When a committee chair has a bill he or she considers appropriate for suspension, the chair makes a request to the leadership. The Speaker is guided by party rules restricting the use of the procedure. The Republican Conference rule in the 109th Congress read

> The Majority Leader shall not schedule any bill or resolution for consideration under suspension of the rules which: 1) fails to include a cost estimate; 2) has not been cleared by the minority; 3) was opposed by more than one-third of the committee members reporting the bill; 4) creates a new program; 5) extends an authorization whose originating statute contained a sunset provision, or, 6) authorizes more than a 10% increase in authorizations, appropriations, or direct spending in any given year.

The Democratic Caucus rule is similar in thrust. These rules can be waived, but the requirement of a two-thirds vote for passage limits what can be successfully passed under suspension of the rules. The minor measures typically so considered can be very helpful to members as they seek reelection. As the opportunities to offer amendments on the floor have decreased, the chance to get measures passed via suspension has become more valuable for tending the constituency, pleasing interest groups, or pursuing a policy interest, albeit a narrow one that can garner a two-thirds vote.

The two-thirds passage requirement also gives the minority party one of its few points of leverage under House rules. Minority Democrats used that leverage to assure themselves of getting a reasonable proportion of Democratic-sponsored measures considered via the suspension procedure. Dissatisfied with the allocation of suspension measures to the minority, Democrats on October 1, 1997, defeated six suspension measures in a row and forced the majority to postpone consideration of ten others. Thereafter Republicans were more generous (Wolfensberger 2002). The minority can thus inconvenience the majority; approving bills under the suspension procedure is much less time consuming that other routes. The leverage is, however, limited by the majority's ability to bring up even a measure defeated under the suspension procedure via a special rule.

Special Rules

Most major legislation is brought to the House floor by a special rule that allows the measure to be taken up out of order. The Rules Committee reports such rules, which take the form of House resolutions—designated H.Res. A majority of the House membership must approve each one.

The rule sets the terms for a measure's floor consideration. A rule always specifies how much time is to be allowed for general debate and who is to control that time. One or two hours of general debate are typical, although major measures occasionally are granted considerably more time. The time is always equally split between the chair and the ranking minority member of the committee that reported the legislation; if several committees worked on the bill, each will control some of the general debate time.

A rule may restrict amendments, waive points of order (against what would otherwise be violations of House rules in the legislation or in how it is brought up), and include other special provisions to govern floor consideration. The extent to which a rule restricts amendments and the manner in which it does so also may vary. An open rule allows all germane amendments, whereas a closed rule prohibits all amendments other than those offered by the reporting committee. Between the two extremes are rules that allow some but not all germane amendments to be offered;[9] the Rules Committee labels such rules as modified open, structured, or modified closed, depending on just how restrictive the rule is. The committee defines those rule types thus:

> Modified Open: Allows any Member to offer a germane amendment under the five minute rule subject only to an overall time limit on the amendment process, and/or a requirement that amendments be pre-printed in the *Congressional Record* (www.rules.house.gov).

That is, modified open rules allow all germane amendments that are printed in the *Congressional Record* by a specific time (always before floor consideration begins) or set a time limit on the amending process and allow all germane amendments that can be offered during that time period.

A "Modified Closed/Structured [rule]—Permits only those amendments designated by the Rules Committee." The committee increasingly tended to use the term "modified closed" to refer to rules that allow only one amendment, usually a substitute from the minority party, and the term "structured" to refer to rules that allow more amendments. In the 109th Congress, however, no rules were labeled "modified closed." The committee's definition continues

> In the case of a structured rule the Committee will often notify Members by a Dear Colleague letter and an announcement on the House Floor. In such instances, Members are encouraged to file their amendments with the Rules Committee.

That is, members send to the Rules Committee the amendments that they would like to offer and Rules then decides which will be allowed.

In the contemporary House most rules are somewhat restrictive; since 1989, on average 64 percent of rules have been modified open, structured/modified closed, or closed. Restrictive rules are even more likely to be used on major legislation. In the period 1993–2004, on average 71 percent of major bills were considered under a *substantially* restrictive rule, that is, a structured, modified closed, or closed rule.

When major legislation is ready for floor consideration, a decision on what type of rule to use must be made. Given the variety in contemporary rules, the choices are many. The Rules Committee is officially charged with making the decision, and the leaders of the reporting committee make their preferences known. But since the majority party members of Rules are selected by the Speaker, the party leadership strongly influences

---

9. The Rules Committee can and sometimes does allow nongermane amendments to be offered.

what is decided. On major legislation the decision on the character of the rule is considered crucial to the bill's success; not surprisingly, the leadership decides.

Because there are many options in the design of a rule, special rules can increasingly be tailored to the problem at hand. Thus, when a bill is referred to several committees, setting the ground rules for floor consideration can present a host of complicated and delicate problems (Bach and Smith 1988, 18–23). Debate time must be divided. When two or more committees have reported different provisions on a given matter, a decision also must be made about which committee's language will constitute the base text and how the other committees' versions will be considered. The first rule for the consideration of the 1992 energy bill, which had been referred to nine committees, split five hours of general debate among the committees. The Energy and Commerce Committee received one hour; the other eight were allotted a half hour each. The committees worked out as many of the conflicts among themselves as they could. In the remaining cases, the Rules Committee decided which committee's version would go into the base bill that would serve as the original bill for the purpose of amendment on the floor. Other committees could offer their language as amendments to that text. The rule limited the amendments to those listed in the Rules Committee's report, set debate time for each amendment—ranging from five to twenty minutes per side—and specified that those amendments "shall not be subject to amendment except as specified in the report" (*Congressional Record,* May 20, 1992, H3462). The Rules Committee's summary of its rule for the Energy Policy Act of 2003 reads as follows:

1. Structured rule.
2. Provides one hour and 30 minutes of general debate with 30 minutes equally divided and controlled by the chairman and ranking minority member of the Committee on Energy and Commerce and 20 minutes equally divided and controlled by the chairmen and ranking minority members of each of the following Committees: Science, Resources, and Ways and Means.
3. Waives all points of order against consideration of the bill.
4. Makes in order only those amendments printed in the Rules Committee report accompanying the resolution.
5. Provides that the amendments made in order may be offered only in the order printed in the report, may be offered only by a Member designated in the report, shall be considered as read, shall be debatable for the time specified in the report equally divided and controlled by the proponent and an opponent, shall not be subject to amendment, and shall not be subject to a demand for division of the question in the House or in the Committee of the Whole.

6. Waives all points of order against the amendments printed in the report.
7. Provides one motion to recommit with or without instructions (rules. house.gov).

That rule made in order twenty-two amendments with debate times ranging from ten to thirty minutes.

The rule for the juvenile justice/gun control legislation considered in June 1999 demonstrates that complex rules are not limited to multiply referred legislation. Speaker Hastert decided the House needed to respond legislatively to the Columbine High School shootings. The Senate had passed gun control legislation, and Democrats and moderate Republicans were clamoring for the House to follow suit. Yet a host of procedural and political problems confronted Hastert. The only legislation a committee had so far reported was HR1501, a noncontroversial bill providing grants to combat juvenile crime. A big majority of House Republicans opposed gun control, but moderate Republicans believed their electoral survival depended on a response to the public's demand to do something after the shootings; even conservatives felt the need to respond, although not by passing gun control legislation.

Hastert decided to bring gun control provisions and other measures aimed at combating juvenile crime to the floor, even though they had not been reported by committee. The rule specified that HR1501, the noncontroversial bill, be considered first; forty-four specific amendments were made in order to HR1501, each with a time limit. One of these was the McCollum amendment, which incorporated the Republicans' new juvenile crime measures, such as increasing minimum sentences for juveniles and allowing prosecutors to try juveniles as adults in federal courts; thirty-eight of the other amendments allowed were made in order as amendments to the McCollum amendment, meaning that the McCollum amendment was in effect the base bill. Many of the amendments were intended to give their sponsors and others who voted for them something to tell their constituents when asked about their response to Columbine. For example, an amendment allowed states and municipalities to display the Ten Commandments on public property. (It was approved 248–180.)

After HR1501 was disposed of, the rule specified that HR2122, the Speaker's gun control bill, be considered. Eleven amendments were made in order, and consideration was governed by a provision that specified who had the right to offer each amendment and set time limits. The most important amendments were the NRA-backed Dingell amendment, which would weaken the bill's gun control provisions, and the Democrats' McCarthy amendment, which would strengthen them. The Republican leadership wanted to make sure that Republican members had a menu of proposals to choose from. They believed that if the Dingell amendment were adopted, it would sink the bill. Republicans chose to allow John Dingell, a senior Democrat (and in the minority of his party in regard to this issue), to offer his amendment rather than have a Republican offer the weakening amendment in order to obscure partisan responsibility for weakening or killing gun control.

Finally, the rule stipulated that if both bills passed, they would be combined and sent to the Senate as one bill. The bills had been split so that the gun control provisions would not endanger the juvenile justice measures. As it turned out, the gun control bill failed. When the Dingell amendment was adopted and the McCarthy amendment failed, the resulting legislation was too weak for pro–gun control Democrats but still too strong for adamantly anti–gun control Republicans.

The Uses of Special Rules

Special rules can be used to save time and prevent obstruction and delay, to focus attention and debate on the critical choices, and sometimes to structure the choices members confront on the floor in a way that promotes a particular outcome.

Rules that restrict amendments and waive points of order save time and prevent obstructionism. Before Republicans gained a House majority in the 1994 elections, they had promised that if they took control of the chamber they would use less restrictive rules than had the Democrats when in power. Yet House Republicans also promised to pass the Contract with America during the first one hundred days of the 104th Congress. When they brought one of the early Contract items to the floor under an open rule, Democrats naturally enough offered multitudes of amendments. Thereafter, the Republican-controlled Rules Committee usually included (in otherwise unrestrictive rules) a time limit on total amending activity.

Any restrictions on amendments, even simply the requirement that amendments be printed in the *Congressional Record* several days before being offered on the floor, help the bill's proponents by reducing uncertainty. Proponents can focus their efforts and plan strategy more efficiently. Opponents lose the element of surprise.

When the rule gives members a choice among comprehensive substitutes but bars votes on narrow amendments, it is focusing the debate on alternative approaches, on the big choices rather than the picky details. Since the late 1980s rules allowing a choice among comprehensive substitutes have been used to bring to the floor tax bills, budget resolutions, civil rights bills, and social welfare legislation on such issues as parental leave, the minimum wage, and child care. The rule for the consideration of the 2004 budget resolution, which sets an overall spending plan for the next year, made in order votes on four substitute versions: one sponsored by the

Congressional Black Caucus; another by the Blue Dogs, a group of conservative Democrats; a third by the Republican Study Committee, a group of very conservative Republicans; and a Democratic Leadership substitute. Debate time for the first three was set at forty minutes; the Democratic substitute was given sixty minutes.

In addition to reducing uncertainty and focusing debate, carefully crafted rules can structure choices to advantage a particular outcome, that is, rules can be strategic tools. The rule for welfare reform legislation in 1988 illustrates how. Most Democrats—enough to constitute a clear majority of the House—favored passing a welfare reform bill; they believed it constituted good public policy. Many, however, believed that, for reelection reasons, they had to go on record as favoring a reduction in the costs of the program. By allowing a vote on an amendment to cut the program moderately but barring one on an amendment that made draconian cuts, the rule gave those members who needed it the opportunity to demonstrate fiscal responsibility and also ensured that legislation most Democrats favored would be enacted.

In 1995 Republicans, now in the majority, used a cleverly constructed restrictive rule to protect their rescission bill. The rule specified that anyone wishing to restore spending that had been cut in the bill had to offset the cost by cutting something else in the same section of the bill. Thus, no money could be transferred to social programs from defense spending or from disaster relief for California, for example, since these programs were in different sections of the bill.

The Republican leadership frequently used highly restrictive rules to protect legislation and to shield its members from having to cast tough votes. In 2001–2002, 44 percent of all rules allowed only one Democratic substitute (Wolfensberger n.d.). Amendments that the leadership opposed but that might pass often were disallowed. Expressing the consensus Democratic view, Rep. George Miller of California charged, "We are not allowed to offer amendments if we can win those amendments. We are not allowed those amendments if it means Republicans must take a tough vote" (*CR,* July 16, 2002, H4702).

In 2004, for example, the Workforce Investment Act, the country's main job training legislation, included a provision that would allow religious groups that run federally funded job training and literacy programs to hire and fire employees based on their religious beliefs. Republicans had failed to enact Bush's faith-based initiative as a separate bill and were attempting to enact it piecemeal. This provision was politically tricky for some Republicans. So the rule for the bill simply barred the Democratic amendment that would have knocked out that provision.

The rule for the Broadcast Decency Enforcement Act of 2004 barred an amendment supported by a considerable number of Republicans and all Democrats to roll back the Federal Communication Commission's loosening of media ownership rules. And the resolution to establish a congressional committee to investigate the governmental response to Hurricane Katrina was brought up under a closed rule, thereby preventing Democrats from offering an amendment making the investigative body an independent commission rather than a congressional committee with a Republican majority.

The Federal Housing Finance Reform Act of 2005 (HR1461) was reported out of the Financial Services Committee on May 25 by a vote of 65 to 5. Democrats backed the bill and made the strong bipartisan vote possible because the bill included an affordable housing fund. Many conservative Republicans opposed this fund—one called it an "experiment in socialism"—but failed in their attempt to remove it in committee (*CQW,* June 6, 2005, 1453). To overcome the objections of these individuals, the leadership negotiated and the Rules Committee made in order a manager's amendment making major changes in the bill and prohibited Democrats from amending the amendment. Among the provisions included was one that basically barred nonprofit groups that applied for or received housing grants from using their own funds to engage in nonpartisan voter registration or get-out-the-vote activities. These provisions placated conservative Republicans but infuriated Democrats.

Majority party members vote for such rules not only because the expectation of supporting your party on procedural votes is now very strong, but also because the amendments at issue often are ones the member believes to be bad public policy but politically difficult to vote against. (For Democrats, amendments on such hot button issues as homosexual rights or flag burning are often problematic; for Republicans, amendments that increase spending or benefits under popular domestic programs are.)

If barring a vote altogether is politically infeasible, a rule can force an amendment's proponents to offer it in a parliamentary guise that makes the vote highly obscure. So, for example, rather than allowing the minority party to offer a substitute for the majority's bill, a rule can force the minority party to offer its alternative through a motion to recommit with instructions. When House Republicans brought their prescription drug bill to the floor in summer 2002, for example, they forced Democrats to offer their alternative, which provided more generous drug benefits, through such a motion. In April 2006, although nine amendments were made in order, the Rules Committee did not provide an opportunity for the Democrats' much tougher substitute to their lobbying reform bill to be offered as an amendment, thus making the motion to recommit the only way Democrats could get a vote on the Republicans' substitute. Democrats were even denied a motion to recommit with instructions on a June 2006 resolution on the war in Iraq.

Legislation that the majority party leadership opposes seldom gets to the floor but, under those rare circumstances when it does, rules can serve as strategic tools as well. In 1997, to get the necessary support for the rule bringing the budget reconciliation bills to the floor, the Republican leadership had to promise a group of deficit hawks a floor vote on their budget enforcement bill. That bill, which even its supporters conceded needed refinement, was brought to the floor under a closed rule, which made it impossible for supporters to improve it through amendments; it went down in flames on an 81–347 vote (*Congressional Quarterly Almanac* 1997, 2–49).

Under intense pressure to bring the campaign finance reform bill to the floor in 2001, Speaker Hastert did so but under a rule that campaign reform supporters claimed doomed them to failure. To build support, proponents of the Shays-Meehan bill had made a number of changes in their bill after they introduced it. Instead of allowing the compromise bill to be brought to the floor, which would have been the normal procedure, the rule brought the original bill to the floor and specified that each of the compromises would have to be offered separately as an amendment. To succeed, proponents would have to win twenty-two votes on amendments in a row. Bill supporters themselves voted down the rule and thus seemed to kill the bill. (Supporters did force the bill to the floor again later through a discharge petition, as discussed earlier.)

New Parliamentary Devices

New parliamentary devices developed in recent years have made special rules even more flexible and potent tools for structuring choices. A "king-of-the-hill" provision in a rule stipulates that a series of amendments or entire substitutes are to be voted on ad seriatim and the last one that receives a majority prevails. This device makes possible a direct vote on each of several alternatives; in ordinary parliamentary procedure, if an amendment or substitute receives a majority, no further alternative amendments to that part of the bill already amended can be offered. Clearly, when the king-of-the-hill procedure is employed, the amendment or substitute voted on last is advantaged. The procedure also makes it possible for members to vote for more than one version, which is sometimes politically advantageous. When Democrats were in the majority before 1995, budget resolutions were often considered under king-of-the-hill rules. Members were thus guaranteed a vote on each of the substitute versions of the resolution made in order by the rule. The House Budget Committee version was always placed in the advantageous last position.[10]

---

10. When the leadership was confident that it could defeat all the alternatives and no postcommittee adjustments in the budget resolution were needed, the Budget Committee version was not offered as an amendment at all but constituted the base bill.

The rule for the 1991 civil rights bill illustrates how the procedure can be used strategically. It stipulated that the three substitutes made in order were to be offered in a specific order under the king-of-the-hill procedure. The rule gave liberals a vote on their much stronger version but put that substitute first in line. Having cast a vote in favor of the tough bill favored by civil rights activists, these members then could support the leadership's more moderate compromise. The rule next gave House Republicans and the George H. W. Bush administration a vote on their preferred version. It put the Democratic compromise last—that is, in the advantaged position.

In the 104th Congress Republicans began using a "queen-of-the-hill" variant, which allows a vote on all the versions but specifies that whichever version gets the most votes, so long as it receives a majority, wins. The rules for the welfare reform bill and the term-limits constitutional amendment took this form; in the former case, a liberal Democratic substitute, a more conservative Democratic substitute, and the Republican version were considered under the queen-of-the-hill procedure. On term limits, votes on four versions were made in order. In both cases the option the Republican leadership supported was placed last, which is still the preferred position. Supporters of the last option, unlike those of earlier ones, know how many votes they need in order to win.

In the 105th Congress, a queen-of-the-hill rule again was used on a term-limits constitutional amendment. Rules Committee Chair Gerald Solomon, R-N.Y., explained the political rationale:

> The Committee on Rules was faced with a situation where there are nine States which have passed ballot initiatives requiring Members from those States to support a particular version of the term limits constitutional amendment specified in the ballot initiative, or else they would have to have a special designation next to their names on the ballot the next time they run at the next election which would read "disregarded voter instructions on term limits" (*CR*, February 12, 1997, H459).

The queen-of-the-hill procedure allowed members from these states to vote for their state's specific version. The various versions were even labeled by state; the first to be voted on was the Arkansas version.

Although queen-of-the-hill rules have been used less frequently in the last few years, the device is nevertheless still available to leaders. Interestingly, the rule for the consideration of the campaign finance reform act in 2002 was a queen-of-the-hill rule, with a substitute offered by the majority leader, one offered by Rules and Administration Committee Chair Robert Ney, and the Shays-Meehan version presented as the three options.

Another new device—a self-executing rule—provides that when a rule is adopted by the House, the accompanying bill is automatically amended to incorporate the text of an amendment either set forth or referenced in the rule. The new language is "considered as adopted," and no separate vote on it is held. Rules with self-executing provisions are increasingly frequent. In the last three Democratic Congresses of the 1990s (1989–1994), 19 percent of rules had self-executing provisions; in the five Republican-controlled congresses from 1995 through 2004, 28 percent of rules had them. Some self-executing rules simply substitute the committee's bill for the original bill; thus a rule that states "the amendment in the nature of a substitute recommended by the Committee on Education and the Workforce now printed in the bill shall be considered as adopted" is essentially "a time saver and vote saver," in the words of former Rules Counsel Don Wolfensberger. "By self-executing adoption of the committee amendment in the House you avoid two votes on the exact same matter (assuming the minority substitute fails) and instead go to the motion to recommit" (Wolfensberger, personal communication, March 2006).

If rules that self-execute only committee amendments are excluded, an increase in the frequency of self-executing rules is still evident—from 16.7 percent of rules during the last three Democratic Congresses to 21.2 percent in the following five Republican-controlled Congresses. The procedure provides a simple way of inserting last-minute corrections into a bill, and some of the self-executing provisions make only technical changes.

But postcommittee compromises of considerable substantive significance and even totally new provisions also can be inserted into a bill without a floor vote through a self-executing provision. Thus, in 1999 after the Republicans' tax bill was reported from committee, the leadership, in order to amass the votes needed to pass the bill, worked out a compromise with moderate Republicans. The language was incorporated into the legislation by a self-executing provision in the rule. The major postcommittee adjustments the leaders crafted to the 2005 reconciliation bill were bundled into an amendment sponsored by the Budget Committee Chair; the rule stipulated that the amendment "shall be considered as adopted" and barred all other amendments. The postcommittee adjustment required to pass the 2005 "Gasoline for America's Security Act" discussed earlier was contained in a manager's amendment that the rule specified "shall be considered as adopted."

Because a self-executing provision in the rule allows language to be incorporated into legislation without a vote, it can be used to pass matters that members would be leering of voting for openly. Without a recorded vote, the visibility of the issue is decreased and responsibility for it is obscured. In 2004, $12.8 billion in new tax breaks for business were quietly incorporated into the transportation bill through a self-executing rule (*RC*, April 7, 2004). In 2006, in the rule for a bill to rein in 527 groups' participation in elections, Republicans self-executed an amendment to abolish the limits on party-coordinated expenditures, meaning that a party could spend an unlimited amount of hard money in coordination with its candidates (H.Res.755).

Self-executing provisions also serve as tools in more complex strategic situations. Compelled by political pressure to bring to the floor a Democratic proposal to expand the child tax credit to low-income families, Republicans bundled it with tax breaks for higher-income families. They then brought the bill to the floor under a rule specifying that approval of the rule would automatically and without a separate vote trigger approval of the bill. This forced a conference committee on the bill where House Republicans could kill it.

The rule for the lobby/ethics reform bill the House considered in spring 2006 was, in the words of Don Wolfensberger, "the mother of all self-executing rules," with three separate self-executing provisions (*RC,* June 19, 2006). A Rules Committee version was substituted for the bills reported by the committees of jurisdiction; this version deleted several major provisions in the Judiciary Committee bill that the leadership had been unable to sell to its members. The Rules Committee version was further altered by deleting another Judiciary Committee provision. Finally, the House-passed regulation of 527 political committees was added to the bill that would go to the Senate. All of this was done automatically, without a vote.

On the Floor

Floor consideration of a bill begins with debate on the rule. One hour is allotted, half controlled by a majority member of Rules and half by a minority member. The majority member explains and justifies the rule, the minority member gives his or her party's position, and then both yield time to other members who wish to speak. If neither the rule nor the legislation is controversial, much less than the full hour may be used. If the legislation is controversial but the rule is not, members frequently will use the time to discuss the legislation substantively. Since so many of today's rules are restrictive and complex, they are often highly controversial, and debate may well revolve around the character of the rule itself and consume the entire hour. During this period, no amendments to the rule are in order.

The House must approve the rule before consideration of the legislation can begin. The Rules Committee member managing the debate on the rule for the majority party will move the previous question. If successful, the motion cuts off debate, and the House then proceeds to vote on the rule itself. The only way to amend the rule is to defeat the previous question motion. If opponents defeat the previous question motion, they control the floor and may propose the special rule they would like to see.

Losing on the motion to order the previous question is devastating for the majority party and seldom happens; a member who votes against his or her party on this crucial procedural motion is not quickly forgiven.

One memorable vote on the previous question occurred in 1981 on the reconciliation bill that implemented President Ronald Reagan's economic program. The key battle on that legislation was over the rule. Reagan and House Republicans wanted a single vote on Reagan's package of spending cuts; they could then make the vote a test of whether members supported or opposed the popular president's program to rescue the economy. Democrats, who controlled the House, proposed a rule that forced a series of votes on cutting specific popular programs. Knowing they were likely to lose at least some of those votes and thereby major chunks of Reagan's economic plan, Republicans decided to try to defeat the previous question on the rule. With the help of some conservative Democrats, they were successful and so were able to substitute their own rule that called for a single vote on the package as a whole.

Votes on the previous question are usually far less visible, and disgruntled majority party members can be persuaded by their leadership to vote yes on that motion and show their displeasure, if they must, by voting against the rule. Fearing they lacked the votes to pass their rule for the consideration of the Department of Interior appropriations bill in the summer of 1995, Republicans nevertheless made an attempt to do so—but only after forcefully explaining to their freshman members that they had better not join the minority in voting against the previous question (*RC*, 1995, 22). The rule was, in fact, defeated. The leadership then worked out a compromise among House Republicans, got the Rules Committee to incorporate it in a new rule, brought that to the floor, and passed it. When the majority party lost the rule, it did not lose control of the floor as it would have had it lost the previous question vote.

Once the previous question has been approved, the House votes on the rule itself. When the rule is not controversial, the vote may be by voice; on controversial rules the votes will be recorded. These recorded votes are still often called roll call votes, although the House seldom calls the roll as it did in the days before electronic voting. Because rules are frequently contentious, recorded votes on either the previous question or the rule itself or both are likely. In 2003–2004, for example, 132 measures were brought to the floor under special rules, and on 81 (61 percent) of them, there was a recorded vote on either the previous question, passage of the rule, or both.

The majority party sometimes loses votes on rules but not often. The vote on the Interior appropriations rule was the only one that Republicans lost during the 104th; from 1981 to 1992, Democrats lost on average just over one rule per year. During the highly charged 103rd Congress

(1993–1994) Democrats lost five rules, and during the 105th with its narrow partisan majority Republicans lost five. In the 106th, Republicans lost one rule; in the 107th, two; and in the 108th, none.

Majority party members are expected to support their party on such procedural votes. Republicans in recent years seldom even systematically checked their members' voting intentions on rules. "Basically we ask all our members to signal if they have any problem with the rule. The general presumption is that otherwise you are expected to vote 'Yes'," a leadership aide explained. "If you have a problem, you need to let us know. . . . More often than a Whip Count, we'll ask the Whip to do a spot-check of trouble spots—those members who on similar issues have been a problem, just to make sure that they are okay."

Over the period 1987 to 1996 the mean vote by majority party members in favor on rule passage votes was 97 percent. Especially when the rule is restrictive, most minority party members now vote against the rule. In 2003–2004, every recorded rule vote for a major measure was a party vote, pitting a majority of Republicans against a majority of Democrats. Every Republican opposed every Democrat on 41 percent of these votes, and no more than two members defected from the party position on another 27 percent; the largest number of Republican defections on any one vote was six.

If the House approves the rule, it usually then resolves itself into the Committee of the Whole, where the legislation is debated and amended.[11] A sort of parliamentary fiction, the Committee of the Whole has the same membership as the House but somewhat more streamlined rules. The quorum for doing business in the Committee of the Whole is 100 members, rather than the House quorum of 218 members (half the full membership). In the Committee of the Whole when a member is recognized to offer or speak on an amendment, it is for only five minutes. The Speaker does not preside over the Committee of the Whole, but since he or she chooses the presiding officer and always picks a majority party member, the majority party remains in control of the chair.

General debate begins the consideration of the bill in the Committee of the Whole. The rule has specified who controls the time. The chair of the committee or subcommittee that reported the bill serves as floor manager

---

11. Rules usually have a provision that reads as follows: "Resolved, That at any time after the adoption of this resolution the Speaker may, pursuant to clause 2(b) of rule XVIII, declare the House resolved into the Committee of the Whole House on the state of the Union for consideration of the bill___." That is, the rule specifies that the bill will be considered in the Committee of the Whole at a time of the Speaker's choosing. Occasionally, the rule will specify consideration in the House; this is effectively a closed rule because, in the House, the previous question motion, which cuts off debate, is always in order.

for the majority and actually controls the time allotted to the committee majority; his or her minority counterpart controls the minority's time. If the legislation is the product of several committees, each will have floor managers. The majority floor manager begins with a prepared statement explaining what the legislation does and why it deserves to pass.

The minority floor manager then makes a statement, which may range from wholehearted agreement with his or her opposite number to an all-out attack on the bill. When the committee has come to a broad bipartisan agreement, general debate may be a veritable lovefest, with committee members congratulating each other on the wonderful job they did and on the admirably cooperative way in which they did it. When the committee reporting the legislation is split, especially if it is split along party lines, the tone of floor debate will be contentious and sometimes bitter. Because of the intense partisan and ideological polarization that has developed in recent years, highly charged partisan battles are more likely than lovefests on major legislation. (See Figure 6.1 for the trend in partisanship.)

After opening statements the floor managers yield time—usually in small amounts—to other members who wish to speak. By and large, the majority floor manager (or managers) yields time to supporters of the legislation and to majority party members, while the minority floor manager yields time to minority party members and, assuming the bill is controversial, to opponents of the bill.

When general debate time has expired, the amending process begins. What happens next depends on the rule. If all germane amendments are allowed, members are recognized to offer amendments. House rules give the chair of the Committee of the Whole discretion to determine the order of recognition, but by custom members of the reporting committee are given preference in gaining recognition, and they are recognized in order of seniority (Tiefer 1989, 231). Once a member is recognized to offer his or her amendment, the member has five minutes to explain it. The floor manager has five minutes to reply; then other members may speak. They gain time by offering pro forma amendments "to strike the last word" or "to strike the requisite number of words." The member who offers a pro forma amendment does not actually want it to pass, but by offering it he or she gets five minutes to speak on the amendment that is really at issue.

A House member may offer an amendment to the amendment being considered. Such a second-degree amendment may be intended sincerely to improve the amendment to which it is offered. Alternatively, the purpose behind a second-degree amendment may be to lessen the impact or even negate altogether the effect of the original amendment. If a bill's supporters believe they cannot defeat a popular but, in their view, harmful amendment, they may try to come up with a second-degree amendment to at least weaken its effect.

Debate on an amendment under the five-minute rule may go on for a considerable period of time, but eventually when everyone who wants to has spoken, a vote on the amendment occurs. Sometimes a floor manager has no objections to an amendment or actually supports it and will simply "accept" the amendment without asking for a recorded vote. In that case the amendment is usually approved by voice vote. If the floor manager— or another member—opposes the amendment, a vote will be demanded. The first vote may be by voice, but if the amendment is at all controversial, the losing side in a voice vote will demand a recorded vote. Only twenty-five members are needed to force a recorded vote.

The House uses an electronic voting system. Members have individualized cards that look rather like a credit card; they insert their cards into one of the ten voting stations attached to the backs of seats on the House floor and punch the "yea," "nay," or "present" button. The vote is recorded by a computer, and it also shows up as a green, red, or amber light next to the member's name on a huge lighted display behind the Speaker's dais.

After the amendment has been disposed of, another member is recognized to offer another amendment. Under an open rule the amending process continues as long as there are members who want to offer amendments and who are on the floor prepared to do so. The House can by majority vote cut off debate, although amendments that have been "preprinted" in the *Congressional Record* at least one day before floor consideration are guaranteed ten minutes of debate (Tiefer 1989, 401–403). Unlike senators, House members have limited patience for protracted floor debate. In January 1995 Republicans brought the unfunded mandates bill to the floor under an open rule; after six days of debate and votes on numerous politically dicey amendments and with 170 amendments still pending, they voted to cut off debate.

A more frequently used way of controlling the length of the amending process is through the rule. Under many rules the amending process proceeds pretty much as described above except that the amendments allowed are limited, perhaps to those preprinted in the *Congressional Record*. Often now the rule specifies which amendments are in order and which member may offer each. In these cases the rule frequently specifies a time limit on debate on a specific amendment—usually ten or twenty minutes, or an hour for a major amendment. The rule also is likely to prohibit amendments other than the amendments made in order.

What happens in the Committee of the Whole thus varies depending on the number of committees involved and the character of the rule. Since most rules for major legislation are restrictive, the amending process is seldom prolonged. Even when the Rules Committee allows a number of amendments to be offered, the debate time it allots is usually short—most often ten minutes for amendments other than a minority party substitute, which may be given an hour. The Department of Defense authorization bill for 2007, for example, was considered under rules that allowed thirty-one amendments; the first rule specified one hour of general debate and made in order eight amendments; the second made in order twenty-three more. However, all but one of these amendments were allotted only ten minutes of debate time; the exception was allotted twenty minutes. Such rules assure the expeditious processing of most legislation on the floor; they make floor proceedings more orderly and predictable. But the sort of free-wheeling, unscripted amending process that was still common in the late 1980s is largely a thing of the past.

After general debate and whatever amending is allowed have been completed, the Committee of the Whole rises and reports back to the House. The Speaker again presides and the rules of the House again are in effect. Amendments adopted in the Committee of the Whole must be approved by the House, which gives opponents of an amendment a second chance to defeat it. Usually, however, the House votes on all the amendments adopted as a package and approval is certain. Occasionally, if a vote was very close and the amendment makes major and unacceptable changes in the legislation, an effort to change the outcome will be made. In 1995 Democrats, with some help from moderate Republicans, successfully passed in the Committee of the Whole an amendment to an appropriations bill that deleted controversial language barring the Environmental Protection Agency from enforcing various environmental laws. The amendment won on a close 211–206 vote and the provision was important to many staunchly antiregulatory Republicans, so the leadership called for a second vote in the House and defeated the amendment on an even closer 210–210 vote. (Motions die on a tie vote.) In that case the leadership used a bit of strategic scheduling and also got lucky; although no Republicans switched their votes, several Democrats who had supported the amendment the first time were absent for the second vote. Usually, however, amendments that win in the Committee of the Whole win again in the House. After all, the membership of the two bodies is identical.

The minority may then offer a motion to recommit the legislation to committee with or without instructions. A motion to recommit without instructions is essentially a motion to kill the bill and seldom prevails. By this point too many members have a stake in the legislation's enactment; if it lacked majority support, it would probably not have gotten so far. A motion to recommit with instructions—that is, instructions to report the bill back with specified changes—is, in effect, a motion to amend the bill. It is the minority's last chance to change the legislation. The motion may propose substituting the minority's version of the bill for the majority's, or it may propose much more modest changes. Again, because it is the minority's motion, it seldom wins—although more frequently than the motion to recommit without instructions. Since 1995 less than 5 percent of motions to recommit of either type have prevailed (Roust 2005, 13).

Assuming the legislation survives, a vote on final passage is taken, usually by recorded vote. Legislation that gets this far will almost certainly pass. The majority party leadership seldom brings a bill to the floor if it does not have the votes to pass it. In the early 2000s, however, Republican leaders found themselves in a situation that induced them to ignore that maxim on a number of occasions. They were charged with passing President George W. Bush's often ambitious and contentious program, and yet their majority was narrow. The Republican leadership brought to the floor several key elements of Bush's agenda, even though they were not sure of sufficient votes for passage, and then held open the recorded vote until they could pressure or persuade enough party members to support the bill to pass it. A normal recorded vote lasts fifteen minutes and is often extended to seventeen so as to give stragglers time to get to the floor to vote. After all, most members are not on the floor continuously during bill consideration but instead are in committee rooms or in their offices conducting other business. The House rule simply stipulates that a recorded vote must be held open for fifteen minutes and does not specify a maximum time.

The Republican House leadership took advantage of that lacuna. The most blatant example was the vote on the conference report for the Medicare/prescription drug bill that lasted about three hours (see Chapter 8). The vote on passage of that bill also had been extended, to about an hour. Legislation giving the president trade promotion authority in 2001 and approval of the Central American Fair Trade Agreement and the "Gasoline for America's Security Act," both in 2005, all got the same treatment. Republican leaders figured correctly that the imminent prospect of a very public defeat for their president and their party would soften up enough Republican members to allow the party to squeak out a victory.

Constitutional amendments requiring a two-thirds vote often are defeated on a floor vote in the House, but bills that require only a majority seldom are; in the 100th, 101st, 103rd, and 104th Congresses, the only major bills to be defeated at this stage were two competing proposals to aid the Nicaraguan contras, one President Reagan's and the other sponsored by the Democratic leadership in 1988; the first 1990 budget summit agreement (although that technically was the defeat of a conference report); and the campaign finance bill in the 104th, legislation the Republican leadership opposed. The narrow partisan majority in the 105th resulted in a higher number of defeats; four bills lost at this stage, including two that were leadership priorities (school vouchers and the waiving of environmental regulations on emergency flood control projects).

In the 107th Congress, the bankruptcy reform bill died on a House floor vote when the rule for consideration of the conference report failed, a case discussed more in Chapter 4. A bill to set severe limitations on federal spending was badly defeated—146 to 268—on the House floor in 2004. To get enough votes to pass the budget resolution that year, the Republican leadership had promised conservatives a vote on their budget process reform proposals. To fulfill their pledge, the leaders brought the bill to the floor even though it badly split Republicans and, given unanimous Democratic opposition, was doomed to defeat. Thus, when a bill is defeated on the House floor, extraordinary circumstances are almost always involved; bills that get to the House floor almost always pass.

If the legislation does pass, a motion to reconsider is made and laid upon the table. This ensures that the issue cannot be reopened. The legislation is then sent to the Senate.

Unorthodox Lawmaking in the House

If the textbook legislative process can be likened to climbing a ladder, the contemporary process is more like climbing a big old tree with many branches. The route to enactment used to be linear and predictable; now it is flexible and varied. To be sure, the textbook model was never a complete description of how bills became laws. There have always been alternative routes. In the past, however, the alternatives were infrequently used on major legislation. Now variation is the norm. As the case studies in Chapters 7 through 12 show, no two major bills are likely to follow exactly the same process.

Although the new practices and procedures arose in response to different problems and opportunities (see Chapter 6), their consequences are similar. The new practices and procedures in the House facilitate lawmaking. Most make it easier for the majority party's leadership to advance its members' legislative goals. The leadership now has more flexibility to shape the legislative process to suit the particular legislation at issue. However, as is becoming increasingly clear, unorthodox lawmaking also entails costs. This is especially true of the way in which the House Republican leadership used the new tools and techniques in recent years. With the political parties polarized along ideological lines and Republican margins of control narrow, unorthodox lawmaking too often was used to exclude—or at least had the result of excluding—the minority from meaningful participation in the legislative process.

Routes and Obstacles: The Legislative Process in the Senate

IN THE SENATE LEGISLATION MUST TRAVERSE the same basic path as in the House, and the alternatives at the various stages are, in many cases, similar—at least on the surface. Yet the Senate is a quite different body from the House (Matthews 1960; Sinclair 1989, 2006; Smith 1989; Koger 2002). Smaller in membership, the Senate is less hierarchical and less formal. Senate rules give senators as individuals great power: a senator may hold the floor indefinitely unless the Senate invokes cloture, which requires an extraordinary majority; further, any senator may offer an unlimited number of amendments to almost any piece of legislation, and those amendments need not even be germane. Current norms allow senators to use extended debate and floor amendments expansively (Sinclair 1989). Like the House, the Senate is now polarized along coinciding partisan and ideological lines, and it is often the minority party that makes use of these Senate prerogatives.

The differences in the two bodies are reflected in their legislative processes. The Senate does much of its business by unanimous consent—both an acknowledgment and an augmentation of the power of senators as individuals. Any one senator can block a unanimous consent request. The Senate is not a majority-rule chamber like the House. In the House the majority can always prevail; in the Senate minorities can often block majorities.

Bill Introduction

In the Senate, as in the House, only members—that is, senators—may introduce legislation, and each may introduce as many measures as he or she pleases. Senators may introduce their bills from the floor or just submit them to the clerks while the chamber is in session. The sources of ideas for legislation—the executive branch, interest groups, constituents, the legislator's own issue interests—are similar in the two chambers. Because senators represent whole states and serve on more committees than the typical House member, they tend to offer legislation concerning a broader range of issues.

Bill Referral

When a bill is introduced or arrives from the House of Representatives, it is normally referred by the presiding officer, on the advice of the parliamentarian, to the committee of predominant jurisdiction. Senate rules do not encourage multiple referral as House rules do.

Multiple Referral and Multiple Committees

Sometimes bills are sent to more than one committee in the Senate. A 1977 rule provides that the joint party leadership (that is, the majority and the minority leaders acting together) can by motion propose that legislation be multiply referred, but this route is never used (Davidson 1989, 379–380). When legislation is multiply referred, it is done by unanimous consent; the consent request may specify time limits for each committee's consideration of the legislation as the 1977 rule allows. Agreements are usually negotiated by the affected committee leaders; in the Senate party leaders seldom take an active role (Davidson 1989, 388). As one knowledgeable observer explained in an interview with the author,

> One just can't imagine the Senate giving its leaders the kind of power the Speaker has with respect to referral—determining what committees can do what to legislation, sometimes even to specifying what language they can work on, specifying committee reporting deadlines, and the like.

Multiple referral is less frequent in the Senate than in the House; less than one in twenty bills is multiply referred and the proportion has been dropping in recent Congresses (see Table 6.2). Even major measures are only a little more likely to be multiply referred, with less than one in ten sent to more than one committee in recent Congresses. Much of the legislation sent to multiple committees in the House is referred to only one committee in the Senate; the reverse is seldom the case.

Legislation that is multiply referred in the Senate is also less likely than in the House to be sent to a large number of committees. The big trade bill in the 100th Congress was referred to nine committees in the

Senate, and the bills implementing the North American Free Trade Agreement (NAFTA) and the General Agreement on Tariffs and Trade (GATT) in the 103rd were each sent to six. More typical, however, is referral to two committees.

In the Senate several different committees sometimes consider bills that, while not identical, deal with the same topic. For example, in 1995 three committees—Judiciary, Governmental Affairs, and Energy and Natural Resources—reported regulatory reform legislation (Sinclair 1997, chap. 8). Even when not technically multiply referred, such legislation entails many of the same complications. A bill also may be a composite of the work of several committees, as was the big transportation bill the Senate passed in 2004. The bulk of that measure was considered and reported by the Environment and Public Works Committee, but tax provisions drafted by the Finance Committee and a section authorizing mass transit programs drafted by the Banking Committee were incorporated into the bill after floor consideration began.

Part of the difference in the frequency of multiple referral in the Senate and the House is a result of differences in how jurisdictional boundaries are drawn in the two chambers; the Senate made significant changes in 1977, and its committee jurisdictions are somewhat more consonant with contemporary issues. But the difference also reflects more basic differences between the chambers; in the Senate when legislation impinges on the jurisdiction of more than one committee, the committee chairs often informally work out any problems among themselves. Thus, in 2005, legislation overhauling federal pension laws was multiply referred in the House: to the Education and the Workforce Committee and in addition to Ways and Means; in the Senate, the Health, Education, Labor and Pensions Committee and the Finance Committee each approved its own draft bill, and then the leaders of the two committees agreed to combine their bills before taking the legislation to the floor (HR2830; *CQ Weekly,* October 3, 2005, 2625).

Senate Committee Decision Making

Judged by floor voting patterns, the Senate is about as highly polarized along partisan lines as the House is. (See Figure 6.1.) Polarization affects committee decision making in the Senate but to a considerably lesser extent than it does in the House. In the Congresses of the 1960s and 1970s, the Senate committee process was partisan on less than one in ten major measures; that increased to about one in seven in the 1980s. In the Congresses of the 1990s and early 2000s, the Senate committee process was partisan on about a quarter of the major measures considered. So, certainly, Senate committee decision making is now more likely to be partisan than it used to be; yet, compared to the House, where about half of the major measures are the product of partisan committee processes, partisanship in Senate committees is still moderate.

Senate rules largely account for this difference between the two chambers. In the Senate, unlike in the House, partisan ratios on even the most powerful committees closely reflect chamber ratios and, in recent years, the Senate has been narrowly split. The 2000 elections, in fact, returned a 50–50 Senate and, so long as that lasted, committees also had equal numbers of Democrats and Republicans. Most Senate committees are relatively small, so when the chamber margin is narrow, the majority party may have only one more member on each committee than the minority, as was the case during most of the early 2000s. Under those circumstances, excluding the minority party from committee decision making and relying on a purely partisan coalition in committee is problematic.

Furthermore and more important, because Senate rules give individual senators so much power, any senator, whether a committee member or not, can cause problems for legislation later in the legislative process. Consequently, a bill's supporters have a strong incentive to put together a broad support coalition at the committee stage, one that accommodates interested senators who are not committee members as well as those who are, and that means a bipartisan coalition.

Senators hold multiple committee assignments and usually at least one and often more subcommittee leadership positions. In the 108th Congress, senators averaged 3.9 committee assignments and 8.1 subcommittee assignments each; majority party members averaged 1.7 chairmanships.[1] Thus, senators are stretched very thin. The time pressure this creates, combined with the openness of Senate floor proceedings, contributes to Senate committees' tendency to explicitly put off conflict, including partisan conflict, until the floor stage; that is, major divisive amendments are held to be decided on the floor. Committee chairs may "figure that if they get into these controversial subjects in committee, they'll never get the bill out," as a leadership staffer explained. Committee members are willing to go along because they know they will get their chance on the floor. And, further, why have a time-consuming fight in committee when the battle will have to be refought on the floor, the reasoning goes.

Still, Senate committee decision making has been considerably more partisan since the mid-1990s than it was before. Despite incentives in Senate procedures to avoid narrow supportive majorities, partisan polarization has made finding compromises acceptable to both political parties much more difficult.

---

1. *CQ Weekly*, April 12, 2003, C2–C17.

Bypassing Committee

In the Senate, as in the House, committees are sometimes bypassed altogether. In the Congresses of the 1990s and early 2000s, the proportion of major measures that were considered on the Senate floor without first going through committee varied widely from a low of 11 percent in the 101st Congress (1989–1990) to a high of 41 percent in the 107th (2001–2002). In the Senate bypassing a committee is technically simple; under Rule 14, if any senator objects to committee referral (more precisely, objects on the floor to further proceedings on the measure after the second reading, which occurs right before the bill would be referred to committee), the bill goes directly to the calendar (Tiefer 1989, 594). When legislation reported by a Senate committee awaits floor action and a companion House-passed bill arrives in the Senate, this procedure is frequently used to put the bill directly on the calendar rather than sending it to a committee that has already dealt with the issue. In a similar vein, when a Senate committee is still working on a bill and the House sends over its version, the House-passed bill is commonly held at the desk by unanimous consent. The use of these procedures does not, of course, constitute bypassing the committee in any real sense.

Any senator's power to put legislation directly on the calendar simply by objecting to the bill's being referred to committee would seem to make bypassing committee easy. However, the majority leader, through the position's scheduling powers, effectively has a veto over other senators bringing bills to the floor directly by this route. Although procedurally simple, the direct route really requires the majority leader's assent to work.

The majority leader or a Senate committee chair, with the majority leader's agreement, sometimes uses this rule to speed up the legislative process, particularly on relatively uncontroversial legislation. In 1988 legislation protecting whistleblowers had passed, but late in the year, and President Reagan killed it by pocket veto. When the sponsors and the new George H. W. Bush administration worked out a compromise the following year, the bill was no longer at all controversial, so supporters took it directly to the floor. Republicans, newly in the majority in 1995, were determined to pass quickly legislation requiring that Congress abide by various regulatory laws; the House had passed its bill on the first day of the session. A similar bill had passed before and had bipartisan support, so the Senate by unanimous consent placed the legislation directly on the calendar. Despite this maneuver, the Senate still took a week to pass the bill.

In recent years, debt limit increase bills frequently bypass committee. There is usually some time pressure and they are sufficiently straightforward that committee consideration seems to be seen as a waste of time. To ensure immediate action, Senate leaders took the resolution authorizing the use of force to respond to the September 11 attacks directly to the floor.

Political considerations may dictate bypassing committee. In 1999 Majority Leader Trent Lott of Mississippi took a "partial-birth" abortion bill and a bill to establish a "Social Security lockbox" directly to the floor, bypassing committee. In both cases, the desire to score political points dictated the timing; in the latter case, Lott also bypassed the committee because Finance Committee Chair William Roth of Delaware opposed the bill.

In 2001, the evenly split Senate Budget Committee was unable to agree on a budget resolution, so Majority Leader Lott bypassed the committee and brought a Republican resolution directly to the floor. Tom Daschle, the majority leader in late 2001, got Committee Chair Jeff Bingaman, D-N.M., to cancel further energy legislation mark-ups in the Energy and Natural Resources Committee when it appeared that the committee might approve drilling in the Arctic National Wildlife Refuge, a position opposed by most Senate Democrats. Daschle and Bingaman put together a Democratic bill, and Daschle used Rule 14 to get it directly to the floor. In 2003, at President George W. Bush's urging, Majority Leader Bill Frist and Foreign Relations Committee Chair Richard Lugar dropped the HIV/AIDS bill that Lugar's committee was working on in a bipartisan fashion and instead considered and passed the House bill.

Occasionally, the Senate bypasses committees to, in effect, avoid multiple referral. An omnibus drug bill in 1988 involved the jurisdiction of more than half the committees; rather than referring the legislation to all the various committees with jurisdiction, Senate leaders bypassed committee consideration. Instead, the bill was based on the recommendations of party task forces and drafted through months-long, bipartisan negotiations among key senators. Although the senators who were involved were largely the ones who would have taken the lead had the legislation gone to the committees, the informal process allowed for more flexibility (Sinclair 2000, chap. 9).

Senators have available another—and, in some ways, even easier—way to bypass committee; they can offer their legislation as an amendment to another bill on the floor. In most cases the "amendment" need not even be germane. The original Gramm-Rudman budget-balancing legislation was never considered by committee; Texas Republican Phil Gramm, its lead sponsor, simply offered it on the floor as an amendment to legislation raising the debt ceiling. During the 108th Congress, Democrats repeatedly attempted to attach an increase in the minimum wage and a rejection of President Bush's administrative changes in overtime pay rules to unrelated legislation. They succeeded several times with the overtime pay rules amendment but it never became law. Arizona Republican John McCain's amendment barring the "use of cruel, inhuman, and degrading treatment against detainees," which President Bush vigorously opposed, was added to the Defense appropriations bill on the floor in late 2005; despite a veto threat, it did become law (*CQW,* October 10, 2005, 2725).

As these examples suggest, the legislative process is often less formal in the Senate than in the House. Individual members are more important and committees less important than in the House. Given the power that senators as individuals wield and each senator's enormous workload, informal negotiations and agreements sometimes supplant more formal procedures.

Postcommittee Adjustments

To enhance its chances of passage, legislation in the Senate, as in the House, may be altered after it has been reported from committee. In recent Congresses about a quarter to a third of major measures were subject to such postcommittee adjustment; in the 104th Congress (1995–1996) the proportion shot up to 60 percent but, in succeeding Congresses, it fell again.

More frequently than in the House, Senate committee leaders or even individual senators take the lead. In 1993, for example, Senate Banking Committee leaders faced the daunting task of passing highly unpopular legislation to provide funds to finish the savings and loan bailout. In a time of big deficits and not enough money for popular programs, no senator relished voting for what appeared to be a bailout of the greedy savings and loan industry, even though, in effect, the bailout was an obligation resulting from the federal government's guarantee of the safety of deposits. After the Senate Banking Committee had reported the legislation, it became clear it would not pass, so the chair and the ranking minority member, after negotiations with President Bill Clinton's administration, offered a less generous substitute on the floor and thereby engineered passage. In 1999, Senator McCain, as chair of the Commerce Committee, had to make a number of postcommittee compromises to pass legislation setting liability limits for potential Y2K problems, thus protecting high-tech companies. As he explained on the Senate floor:

> Mr. President,[2] we are about to culminate the work of many months: investigation, drafting, negotiation, and compromise. . . .
>
> I want to remind my colleagues that many compromises have been made in this bill since it passed out of the Commerce Committee. It is certainly not as strong a bill as that passed by the House. These compromises have been

---

2. The Constitution designates the vice president of the United States as the president of the Senate; the presiding officer of the Senate is always addressed as "Mr. President," even though the vice president seldom presides.

made in order to get a bill that can have bipartisan approval and can be signed into law (*Congressional Record*, June 15, 1999, S6976).

Agriculture Committee Chair Tom Harkin took the lead in negotiating postcommittee compromises to the farm bill in 2002, and Finance Committee Chair Charles Grassley worked out a package of sweeteners that made possible Senate passage of a big corporate tax bill in 2004. In both of these cases, however, party leaders were also involved.

The effort to craft a postcommittee compromise may be led by the party leadership. On the clean air bill in 1990, Majority Leader George Mitchell, a Democrat from Maine, orchestrated the complex negotiations that finally produced a bill that could pass the Senate (Cohen 1992, 81–98). He was similarly active on child care legislation in 1989; when it became clear the liberal Labor Committee's bill could not pass on its own, he put together a substitute based on elements of the Finance and Labor Committees' versions. In 1995, when Republican supporters of two line-item-veto bills could not work out their differences, Majority Leader Bob Dole of Kansas helped craft a draft quite different from either one.

With margins of control narrow and partisan polarization escalating, party leaders have become increasingly involved in the legislative process on major legislation. On "flagship" legislation, "it's kind of cradle-to-grave," a leadership aide explained. The aide went on to say:

> On the really big bills, he [the Majority Leader] starts meetings right away, as soon as the issue comes up, well before committee mark-up. On ___, he had [the chairman] in right away and he talked to [a committee member active on the issue] and to others. On this sort of flagship effort, he reaches out to dissenting parts of the committee and tries to help the Chair.

The working out of postcommittee compromises is often a significant part of the majority leader's effort to pass major legislation. Thus, Tom Daschle as minority and majority leader took a very active role on issues ranging from farm legislation to energy to trade promotion authority. Frist also was frequently engaged in attempts to work out compromises on priority legislation. In the 108th Congress, he brokered a postcommittee deal on a measure limiting class action lawsuits that picked up a number of Democratic votes; a partisan fight over nongermane amendments stalled the bill but the deal allowed it to pass in early 2005.

Of course, the strategy of altering the bill substantively to increase support is not always successful; it may not be possible to make sufficient changes to pick up needed new votes without altering the measure in a way that alienates its supporters. In 1995 Senate supporters of a balanced budget constitutional amendment engaged in a succession of very public negotiations as they scurried to get the necessary votes. Majority Leader Dole and the chair of the Judiciary Committee, as well as other core supporters, crafted an amendment restricting the judiciary's power over the constitutional amendment's enforcement and thereby won the support of Sen. Sam Nunn, D-Ga. Despite lengthy attempts, they were never able to satisfy senators concerned about the impact of the balanced budget amendment on the Social Security system, and the amendment failed.

Passage of a constitutional amendment requires a two-thirds vote, an intentionally high barrier to success. Ordinary legislation, if it is controversial, may well need an extraordinary majority as well. Senators now use their right of extended debate—their right to talk and thus block action indefinitely—much more frequently than in the past. Since cutting off debate requires sixty votes, supporters of legislation must build a coalition that is bigger than a simple majority. Doing so will likely require considerable compromise and may require the sort of postcommittee adjustments discussed here. On national service legislation in 1993 sponsors never had a problem getting a majority; Democrats had to make concessions in order to amass the sixty votes it takes to overcome a threatened filibuster. Republicans could have passed strong Y2K legislation and the class action lawsuit bill in their preferred form if only a majority had been required.

Scheduling Legislation for the Floor

The Senate does not use special rules to bring legislation to the floor. The majority leader, by motion or unanimous consent, just takes the bill to be considered off the calendar. Senate precedent provides the majority leader with the right of first recognition; when several senators seek recognition, the majority leader is recognized first and the minority leader second. Otherwise, Senate rules require the presiding officer to recognize the first senator to seek recognition, giving the presiding officer much less discretion than his House counterpart has. (When the Senate is debating legislation, the bill's managers have the right to be recognized after the leaders but before other senators.)

Although the procedure seems simpler than that used by the House, the Senate majority party leadership actually has much less control over the scheduling of legislation and over the terms for its consideration. On any debatable motion any senator can hold the floor indefinitely unless or until sixty senators vote to shut off debate. The motion to proceed to consideration of a bill is debatable, so senators can filibuster against bringing legislation they oppose to the floor.

This fact shapes the process by which legislation is actually scheduled for floor debate in the Senate. The majority leader usually moves bills off the calendar for floor consideration by unanimous consent; a study of 247 matters considered by the Senate in the 98th Congress (1983–1984) found that 98 percent came up by unanimous consent (Tiefer 1989, 563). Another study shows that between 1981 and 2002, only eleven motions to proceed per year were made on average (Beth 2003, 3).

The Consultation Process

Since any senator can block a unanimous consent request, the majority leader, if he or she wishes floor business to proceed smoothly, must check with all interested senators before bringing legislation to the floor. Leaders of the reporting committee and the minority leader always are consulted; in the Senate effective scheduling requires bipartisan cooperation, and that requires intensive consultation between the majority and minority leaders. Unlike the House, where floor scheduling is a task of the majority party leadership alone, the Senate cannot function if the two leaders do not work together.

The more contentious and partisan the issue, the more consultation is required. During the impeachment trial of President Clinton, Majority Leader Lott and Minority Leader Daschle checked with each other multiple times a day. Partisan battles strained their relationship, yet Majority Leader Bill Frist and Minority Leader Harry Reid worked together on a daily basis during the 109th Congress (2005–2006).

Since any senator can object to considering the legislation and since time constraints make it impossible for the leaders to check with every senator on every piece of legislation, senators without an obvious interest in the bill are expected to inform their party leadership if they do have an interest. For every bill, the party secretaries, who are employees of the majority and minority leaders, keep a record of senators who have asked to be informed before the bill is brought to the floor, and these senators must be consulted. In addition, once the majority and minority leaders have tentatively agreed on a unanimous consent agreement, that information is put on the "hot line," an automated telephone line to all senators' offices; the recorded message specifies the terms of the agreement and asks senators who have objections to let their leader know in a given period of time. Today, e-mail is increasingly being used for hot-lining.

Senate party leaders contend that their only responsibility to senators who have asked to be informed is to tell them when the leaders are ready to bring a bill to the floor, and that may well be all a particular senator expects. The senator may simply want to be sure he or she is prepared to offer an amendment when the legislation comes up. In other cases, however, a senator may object to the legislation's floor consideration at any time or until the bill's supporters have altered it to his or her liking. The notification by a senator to his or her party leader is called a hold; a typical hold letter, addressed to then Majority Leader Lott and copied to the majority secretary, reads:

> Dear Trent:
>
> I will object to any time agreement or unanimous consent request with respect to consideration of any legislation or amendment that involves [the matter in question], as I wish to be accorded my full rights as a Member of the Senate to offer amendments, debate and consider such legislation or amendment.
>
> Many thanks and kindest personal regards.
>
> [signature]

The party secretaries confer every morning and inform each other about new holds on legislation or nominations. They do not, however, reveal the names of their members who have placed the holds, so a hold may remain anonymous. The Intelligence reauthorization bill "has now been held up for months as a result of a secret hold," Sen. Ron Wyden, D-Wash., charged in March 2006 (*CR*, March 8, 2006, S1872). Of course, if the purpose of a hold is to invite negotiations, senators make their identity known.

Holds are frequent, and placing them has become standard operating procedure in the Senate. This little story appeared deep in *CongressDaily*'s roundup of Capitol Hill news on July 2, 2003; it was reported with almost a yawn, even though there was little news competition since Congress was home for the 4th of July recess:

> Senate Majority Leader Frist and Finance Chairman Grassley are continuing to negotiate with Alabama Republican Sens. Richard Shelby and Jeff Sessions over a hold they have placed on a bill that benefits hundreds of U.S. businesses by cutting tariffs on products they import, according to a Senate leadership aide. Sixty-six senators wrote Frist late last week urging him to bring the bill to the floor "without further amendments" to force a cloture vote to beat the holds. While the letter gives Frist more leverage in negotiating with the Alabamians, he "wouldn't bring it up until he has exhausted his ability to work things out amicably," the aide said. Shelby and Sessions want provisions added to the bill that would require country-of-origin labeling on packages of socks, among other demands (*CongressDaily*, Wednesday, July 2, 2003).

Holds are not specified in Senate rules; they are an informal custom. What gives holds their bite is the implicit or explicit threat to filibuster the motion to proceed. Of course, a hold cannot block consideration of such must-pass legislation as appropriations bills. The majority leader will also sometimes go ahead with less essential legislation despite a hold, and may find that the threat implicit in the hold was a bluff.

On the other hand, the majority leader may face a filibuster on the motion to proceed and, if that is overcome, a filibuster on the bill itself.

Even if both filibusters can be overcome, the time consumed is substantial. Especially when floor time is short—before a recess or near the end of the session—most legislation is not likely to be considered worthy of so much time. After all, if scarce time is used trying to end a filibuster, other legislation will be sacrificed. Supporters of legislation are under increasing pressure to make concessions that will remove the threat of a filibuster. In July 2006, Senator Wyden put a hold on a major telecommunications bill because he objected to its weak language on "Net neutrality." *Congressional Quarterly* reported matter-of-factly, "Senate leaders have said they will not bring the bill to the floor until sponsors line up enough votes to overcome a potential Democratic filibuster" (*CQW*, September 4, 2006, 2321). As time becomes scarcer, a hold increasingly becomes a veto.

Senators' willingness to hold up one matter in order to extract concessions on another, sometimes known as hostage taking, has further complicated Senate floor scheduling. A particularly Byzantine instance occurred in 1995 when Jesse Helms, R-N.C., chair of the Senate Foreign Relations Committee, sponsored a State Department reorganization bill that the Clinton administration and many Democrats opposed. Helms brought the legislation to the floor, but after two attempts at imposing cloture failed, Majority Leader Dole stopped floor consideration. Frustrated, Helms began bottling up ambassador nominations, the START II treaty, and the Chemical Weapons Convention. Democrats responded by blocking action on a flag desecration constitutional amendment and a Cuba sanctions bill, both priorities for Helms. Negotiations and concessions eventually unstuck the impasse, although only the Cuba sanctions bill actually became law.

The majority leader thus schedules legislation under severe constraints. When he or she rises to make a unanimous consent request that the Senate proceed to consider a particular bill, this action has almost always already been cleared with the leader's party colleagues and has received agreement from the minority leader who has cleared it with minority party members.

Nominations

The Constitution gives the Senate the power to advise and consent on high-level presidential appointments. This has come to mean that the Senate must approve by majority vote the president's nominations of cabinet secretaries and other high-level executives, ambassadors, and judges, including Supreme Court justices. A motion to proceed to consider a nomination is not debatable, but the motion to approve the nomination is and, consequently, it can be filibustered.

Party polarization has made the confirmation process an increasingly confrontational one. Senators use holds to block nominations they oppose, even if a Senate majority clearly supports the nomination. Thus cloture votes showed a sizable majority for the confirmation of Henry Foster as surgeon general, but lacking the sixty votes necessary to cut off debate, the nomination died. James Hormel, an openly homosexual man nominated by President Clinton as ambassador to Luxembourg, almost certainly commanded majority support, but opposition from extreme conservatives led Majority Leader Lott to refuse to bring the nomination to the floor for a vote. (Using his power to make recess appointments, Clinton appointed Hormel to the post "temporarily" while Congress was out of session.)

During the Reagan and George H. W. Bush administrations, Democrats blocked judicial nominees who they considered too conservative; in the second half of the 1990s, Republicans blocked many of Clinton's nominees because they believed them too liberal. (See Epstein and Segal 2005 on the judicial confirmation process.) When the opposition party controls the Senate, it often can block presidential nominees it finds offensive in committee so that the nomination never makes it to a floor vote. Since George W. Bush has been president, Democrats have blocked a number of appellate court nominees. In the 108th Congress, Republicans were in the majority so they could vote Bush nominees out of the Judiciary Committee, but they could not overcome Democratic filibusters.

Frustrated, Senate Republicans threatened to change Senate rules to disallow filibusters on presidential nominations. The Republicans did not have the two-thirds vote that changing Senate rules in the ordinary way requires; however, their plan entailed having the Senate's presiding officer (presumably, Vice President Dick Cheney) rule that cutting off debate on nominations only requires a simple majority. Democrats would, of course, appeal the ruling, but only a simple majority is required to uphold a ruling of the chair. The plan was dubbed the "nuclear option" because of its likely explosive consequences (see Chapter 13).

Since implementing the plan would require the presiding officer to make a ruling that contravenes Senate precedent, one can consider the plan a highly unorthodox response to what Republicans considered the Democrats' unorthodox use of Senate rules (see Beth 2005). The showdown was averted at the last moment by a bipartisan group of fourteen senators. The Democrats in the group agreed to not support filibusters of judicial nominations except under extraordinary circumstances; the Republicans, in return, promised not to support the nuclear option. This agreement held throughout the 109th Congress. In 2005 the Senate approved two Bush Supreme Court nominees, even though both were seen as quite conservative; the agreement played a part, but most Democrats also feared that public opinion would not support filibusters against the nominees since both were perceived as highly qualified.

Increasingly often in recent years senators have taken to holding nominations hostage in order to extract concessions on other matters from the administration. That is, senators block nominees they do not oppose in order to gain a bargaining chip vis-à-vis the administration. The nomination of Richard Holbrooke as ambassador to the United Nations in 1999 was held up over matters having nothing to do with him. Sen. Charles Grassley, R-Iowa, wanted the administration to respond to his concerns about the treatment of a State Department whistleblower; Senators Mitch McConnell, R-Ky., and Lott hoped to extract from the president a promise to appoint their candidate to the Federal Election Commission. Sen. Orrin Hatch, R-Utah, chair of the Judiciary Committee, held up most judicial nominees during the first half of 1999 in order to force the president to appoint his choice, a person strongly opposed by environmentalists, to the bench.

Even members of the president's own party sometimes use the strategy. In 2003, Sen. Larry Craig, R-Idaho, put holds on every Air Force promotion—which are normally routinely approved. He really did not have anything against any of the Air Force personnel up for promotion; he simply wanted to force the Air Force to deliver on a promise he claimed had been made to station several planes at a base in Idaho.

Senators also use the holding hostage strategy for broader policy purposes. Thus Senators Hillary Rodham Clinton, D-N.Y., and Patty Murray, D-Wash., put a hold on the nomination of the Food and Drug Administration commissioner until after they had extracted a promise that the long-delayed decision on the morning-after emergency contraceptive would be made by September 1, 2005. The promise was made but not kept, so when President George W. Bush nominated a successor commissioner, the senators insisted on a decision before allowing a vote. Sen. Barack Obama, D-Ill., put holds on Environmental Protection Agency nominees until the agency promised to issue expeditiously its long-overdue regulation limiting exposure to lead paint. He insisted on getting a promise in writing (*Washington Post*, November 5, 2005).

Processing Noncontroversial Business

Congress considers and passes many bills and nominations that are not at all controversial. To expedite such business, the House uses suspension of the rules; the Senate uses unanimous consent.

To determine if a measure is sufficiently noncontroversial that it can be passed by unanimous consent, it needs to be "cleared," a process handled by staff in the party secretaries' offices. "The first I hear about a bill will usually come either from the sponsor or from a committee," a majority aide explained. "And they will say, 'we want to pass such-and-such a bill.

Can you hotline it?' " The aide will check the calendar to see if a senator has sent a hold letter on the matter. Then, as the aide went on to explain:

> I'll call that person or those people and see what's going on. Either they'll say "I just hate that bill" or they'll say "[it has] this sort of problem or that sort of problem." Or maybe it was just that they wanted to be apprised of the fact that it was going to come up. I will allay their concerns or maybe find that there are other problems, and that might mean that I have to kick it up to someone else.

If the problems can be taken care of at the staff level, the aide will ask the majority leader and the appropriate committee, "Is this okay to hotline?" At that point, the staffer's minority counterpart will be informed, and much the same process then takes place on the minority side. "Then I'll hotline the item. After the hotline, then any office with problems will have to call us. I'll call those offices and then, if it's cleared by both sides, then it will go on wrap-up," the staffer concluded.

The "wrap-up" occurs at the end of the day. One measure after another is brought up by the majority leader or a designee, no debate occurs, and the measure is passed by unanimous consent; the minority leader or the designee is always present to protect minority members' rights but, in fact, everything brought up has already been cleared (Oleszek 2004, 198; Gold 2003, 79–80). On November 18, 2005, for example, Senate Majority Whip Mitch McConnell, R-Ky., called up and the Senate passed in quick succession twenty measures that ranged from the naming of post offices to land conveyance in Utah (HR680) to the Vessel Hull Design Protection Amendments of 2005 (S1785).

Unanimous Consent Agreements

The Senate often considers legislation under formal unanimous consent agreements (UCAs). The majority leader and senior staff, especially the party secretary, negotiate an agreement setting terms for the consideration of the legislation. A UCA may specify time for general debate and time limits for the debate of specific amendments; it may completely bar nongermane (or, more frequently, nonrelelvant) amendments or those not explicitly listed;[3] and it may specify the time for votes on specific amendments and on final passage (Tiefer 1989, 573–584; Smith and Flathman 1989). Here is an example of a fairly typical comprehensive, complex unanimous consent agreement. It was offered and agreed to on June 10, 1999:

> Mr. President, I ask unanimous consent that the Senate proceed to the consideration of Calendar No. 91, S. 886, the State Department reauthorization bill, at a time determined by the two leaders, and that the bill be considered

---

3. Relevance is, in most cases, a less strict standard than is germaneness.

under the following limitations: that the only first-degree amendments in order be the following, and that they be subject to relevant second-degree amendments, with any debate time on amendments controlled in the usual form [between the sponsor and an opponent, generally, the bill manager], provided that time for debate on any second-degree amendment would be limited to that accorded the amendment to which it is offered; that upon disposition of all amendments, the bill be read the third time, and the Senate proceed to vote on passage of the bill, as amended, if amended, with no intervening action.

I submit the list of amendments.

The list is as follows:

Abraham-Grams: U.S. entry/exit controls.
Ashcroft: 4 relevant.
Baucus: 3 relevant.
Biden: 5 relevant.
Bingaman: Science counselors—embassies.
Daschle: 2 relevant.
Dodd: 3 relevant.
Durbin: Baltics and Northeast Europe.
Feingold: 4 relevant.
Feinstein: relevant.
Helms: 2 relevant.
Kerry: 3 relevant.
Leahy: 5 relevant.
Lott: 2 relevant.
Managers' amendment.
Kennedy: relevant.
Moynihan: relevant.
Reed: 2 relevant.
Reid: relevant.
Sarbanes: 3 relevant.
Thomas: veterans.
Wellstone: 3 relevant.
Wellstone: trafficking.
Wellstone: child soldiers (*CR*, June 10, 1999, S6821).

As this list of amendments suggests, unanimous consent agreements have become increasingly individualized as Senate leaders seek to accommodate individual senators' demands (Smith and Flathman 1989, 361). Each interested senator may bargain for particular amounts of debate time on his or her amendments and even expect to have the date and time when those amendments will come up specified.

Comprehensive unanimous consent agreements that are worked out before the bill comes to the floor and that govern the entire process of consideration are increasingly rare (Smith and Flathman 1989, 366; Evans and Oleszek 1999). In the 108th Congress, for example, only two major measures were brought to the floor under what could be considered comprehensive UCAs. These days, the leader more often will be able to work out only a partial agreement before debate begins. The agreement may just stipulate that the bill will be brought up; in effect, that no one will object to the motion to proceed to consider the bill.

As consideration progresses, senators are likely to become clearer about what amendments they want to offer and how much time they will need, and further agreements may become possible. Thus, several partial UCAs may govern a bill's consideration. The major measures that came to the floor in the 108th averaged about six UCAs each. As an expert participant explained:

> Usually you have a UCA only to bring something to the floor, and then maybe you have another one that will deal with a couple of important amendments, and then perhaps a little later, one that will start limiting amendments to some extent, and then perhaps one that specifies when a vote will take place. So it's done through a series of steps, each of which sort of leaves less and less leeway.

This is the series of UCAs for consideration of S1689, a bill making supplemental appropriations for Iraq and Afghanistan:

9/30/03
Supplemental Appropriations—Agreement: A unanimous-consent agreement was reached providing that at 10:30 a.m., on Wednesday, October 1, 2003, Senate begin consideration of S. 1689, an original bill making emergency supplemental appropriations for Iraq and Afghanistan, for the fiscal year ending September 30, 2003, for debate only, and that the time until 12:30 p.m. be divided equally.

10/1
A unanimous-consent agreement was reached providing that at 10:30 a.m., on Thursday, October 2, 2003, Senate continue consideration of the bill and that there be 40 minutes of debate remaining on the McConnell Modified Amendment No. 1795 (listed above) and the Senate then vote on or in relation to the amendment.

10/2
A unanimous-consent agreement was reached providing for further consideration of the bill at 10 a.m., on Friday, October 3, 2003.

10/3
A unanimous-consent agreement was reached providing for further consideration of the bill at 10:30 a.m., on Tuesday, October 14, 2003.

10/14
A unanimous-consent agreement was reached providing for further consideration of Corzine Amendment No. 1811 (listed above) and Reed/Hagel Amendment No. 1834 (listed above) on Wednesday, October 15, 2003; and

the Senate will then vote on or in relation to each amendment beginning at approximately 10:40 a.m.

A unanimous-consent agreement was reached providing for further consideration of the bill at approximately 10:30 a.m., on Wednesday, October 15, 2003.

10/15
A unanimous-consent agreement was reached providing for further consideration of the bill at 10:30 a.m., on Thursday, October 16, 2003.

10/16
A unanimous-consent agreement was reached providing that at 9 a.m., on Friday, October 17, 2003, Senate will begin a series of votes on certain pending amendments.

A unanimous-consent agreement was reached providing for further consideration of the bill at 9 a.m., on Friday, October 17, 2003 (excerpted from the *Daily Digest*).

On October 17, 2003, the bill passed the Senate 87–12.

A unanimous consent agreement provides some of the predictability that a special rule provides in the House. The difference is that a simple majority can approve a special rule whereas a UCA requires unanimous consent—one senator can veto it. This difference, of course, has an enormous impact on the legislative process in the two chambers.

Clearly, unanimous consent agreements make the majority leader's job easier; a comprehensive UCA gives the leader a much better idea of how long the legislation will take on the floor. Even a partial one provides some predictability. The bill's supporters value the reduction in uncertainty that UCAs accomplish. But why do other senators agree to unanimous consent agreements? For other senators, with their extremely busy schedules and their own legislative priorities, the more predictable schedule and the more efficient use of time that UCAs make possible are important benefits and may dictate acquiescing to a UCA even for a bill the senator does not support. But, if the senator strongly opposes the legislation, he or she can always object.

In recent years, the minority party sometimes objected to the consideration—not just the passage—of major legislation it strongly opposed (see following and Chapter 5 for some reasons). The majority leader in some instances brought such legislation to the floor without an agreement and so, instead of asking unanimous consent that the bill be considered, moved to proceed to consider the bill. The leader usually knew that the votes to break a filibuster against the motion to proceed were lacking but wanted to make a political point by at least having a debate on the issue. During the 108th Congress, three major measures were killed when Democrats filibustered and so blocked an up-or-down vote on the motion to proceed to consider the bill in question. Yet even under these highly contentious and partisan circumstances, the party leaders reached UCAs specifying when the debate would take place, how much time for debate would be allowed, and when the cloture vote would occur.

The minority party now is seldom willing to agree to UCAs that limit amendments or debate initially. In the 108th Congress, only five initial UCAs for major measures restricted amendments in some way. The Global HIV/AIDS bill UCA required amendments to be relevant, and the Victims' Rights bill barred all amendments. Both bills passed overwhelmingly. The Victims' Rights bill was the product of extensive consultation among senators of both major parties; its primary sponsors were Jon Kyl, R-Ariz., and Dianne Feinstein, D-Calif.; among its twenty-one cosponsors were Orrin Hatch and Patrick Leahy, chair and ranking minority member of the Judiciary Committee, respectively; Republican Party leader Frist; Ted Kennedy, D-Mass.; Democratic Party leader Daschle; and eleven other Democrats.

The first UCA for the FY04 Department of Defense (DoD) authorization bill required all amendments to be relevant; that for the Homeland Security appropriations bill in 2004 also limited the character of amendments but by a standard looser than "relevant."[4] The UCA for the 2003 debt limit increase bill "limited" amendments as follows: "that first degree amendments be limited to 12 per side, with relevant second degree amendments in order; that no amendments relative to gun liability or hate crimes be in order on either side" (*Daily Digest,* May 7, 2003).

In this case, Democrats wanted to use the consideration of this must-pass measure to get floor votes on a number of their issues, and they mostly succeeded. On the other hand, Frist scheduled the debate right before a recess, so senators' desire to get out of town forced Democrats to keep the debate fairly short. Only after a period of debate and amending activity is the minority at all likely to entertain the possibility of limiting amendments in any way. As a consequence, both in the abstract and in practice, the majority party's floor agenda control is very limited.

The Senate Floor

Assume the Senate has agreed to consider the legislation. Floor debate begins in the same way it does in the House: with opening statements by the majority and minority floor managers. As in the House, the chair and the ranking minority member of the committee or subcommittee usually

---

4. Senate rules specify that amendments to general appropriations bill be germane but the Senate can override its rules in UCAs and, in any case, tends to interpret the rule loosely.

manage the legislation on the floor, but in the Senate a bill sponsor who holds no such official position may act as floor manager.

Debate is unlimited unless constrained by a unanimous consent agreement, and even then it will not be as restricted as in the House. Senators' statements are likely to be considerably longer than those of representatives. When the Senate is engaged in a great debate, such as on the resolution in 1991 to authorize the Persian Gulf War, the lack of tight time limits makes for better and certainly more dramatic debate. On less momentous occasions Senate debate can drag on interminably.

Especially if the Senate is operating without a complex UCA, debate on amendments is quite unstructured. Even when the House is operating under an open rule, it often amends bills by section or title so that, at any given time, only amendments to a particular section or title are in order. In the Senate measures are open to amendment at any point. Although it is not required, senators often do submit their amendments to be printed in the *Congressional Record* before offering them on the floor. The floor manager may know when a senator intends to offer an amendment, and if that senator is not on the floor at the planned time, the floor manager is likely to wait! The House, in contrast, waits for no member and certainly not for a rank-and-file member who wants to offer an amendment.

Quorum calls are used to kill time. A senator can make a point of order that a quorum is not present, and the presiding officer will ask the clerk to call the roll.[5] The Senate does not use electronic voting. The clerk will very slowly call the names of the senators while everyone waits for the senator who is supposed to be offering the amendment to show up. When the senator comes in, the quorum call is vacated (that is, called off), usually without a quorum ever having shown up. Similarly, when senators need some time in the midst of floor consideration to negotiate in private, quorum calls make possible a kind of time-out. For example, the floor manager and a senator offering an amendment may want to see if they can work out a compromise version of the amendment that both find acceptable.

Amendment Rules and Their Consequences

Senate rules, under most circumstances, allow any senator to offer as many amendments as he or she wishes to legislation on the floor. For most bills the amendments need not even be germane to the legislation; that is, if a senator wants to offer a civil rights provision to an agriculture bill or vice

---

5. In fact, a quorum is seldom present since senators are in their offices or in committee working. Even if a quorum is present, the presiding officer must have the roll called; only under cloture may the presiding officer determine the presence of a quorum by counting.

versa, Senate rules do not prohibit it. Senate committees, therefore, have considerably less power than their House counterparts to kill legislation by refusing to report it. The language can be offered as an amendment to some other bill on the floor. Amendments to general appropriations bills (that is, spending bills) must be germane according to Senate rules, but senators often prefer not to enforce the rule. Some unanimous consent agreements require that amendments be relevant (a less stringent standard than germaneness) unless they are explicitly listed, and after cloture is invoked amendments must be germane. The Congressional Budget and Impoundment Control Act of 1974 (hereafter the Budget Act) requires that amendments to budget resolutions and reconciliation bills be germane.

In fact, senators frequently offer nongermane amendments. Throughout his long Senate career Jesse Helms used nongermane amendments on such hot-button topics as busing, homosexuality, pornography, and abortion to get his issues to the floor and force senators to vote on them. In the late 1980s he successfully attached to an education bill an amendment outlawing dial-a-porn services (900-number telephone services that provide explicit sexual messages for a fee).

But Helms was by no means an anomaly; most senators use the tactic at least occasionally. In early 1993 then Minority Leader Dole attempted unsuccessfully to attach an amendment on homosexuals in the military to family and medical leave legislation. His purpose was to embarrass President Clinton and, if possible, to impede passage of the bill. In this case Majority Leader Mitchell successfully countered Dole's strategy by offering an amendment to Dole's amendment that, in effect, removed its sting. In 2004, senators offered amendments to the annual defense authorization bill that set higher monetary penalties for broadcast indecency (Sam Brownback, R-Kans.), increased the top income tax rate to 36 percent (Joseph Biden, D-Del.), broadened the categories covered by federal hate crime laws (Gordon Smith, R-Ore.), and declared it the sense of the Senate that legislation should be enacted imposing an excise tax on plaintiffs' attorneys in tobacco litigation (Jon Kyl, R-Ariz.).

Senators' ability and willingness to offer nongermane amendments have major implications for the majority leadership's control of the schedule and of the agenda more broadly. The leadership cannot keep issues off the floor by refusing to schedule legislation. A senator can simply offer the legislation as a nongermane amendment. In the 104th Congress Majority Leader Dole and most Republicans would have dearly loved to keep off the floor the issue of open hearings on the ethics case involving Sen. Bob Packwood, R-Ore. But Sen. Barbara Boxer, D-Calif., offered it as a floor amendment to the defense authorization bill and forced a recorded vote.

As the Senate became more partisan in the 1990s, the Senate minority party became increasingly adept at using the Senate's permissive amending rules to force its issues onto the floor. In 1996 Senate Majority Leader Dole and most Senate Republicans did not want to vote on a minimum wage increase that most opposed but that was popular with the public. Senate Democrats were prepared to offer the minimum wage increase as an amendment to every important piece of legislation brought to the floor and, to avoid a vote, Dole was forced to put off votes, bringing the legislative process in the Senate to a standstill. Eventually, Dole's successor as majority leader, Senator Lott, capitulated, the bill came to a vote, and it passed handily.

Using similar tactics, the minority Democrats, sometimes with the help of dissident Republicans, forced debates on campaign finance reform, gun control, tobacco taxes, HMO regulation, Bush administration rules limiting overtime pay, and further minimum wage increases, all issues the majority party would rather have avoided. In 2004, Democrats used the debate on the defense authorization act discussed earlier to highlight their concerns about the war in Iraq by offering amendments that required President Bush to submit a report on U.S. strategy for stabilizing Iraq and specifying the number of troops that would be needed (Kennedy, D-Mass.) and that ordered the Department of Defense to prepare and give Congress a number of reports related to the treatment of detainees in U. S. military prisons around the world (Leahy, D-Vt.).

Amending rules make it much more difficult for the majority party and the leadership to control the agenda in the Senate than in the House. Senate leaders sometimes bring bills that they oppose to the floor because attempts to keep them off would be highly disruptive to their schedule and likely not successful. In 2001, for example, Majority Leader Lott did not attempt to keep campaign finance reform legislation off the floor, even though most Republicans (including President Bush) strongly opposed the bill. Republican John McCain and his Democratic allies had threatened to add the bill as a nongermane amendment to every bill Lott did bring to the floor. The result of trying to block it would have been gridlock on the new president's program.

That limited agenda control can also create problems for legislation the majority wants and has the votes to pass. The minority can sometimes come up with "killer" amendments that result in the defeat of a bill that otherwise would command a majority. Thus, in March 2004, Republicans brought to the Senate floor legislation to shield the firearms industry from lawsuits; the bill had more than sixty supporters and seemed assured of passing. And, had the House's restrictive rules been available, it surely would have. Democratic opponents of the bill failed to stop floor consideration when cloture on the vote to proceed to consider the bill was invoked 75 to 22.

Then, however, an amendment sponsored by Dianne Feinstein, John W. Warner, R-Va., and Chuck Schumer, D-N.Y., passed on a 52 to 47 vote.

The amendment extended for ten years the ban on nineteen types of military-style, semiautomatic assault weapons, which was set to expire in September. Minutes later, the Senate approved, 53 to 46, a proposal by John McCain and Jack Reed, D-R.I., to require criminal background checks for purchases from unlicensed as well as licensed dealers at gun shows, closing a loophole in existing law blamed by gun-control advocates for sales of weapons to criminals and terrorists. After the National Rifle Association let the bill's chief sponsor, Larry E. Craig, R-Idaho, know that the amended bill was worse than no bill from their perspective, he took the Senate floor to say the bill had been "so dramatically wounded it should not pass" and the bill was defeated on a 90 to 8 vote (*WP,* March 3, 2004).

Senators today fully exercise their right to offer as many amendments as they wish on the floor, although the majority of these are relevant to the legislation at issue. On major legislation the number of amendments offered and pushed to a recorded vote is often high, and amending marathons (when ten or more amendments are offered and pushed to a recorded vote) are far from rare.[6] In the Congresses from 1993 to 1998 and 2001 to 2004, on average more than 30 percent of the major measures considered on the Senate floor were subject to ten or more amendments decided by recorded vote.

What sort of legislation is likely to provoke a high rate of amending activity, and does such activity usually represent an attempt to legislate or to stop legislation? Legislation that must pass, as well as legislation that seems highly likely to pass, more often than other legislation evokes high amending activity, suggesting that senators are using such bills as vehicles for legislating. Appropriations bills, which must be enacted to keep the government functioning, make up a regular part of legislation on which amending marathons take place. Legislation that is very broad in scope often provokes extensive amending activity; budget resolutions, major tax bills, and omnibus appropriations bills are examples. More than forty amendments were offered and pushed to a recorded vote on the budget resolutions of 1993, 1995, and 1997; forty-four were on the 1995 reconciliation bill and fifty on the 2003 budget resolution.

And, of course, controversial legislation stimulates amending activity as opponents attempt to alter or even kill it, or at least to place supporters on the record on controversial provisions. The Medicare/prescription drug bill that passed the Senate in 2003 occasioned thirty-four amendments pushed to a roll call vote. There were roll calls on eighteen amendments on the very controversial energy bill—and hundreds more amendments pending—in 2003 before Majority Leader Frist gave up on passing the Republican version of the bill.

---

6. This is my term, not an official designation.

One must remember that amendments that are pushed to a roll call are only the tip of the iceberg. For example, the 2004 intelligence reform bill was subject to only 7 amendments that were decided on a roll call vote, but a total of 262 amendments were proposed, and the bill was on the Senate floor for nine days. Defense authorization bills have stimulated high amending activity in recent years because they are quite broad in scope, parts are highly controversial (missile defense, for example), and since they are considered nearly must-past legislation, the minority party has seen them as a convenient vehicle for getting votes on issues it wants to highlight. There were thirty amendments pushed to a roll call vote on the 2004 DoD authorization bill, including a number, such as the Kennedy and Leahy amendments mentioned earlier, that were intended to draw media attention to Democratic critiques of Bush administration policies regarding Iraq and to put Republicans on the spot.

To expedite the legislative process on the Senate floor, a floor manager will often agree to accept many pending amendments, either as is or with some negotiated changes, and roll them into a big "manager's amendment" that the floor manager then offers. After a number of grueling days on the floor, the manager may be willing to accept "just about anything," staff report (only half jokingly). Some of these amendments, everyone knows, will be dropped in conference. Even so, senators are able to claim credit for an amendment passing the Senate.

If a senator wants a recorded vote on his or her amendment, the senator can almost always get one. Senate party leaders cannot protect their members from tough votes in the way that House leaders sometimes can. To be sure, bill proponents often move to table an amendment. This is a nondebatable motion, and if an amendment is successfully tabled—which requires only a majority vote—debate on it is cut off and it is killed without a vote ever being taken on the amendment itself. However, the tactic makes an ineffective fig leaf for senators who oppose the amendment but fear the political consequences of voting against it.

The consideration of reconciliation bills is governed by Budget Act rules that are highly complex and require sixty votes to waive. Many of the amendments offered to reconciliation bills can be killed by making a point of order against them for violating the Budget Act, and this is routinely done. The amendment's sponsor can, however, demand a recorded vote on waiving the act. While the requirement of sixty votes to waive makes it relatively easy to defeat the motion, senators are forced to go on the record. The parliamentary language does not provide much of a screen to hide the opposition of senators to the substance of the amendment. (In fact, a senator who believes that waiving budget rules is a mistake, and thus votes against such motions on principle regardless of the substance of the amendment at issue, may have a hard time convincing constituents of his or her motives.)

Each senator's prerogative under the rules to offer as many amendments as she or he desires on almost any piece of legislation has many uses and, in fact, is employed to a variety of ends. Committee and party leaders know that the Senate's permissive amending rules give disgruntled senators a potent weapon. Therefore, before the bill reaches the floor, leaders have a considerable incentive to bargain and compromise with any senator who expresses dissatisfaction. Senators not on the committee of jurisdiction can influence the shape of legislation at the pre-floor stage in a way not possible for similarly situated House members. If senators alert a bill's sponsor, informally or through a hold, that they have a problem with certain of a bill's provisions, the sponsor must seriously consider trying to placate them. A single dissatisfied senator, even a junior senator who is a minority party member, can cause a great deal of trouble.

Extended Debate and Cloture

A bill's supporters must concern themselves not just with the barrage of amendments opponents may offer on the floor but also with the possibility that opponents will use extended debate to block action altogether. In the Senate debate ends on a matter when every senator has said all he or she wants to say or after cloture is invoked. The cloture process is the only way in which debate can be shut off in the Senate over any senator's objection.

Any senator may circulate a cloture petition. When the senator has gathered sixteen signatures the petition is filed; after a one-day layover, the Senate votes. On most matters three-fifths of the entire Senate membership (usually sixty) must vote for cloture for the motion to pass. If the measure at issue changes Senate rules, two-thirds of those present and voting are required to shut off debate.

Even after a successful cloture vote, debate does not necessarily end immediately. Senate rule 22, the cloture rule, places a cap of thirty hours on consideration after the cloture vote. The thirty hours does include time spent on quorum calls and voting as well as on debate. The rule also requires that amendments considered after cloture must be germane.

If cloture fails, the bill's supporters may try again. There is no limit on the number of cloture petitions that may be filed on one measure, and sometimes supporters file a new petition even before a vote has been taken on a previous one so as to minimize the delay caused by the requirement that there be a day in session between the filing of the petition and the vote. In 1987 and 1988 Majority Leader Robert C. Byrd, D-W.Va., made eight attempts to impose cloture on campaign finance reform legislation before he gave up. In 1999 Republicans tried and failed to impose cloture three times on Y2K legislation before McCain decided he had to compromise; on the Social Security "lockbox," Republicans tried unsuccessfully five times. In the 108th Congress, Majority Leader Frist attempted seven times to impose cloture on the nomination of Miguel Estrada to an appellate judgeship; he was never successful.

The cloture process is time consuming and cumbersome. Furthermore, if the opponents are determined, supporters may need to impose cloture at more than one stage in a bill's progress through the chamber. Thus, extended debate can occur on the motion to proceed to consider the measure, on specific amendments, on the measure itself, on various motions related to going to conference, and on the conference report. No single measure has ever been subject to filibusters at all these stages, but it is not uncommon for cloture to be sought at several stages. On the "motor voter" bill in 1993, for example, cloture votes took place on the motion to proceed, on the measure itself, and on the conference report.

The purpose of the cloture rule is to give the Senate some way to end a filibuster—the use of extended debate to block or delay legislation. Yet filibusters are not as easy to identify as one might think, especially since modern filibusters seldom resemble the famous ones of the past (Beth 1995). The word *filibuster* conjures up images of Sen. Huey Long, D-La., in the 1930s reading from the Constitution, quoting the Bible, and offering "pot liquor" recipes; of Sen. Strom Thurmond, D-S.C., in the 1950s holding the floor for twenty-four hours at a stretch; or of round-the-clock sessions with senators sleeping on cots in the Capitol as occurred during the great civil rights battle of 1964. Modern filibusters are seldom so dramatic, and threats to filibuster now frequently take the place of actual filibusters. A hold may keep legislation off the floor altogether.

Sometimes after a bill is brought to the floor, nothing happens: no senators step forward to offer their amendments, but proponents make no move to call a vote on passage. This occurred with the 1990 clean air bill reported by the Environment Committee (discussed in Chapter 1). In such cases supporters of the legislation know they lack the votes to invoke cloture and so refrain from forcing a showdown; opponents are consequently saved the trouble of staging an overt filibuster. Eventually, supporters must take their chances, give up on the bill, or negotiate with opponents, as happened on the clean air bill.

Because filibuster threats are frequent and may also be nebulous, a bill's supporters may file for cloture before opponents have clearly indicated they intend to engage in extended debate, and undoubtedly sometimes when opponents actually had no such intention. The requirement that all amendments must be germane after cloture is invoked sometimes encourages supporters to try for cloture. Finally, when senators spend a long time debating and amending a measure, they may simply be performing their deliberative function rather than trying to kill the measure. Many filibusters have as their purpose forcing a compromise on the legislation rather than killing it outright. Therefore, distinguishing between deliberating and filibustering becomes even harder.

Filibusters, defined as those instances where an attempt to invoke cloture on a given measure or nomination has been made, are now very frequent in the Senate. Recent Congresses (103rd through 108th) have averaged twenty-nine each (Beth 1995; DSG 1994; *Congressional Quarterly Almanac,* various years). The number of cloture votes averaged fifty-two per Congress, indicating that on many measures more than one cloture vote was taken.

Filibusters occur on a broad variety of matters. Not just legislation but presidential nominations may be subject to extended debate. In 1995 Republicans killed by a filibuster the nomination of Henry Foster to be surgeon general of the United States. A majority of senators was ready to confirm Foster, but since only fifty-seven voted to cut off debate, no vote on confirmation ever took place. Democrats blocked ten of Bush's appellate court nominees in 2003–2004, including Estrada. The twenty-one cloture votes all failed, although in every case more than half of the senators voting voted in favor of invoking cloture.

Extended debate is not confined to the great issues of the day; senators sometimes hold up minor and parochial legislation or more major bills for parochial reasons. A bill adjusting Hoover Dam rates was filibustered; senators concerned that Cuba would interfere with radio broadcasting in their states filibustered a bill setting up Radio Marti to broadcast to Cuba; and a Maryland senator filibustered the Metropolitan Washington Airports Transfer Act. As the 102nd Congress was rushing to adjourn in October 1992, Sen. Alfonse D'Amato, R-N.Y., held the floor for fifteen hours and fifteen minutes to protest the removal from an urban aid tax bill of a provision he said could have restored jobs at a New York typewriter plant (*CQW,* October 10, 1992, 3128). The bill containing the agreement on appropriations bills between President Clinton and Congress in November 1999, a bill that had to pass before the Congress could adjourn for the year, was filibustered by the senators from Minnesota and Wisconsin because it included the Northeast Dairy Compact, which they claimed hurt their dairy farmers, and by Sen. Max Baucus, D-Mont., because the bill excluded provisions making satellite TV more accessible to rural areas.

Major legislation is especially likely to encounter an extended debate–related problem—a hold, a filibuster threat, or a filibuster. Since the early 1990s, about half of all major measures have. In 1999, Y2K legislation passed the Senate only after Republicans agreed to compromises and the Social Security lockbox bill failed because Republicans were unwilling to satisfy Democrats. In 2002, Republicans, then in the minority in the Senate, refused to allow a vote before the elections on the Democrats' version of the bill setting up the new Department of Homeland Security; Democrats had the votes to pass the bill in a form Bush disliked, and Republicans wanted to use the fact that a bill had not passed as a campaign issue. In the 108th, Democrats used the Senate super-majority requirement to kill energy legislation, welfare act reauthorization, legislation tightening class action lawsuits, and malpractice law changes. At the beginning of the 110th Congress, Republicans held up the new Democratic majority's signature ethics reform legislation until they extracted a promise from Majority Leader Harry Reid for a future vote on their line-item veto legislation.

The filibuster is not a tool of the minority party alone, however. Majority Republicans repeatedly filibustered campaign finance legislation in the late 1990s. In June 1999, Phil Gramm, a senior member of the majority party, blocked passage of a broadly supported bill allowing the disabled to keep their Medicaid and Medicare benefits when they take paid jobs, until supporters agreed to drop the funding mechanism he disliked (*WP,* June 17, 1999). In the 108th Congress, the Internet tax moratorium bill was initially held up by Lamar Alexander, R-Tenn., a former governor concerned about the bill's impact on state and local taxing powers. He was joined by three other former governors, two Democrats and one Republican, in leading the charge for the states. After months of stalemate, they forced proponents to accept a major compromise.

Even more than the Senate's permissive amending rules, the right of extended debate provides the individual senator with a powerful weapon few can refrain from using. Extended debate has become a routinely employed partisan tool as well. As a consequence, controversial measures almost always need sixty votes to pass the Senate, and amassing the necessary support often requires significant concessions.

Majority leaders are not completely without weapons to counter senators' use of Senate rules for partisan and individual advantage, but the weapons are more effective as negative than as positive tools. Any senator can make a motion to proceed to consider but, in more than half a century, only two such motions that the majority leader opposed have won. The majority leader can file for cloture in the hopes of speeding debate and avoiding embarrassing amendments. In July 2005, for example, Majority Leader Frist attempted to impose cloture on the defense authorization bill because he wanted to finish it quickly, and a germaneness requirement would have greatly speeded up consideration. It also would have prevented Democrats from offering some of their amendments that Republicans did not want to vote on. In 2004 he attempted to impose cloture on the class action lawsuit bill to prevent Democrats from offering their signature amendments, including one to raise the minimum wage. Neither attempt was successful. In fact, in the 108th Congress, only twelve of forty-nine cloture votes amassed the necessary super-majority to cut off debate; in only three cases was cloture invoked when a majority of Democrats voted against it.

The majority leader can "fill the amendment tree," that is, use the majority leader's prerogative of first recognition to offer amendments in all the parliamentarily permissible slots, thus preventing other senators from offering their amendments. However, unless cloture can be invoked, the bill at issue cannot be brought to a passage vote. In the late 1990s, Majority Leader Lott used the tactic a number of times, and Frist tried it a couple of times in the 109th Congress. Because Democrats maintained high cohesion on cloture votes, it usually just led to gridlock.

Amendment Tree

Senators' desire to—in the words of a knowledgeable participant—"have a life" also gives the majority leader some leverage. Senators' enthusiasm for offering their less crucial amendments tends to lessen on Friday afternoon when the airport beckons. Similarly, if the majority leader schedules a bill right before a recess and insists it be finished before the Senate can depart, action tends to speed up. A former high-ranking leadership aide explained:

> Many times now you bring bills to the floor without a [comprehensive] consent agreement. And this is a kind of informal assessment period. You have a couple of days of debate. If you see it's not going anywhere, you go to the Democrats. You see how many amendments they have.... And then ... say, on Thursday, things are just not seeming to go anywhere. You'll go to the Democrats and say, how much more do you have? The Democrats will say, well, we've got another hundred amendments. You let it go fairly far into the evening, then essentially they'll want to get out; they'll want to go home. So you kind of grind them Thursday nights. And, soon enough, they'll say, well, we've got one more amendment. And that'll be it.

Yet these tactics only work when no senator feels really intensely on the matter at issue.

Finally, senators have to consider whether their exploitation of Senate prerogatives is likely to entail an electoral cost. If legislation is widely popular, being seen as responsible for its demise is a high-risk strategy, and few elected politicians are risk takers. Thus if a measure is popular and if its supporters can raise the visibility of the process sufficiently to pin public responsibility on the blockers, the costs may become too high.

If legislation reaches the point of a passage vote, it almost certainly will pass. In recent Congresses almost all of the major measures that lost on passage votes in the Senate were constitutional amendments, which require a two-thirds vote. Among the few exceptions were a bill barring employment discrimination against homosexuals, which was opposed by most majority party senators and was only brought to the floor as part of a package deal, and the gun liability bill, after killer amendments won and its sponsor called for its defeat.

Unorthodox Lawmaking in the Senate

Because the Senate's legislative process has always been less formal than the House's and thus more flexible, the distinction between the orthodox and the unorthodox is less clear in the Senate than in the House. Senators have always had the right under the rules to talk as long as they wished, offer multitudes of amendments, and propose nongermane amendments. They have always used those prerogatives. Yet all the evidence indicates that the frequency of such behavior has increased enormously in recent decades. The contemporary legislative process in the Senate is of necessity predicated on the assumption that senators will regularly and fully exploit their prerogatives. The extensive consultation that is a standard part of legislative scheduling, the "individualized" unanimous consent agreements, and the deference to senators as individuals are all responses to senators' hyperexploitation of their prerogatives under the rules. In addition, in recent years, the parties—especially the minority party—are fully exploiting Senate rules to further their partisan objectives. When employed by an organized and sizable group of senators, the Senate's permissive rules become a formidable weapon.

Unlike unorthodox lawmaking in the House of Representatives, the changes in the legislative process in the Senate, on balance, make legislating more difficult. Given senators' willingness to exploit their prerogatives and the lack of much cost to them within the chamber of doing so repeatedly, successful lawmaking requires accommodating individual senators and the minority party, and most controversial legislation requires a supermajority for Senate passage. Yet there is an upside to unorthodox lawmaking in the Senate. The greater necessity of building oversized coalitions has made excluding any sort of minority from meaningfully participating in the legislative process more—rather than less—difficult. Minorities, partisan or otherwise, can make themselves heard. And, for better or worse, they can often influence outcomes.

c h a p t e r   f o u r

Getting One Bill: Reconciling House-Senate Differences

SINCE THE HOUSE AND SENATE differ in membership and rules, major legislation is unlikely to emerge in identical form from the two chambers. Even if exactly the same bill were introduced in the House and the Senate, the changes necessary to pass it would likely result in differences by the time it worked its way through the two chambers' quite different legislative processes. Yet, before the bill can become law, both chambers must approve the identical wording; after all, a law cannot exist in several different versions. How would people know which they were expected to obey?

A number of alternative ways of reconciling House-Senate differences are used. One chamber can simply accept the other chamber's version of the legislation. A procedure based on amendments between the chambers entails a kind of public bargaining back and forth. A conference committee of members from both chambers can be appointed and charged with coming up with a compromise, which is then taken back to both chambers for approval.

Nonconference Reconciliation Procedures

On minor legislation or when the differences between the two chambers' bill versions are small, one chamber may be willing to accept the other's bill. Early in 1995, for example, the House accepted the Senate's version of legislation applying labor and other regulatory laws to Congress. The two chambers' bills were very similar, and House and Senate Republicans were eager to complete an early legislative victory.

Sometimes political expediency dictates that one chamber simply pass the other's bill. Such was the situation when the Lacy J. Peterson case created great pressure for the passage of fetal protection legislation; the Senate just passed the House bill. Similarly, the judicial threat to the enormously popular do-not-call registry led the House to immediately pass a bill and prompted the Senate to accept that legislation without change only hours later.

Late in a Congress, when time is tight and the alternative is the probable death of the bill, one chamber may accept the other's version of even major legislation; if the choice is to let the legislation die and start over in the next Congress or to take a less preferred version, supporters may well opt for the latter. In late 2004, for example, the House agreed to the Senate version of a bill extending the moratorium on Internet taxes even though that meant accepting a temporary rather than a permanent ban.

In 1980, in a more striking example, the House in a lame-duck (that is, post-election) session accepted the weaker Senate version of the massive bill on Alaskan lands. Since Republicans had won control of the Senate in the elections, House supporters of a strongly pro-environment bill knew they would fare worse if they waited until the next year. They also knew that, if they did anything other than simply accept the Senate bill, Senate opponents of a strong bill could easily use extended debate to kill the legislation in the few remaining days of the session. Similarly, during the lame-duck session in 2006, the House grudgingly accepted a much more restrictive Senate version of a bill allowing expanded drilling off of the Gulf Coast. House Republicans had intended to hold out for their more permissive bill, but when the Democrats won control of both chambers, they knew the Senate bill was the best they were going to get. The power of extended debate as an obstructionist tool, especially late in a session, can put the House at a disadvantage, confronting the chamber with the choice of accepting Senate legislation as is or taking a chance that opponents in the Senate will kill it if more action is required.

Sometimes, however, strategic considerations dictate that the Senate accept the House bill. Thus, in 2004 when the Republican-controlled House passed the Shays-Meehan campaign finance reform bill over the Republican leadership's objections, Senate Minority Leader Tom Daschle, D-S.D., engineered passage of that bill without change in the Republican-controlled Senate. The bill's supporters knew that, were the bill to go to conference with the Senate-passed McCain-Feingold bill, Republican opponents would kill it.

House-Senate differences on most minor and some major legislation are reconciled through a process known as amendments between the chambers. Assume the House has passed legislation and sent it to the Senate. The Senate then amends the bill, perhaps by substituting its own version for the House's, and sends it back to the House. At this point the House floor manager of the bill may ask that the House by unanimous consent (or under suspension of the rules or by a special rule) "agree to the

Senate amendment with an amendment." The Senate amendment referred to is actually the Senate version of the bill, and the amendment the House is adding is the House's initial offer of a settlement of interchamber differences. Generally, the House will stick to its own position or move least on those issues its members care about most. If the House agrees to the motion, the bill as amended goes back to the Senate, and the Senate can either accept the House offer or respond with an offer of its own.

Although the parliamentary language soon becomes mind-bogglingly complex, what is actually going on is fairly straightforward bargaining, with each chamber making offers in succession. The legislation may go back and forth between the chambers several times (Tiefer 1989, 778; Oleszek 2004, 257–258). The process on a bill banning junk e-mail went like this:

11/22/2003
Message on House action received in Senate and at desk: House amendment to Senate bill.

11/25
Senate concurred in the House amendment with an amendment by Unanimous Consent.

12/8
Message on Senate action sent to the House.

12/8/2003: 5:04 p.m.
Mr. Tauzin asked unanimous consent that the House agree to the Senate amendment to the House amendment.

12/8/2003: 5:05 p.m.
On motion that the House agree to the Senate amendment to the House amendment Agreed to without objection (excerpted from Thomas Bill Status Report for S877 at thomas.loc.gov).

Often differences are resolved through informal, behind-the-scenes negotiations between House and Senate committee leaders and then incorporated in the amendment one house sends the other. For example, in late 1988 a marathon series of informal negotiations settled the differences between the chambers on the omnibus drug bill. The highly complex deal was then incorporated into an amendment that the House adopted and sent to the Senate in the last hours of the session, and the Senate then accepted (Sinclair 2000, 149–151).

In still another variation on nonconference procedures for settling interchamber differences, the process on several recent important bills consisted of informal negotiations followed by a "clean" bill being introduced and passed. After the Senate and House passed their versions of the USA PATRIOT Act in 2001, no formal conference was held. Rather, key lawmakers met with administration officials to resolve differences and then introduced a clean bill that incorporated their agreements. Both chambers passed this new bill in identical form.

On the bill setting up the Department of Homeland Security, union representation for employees was the most controversial issue and was the sticking point that prevented resolution of the legislation before the 2002 midterm elections. When Republicans prevailed in the elections, Democrats were forced to retreat on their demands and an agreement was reached. The House incorporated that agreement into a clean bill that it and then the Senate passed.

Conference Committees

The most common way of resolving interchamber differences on major legislation is by conference committee (Longley and Oleszek 1989). In Congresses of the 1990s (103rd, 104th, and 105th), an average of 78 percent of major measures that got to the resolution stage were sent to conference; in some of these cases, amendments between the chambers were also used. In the early 2000s (107th and 108th Congresses), the figure dropped a bit as some of the informal procedures became more frequent; nevertheless, 67 percent of major measures that got to the resolution stage went to conference. By and large, conferences are restricted to settling differences on major legislation. Studies that examine all bills that passed or all those that became law in a specific Congress have found that only 9 to 13 percent of these went to conference (Smith 1995, 406; Oleszek 2004, 255).

Both chambers must approve sending legislation to conference; the first house requests a conference and the second agrees. Usually this approval is obtained by unanimous consent, but it can be done by motion and a majority vote, although in the Senate the motion can be filibustered.

The Appointment of Conferees

In both chambers the presiding officer appoints conferees; House rules give the Speaker sole power to do so; the Senate's presiding officer must receive unanimous consent. In the Senate, with its weak presiding officer, committee leaders, increasingly with the participation of the party leaders, actually make the choice. The chair of the committee of origin, after "consultation" with the ranking minority member, "recommends" a list of conferees to the presiding officer, who accepts it without change. By tradition, conference committees are bipartisan; the ratio of majority to minority members roughly reflects the ratio in the chamber, and the majority allows the minority to choose its own members.

The process is similar in the House, except the Speaker has more discretion. House rules explicitly require the Speaker to appoint "no less than a majority of members who supported the House position as determined by the Speaker." The rule continues: "The Speaker shall name Members who are primarily responsible for the legislation and shall, to the fullest extent feasible, include the principal proponents of the major provisions of the bill as it passed the House" (Gold et al. 1992, 339). Since the decision about which members meet these criteria is solely the Speaker's, the rule actually gives more leeway to choose, if so desired, junior members or members not on the committee of origin.

During the 104th Congress, Speaker Newt Gingrich, R-Ga., was unusually assertive in exercising the Speaker's discretion; he appointed freshmen and even, on occasion, Democratic supporters of the legislation that the minority had kept off its conference delegation. In 1999, after managed care legislation that the Republican Party leadership opposed passed the House, Speaker Dennis Hastert, R-Ill., employed his discretion to keep Republican supporters of the successful bill off the conference committee. Despite protests from a number of the sixty-eight Republicans who broke ranks to support the Norwood-Dingell bill, neither Charlie Norwood, R-Ga., the chief sponsor, nor Greg Ganske, R-Iowa, another prominent backer, was appointed.

Senate leaders have also, from time to time, attempted to stack conference delegations, as Majority Leader Bob Dole, R-Kans., did on the Kennedy-Kassebaum health care reform bill in 1996. However, the fact that so many conference-related motions are debatable and can be filibustered holds Senate leaders in check. Dole's attempt to stack the conference delegation with supporters of medical savings accounts, which he favored but a majority of the Senate had voted against, was stymied by Senator Ted Kennedy's, D-Mass., threat to filibuster the naming of conferees.

In 2002, Minority Leader Trent Lott, R-Miss., passed over a senior committee Republican to select a senator "who is close to Republican leaders" to serve as conferee on the terrorism insurance bill (*CQ Weekly,* July 27, 2002, 2061). Lott had tried and failed to produce a conference delegation that might agree to the House's cap on punitive damages. He now wanted to be sure the conferees agreed to a bill.

In both chambers most of the conferees will be members of the committee (or committees) that reported the bill and, by and large, fairly senior ones. Today, both chambers include leaders of the subcommittee responsible for the bill. The conference delegation will not simply consist of the most senior members of the committee, as was often the case before the mid-1970s.

When several committees have considered the legislation, all expect representation on the conference committee. Even if a committee was discharged, it still regards itself as entitled to conference representation and, in fact, when committees agree to be discharged they are not waiving their jurisdictional rights. Frequently, the chair of the discharged committee sends a letter to that effect to the lead committee, and the letter is then printed in the *Congressional Record*. The prevalence of multiple referral since the 1980s has led to very large conference delegations, especially from the House, where multiple referral is more common. On the conference committee for the 1988 trade bill were 44 senators from nine Senate committees and 155 House members from 14 House committees (Tiefer 1989, 798–799). Although this is an extreme example, multicommittee conference delegations are common. In addition to multiple referral putting pressure on the size of conferences, so does the Senate's penchant for added nongermane amendments to bills. The House committees whose jurisdictions these amendments impinge on expect to be included in the conference.

When Republicans took control of the House, Gingrich attempted to reduce the size of conference delegations to speed action, with some success. On the line-item veto bill, the House delegation of eight was actually considerably smaller than the Senate delegation of eighteen. Speaker Hastert also kept conference delegations small when he could. He appointed only three conferees for both the 2001 and the 2003 tax reconciliation bills and for the 2001 and 2003 budget resolutions and only eight, from two committees, on the Medicare/prescription drug bill. Yet some bills are so broad in scope and affect the jurisdiction of so many committees that large conference delegations are unavoidable. The reconciliation bill that implemented the spending provisions of the 1997 balanced budget deal was the product of eight committees in each chamber. The conference numbered seventy-three members in total.

Speaker Hastert responded to the problem of very large conferences on bills impinging on the jurisdiction of a number of committees by instituting a "2–1" rule. Any committee that made a jurisdictional claim recognized as valid by the nonpartisan parliamentarians got conference representation. Only the lead committee (or, occasionally, committees) received more than three conferees. The other committees all were granted two majority party conferees and one minority party conferee. The House conference delegation for the big transportation reauthorization bill in 2005 consisted of Majority Leader Tom DeLay, R-Tex., thirty-four members of the Transportation Committee, and three members of each of the following ten committees: Budget, Education, Energy, Government Reform, Homeland Security, Judiciary, Resources, Rules, Science, and Ways and Means.

Typically, only the conferees from the lead committee have the authority to negotiate on the entire bill. In the case of the 2005 transportation bill only DeLay had authority over the entire bill, and the Transportation Committee members had authority over all but two tax titles of the bill. House conference appointments for large, complex bills often specify in great detail the precise titles or sections that particular conferees can negotiate, as they did for each of the other committees' conferees for the transportation bill. Thus, for example, the conferees from the Committee on Education and the Workforce were appointed "for consideration of secs. 1118, 1605, 1809, 3018, and 3030 of the House bill, and secs. 1304, 1819, 6013, 6031, 6038, and 7603 of the Senate amendment, and modifications committed to conference" (Thomas Bill Status Report for HR3). The authority of House conferees has always been jurisdiction specific, but the extent to which that is spelled out in the appointment process seems to have increased considerably.

On the most important and controversial legislation—especially top priority items on the party's and the president's agenda—Hastert regularly appointed a member of the House party leadership to the conference and made that individual a general conferee who had authority over the entire bill. Thus, Majority Leader Dick Armey, R-Tex., was a conferee on the 2001 reconciliation tax bill. Tom DeLay, as whip and then as majority leader, served on conferences on energy bills, the Medicare/prescription drug bill, and transportation bills. None of this is completely unprecedented. Speaker Jim Wright, D-Tex., appointed Majority Leader Tom Foley, D-Wash., to the conference rewriting the Gramm-Rudman budget balancing law in 1987. Yet a routine leadership presence on such conference delegations is new.

Senate conference delegations are usually—although not always—quite small. The Senate conferees on the 2002 farm bill numbered seven, whereas the House delegation included fourteen members of the Agriculture Committee plus three members from each of nine other committees. The latter were all limited jurisdiction conferees. In contrast, the Senate delegation on the 2005 transportation bill numbered thirty. Furthermore, the Senate seldom spells out the sections or titles over which a conferee has authority. Often the committee the conferee represents is not even specified.

Reaching Agreement

The conferees are charged with coming up with a compromise between the House and Senate positions that can win the assent of a majority in both chambers. Sunshine rules instituted in the mid-1970s require that conference committee meetings be open to the public. However, because a public forum inhibits the hard bargaining that is often necessary, much negotiation takes place informally behind the scenes. To reach a compromise, members may need to retreat from positions they have advocated, often ones they have argued for strongly and ones with ardent interest group and constituency support; that is easier done behind closed doors. Staff typically work to resolve the often myriad minor differences between the bills; members become directly involved in the behind the scenes negotiations when major, controversial provisions are at issue. Often formal, open conference meetings simply ratify deals worked out elsewhere.

The difficulty of reaching agreement depends, of course, on how far apart the two chambers' bills are, as well as on how strongly the participants feel about their positions. Certain kinds of differences lend themselves to compromise more easily than others. When an appropriations bill goes to conference, it typically includes hundreds of items in disagreement, but the differences in dollar figures usually are resolved easily by splitting the difference or trading off among items. The tough fights are more likely to be over substantive provisions (for example, the Hyde amendment barring federal funding for abortions with certain, often contested exceptions).

When the two chambers take completely different approaches to a problem, the conference faces the most difficult task; splitting the difference is meaningless in this context. In 1995 the House passed a line-item-veto bill that would allow the president to make a proposal to rescind spending for specific items previously approved by Congress. Unless both chambers of Congress voted to overturn the proposal, it would become law. The Senate's line-item-veto bill was very different. The Senate proposed that, after passage, appropriations bills be broken down and sent to the president as hundreds of separate bills, thus enabling the vetoing of individual items. Clearly, there was no way of splitting the difference between the two approaches; the conferees had to choose one or the other or come up with a different approach altogether.

Differences between the two chambers' bills on volatile political issues also can complicate resolution. The bankruptcy law overhaul bill the Senate passed in the 107th Congress included a provision preventing anti-abortion groups from using the bill to avoid paying court judgments, and many senators were strongly committed to keeping that language in the final bill. The House bill had no such language, and many House members were just as strongly committed to barring it from the final bill.

The "torture" issue split the chambers for most of 2005. The Senate added to several bills a provision sponsored by John McCain, R-Ariz., that would prohibit torture or cruel and inhumane treatment of enemy combatants. House Republican committee and party leaders opposed the McCain amendment, and the House defense authorization and appropriations bills did not contain the McCain language. (In late 2005, after the House voted overwhelmingly for a motion to instruct conferees to the DoD appropriations bill to accept the anti-torture language, the House Republican leaders could no longer maintain their opposition, and the conferees included the provision in the conference report.)

Conferences with many conferees from a number of different committees can be much more unwieldy than the traditional small, one-committee conference. The House's current standard operating procedure of spelling out the sections or titles of the bill over which the "limited jurisdiction" conferees have authority eases the problem to some extent. Conferences with a number of sets of limited jurisdiction conferees ordinarily work through subconferences, with the House's limited jurisdiction conferees negotiating with their Senate committee counterparts.

Although they have authority over the entire bill, the House general jurisdiction conferees get involved in the provisions under other committees' jurisdiction only if the matter threatens the success of the conference. Since the Senate seldom expressly limits its conferees' authority to specific parts of a bill, senators can, if they wish, dabble in any aspect of the legislation. In fact, staff report that even senators not on the conference may insert themselves into the negotiations if they feel strongly about an issue. Time constraints do tend to keep Senate conferees focused on the parts of the bill that fall within their committees' jurisdiction.

Subconferences do provide some structure, but when conferees from a number of different committees are involved, someone still must coordinate the work, making sure progress is made and that the parts are reassembled into a coherent whole at the end. The committee chairs of the lead committee have the primary responsibility for this, but the party leadership and the leaders' senior staff often are actively involved as well.

As the legislative process has changed, drawing party leaders more deeply into the process, members have come to expect that their leaders will take a hand on major legislation at the conference stage. Speaker Hastert routinely discussed upcoming conferences with the relevant committee chairs, laying out the parameters of an acceptable agreement: "what's got to be in it, . . . [and] things that can't be in it." The Senate leaders also keep a careful eye on conference negotiations.

Stalemate between the two chambers often requires direct leadership intervention. When conferences on four appropriations bills bogged down in late 1995 over the abortion issue, House Majority Leader Dick Armey and Senate Republican Whip Trent Lott stepped in to broker agreements that both adamantly anti-abortion House Republicans and more moderate Senate Republicans could accept. In March 1996 Senate Majority Leader Dole almost single-handedly broke the stalemate on the line-item-veto bill. Having established himself as the almost certain presidential nominee of the Republican Party, Dole made getting a bill out of conference and to the president a top priority and so a test of his ability to get things done. Under these special political circumstances Republican senators, even those with severe substantive doubts about the bill, were unwilling to hold out against Dole's position of basically agreeing to the House version of the bill. Doing otherwise would have crippled their nominee. The line-item-veto bill was approved by the conferees and signed by the president, who in negotiations with Majority Leader Dole and Speaker Gingrich had decided what the effective date of the legislation would be. It was Speaker Hastert and Majority Leader Bill Frist who broke the impasse on the Medicare/prescription drug legislation in late 2003 and negotiated the final bill. (See Chapter 8.)

When the choices facing conferees are highly salient and consequential ones that affect the political fate of members and of their party, party leaders are likely to make the final decisions, as they did on the Medicare/prescription drug bill. In 2002, 2003, and again in 2004, Congress enacted an omnibus appropriations bill because various political problems made it impossible to pass thirteen bills separately. When it came to putting together those huge and consequential spending bills, deciding what provisions would be included and which would be dropped, the party leaders made the final determinations.

High partisan polarization has affected the process of resolving interchamber differences. During the period of split partisan control of the House and Senate from June 2001 through the end of 2002, major legislation, such as the patients' bill of rights and an energy bill, died at the conference stage; the differences between the Democratic Senate bill and the Republican House bill were irreconcilable. But even when the two chambers are controlled by the same party, the Senate's supermajority requirement can complicate the process.

Republicans controlled both chambers during most of 1995 through 2006, but even then, the Senate's bill was usually considerably more moderate than congressional Republicans as a group preferred. The Republicans' strategic response to this problem dictated that the House pass extremely conservative bills so that, when it came time to negotiate with the Senate, conservatives would be in the strongest position possible. Republicans gambled that Senate moderates of both parties would be loathe to vote against bills on such important issues, even if the bills that emerged from conference were considerably further to the right than they preferred. On the Medicare/prescription drug legislation, the wager paid off, at least in the short run, and the conference report passed the Senate. The energy bill, in contrast, was blocked by a filibuster.

No longer constrained by a possible Clinton veto once George W. Bush became president in 2001, Republicans went further in trying to use conferences to recoup losses they suffered in the Senate. "[I]f you can get a bill to conference," Senate Republican Whip Mitch McConnell explained, "you have wide latitude to produce a bill the majority is comfortable with and the president is comfortable with" (*New York Times*, August 2, 2003).

To accomplish that, Republicans took to excluding most Democrats from conference negotiations altogether. When Democrats complained about being excluded from the negotiations on the budget resolution in April 2001, Senate Budget Committee Chair Pete Domenici, R-N.M., baldly replied, "We don't expect you to sign [the conference report], so we don't expect you to be needed" (*CQW,* April 28, 2001, 904). In 2003, no Democrats were allowed to participate in the energy bill conference and only two Senate Democrats who were considered accommodating were admitted to the negotiations on the Medicare/prescription drug bill.

In the Senate, the minority party usually has strategic options to employ when it feels misused by the majority. The motions necessary to go to conference can be filibustered. "The three steps [necessary to go to conference] are usually bundled into a unanimous consent agreement and done within seconds," former Senate parliamentarian Robert B. Dove, explained. "But if some senators do not want a conference to occur and if they are very determined, they can force three separate cloture votes to close debate, and that takes a lot of time. It basically stops the whole process of going to conference" (*Roll Call,* May 3, 2004). Democrats responded to their exclusion from conference committee decision making by blocking conferences.

In 2004, Democrats blocked all conferences until early April, when they allowed conferees to be appointed on the Coast Guard reauthorization bill. Among the legislation stopped were bills on charitable giving and job training. Later in the spring, a massive highway bill was stopped. Explaining his objection to the Republican motions to go to conference, Democratic Whip Harry Reid of Nevada said, "Maybe we can reflect back on what happened on the energy bill. . . . We not only were not allowed to go to conference, we did not even know where the conference meetings were being held" (*CQW,* May 8, 2004, 1080). In each case the Democrats' demand was a guarantee that they be included in the negotiations. In late May, Democrats did allow the highway bill to go to conference in return for a promise from Majority Leader Bill Frist. Daschle and Frist explained— and put on the record—the agreement through this floor colloquy:

FRIST: . . . The transportation bill we passed this year was a model of bipartisan cooperation that was marked by good faith on both sides. That is the essence of the agreement I am proposing, a commitment from both sides that they will work in good faith in conference to get the best possible result. I have spoken to Senator Inhofe, who will chair the conference. He has agreed he will not pursue a conclusion to the conference, nor sign any conference report that would alter the text of S. 1072 in a way that undermines the bipartisan working relationship that has existed in the Senate.

DASCHLE: . . . I have discussed this with my colleagues and can commit whole-heartedly to the good-faith process he has proposed. Our side understands that changes will have to be made, and we are not entering this process demanding a specific outcome on any provision. Instead, we are asking any changes to S. 1072 be the result of the mutual agreement of the lead Senate conferees acting in good faith. By moving S. 1072 through the Senate, Senators Inhofe, Bond, Jeffords, and Reid have already demonstrated they can make that process work. If the process should break down due to disagreements over either transportation policy or extraneous provisions, then we understand he and I will not bring such a conference report to the floor.

FRIST: That is correct, so long as the Democratic conferees are acting in good faith, and I have every expectation they will. Our goal is to reach a conference agreement that reflects the balance and broad bipartisan consensus S. 1072 achieves. That will be the test of good faith for both sides. I think we can do that, and we will not bring a bill to the Senate floor if it does not reflect that commitment (*Congressional Record*, May 19, 2004, S5838).

In 2005, the legislative process on the energy bill was bipartisan both initially in the Senate and in conference, and a bill finally was enacted. (See Chapter 7.) However, the often unpalatable compromises required to get the support of more than a handful of the minority party in a period of high partisan polarization tempts the majority party to use conferences to attain its ends.

The executive branch is often an important participant in conference. During periods when control of the White House and Congress is divided between the parties, especially in times when the parties are highly polarized, the president is often another source of difficulty in reaching agreement. The president has no official role, but, if conferees want their legislation to become law, they must satisfy the president sufficiently to avoid a veto or be prepared to muster a two-thirds vote in both chambers. Under divided control presidents often wield their greatest power over legislation at the conference stage. The term *veto bargaining* became current during George H. W. Bush's presidency to describe that Bush administration's frequent attempts to extract concessions from the Democratic Congress by threatening a veto.

After Republicans gained control of Congress in the 1994 elections, President Clinton showed himself to be an adept veto bargainer. Most bills and all major legislation showed the effects of administration involvement, usually at the conference stage. In 1998 the conferees for a bill authorizing funds for agricultural research and making up a shortfall in the federal crop insurance program added a provision restoring food stamp eligibility for 250,000 legal immigrants who had been denied such eligibility by the 1996 welfare reform bill; they did so because Clinton persuaded them that otherwise he would veto the bill, which was of great importance to their constituents. The Clinton administration was especially effective in conferences on appropriations bills, often extracting more money for education and other favored programs from a less than amenable Republican Congress.

When the same party controls Congress and the White House, the administration wields influence throughout the legislative process. It may send Congress draft legislation. Administration officials, of course, testify at committee hearings, but less formal consultation is ongoing and probably more influential. Nevertheless, the House/Senate resolution stage gets special administration attention just because it is the final stage. What emerges goes to the president. White House involvement allowed the airline assistance bill passed in the wake of the 9/11 attacks to avoid conference altogether. Formally, the Senate passed the House bill without change. In actuality, the bill was drafted by the White House and congressional leaders from both chambers.

In the tough conference on the terrorism reinsurance bill in 2002, the Republican House's counteroffer to the Democratic Senate's offer was "written in cooperation with the White House" (*CongressDaily AM,* October 8, 2002). "More often than any other senior administration figure, [Vice President Dick] Cheney is frequently the big gun who enters Congressional negotiations at a key stage to cut a deal, Hill sources [reported]." According to reports, in 2005 he was active on the extension of the PATRIOT Act, the torture issue, and economic policy among other issues (*RC,* December 14, 2005). As in previous administrations, the White House chief of staff and the director of the Office of Management and Budget also often are involved at the conference stage.

Even though Republicans controlled both chambers of Congress in the 108th Congress, President George W. Bush used veto threats quite frequently; he threatened at least eighteen relatively major bills with vetoes.[1] These veto threats were, by and large, directed at specific provisions in bills that he otherwise supported. Attempts to overturn new FCC media ownership rules, to lift the ban on travel to Cuba, to prevent the administration from revising overtime rules in such a way as to deprive some of those currently eligible of overtime pay, to delay military base closings, to allow concurrent receipts for veterans, and to block the administration's efforts to outsource federal jobs to private companies were the target of veto threats—in some cases, of repeated threats.

Bush's veto threats may well have been intended to give the Republican leadership ammunition against majority-supported provisions the president opposed. On some issues, Bush was forced to compromise but, in every instance, the veto threat moved the bill toward his position. Party leaders repeatedly removed offending provisions in conference. Hastert made sure a transportation bill Bush would feel it necessary to veto did not emerge from conference in 2004. In fact, "[Hastert] made it clear that

---

1. "Relatively major" includes appropriations bills as well as major measures as defined earlier. Veto threats are identified by their being mentioned in *CQW.*

they would not allow bills that would be vetoed to reach the president's desk," according to Nick Calio, former head of White House liaison for Bush (*RC*, December 15, 2003). Bush did not veto a single bill during his first term and only one before Republicans lost control of Congress in the 2006 elections.

In conference, decisions require the assent of both the House and the Senate. Traditionally, the position of a chamber has been determined by the majority of its conferees and the final agreement also has required a simple majority of the conferees of each chamber. That is still the Senate's interpretation. The House, however, requires, that on each part of the bill a majority of the total of the general conferees plus the jurisdiction-specific conferees must sign (Beth and Rybicki 2003). Conferees formally indicate their approval by signing the conference report, which consists of the compromise legislative language agreed on by the conferees. The House form is broken down by sections that coincide with the jurisdiction-specific authority for which conferees were appointed.

Rarely, at least when both chambers are controlled by the same party, are conferees unable to reach an agreement and the legislation dies in conference. In recent Congresses fewer than one major measure on average died in conference per Congress. In the 108th Congress, the big transportation reauthorization measure never emerged from conference, but the problem was finding a deal that satisfied the president, who was unwilling to go along with as high a spending figure as both the House and Senate wanted. By the time legislation gets to conference, many people, and especially many of the conferees who may well have worked on the bill for months, have a considerable stake in the legislation's enactment. Therefore, a compromise is usually found even when House and Senate versions are very different.

Conferees' Power and Its Limits

Conferees have considerable power over the substance of legislation. House and Senate rules specify that conferees are limited in the agreement they reach to the differences between the House and Senate versions of the legislation. However, in those cases—the majority—in which the Senate has passed a substitute to the House bill (rather than a series of specific amendments to the House bill), Senate rules interpret this requirement quite broadly. In the House the conferees can get around the rule by taking their conference report to the floor under a special rule from the Rules Committee that waives the requirement. Since many conference committees finish their work late in a Congress, when everyone works under severe time constraints, senators and representatives not on a conference committee often lack the time to study the conference report and thus to be able to challenge it. Furthermore, the "layover" requirements that stipulate that members have the conference report available for a period of time before floor consideration often are waived, further limiting access to the report.

Although House members or senators can (by majority vote) instruct their conferees about the substance of the legislation, these instructions are not binding (Tiefer 1989, 780–833; Gold et al. 1992, 337–347). Motions to instruct are frequently offered, more than ninety in the House during the 108th Congress and an average of forty-nine per Congress in the House from 1991 through 2002. In response to the majority's increased use of highly restrictive rules, the minority party in the House often turns to motions to instruct conferees to force floor debate on its issues. A considerable number of such motions do pass—thirty-four in the 108th. Occasionally they do have an effect, as the 308–122 House vote on the Murtha motion to instruct conferees to accept the Senate's anti-torture language did in 2005. Of course, since the motions are not binding, voting for a popular provision can be a cheap vote for a majority party member.

Not only can conferees ignore instructions, they can and sometimes do jettison provisions that both chambers have approved. Party leaders dropped a number of provisions that Bush opposed but both chambers had voted for from the omnibus appropriations bills in 2002, 2003, and 2004. Democrats complained bitterly but, given that appropriations bills are must-pass legislation, had little recourse. In June 2006, a bar on the funding of permanent U.S. military bases in Iraq, a version of which was included in both chambers' bills, was deleted from the emergency supplemental Iraq-war appropriations bill even before conference. The Bush administration had opposed any such language.

On occasion a provision that neither chamber included in its respective bill gets added in conference. The conference report for the agricultural appropriations bill that passed in late 2005 contained totally new language rewriting and weakening the legal definition of "organic food"; the bills that went to conference did not deal with the issue even peripherally (*RC*, November 16, 2005). (The language was inserted by someone, presumably a senior conferee.) Earmarks—projects for specific districts or states—seem to be regularly added at the conference stage (Lilly 2005, 2006). Sometimes even most majority party conferees are unaware of what is being inserted into the conference report. In fact, there often is no formal meeting of the conference to approve the report. Rather, the necessary signatures are gathered by staff and members sign without actually seeing the final language.

Once a majority of the House conferees and a majority of the Senate conferees have formalized their approval by signing the conference report, it is returned to both chambers, where the full membership must decide whether to accept what their representatives have done. At this point no amendments are in order; the membership votes up or down on the compromise as a package.[2] Although the overwhelming majority of conference reports are approved, occasionally one is sent back to conference—a parliamentary move available only to the chamber that acts first—or simply is voted down.

When the conference report for the 2002 bankruptcy bill came back to the House containing language that prohibited abortion protestors from using bankruptcy to escape fines for harassing staff and prospective clients of abortion clinics, committed anti-abortion Republicans joined with those Democrats who opposed the bankruptcy provisions to defeat the rule. That killed the bill for the 107th Congress.

When House and Senate conferees deleted a pay-as-you-go (PAYGO) provision from the 2004 budget resolution, the resolution became impossible to pass in the Senate. Moderate Senate Republicans had insisted on the provision as their price for supporting it, but House Republicans and the Bush administration strongly opposed PAYGO. Frist hoped the moderates would back down but, when they refused, he knew he lacked the votes to pass the conference report and never brought it to the floor. To the Republicans' considerable embarrassment, Congress had to function without a budget resolution in 2004.

In fall of 2005, the House voted down the conference report on the Labor, Health and Human Services, Education appropriations bill, with twenty-two Republicans joining all the Democrats in opposition. Democrats vehemently disliked the cuts in spending for education and health programs, as did some moderate Republicans, and there were ten different issues motivating the other Republican opponents, according to a Republican leader (*CQW*, November 18, 2005, 3133). The Labor-H bill, as it is called, is huge, funding hundreds of programs, and the 2005 budget resolution had mandated a tight spending ceiling, ensuring that many popular programs would suffer. Reportedly, the conference committee's dropping of all earmarked projects for specific districts also infuriated some members. Of course, everyone knew that defeat of the conference report was not the last word. The programs the bill funded could not be allowed to go without any money for a year. The Speaker reappointed conferees, and the

---

2. The exceptions are appropriations bills on which the conferees have exceeded the scope of the differences between the two chambers' bills or to which the Senate has added amendments that constitute unauthorized appropriations or legislation and bills on which the Senate has added nongermane amendments, so long as the Senate has constructed its appropriations bill via a series (often one hundred or more) of amendments to the House bill. House rules allow separate votes on those matters, but this can be waived by a rule from the Rules Committee. Since the mid-1990s, the Senate has instead produced a substitute for the House bill and this precludes demands for separate votes (Tiefer 1989, 833–848; Oleszek 2004, 276).

House sent the bill back to conference with the Senate. Increases in funding for rural health care and a few other changes allowed the Republican leadership to narrowly pass the new conference report a month after the first had failed.

These cases (and occasionally others) notwithstanding, the recommittal or defeat of a conference report is rare. Yet, as infrequent as the rejection of a conference report is, its occasional occurrence serves to remind conferees that they must be sensitive to the policy preferences of their chambers' membership. Conferees have considerable discretion but only within the limits set by the full membership's tolerance.

The Final Step

After both the House and Senate have approved legislation in identical form, it is sent to the president, who can sign it, do nothing, or veto it. If he signs it or holds it for ten weekdays while Congress is in session, the legislation becomes law. However, if Congress has adjourned sine die (that is, indefinitely, which happens at the end of a Congress), the president can kill legislation by holding it for ten weekdays without signing it. In those cases the president is said to cast a pocket veto.[3]

When the president casts a formal veto, the legislation is sent back to the Congress with the president's message of disapproval and his reasons for having cast the veto. For the legislation to become law, both houses must override the veto by a two-thirds vote.

No rules require that Congress vote to override a president's veto within a specified period of time. In the past the vote tended to come fairly soon after the veto. For years this was the expectation and the practice. More recently, however, the chamber that originated the bill (which must be the first to vote to override) has sometimes held the bill to gain political advantage. In 1996, for example, Republican leaders did not schedule veto override votes on the "partial-birth" abortion bill until late September, only weeks before the elections. This was a bill that had passed both houses way back in March and had been vetoed in April.

Mustering a two-thirds vote in both chambers on a controversial matter is a formidable task. George H. W. Bush had only one veto overridden during his four years as president even though politically he was quite

---

3. For the controversy over whether presidents have the right to pocket veto legislation when the Congress has adjourned but not sine die (between the two sessions or over recesses, for example), see Gold 2004, 130–131. Congress seems to have successfully countered this strategy by authorizing an agent to receive messages from the president.

weak during much of his presidency. In 1995, despite being enormously weakened by the 1994 elections, Clinton suffered only one override; from 1996 through 2000, only one more of his vetoes was overridden. A bill's supporters know that if they want to enact legislation, they must either satisfy the president or be prepared to amass enough support in both houses to override his veto. The former will usually seem the easier task. Thus, the veto gives the president considerable influence in the legislative process as explored earlier in this chapter.

Reconciling Differences: How Much Change?

Change in the legislative process within the two chambers has spilled over and affected the process of reconciling interchamber differences. Multiple referral and members' desire for broad participation has led to bigger conference delegations, especially on the part of the House. Although House leaders have reined in the size of conference delegations, conferences still often have multicommittee representation; such conferences work in subconferences, which on the House side have authority to make decisions only on specifically delineated parts of the legislation. The coordinating problems such an undertaking entails draw the party leadership, the only central leadership in the chambers, into a process that used to be committee dominated. The party leaders' greater involvement in the legislative process within their chamber—in working out postcommittee compromises that facilitate passage, for example—leads to a greater role for them at the resolution stage as well. If it took leadership intervention to put together the compromise necessary to pass the bill, sustaining the compromise in conference and passing the resulting conference report often will require leadership involvement, too.

Furthermore, the party leadership's more central role also seems to have stimulated the use of various informal routes to resolving interchamber differences, ones that often involve the administration and that sometimes avoid conference altogether. Data gathered by Elizabeth Rybicki show that in recent years the number of conferences has dropped significantly: from a mean of eighty-one conferences per Congress for the 97th through the 103rd (1981–1994), the number drops to sixty-three in the 104th; then it falls to a mean of fifty-one for the 105th and 106th and a mean of thirty-seven for the 107th and 108th Congresses.

Omnibus Legislation, the Budget Process, and Summits

UNORTHODOX LAWMAKING IS NOT CONFINED to the sorts of innovations and modifications to what were once standard procedures and practices that the previous chapters examined. Omnibus bills, the budget process and summits, and forms of legislation—ways of making decisions that either did not exist at all or were rarely used several decades ago—are now prominent. Contemporary Congresses often legislate through enormous omnibus bills, something rarely done before the 1980s. The budget process, established in the mid-1970s but peripheral to legislative decision making until the 1980s, has become central. And on big issues that must be resolved, summits—relatively formal negotiations between congressional leaders and high-ranking administration officials representing the president directly—have become a fairly standard mode of decision making when control of the national government's branches is divided between the parties.

When legislative decisions are made through omnibus legislation, the budget process, and summits, decision making is more centralized than it is on other major legislation; central leaders—congressional party leaders and often the president—play a more important role, frequently the decisive role. These modes of legislating make it possible for Congress to enact comprehensive policy change, always a difficult task for what has usually been a decentralized institution; they also may reduce the opportunities for careful scrutiny of the legislation's provisions and for broad participation by rank-and-file members.

Divided government, partisan polarization, and big deficits are the most important of the environmental factors that fostered these developments. As long as intense partisanship and big deficits persist, the major political conflicts of a Congress likely will continue to revolve around omnibus legislation and the budget process. With the return of divided government, summits too may again become prominent.

Omnibus Legislation and the Budget Process

The legislation that Congress deals with varies from the short and simple—the one-sentence bill, HR3989, "To designate the facility of the United States Postal Service located at 37598 Goodhue Avenue in Dennison, Minnesota, as the 'Albert H. Quie Post Office' "—to the extraordinarily long and complex.[1] The 1990 Clean Air Act was about 800 pages long, and the 2005 energy bill was 550 pages; in both cases, nonexperts would need a translator to make sense of the legislation. The bills enacting President Ronald Reagan's economic program in 1981 and President Bill Clinton's in 1993 were even longer.

Legislation that addresses numerous and not necessarily related subjects, issues, and programs, and therefore is usually highly complex and long, is referred to as omnibus legislation. Although there is no consensus technical definition of what constitutes an omnibus bill, every Congress watcher would classify as omnibus the 1988 trade bill that spanned the jurisdiction of thirteen House and nine Senate committees and the anti-drug bill passed the same year. The latter covered drug abuse education and prevention; treatment; punishment of abusers and sellers, big and small; and the interdiction of drugs flowing into the United States from abroad by air, sea, and land.

Although perhaps not quite as disparate in subjects covered, the 2002 bill setting up the Department of Homeland Security and the 2004 bill reorganizing U.S. government intelligence operations also can be considered omnibus legislation, and the process on each illustrates the problems such bills create and the unorthodox fixes the leadership employs to pass them. When President George W. Bush requested that Congress quickly establish a Department of Homeland Security in the spring of 2002, the House Republican leadership could anticipate some significant problems. What Bush proposed was the largest reorganization of the federal bureaucracy in a half century, a reorganization that combined all or part of twenty-two federal agencies responsible for counterterrorism. A large number of House committees would have to be involved because they had jurisdiction over programs that Bush wanted moved into the new department, and

---

1. Albert H. Quie is a former member of the House; Congress frequently names federal buildings after former members.

some of them would likely resist giving up any of their jurisdiction. Yet if the House did not move expeditiously, the chamber's and the party's reputation would be damaged.

To handle the political problems as well as the major coordination task of melding the work of a dozen or so committees into a coherent whole, Speaker Dennis Hastert, R-Ill., proposed and the House approved a select committee of nine members. Hastert chose Majority Leader Dick Armey, R-Tex., to chair the committee and appointed members of the leadership to the remaining Republican slots (*CQ Weekly*, June 22, 2002, 1651). On June 24, the legislation was referred to twelve standing committees under a deadline; on July 16 and 17, ten of these committees presented their recommendations to the Select Committee, which made significant changes to some of the recommendations. Floor consideration on the combined bill began on July 25, and the bill passed on July 26.

The bill reorganizing government intelligence operations in response to the recommendations of the 9/11 Commission was also a far-reaching measure and, on the House side, included a myriad of loosely related proposals—on such matters as law enforcement and immigration, for example. In the House the bill was referred to thirteen committees, five of which reported. These formal processes, however, masked what really happened. The bill was actually drafted by the chairs of the affected committees under leadership auspices. Only then was the bill introduced—by Speaker Hastert—and sent to the committees, all of which reported or were discharged within ten days.

Revealing the differences between the chambers, neither bill was handled through such unorthodox processes in the Senate. Both were reported by a single committee—Government Affairs. The Homeland Security Department bill did run into a typical Senate problem when minority Republicans, using their right of extended debate, refused to allow a passage vote on a version Bush opposed. (See Chapter 3.)

Many of the bills generally labeled omnibus are money bills of some sort. The most common omnibus measures in contemporary Congresses are omnibus appropriations bills, budget resolutions, and reconciliation bills. Omnibus measures have made up about 14 percent of major legislation in recent Congresses.[2]

The Congressional Budget and Impoundment Control Act of 1974 created an entirely new process and superimposed it on the old process by which Congress had made spending and taxing decisions. The new budget process made omnibus measures a regular part of the annual congressional workload and influenced the legislative process in other direct and indirect ways. Although a detailed examination of the budget process and

---

2. The 103rd, 104th, 105th, 107th, and 108th.

its ramifications cannot be undertaken here, a discussion of the contemporary legislative process would not be complete without some discussion of the budget process. (On the budget process, see Schick 1980; Oleszek 2004; and Thurber and Durst 1993.)

Understanding the budget process requires first grasping the difference between authorizations and appropriations. It is the subject matter committees, such as Agriculture or Education, that are empowered to report legislation that creates new programs or alters existing ones. Such a bill typically also authorizes Congress to appropriate the money that will be needed to implement the program. Most of these authorization bills, as they often are called, now authorize specific maximum amounts of appropriations for one or more fiscal years. If the program is going to continue being implemented beyond those fiscal years, Congress is supposed to reauthorize appropriations for it for additional fiscal years. Congress moved from mostly permanent authorizations to mostly temporary, but multiyear, authorizations in the 1960s and 1970s in order to encourage more program oversight and to increase the influence of the subject matter, or "authorization," committees.

The Constitution requires that funds for government programs must be appropriated by law. Congressional rules, especially House rules, require that those appropriations first must be authorized. Once a program has been created by law, the provisions governing its organization, purposes, activities, and so on remain in force unless that law is amended or repealed, or unless the law includes a "sunset" provision that causes the provisions to expire on a certain date or after a certain number of years. It is the authorization of appropriations for a program that is limited to one year or a finite number of fiscal years.

The reason people talk as if the program itself would cease to exist if it were not reauthorized when its limited-year authorization of appropriations expires is because a program without money (appropriations) in effect does not exist. However, the internal congressional rules that bar unauthorized appropriations can be waived and now often are. Thus, for various political reasons, U.S. foreign aid programs were not reauthorized for many years, even though they were supposed to be reauthorized every year. However, those programs continued to function because money for them was appropriated after the rules prohibiting unauthorized appropriations were waived in the House, via a rule reported from the Rules Committee.

Appropriating funds is the task of the House and Senate Appropriations Committees; every year they must report out and see enacted a series of bills that appropriate money for the federal government's multitude of programs and agencies. The two committees are organized into a number of subcommittees, each of which reports a general appropriations bill that funds a number of government programs and agencies. For example, the

Labor, Health and Human Services, and Education Subcommittee reports a bill that appropriates funds for the programs and agencies that fall under these three cabinet departments.

For many years, the House and Senate Appropriations Committees each had thirteen subcommittees with identical jurisdiction. In 2005, the House and Senate committees reorganized and reduced the number of subcommittees; in the 109th Congress, the number of general appropriations bills was eleven. When Democrats took control of both chambers after the 2006 elections, they reorganized again, establishing twelve subcommittees. There are currently twelve general appropriations bills.[3]

Appropriations bills fund their programs for only one year. Were Congress to fail to pass the Labor-HHS-Education appropriations bill, many of those departments' programs as well as the administrative structure would have to shut down. (Programs such as Social Security that are funded through a mechanism other than annual appropriations would not be directly affected.) The prospect of shutting down programs that people want and depend on is sufficiently horrendous that Congress always passes appropriations bills—although in late 1995 it did so only after a hiatus of several weeks (see the discussion of the 1995 budget process in Chapter 11).

Frequently, Congress cannot pass all the general appropriations bills by the annual deadline of October 1, the beginning of the fiscal year (abbreviated FY); in that case it passes a continuing (appropriations) resolution, referred to as a CR, that temporarily continues funding.[4] Continuing resolutions may cover the few appropriations bills that have not yet passed and extend for only a few days or weeks. Sometimes, however, Congress passes a bill that encompasses half or more of the regular appropriations bills and extends through the remainder of the fiscal year—such legislation truly qualifies as omnibus. In 2002, for example, Congress failed to pass eleven of the regular appropriations bills; after multiple CRs, all eleven were wrapped into one omnibus bill and passed in February 2003, more than four months after the beginning of the fiscal year. Similarly, seven regular appropriations bills for FY2004 were packaged into one omnibus bill and finally passed in January 2004. The FY2005 Omnibus Appropriations bill included nine of the regular appropriations bills. The next year, however, Congress managed

---

3. The 2005 House committee reorganization reduced the number of subcommittees to ten. The Senate committee only cut its subcommittees to twelve. Consequently, the subcommittees in the two chambers were no longer entirely parallel. The Democratic reorganization in the 110th Congress reestablished a parallel structure.

4. Funding is usually set at the previous year's level or at the lower of the levels proposed by the House and Senate.

to pass all of its appropriations bills separately, although some were passed well after the beginning of the fiscal year.

In the beginning of the 110th Congress, only two of the eleven general Appropriations bills for FY2007 had been enacted. At a lame-duck session, the outgoing Republican majority had passed a CR funding the programs covered by the other bills through February 15. That CR set funding for each program at its previous year's level. The new Democratic majority was confronted with having to pass nine contentious Appropriations bills four months into the fiscal year or doing one big bill. Since the new majority had an ambitious agenda, and the Appropriations Committees would soon have to start work on the FY2008 bills, the chairs of the Appropriations Committees negotiated a combination CR/omnibus Appropriations bill that mostly funded programs at the previous year's level for the rest of fiscal 2007 but did make some adjustments to take into account Democratic priorities and to avoid hardships in underfunded programs. This bill never went through committee in either chamber and was considered under a closed rule on the House floor. Here again, severe policy and political problems prompted the use of unorthodox processes.

In addition to regular appropriations bills, Congress may pass supplemental appropriations bills. These bills are supposed to address unexpected contingencies—emergencies such as Hurricane Katrina relief (Oleszek 2004, 44). The George W. Bush administration used emergency supplementals to fund the wars in Afghanistan and Iraq, arguing that the amounts needed could not be predicted and so could not be included in the regular budget. The amounts appropriated by supplementals do not count against spending ceilings set by the budget resolution and do not figure into predictions about future budget deficits. Furthermore, the president's request usually is much less detailed and less thoroughly justified than are funding requests in his budget. For these reasons, the administration's use of supplementals to fund the wars became increasingly controversial, even among congressional Republicans. After the 2006 elections, the administration promised to include war funding in the regular budget—after one more big supplemental in early 2007.

Not all programs are funded through annual appropriations. Some of the federal government's biggest programs are entitlement programs—programs that stipulate that people who meet certain criteria are entitled to a specified benefit. Social Security, Medicare, Medicaid, agricultural commodity programs, and food stamps are all entitlement programs. Funding for many of these programs is not under the control of the Appropriations Committees. Some of the biggest—Social Security and a part of Medicare—are funded by trust funds, and some have permanent appropriations. Even in those cases, such as food stamps, for which annual appropriations are required, the Appropriations Committees' discretion is highly limited. If the money appropriated runs out before the end of the year, Congress must pass a supplemental appropriations bill to fund food stamps for eligible people. Cutting spending for entitlements requires changing the legislation that authorized the program, and that is in the jurisdiction of the authorizing committee, not the Appropriations Committee.[5]

To provide some coherence to the process of making spending decisions, the Budget Act requires that before the appropriations bills are drafted, Congress must pass a budget resolution setting guidelines. The budget resolution specifies how much the federal government will spend in the next fiscal year, how much it expects to collect in taxes, and how large the deficit or surplus (the difference between the two) is expected to be. It also specifies how much is to be spent in each of twenty broad functional categories—health or agriculture, for example. The Budget Committee report accompanying the resolution may contain detailed suggestions about policy changes that would produce the overall figures. Although it may suggest that spending on particular programs be cut in order to reach the overall spending figure, its suggestions have no binding effect.

Estimating the deficit or surplus is not a routine technical exercise and may well be the source of controversy. The deficit or surplus depends on expected expenditures and revenues, both of which depend in turn on a number of economic assumptions. Tax receipts, for example, depend on the state of the economy; when the economy is growing, more people have jobs, wages are likely to be going up, and more businesses are making money, and thus people and business pay more in taxes. Federal expenditures depend on economic estimates as well; for example, when the economy is bad, more people will qualify for unemployment benefits and food stamps, so spending for such entitlement programs will go up.

In addition to estimates for the upcoming year, the budget resolution projects expenditures, revenues, and deficits or surpluses for either five or ten years into the future, an even trickier enterprise. Congress relies on the Congressional Budget Office, staffed by nonpartisan experts, for its estimates. The Office of Management and Budget provides estimates for the president. In 1995 a dispute over which set of figures to use was at the center of the budget battle. Small differences in assumptions about the growth rate of the American economy over the following seven years made a huge difference in the estimate of how much needed to be cut from spending in order to achieve a balanced budget by the year 2002.

Drafting the budget resolution is the task of a Budget Committee in each chamber. The committees take into consideration the president's

---

5. Aid to Families with Dependent Children (AFDC) was an entitlement program; the 1996 welfare bill changed it from an entitlement to a block grant program that requires annual appropriations.

budget request that by law must be submitted to Congress by the first Monday in February. As the Senate committee's description of the budget process explains, "One of the first things Congress needs to know when crafting a budget is what the executive branch believes is necessary to fund the operations of the Federal government" (Committee on the Budget, United States Senate 1998, 10). Other committees send their views on spending on programs within their jurisdictions to the Budget Committees, and the Congressional Budget Office provides reports on the budget and economic outlook as well as an analysis of the president's budget request. Since the resolution sets overall budgetary policy, drafting it is too important and often too difficult a task for the committee to undertake on its own. A budget is a statement of priorities and, when resources are tight, involves painful trade-offs. Congressional party leaders always are involved, and the president may be as well.

The legislative process on a budget resolution looks similar in many ways to the process followed on ordinary legislation. After the committees report, each chamber must pass its respective version. In the House the majority party leadership always brings up the resolution under a special rule that restricts amendments; usually, only a limited number of comprehensive substitutes are allowed. The Budget Act limits Senate debate to fifty hours and requires that amendments be germane. Thus, a budget resolution cannot be filibustered. A conference committee is appointed to come up with a compromise between the two chambers' versions, which must then be approved by both houses. The budget resolution, however, is not legislation; it is a concurrent resolution that does not require the president's signature.

In essence, the budget resolution is a set of guidelines that Congress has agreed on to guide its own—specifically, its committees'—spending and taxing decisions for the year. The budget resolution serves as a framework within which the Appropriations Committees make their spending decisions. The conference report on the resolution divides up total spending by committee. Since the Appropriations Committees are responsible for all spending done through appropriations, they receive the largest allocation. The spending that the Appropriations Committees control is referred to as "discretionary" because in law if not in political reality the committees could simply cut that spending at will. Discretionary spending now accounts for only about 27 percent of federal spending; entitlements account for 64 percent and interest on the national debt, 9 percent (Senate Appropriations Committee estimate for 2006 at http://appropriations.senate.gov/budgetprocess.cfm).

The resolution may—and in recent years often does—include binding instructions to other committees to bring law within their jurisdiction into conformance with the dictates of the budget resolution. If the aim is to cut the increase in spending, as is often the case, entitlements are likely to be targeted. The resolution may instruct an authorizing committee to reduce expenditures in the programs under its jurisdiction by a given amount; doing so requires the committee to change legislation under its jurisdiction. For example, the budget resolution for FY2006 stipulated that

> The House Committee on Agriculture shall report changes in laws within its jurisdiction sufficient to reduce the level of direct spending for that committee by $173,000,000 in outlays for fiscal year 2006 and $3,000,000,000 in outlays for the period of fiscal years 2006 through 2010 (House Report 109-062 — Concurrent Resolution on the Budget for Fiscal Year 2006).

The budget resolution instructions do not prescribe the details of the changes, only the amount of savings. Similarly, if the resolution specifies that tax revenues need to increase over what current law would bring in, the tax-writing committees—House Ways and Means and Senate Finance—will be instructed to draft a tax bill that raises a specific amount, but they will not be told how to do it—whether by raising the gasoline tax or by increasing income tax rates, for example. Conversely, if the budget resolution instructs the tax committees to cut taxes, the instructions consist of an amount taxes are to be reduced; the report may offer suggestions as to which taxes might be cut, but these are not binding. The instructions in a budget resolution are called reconciliation instructions; they instruct the various committees to reconcile legislation under their jurisdictions with the figures in the budget resolution. Reconciliation instructions also specify a deadline for committee compliance.

When the budget process is used as a vehicle for making comprehensive policy change, the number of committees instructed is often large. The budget resolution in 1981, which carried Reagan's economic program, instructed fifteen House and fourteen Senate committees. The 1993 resolution containing Clinton's program instructed thirteen House and twelve Senate committees. The 1995 resolution encompassing the new Republican majority's economic plan instructed twelve House and eleven Senate committees. The budget resolutions of 2001 and 2003, which carried George W. Bush's economic program, only specified tax cuts, although enormous ones, so they only instructed the tax-writing committees. By 2005, the growing deficit pressured Republicans to attempt to control spending growth, and the budget resolution instructed eight committees in each chamber to cut spending, but it also instructed the tax committees to cut taxes.

The instructed committees draft their legislation and then send it to the Budget Committee, which packages it into an omnibus reconciliation bill.[6] The legislation must then win approval by each chamber. In the House special rules that tightly restrict amending activity always are used to protect these big and usually controversial packages. The Budget Act protects the reconciliation bill against a filibuster in the Senate by limiting initial floor debate to twenty hours and debate on the conference report to ten hours; in addition, amendments must be germane and deficit neutral, that is, they can not increase spending. Sixty votes are required to waive these rules.

Conference committees on reconciliation bills have sometimes been huge. All the committees with provisions in the legislation as well as the Budget Committees are represented, and the totals have run into the hundreds. The conference committee on the 1981 reconciliation bill consisted of 208 House conferees from 17 committees and 72 senators from 14 committees (Tiefer 1989, 798). In 1993, 164 House members from 16 committees and 53 senators from 13 committees served on the reconciliation bill conference committee. Generally, such conferences work in subgroups; the 1981 conference, for instance, met in fifty-eight subgroups (*CQW* 1984, 1298). Most conferees have authority to make decisions only about the provisions their committee or subcommittee drafted. The House conference delegation for the 1997 spending reconciliation bill, for example, consisted of thirteen subgroups from eight committees, each with authority to negotiate on only a specific title or subtitle of the bill. Conferees from the Budget Committees usually have authority over the entire bill and take on the formidable task of coordination.

Because reconciliation bills are so substantively and politically important, the party leadership is always involved. When the Democrats were in the majority before 1995, the House majority leader served as the leadership representative on the Budget Committee and was routinely appointed a conferee. Speaker Newt Gingrich, R-Ga., appointed Majority Leader Armey, Majority Whip Tom DeLay, and Chief Deputy Whip Hastert to the 1997 spending reconciliation bill conference; they were three of the five Republican general conferees with authority over the entire bill. The conference delegation for the 2005 reconciliation bill illustrates contemporary practices. The Senate appointed twenty conferees without specifying the committees each represented. The House delegation was forty strong but only fifteen of those were general conferees; three members from each of eight committees were appointed to negotiate on the matters under their committee's jurisdiction, which was spelled out in detail. Of the fifteen conferees with jurisdiction over the entire bill, thirteen were from the

---

6. Occasionally, two reconciliation bills will be used, one that includes the programmatic changes intended to cut spending, the other that deals with taxes. This was the case in 2005.

Budget Committee; the other two were from the party leadership—Roy Blunt, R-Mo., whip and acting majority leader, and Tom DeLay.[7] Unlike the budget resolution, the reconciliation bill is legislation, so the president can veto it. This possibility gives the president influence in the process of putting the bill together, even if Congress is controlled by the other party. Unless the congressional majority party has huge majorities in both chambers, its chances are exceedingly dim of amassing a two-thirds vote to override the president on legislation that goes to the heart of the differences between the parties. If the president's own party is in the majority, the president and congressional party leaders likely will work together closely on such a major piece of legislation. The 1993 reconciliation bill followed the outlines that President Clinton had laid out, even though he had to compromise on specific provisions. In 2001 and 2003 the Republican congressional majorities gave Bush most of what he had requested. In both cases, majority party leaders played a crucial role in delivering for the president of their party. (See the case studies in Chapters 10, 11, and 12.)

The budget process provides Congress with a tool for making comprehensive decisions. Before the 1974 Budget Act, Congress made spending and taxing decisions in a piecemeal and uncoordinated fashion. To pass an economic program embodying a significant change in direction, such as Reagan's in 1981 or Clinton's in 1993, would have required enacting a dozen or more separate bills.

Reconciliation bills make a multitude of policy decisions through an abbreviated legislative process in which many provisions receive limited scrutiny. It is possible that no committee hearings were held on the changes included in the legislation. With the committees operating under time constraints, many provisions may have received only perfunctory attention during committee markup; as part of a much larger package, they may have been altogether ignored during floor debate. In fact, most members may not have been aware of many of them. Yet the provisions in a reconciliation bill are very likely to become law. The sheer size of the package tends to take attention away from any but the most major provisions. In the House the bill will be considered under a special rule that prohibits most amendments. In the Senate the bill is protected from a filibuster. And a reconciliation bill is considered "must pass" legislation by the majority party.

Given these advantages, the temptation to use a reconciliation bill as a vehicle for enacting extraneous provisions that have nothing to do with

---

7. At that point—December 2005—DeLay had stepped down as majority leader temporarily as the rules dictating that indicted leaders do so required but he had not been replaced and was still acting as part of the leadership.

implementing the reconciliation instructions is enormous. To counter that temptation, in the mid-1980s the Senate adopted the Byrd rule, named after its creator, Sen. Robert C. Byrd, a Democrat from West Virginia. The rule prohibits extraneous matter in a reconciliation bill and requires a three-fifths vote to be waived (Tiefer 1989, 891–894; Gold et al. 1992, 302–303, 326). Since what is extraneous is not self-evident, a set of rules defining what does and does not fall under the Byrd rule has developed.

Application of the rule can have major policy consequences; in 1995, for example, Senate Democrats managed to knock out big chunks of the Republicans' welfare reform legislation from the reconciliation bill. Democrats used the Byrd rule to delete a provision from the 2005 reconciliation bill that granted hospitals immunity from malpractice liability if they refused to treat poor Medicaid recipients who cannot afford a copayment. (*CQW,* December 22, 2005, 3378). Because the conference report was altered by the application of the Byrd rule, the revised version had to be approved in the House; however, most House members had already left town for the Christmas break, so in this case, the move postponed final approval of the bill. The Byrd rule often adds to the strains between the House and the Senate; House members bitterly complain that a Senate rule dictates what can and cannot be included in reconciliation bill conference reports.

The Byrd rule is only one example of the way in which the budget process has superimposed onto the two chambers' rules another set of highly complex rules. In the House the result is that special rules from the Rules Committee, which can waive budget rules, become even more important in managing the business of the chamber. In the Senate, the budget process offers a legislative route protected from filibusters, but it also adds another set of decisions that require a supermajority. For example, the key decision in the Senate's approval of legislation implementing the General Agreement on Tariffs and Trade (GATT) in 1994 was not the vote on passage, which required a simple majority. Before the Senate could vote on approval, sixty votes were needed to waive a Senate budget rule requiring that new legislation be "budget neutral." Since the GATT agreement reduced tariffs, a form of taxes, it did not comply with that rule.

Congress, the President, and Summitry

The veto, their status as head of their political party, and their capacity to command media attention allow presidents to play a major role in the legislative process. Many legislative proposals originate in the executive branch. Executive branch officials testify before congressional committees on most legislation, and they often are present during committee markups and during conference committee deliberations. In addition, executive branch officials let committee and party leaders know through private meetings and frequent informal contacts what the president wants and will accept.

Even if the president is from the other party and has very different policy preferences, the congressional majority party must pay some attention to his wishes if it wants to enact legislation. Presidents under such conditions of divided control have become adept at veto bargaining—at threatening a veto in order to extract the maximum in terms of substantive concessions from an opposition congressional majority. Of course, if the divergence in policy preferences is very wide, the result may be stalemate rather than compromise.

In recent years the president and Congress have resorted to "summits" when normal legislative processes have been incapable of producing a bill and the costs of failing to reach an agreement have been very high. (For a similar argument, see Gilmour 1990.) As relatively formal negotiations between congressional leaders and high-ranking administration officials representing the president directly, summits really have no official status; they occur when the president and the majority party leadership decide to engage in such talks. During the 1980s and 1990s, normal legislative processes often ended in stalemate because of divided control, sharp differences in policy preferences, and the tough decisions that big deficits made necessary. The deficit and the budget process, especially as revised in the mid-1980s by the Gramm-Rudman automatic spending cut provisions, often provided the sense of emergency and the statutory deadline that made inaction politically costly.

In 1987, for example, the Democratic-controlled Congress and the Reagan administration were headed toward a potentially bloody and protracted showdown. Congressional Democrats believed some tax increases were essential and had included them in their budget resolution and in the reconciliation bill; Reagan was adamantly opposed. Then the stock market crashed and everyone realized a quick agreement was essential to restore confidence in the economy. Reagan called for a summit, congressional Democrats agreed, and a small group of high-level negotiators worked out a deal.

In 1990 the Gramm-Rudman requirement—that the deficit be cut by a specified large amount, or a process known as sequestration would take place—meant that the costs if the president and Congress failed to reach an agreement would be very high. Sequestration would involve draconian automatic across-the-board spending cuts. Furthermore, estimates of the deficit were rising, and the economy showed signs of slowing. This situation made decisive action even more necessary.

Most independent experts agreed that a serious budget reduction package would have to include significant revenue increases. Yet in decisions about taxes, the parties saw their future electoral prospects at stake. Attempting to shake the high tax image that Republicans had successfully pinned on them, Democrats were determined to refuse to take the initiative—and the blame—in proposing new taxes. A great many Republicans believed that their "no new taxes" stance accounted for their party's electoral success; George H. W. Bush had pledged himself to that course during his 1988 campaign. As they saw it, Republicans had a great deal to lose by reneging on that promise.

Under these circumstances, normal processes were unlikely to produce results. So President Bush proposed a summit. The congressional party leaders appointed seventeen members as negotiators. The Treasury Secretary, the head of OMB, and the White House Chief of Staff represented the president. The first meeting was held on May 17, 1990, and sessions continued through much of June. Estimates of the likely size of the budget deficit continued to increase, but no progress toward a plan to deal with it was made.

Finally, on September 30, the day before the beginning of the fiscal year, the president and congressional leaders announced that a deal had been reached. Even after Bush had conceded the need for some new revenues, differences over taxes and domestic spending cuts had continued to block progress. Eventually, the congressional negotiating group was pared down to include only the top party leaders, and it was this small group of key leaders and high-ranking administration officials that forged the agreement. Neither Bush nor the Democratic House leadership was able to sell that agreement to their troops, and it was defeated in the House. A revised version, however, was approved soon thereafter and sequestration was avoided (Sinclair 1991). In 1995 a budget summit between the new majority congressional Republicans and President Clinton failed to produce an agreement; but in 1997 they managed to agree on a budget deal that balanced the budget (see Chapter 11).

During the second half of the 1990s, reaching agreement on appropriations bills increasingly came to require summits. Even after the budget reached balance, President Clinton and the conservative Republicans who controlled both houses of Congress differed enough in policy preferences to prevent the normal process from being sufficient. Appropriations bills must pass every year or the government shuts down. Since the president can veto appropriations bills, Congress must either satisfy him or be able to muster a two-thirds vote to override. In the partisan 1990s, the latter was never a realistic possibility for Republicans; but satisfying Clinton meant spending more for programs they disliked. Often, only some of the appropriations bills could be enacted through the regular process; the rest had to be rolled into a big omnibus spending bill, the contents of which were negotiated between congressional leaders and high-ranking White House officials. In 1998, for example, eight of the thirteen appropriations bills were packaged into one omnibus bill; in 1999, five were, including the huge Labor, Health and Human Services, and Education appropriations bill.

Under difficult circumstances, a summit may offer the only hope of agreement between Congress and the president, but as a decision-making mechanism it is relatively expensive for party leaders and the institution; it not only short-circuits the normal decision-making process but also excludes most members and is therefore likely to lead to discontent.

When the president and the congressional majority share a partisan affiliation, summits are much less likely to be necessary. The White House and the majority party leaderships in the House and Senate communicate continuously and work together regularly. The president and most members of his party in Congress share policy preferences. Consequently, informal processes are likely to be adequate for reaching agreements. Not surprisingly, there were no summits during George W. Bush's first six years as president. With the 2006 elections bringing back divided control, summits may return as well. The alternative is likely to be stalemate.

What Is the Regular Process?

The textbook diagram of how a bill becomes a law no longer accurately describes the legislative process on major bills. In the contemporary Congress there are many variations; one can more accurately speak of legislative processes in the plural than of a single cut-and-dried set of steps through which all measures proceed.

While my step-by-step discussion of the legislative process makes the variety obvious, it does not yield any precise sense of the cumulative impact of these procedures and practices. That is best conveyed by a systematic analysis of the legislative process on major legislation. How many of the special process variations characterized the process on major legislation? How frequently did such legislation follow the old textbook process?

For each of the 346 major measures in the Congresses from the late 1980s through the mid-2000s for which I have data, I counted the number of special procedures and practices that the legislation encountered as it worked its way through the House. The procedures and practices enumerated were multiple referral, omnibus legislation, legislation resulting from a legislative-executive branch summit, the bypassing of committees, post-committee adjustments, and consideration under a restrictive rule.

The House legislative process on the 346 major bills of these recent Congresses displayed at least one of these characteristics in 81 percent of the cases and two or more in 50 percent (see Table 5.1). To talk about the "regular order" in the House as the absence of these characteristics is no

TABLE 5.1   Special Procedures and Practices in the House and Senate on Major Legislation, 1987–1990, 1993–1998, 2001–2004

Number of special procedures and practices	Percentage of major measures in which the legislative process was characterized by special procedures and practices	
	House[a]	Senate[b]
0	19	27
1	31	32
2	29	25
3 or more	21	16

[a] The enumerated special procedures and practices that the legislation may have encountered as it worked its way through the House are multiple referral, omnibus legislation, the passage of legislation as a result of a legislative-executive branch summit, the bypassing of committees, postcommittee adjustments, and consideration under a restrictive rule.

[b] For the Senate essentially the same procedures and practices that were counted for the House except consideration under a restrictive rule were enumerated. See note 9. Also counted was whether the bill ran into filibuster trouble and whether it was subject to an amending marathon (ten or more amending roll calls).

Source: Computed by the author.

longer accurate, at least on major legislation. And these figures—and the comparable ones for the Senate—actually underestimate the prevalence of special or unorthodox practices and procedures because a number of bills included in the calculations did not get far enough through the legislative process to encounter some of the practices counted.

Another perspective is provided by calculating the proportion of legislation that followed the once regular process: legislation that was reported by one committee, that was not omnibus nor the result of a summit, that was not subject to postcommittee adjustments, and that was considered on the floor under an open rule. In the House the legislative process on only 6 percent of major legislation—22 out of 346 bills—in these recent Congresses meet these criteria.[8] The "regular order" is no longer the norm; on major legislation it has become the rare exception.

To assess the frequency of the new procedures and practices in the Senate, I counted the same characteristics as for the House, excepting, of

---

8. This figure is less than the 19 percent without any of the special process characteristics in Table 5.1 because the table includes measures that did not get to the House floor and measures considered under procedures other than rules—mostly suspension of the rules.

course, the use of restrictive rules.[9] In the Senate these special procedures and practices are somewhat less pervasive than in the House; the legislative process on a little more than half of major bills displayed at least one special characteristic and 16 percent displayed two or more. This measure, which parallels the one constructed for the House, excludes the most notable changes in the legislative process in the Senate: the increase in floor amending activity and the more frequent use of extended debate. When a second Senate measure of special procedures and practices is created by also counting whether the bill ran into filibuster trouble or was subject to an amending marathon (ten or more amending roll calls), 73 percent of major bills display at least one and 41 percent display two or more special process characteristics (see Table 5.1). In the Senate, as in the House, the legislative process on major legislation frequently no longer conforms to what we still tend to think of as the normal process.

In both chambers, then, the legislative process on major legislation has changed; such legislation is now more likely than not to traverse an unorthodox or nonstandard course. How and why this happened is the subject of the next chapter.

---

9. Instead of counting only technical multiple referral, I also counted bills on which more than one committee worked as subject to an unorthodox process or procedure.

c h a p t e r   s i x

Why and How the Legislative Process Changed

WHY DID THE "TEXTBOOK" LEGISLATIVE PROCESS that seemed so routinized and entrenched change so much? In this chapter I argue that the modifications and innovations can be seen as responses to problems and opportunities that members—as individuals or collectively—confronted, problems and opportunities that arose from changes in institutional structure or challenges in the political environment.

The story is complex and its various strands intertwine in intricate ways, but three factors can be analytically isolated as key: internal reforms that changed the distribution of influence in both chambers in the 1970s; the institution of the congressional budget process, an internal-process reform with sufficiently far-reaching effects to deserve separate treatment; and a political environment in the 1980s and early 1990s characterized by divided control, big deficits, and ideological hostility to the legislative goals of the congressional Democratic Party. I discuss each of these briefly and then analyze how the legislative process was affected by them.

Unorthodox lawmaking, I argue, predates the extreme partisan polarization that characterizes contemporary politics and certainly predates the 1995 Republican assumption of control of Congress. Yet both of these powerfully affected the form that changes with other origins have taken. I close the chapter with an analysis of how partisan polarization and Republican control have shaped the legislative process since the mid-1990s.

From Decentralization to Individualism in the Senate

In the U.S. Senate of the 1950s and before, influence was decentralized but unequally distributed, with committee chairs and other senior members, who were predominantly conservative, exercising the lion's share. Although Democrats were the majority party (except for the first Eisenhower Congress [1953–1954]), southerners, who were mainly conservative, made up a substantial part of the party membership and, being more senior than their northern colleagues, held a disproportionate share of committee leadership positions. The Senate of this era was a relatively closed and inward-looking institution. Typical senators specialized in the issues that came before their committees and participated meagerly on the floor; they were deferential to their seniors, loyal to the institution, and restrained in the use of the powers that Senate rules confer upon the individual (Matthews 1960; Sinclair 1989).

Senate rules then as now allowed unlimited debate and, in most cases, unlimited amending activity. The restraint that characterized the Senate of this period was not a function of rules; rather it depended on norms—unwritten rules of behavior—and on a political environment in which acting with restraint was relatively costless to senators.

That began to change in the late 1950s. The 1958 elections brought into the Senate a big class of northern liberal Democrats who had won competitive elections on a platform promising action; succeeding elections through the mid-1960s augmented the number of such members. These senators could not afford to wait to make their mark, as the old norms had demanded; both their policy and their reelection goals dictated immediate and extensive activism.

An activist style based on participation in a broader range of issues and on the floor as well as in committee became attractive to more and more senators as the political environment and the Washington political community changed radically in the 1960s and 1970s. New issues and an enormous growth in the number of groups active in Washington meant that senators were eagerly sought as champions of groups' causes. The news media played an increasingly important role in politics and needed credible sources to represent issue positions and to offer commentary. These developments made the role of outward-looking policy entrepreneur available to more senators. Successfully playing that role brought a senator a Washington reputation as a player, media attention, and possibly even a shot at the presidency.

With the incentives to exploit fully the great powers that Senate rules confer on the individual increasing so greatly, senators began to offer many more amendments on the floor and to use extended debate more often. As a result, the Senate floor became a more active decision-making arena. The proportion of legislation subject to high amending activity (ten or more amending roll calls) was tiny in the 1950s; for the 84th and 86th Congresses of 1955–1956 and 1959–1960, it averaged 3 percent. During

TABLE 6.1   Increase in Filibusters and Cloture Votes, 1951–2004

Years	Congress	Filibusters per Congress	Cloture votes per Congress	Successful cloture votes per Congress
1951–60	82–86	1.0	.4	0
1961–70	87–91	4.6	5.2	0.8
1971–80	92–96	11	22	9
1981–86	97–99	17	23	10
1987–92	100–102	27	39	15
1993–98	103–105	28	48	14
1999–2002	106–107	32	59	31
2003–04	108	27	49	12

Sources: Data for 82nd–102nd Congresses: Congressional Research Service, comp., "A Look at the Senate Filibuster," in Democratic Studies Group Special Report, June 13, 1994, app. B; Norman Ornstein, Thomas Mann, and Michael Malbin, *Vital Statistics on Congress 1993–1994* (Washington, D.C.: CQ Press, 1994), 162. Data for 103rd Congress: Richard S. Beth, "Cloture in the Senate, 103d Congress," memorandum, Congressional Research Service, June 23, 1995. Data for 104th–108th Congresses: *Congressional Quarterly Almanac* for the years 1995–2004 (Washington, D.C.: Congressional Quarterly).

the 1960s and 1970s, it rose to a mean of 8 percent per Congress, and in the 1980s it averaged 15 percent (Sinclair 1989, 115).[1]

As senators became much more willing to exploit their prerogative of extended debate, filibusters, both overt and covert, increasingly became a routine part of the legislative process in the Senate. As Table 6.1 shows, filibusters were once rare; in the 1950s a typical Congress saw one filibuster. By the 1970s more than ten filibusters occurred per Congress on average, and by the late 1980s and early 1990s filibusters were taking place at a rate of more than one a month.[2] As the number of filibusters grew, so did attempts to stop them by invoking cloture; cloture votes became an ordinary part of the legislative process. While cloture was successfully invoked fairly often, passing legislation that was at all controversial increasingly required sixty votes.

Reform and Its Legacy in the House

In the House changes in chamber and majority party rules during the 1970s transformed the distribution of influence (Dodd and Oppenheimer 1977; Sinclair 1983; Smith 1989; Rohde 1991). Even more than in the Sen-

---

1. These figures are based on data for even-numbered Congresses from the 88th to the 96th Congress and for all Congresses from the 97th through the 99th.

2. See Chapter 3 and Beth 1995 for cautions about these data.

ate, legislative influence in the House had been vested in powerful and often conservative committee leaders—often southerners—over whom party leaders and members had little control. Reformers, who were primarily liberal Democrats, objected to the conservative policy this system produced and to the limited opportunities for participation it afforded rank-and-file members.

Elections throughout the 1960s changed the composition of the Democratic Party in the House as they did in the Senate, increasing the number of northern Democrats, many of whom were liberal reformers, and decreasing the number of conservative southerners. Through a series of rules changes mostly instituted between 1969 and 1975, reformers correspondingly changed the distribution of influence. Powers and resources were shifted from committee chairs down to subcommittee chairs and rank-and-file members and up to the party leadership. For example, the power to appoint subcommittee chairs was taken away from the committee chair and given to the majority party members of the committee; subcommittees were ensured adequate budget and staff. Rather than securing their positions automatically through their seniority on the committee, committee chairs had to win approval by majority vote on a secret ballot of the majority party membership. Junior members gained resources, especially staff, that enormously increased their ability to participate actively in the legislative process. The Speaker, the leader of the majority party, was given the power to select the Democratic members of the Rules Committee, a greater say in the assignment of members to other committees, and new powers over the referral of bills.

During the same period, the House adopted sunshine rules that opened the legislative process to greater public scrutiny. Recorded votes became possible—and easy to force—in the Committee of the Whole, where the amending process takes place. Most committee markup sessions and conference committee meetings were opened to the public. The greater visibility of congressional decision making increased members' incentives for activism.

These reforms had far-reaching direct and indirect effects. By reducing the power and autonomy of the committees, they made legislating more difficult for the majority party. To be sure, Democratic reformers had often been unhappy with the sort of legislation conservative-led committees had produced. By the late 1970s, however, the committee chairs and the membership of the most powerful committees were more representative of the Democratic Party than they had been earlier, and Republicans and dissident Democrats had become adept at using floor amendments to make political points and confront mainstream Democrats with politically difficult votes. Compromises carefully crafted in committee were picked apart on the floor, and floor sessions stretched on interminably.

The number of floor amendments decided on a teller, or recorded, vote had risen gradually from 55 in 1955–1956 to 107 in 1969–1970. With the institution of the recorded teller, it jumped to 195 in 1971–1972, and with electronic voting it jumped again to 351 in 1973–1974 (Smith 1989, 33). During the 94th Congress (1975–1976), 372 such amendments were offered on the floor, and during the 95th, 439. In 1979 floor consideration of the budget resolution took nine days, during which time fifty amendments were offered (Sinclair 1983, 180).

Democrats began to look to their party leaders, the only central leaders in the chamber, to counter these problems. The leaders responded by innovating in ways that led to alterations in the legislative process. The leadership became more involved with legislation before it reached the floor, and this involvement increasingly took the form of negotiating substantive changes in the legislation, often at the postcommittee stage, in order to produce a bill that could pass the chamber. To respond to the barrage of amendments offered on the floor, the leadership developed special rules into powerful devices for structuring floor decision making.

Budget Reform

When President Richard Nixon aggressively challenged Congress's power of the purse, Congress responded by passing the Congressional Budget and Impoundment Control Act of 1974. Presidents had been encroaching on Congress's budgetary powers for decades; lacking a mechanism for making comprehensive decisions, Congress had long used the president's budget as its point of departure for budgetary decision making and usually altered it only marginally. However, when Nixon claimed the right to impound—that is, not spend—congressionally appropriated funds, the Congress had to respond or acquiesce in a severe diminution of its powers. Nixon argued that congressional appropriations were just ceilings and that he was not required to spend any of the money Congress appropriated. In effect, he was arguing that Congress had only negative powers: Congress might be able to prevent the president from doing something by not appropriating funds, but it could not force a president to carry out a policy he opposed.

The Budget Act went far beyond devising a procedure to control impoundments: the budget process that it established provided a mechanism by which comprehensive policymaking in Congress became possible. During its first few years, however, the budget process was not used in that way. In the House the battles over budget resolutions were hard fought and highly partisan; debate did turn on the political parties' different priorities, but the resolutions themselves did not call for significant policy change (Ellwood and Thurber 1981; Schick 1980).

Reconciliation instructions that mandated committees to make changes in legislation under their jurisdiction were first included in the budget resolution in 1980 (Sinclair 1983, 181–190). Frighteningly high inflation in January 1980 convinced President Jimmy Carter and the Democratic congressional party leadership that budget cuts needed to be made, and quickly. The ordinary legislative process, they decided, would take too long and be subject to delay by interests adversely affected by the cuts. Therefore, they decided to use the budget process and to include reconciliation instructions in the first budget resolution. Doing so was highly controversial (in part because the Budget Act envisioned that such instructions would be included in the second budget resolution, which in this and most other cases would be too late), and the committees subject to instructions objected vigorously. Nevertheless, the resolution with the instructions passed, and the committees did comply. To do otherwise was to defy the will of Congress as expressed in its budget resolution.

Although the policy changes required by the 1980 budget resolution were modest by later standards, the experience made clear to perceptive participants that, under certain circumstances at least, the budget process was a mechanism available to central leaders for making comprehensive policy change. David Stockman, a Republican member of the House from Michigan from 1977 to January 1981, was one of those perceptive participants. As President Ronald Reagan's first head of the Office of Management and Budget, he suggested using the budget process to enact Reagan's economic program in 1981 (Stockman 1986). The administration-supported budget resolution included instructions to committees to make substantial changes in policy; supporters forced a single vote on them as a whole and then packaged the policy changes into one massive reconciliation bill where again the key vote was whether to accept or reject them as a whole. This strategy enabled Reagan and his supporters to achieve major policy change quickly in a system resistant to such change.

The budget process has had wide-reaching effects on the legislative process. In the years since 1981, budget politics have remained at center stage. The attempt to control the big deficits Reagan's economic program created shaped the politics of the 1980s and most of the 1990s. Even more significant, the budget process has become the tool of choice for those attempting to bring about comprehensive policy change.

A Hostile Political Climate as a Force for Innovation: The 1980s and Early 1990s

Both the House and Senate entered the 1980s beset by problems resulting from changes in their internal distribution of influence. The highly individualistic Senate, in which each senator was accorded extraordinary latitude, was very good at agenda setting and publicizing problems, but it was less well structured for legislative decision making. The House, which had greatly increased rank-and-file members' opportunities for participation, also had problems legislating, although its central leadership had begun to develop reasonably effective responses.

The political climate of the 1980s and early 1990s exacerbated the problems of legislating, especially for the Democratic House. Ronald Reagan was a conservative, confrontational president whose policy views were far from those of congressional Democrats, and the policy preferences of his successor, George H. W. Bush, were not much closer. In 1981 Reagan and his congressional allies ran over the Democratic House majority and enacted sweeping policy changes over futile Democratic protests. Thereafter, Reagan was never as politically strong again, but he and Bush still had the bully pulpit and the veto.

The growing ideological polarization of the parties exacerbated the conflict. Reagan's nomination had signaled the Republican Party's move to the right. The congressional party, especially the House Republican Party, had begun to change in the mid- and late 1970s. Not only were fewer moderates being elected, more hard-edged, ideological conservatives were entering the House. The elections of 1978 brought a Republican freshman from Georgia named Newt Gingrich to the House.

The Democratic Party in the 1980s became more ideologically homogeneous as its southern contingent changed. Republicans won southern seats, often ones previously held by the most conservative Democrats, and the southern Democrats who remained depended for reelection on the votes of African Americans who tend to be liberal. The Republican Party's increasing conservatism also made any ideological differences that remained among Democrats seem smaller.

The voting cohesion of House Democrats began to increase after the 1982 elections, and in the late 1980s and early 1990s it reached levels unprecedented in the post–World War II era. A member's party unity score is simply the frequency with which the member votes with his or her party colleagues on votes that pit majorities of the two parties against each other. For the period 1951 through 1970, House Democrats' average party unity score was 78 percent; it fell to 74 percent for the period 1971 to 1982.[3] Then after the 1982 elections the scores began rising again and averaged 86 percent for the 1983–1994 period. During this same period, the proportion of party votes also increased, averaging 56 percent compared with 37 percent during the 1971–1982 period. During the 103rd Congress, a

---

3. Party votes are recorded votes on which a majority of Democrats voted against a majority of Republicans. A member's party unity score is the percentage of party votes on which he or she voted with a majority of his or her party colleagues.

FIGURE 6.1   Distance between the Parties on Partisan Votes, 1955–2004

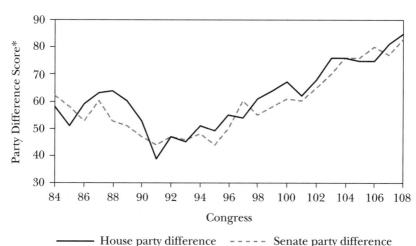

*party distance score = mean Dem pt voting score – (100-mean Rep pt voting score)

majority of Democrats opposed a majority of Republicans on 64 percent of House recorded votes (Rohde 1991; *Congressional Quarterly Almanac,* various years).

Figure 6.1 illustrates the polarization of the congressional parties since the early 1980s. Party voting scores can be used to construct a measure of the difference or distance between the parties. If, on average, 85 percent of Democrats voted against 90 percent of Republicans on party votes, then on average 10 percent of Republicans voted with the 85 percent of Democrats and the difference between these figures (75 = 85–10) provides an indicator of the distance between the parties. As Figure 6.1 shows, that distance increased enormously.

During the 1980s, then, an increasingly cohesive House Democratic majority faced a hostile president, a Republican Senate, and a more aggressive and conservative Republican minority.

After 1981 big deficits became chronic and severely restricted feasible policy options. Democrats often found themselves in the position of fighting to protect past policy successes. Partisan conflict and stalemate in Washington fed public cynicism about government's ability to handle effectively the problems facing the country; many citizens concluded that government could not do anything right. Passing legislation that majority Democrats considered satisfactory became very difficult in such a climate. Even enacting legislation to keep the government going was hard, both because of the ideological gulf between congressional Democrats and

Republican presidents and because the legislation frequently required making unpalatable decisions. This tough climate forced further innovation in the legislative process, especially in the House.

How Internal Reform and a Hostile Climate Spawned Unorthodox Lawmaking

Internal reforms, the hostile political climate, and other lesser changes in the environment altered the context in which members of Congress functioned. As they and their leaders sought to advance their goals within this altered context, they changed the legislative process. Sometimes changes were brought about by formal revisions in chamber rules; more frequently, they were the result of alterations in practices.

Multiple Referral

As our society and economy evolve over time, the issues at the center of controversy change. In the 1950s and early 1960s, for example, environmental protection was an obscure issue, and congressional attempts to deal with it mostly entailed programs to help municipalities build water treatment plants; by the 1970s the environment had become a highly salient issue, and Congress was considering ambitious legislation to protect endangered species and to force automakers and other polluters to clean up the air. As new issues arise and old ones change, the fit between the prominent issues on the congressional agenda and the committee system becomes increasingly poor. Yet Congress, especially the House, has great difficulty in realigning committee jurisdictions. Taking away jurisdiction from a committee reduces its clout; both committee members and affected interest groups that have established good working relationships with the committee will fight the change. Since committee membership is a considerably more important basis of members' influence in the House than in the Senate, realigning jurisdictions so that they fit better with the issues of the day is harder in the House than in the Senate.

By the early 1970s committee jurisdictions that had last been significantly overhauled in 1946 were seriously outmoded; jurisdiction over a number of key issues—energy, the environment, and health, for example—was spread over a number of committees, leading to a lack of coordination and numerous turf fights. The House attempted to reform its committee jurisdictions in the mid-1970s but largely failed (Davidson and Oleszek 1977). The Senate's attempt at committee reform in the late 1970s was considerably more successful (Davidson 1981).

TABLE 6.2   Multiple Referral in the House and Senate, 94th–108th Congresses

Congress	Years	House		Senate	
		Percentage of all bills	Percentage of major legislation	Percentage of all bills	Percentage of major legislation
94th	1975–76	6.5	8.6	3.2	5.2
95th	1977–78	10.9	21.1	4.1	7.3
96th	1979–80	12.6		3.3	
97th	1981–82	10.1	13.7	2.1	3.9
98th	1983–84	12.5		2.1	
99th	1985–86	15.4		1.5	
100th	1987–88	18.6	33.3	1.5	
101st	1989–90	19.6	30.0	1.5	5.3
102nd	1991–92	19.2		4.0	
103rd	1993–94	19.2	27.8	2.0	14.5
104th	1995–96	22.2	50.9	1.5	5.6
105th	1997–98	19.9	26.2	1.4	2.5
106th	1999–2000	20.8		1.2	
107th	2001–02	19.7	34.0	0.6	2.4
108th	2003–04	20.7	25.0	0.4	4.4

Sources: For all bills, compiled by Thomas P. Carr, analyst with the Government and Finance Division of CRS using the Legislative Information System (LIS). For major legislation, compiled by the author.

Unable to realign committee jurisdictions and driven by reform-minded members' desire to increase opportunities for broad participation in the legislative process, the House in 1975 changed its rules to allow multiple referral of legislation (Davidson and Oleszek 1992).[4] In the first Congress with multiple referral, 1975–1976, 6.5 percent of the measures introduced were multiply referred. Over time and driven by the same forces that led to its institution, multiply referred legislation became an increasingly prominent part of the House workload (see Table 6.2). On average 12 percent of measures were multiply referred during the five Congresses

---

4. Actually, even before then, something quite similar to multiple referral occurred under specialized circumstances; when legislation referred to a committee other than Ways and Means contained a revenue component, that section would be sent to the tax committee. In the 91st Congress (1969–1970), for example, three bills primarily under the jurisdiction of a committee other than Ways and Means also were referred to Ways and Means for consideration of their revenue sections; thus, the Interstate and Foreign Commerce Committee was mostly responsible for the Airport Development Act, but the trust fund and tax provisions were handled by Ways and Means.

between 1977 and 1986; the frequency has risen to an average of 20 percent in Congresses since the mid-1980s.

For major legislation, the increase has been steeper. Multiply referred measures have made up a considerably greater proportion of major legislation than they have of all legislation. Beginning in the late 1980s, about 30 percent of major measures were multiply referred. In the 104th Congress, however, 51 percent of major measures were referred to more than one committee—despite a rule change intended to rein in multiple referral.

Multiple referral of legislation has always been possible in the Senate through unanimous consent. The Senate, however, did manage to realign its committee jurisdictions during the 1970s, and because senators can more easily influence legislation outside the committee setting than House members can, they have less incentive to insist on a referral (Fenno 1973; Sinclair 1989). As a consequence, the referral of legislation to more than one committee continues to be much less frequent in the Senate. (See Table 6.2.)

Major measures are more likely than ordinary bills to be sent to more than one committee but even on important and controversial bills, formal multiple referral is much less frequent in the Senate than in the House. In keeping with the Senate's tendency toward less formal procedure, several committees sometimes consider different bills on the same topic. This can create complications much like those that stem from formal multiple referral.

Committees as Shapers of Legislation

By reducing the power of committee chairs and increasing the opportunities and incentives for rank-and-file members to participate in the legislative process, the House reforms of the 1970s diminished the capacity of committees to pass their legislation without change. No longer were bills protected by a powerful chair with the weapons to retaliate against members who challenged legislation in committee or on the floor or by voting rules that prevented most recorded votes on floor amendments. Junior committee members and members not on the committee now had the staff and the access to information that made their participation feasible. The increased prevalence of multiple referral lessened committee autonomy; committee leaders were not always capable of resolving the conflicts among their committees, yet unresolved intercommittee conflicts endangered legislation on the floor. The reformers had given Democratic majority party leaders some new tools, and, as the problems the reforms had wrought became increasingly evident, the now more ideologically homogeneous Democrats began to expect their leaders to use those tools to engineer passage of legislation broadly supported by the Democratic membership.

To respond to their members' demands, the Democratic leadership became more involved in the legislative process in the period before legislation reached the floor. A bill's substance is by far the most important determinant of its fate on the floor. As it became more difficult for the committee or committees of jurisdiction to write a bill that could pass on the floor, the party leaders stepped in more often to help.

Party leaders, of course, may involve themselves informally on legislation during committee consideration; anecdotal and interview evidence indicates that such intervention is much more frequent than it used to be (Sinclair 1995). That kind of involvement is, however, impossible to document systematically across time. Substantive adjustments to legislation after it is reported—whether engineered by the party leadership or others—can be counted with more precision.[5]

Postcommittee adjustments were rare in the pre-reform era. In the 91st Congress (1969–1970) there was no such instance in the House on the fifty-four major measures, although in one case the leadership was involved in making an adjustment of this kind after a veto. Committees were quite successful on the floor, lessening the need for tinkering after they had finished their work. Even when committees lost on the floor and when that loss was no big surprise, leaders seem to have made no attempt to head off the floor defeat by substantive adjustments in the legislation. Presumably, the committee leaders had done what they could and would in committee, and the party leaders lacked the tools to get involved.

In the 94th Congress (1975–1976) there were two clear instances of postcommittee adjustments to major measures; both cases involved the new budget process. In 1975 and again in 1976 it became evident that the budget resolution as reported by the Budget Committee would not pass. In each case the party leadership stepped in and crafted an amendment to the budget resolution to ensure passage in a form acceptable to most Democrats.

In the 1980s and early 1990s the hostile political climate made passing legislation Democrats wanted difficult. Big deficits made it harder for committee leaders to forge broadly acceptable deals; a climate of scarcity begets zero-sum politics in which one group's gain is perceived as a loss by other groups and fewer "sweeteners" to induce support are available. As committee Democrats tried to craft a bill that was passable yet as close as possible to their preferred policy position, they could easily misjudge what was passable.

---

5. I ascertained the presence or absence of a postcommittee adjustment and whether it was directed by the party leadership by doing a case study of each of the major measures for the selected Congresses. The case studies relied primarily on the *CQ Weekly* and the *Congressional Quarterly Almanac*. Thus, instances not ascertainable from the public record could have been missed; however, when I had independent information from interviews or participant-observation available, they confirmed the coding done on the basis of the written record.

TABLE 6.3   The Changing Role of Committees in the Legislative Process, Selected Congresses, 87th–108th

Congress	Years	Percentage of major legislation in which the committee with jurisdiction was bypassed		Percentage of major legislation subject to postcommittee adjustment	
		House	Senate	House	Senate
87th	1961–62	0	6	4	4
89th	1965–66	2	6	8	4
91st	1969–70	2	4	7	9
94th	1975–76	0	4	15	4
95th	1977–78	2	6	13	20
97th	1981–82	7	2	23	27
100th	1987–88	19	14	39	20
101st	1989–90	14	12	39	39
103rd	1993–94	2	8	31	38
104th	1995–96	13	28	48	57
105th	1997–98	10	14	35	30
107th	2001–02	17	41	22	22
108th	2003–04	26	31	20	24

Source: Compiled by the author.

Furthermore, changes in the political environment after the committee had reported—in the salience of the issue or in the public's response to presidential rhetoric—could alter what would pass. Leadership counts of members' voting intentions often showed not enough support for the committee-reported bill. Therefore, major legislation frequently required substantive alterations. As important legislation increasingly involved a number of committees, the compromises that needed to be made among the committees to bring a passable bill to the floor were often beyond the capacity of committee leaders to negotiate. In such a climate postcommittee adjustments, almost always directed by the party leadership, became almost routine (see Table 6.3).

The same forces—internal reforms that decreased the power and autonomy of committees and empowered party leaders and a hostile political climate that exacerbated the difficulties the reforms had produced—led to committees increasingly being bypassed altogether. To be sure, not every instance of the bypassing of committees is directed by the leadership; occasionally a discharge petition is successful. Most often, however, when committees are bypassed, it is the party leadership that made the decision, although not necessarily over the committee's opposition. Sometimes a committee is bypassed with its members' full concurrence simply to speed the process—when identical legislation passed in the previous Congress, for example.

In the pre-reform period and through the 1970s committees were almost never bypassed in the House. In the 91st Congress (1969–1970), for example, the committee was never actually bypassed in the House, although in one case the committee reported only because of a threat of discharge. (That case, an organized crime control bill forced out of a reluctant Judiciary Committee, is counted as a bypass in Table 6.3.) In the 95th Congress (1977–1978), the House Agriculture Committee was effectively bypassed when the House agreed to go directly to conference on a Senate-passed emergency farm bill. As Table 6.3 shows, bypassing the committee has become considerably more frequent since the early 1980s. The circumstances vary widely, but in most cases the decision to bypass the committee is a majority party leadership decision. Leaders became more willing to use informal task forces or even less formal working groups to work out the compromises necessary to pass legislation and to take a direct hand in the process themselves.

If internal reforms had unintended consequences that made legislating more difficult for the House, the Senate's individualism run rampant made the House's problems look picayune. Furthermore, the Senate, unlike the House, did not give its central leadership new tools for dealing with the problems.

In the Senate as in the House, one response was an increase in postcommittee adjustments to legislation. They were rare in the 1960s and 1970s. In the 1980s and 1990s postcommittee adjustments became much more frequent. The Senate majority leader often engineered or at least oversaw the devising of postcommittee changes in legislation, but committee leaders and even individual senators sometimes took on the task, reflecting the wide dispersion of power in the Senate.

Although the frequency of postcommittee adjustments declined a bit in the 103rd Congress in the House, in the Senate it did not. For the majority-rule House, unified control made legislating somewhat easier; at least amassing large margins to dissuade the president from vetoing the legislation was no longer necessary. The Senate, in contrast, still needed sixty votes to pass most controversial legislation. With the return of divided control in the 104th, postcommittee adjustments became more frequent again in both chambers.

In the Senate the frequency with which committees are bypassed also has increased. Committees were seldom bypassed on major legislation before the mid-1980s, although recalcitrant committees occasionally were bypassed on major bills. In the 89th Congress (1965–1966), for example, the Judiciary Committee was bypassed on a highly controversial open housing bill; nevertheless, civil rights opponents managed to kill it by filibustering the motion to proceed.

The frequency of bypassing increased substantially with the 100th Congress and has remained well above its previous level since then. The first two Congresses of the twenty-first century (the 107th and 108th) saw extremely narrow margins of control in the Senate. When the 107th Congress convened in January 2001, it was split evenly between Republicans and Democrats, and only Vice President Dick Cheney's role as president of the Senate allowed Republicans to organize the chamber. When in June 2001, Sen. Jim Jeffords of Vermont left the Republican Party and began caucusing with the Democrats, Democrats became the Senate's majority party. In the 2002 elections, Republicans won enough seats to reclaim majority status, but just barely, with fifty-one senators. Those difficult circumstances, made more problematic by high partisan polarization, led to the extraordinarily high rate of committees being bypassed, as is evident in Table 6.3.

Special Rules in the House

In the pre-reform era most legislation was brought to the House floor under a simple open rule that allowed all germane amendments. Tax bills and often other legislation from the Ways and Means Committee were considered under a closed rule that allowed no amendments (except those offered by the committee itself); tax legislation was regarded as too complex and too politically tempting a target to allow floor amendments. In the 91st Congress (1969–1970), for example, 80 percent of the major legislation was considered under simple open rules; 16 percent—primarily bills reported by the Ways and Means Committee—came to the floor under closed rules. Only two measures were considered under rules with provisions more complex than simply allowing all germane amendments or barring all amendments.

The reforms made legislation much more vulnerable to alteration on the floor. With rank-and-file members having greater incentives and resources for offering amendments on the floor, the number of amendments offered and pushed to a roll call vote shot up. Committee bills were more frequently picked apart on the floor, members often were forced to go on the record on votes hard to explain to constituents back home, and floor sessions stretched on late into the night.

The reformers had given the Democratic leadership the power to name the Democratic members and the chair of the Rules Committee and had thereby made the committee an arm of the leadership. In the late 1970s some Democrats began to pressure their leaders to use special rules to bring floor proceedings under control. Forty Democrats wrote Speaker Thomas P. O'Neill Jr., D-Mass., in 1979 to ask that he make more use of restrictive rules in order to curtail frequent late-night sessions (Smith 1989, 40–41).

TABLE 6.4   Change in the Character of House Special Rules,
95th–108th Congresses

Congress	Years	Percentage restrictive*
95th	1977–78	15
96th	1979–80	25
97th	1981–82	25
98th	1983–84	32
99th	1985–86	43
100th	1987–88	46
101st	1989–90	55
102nd	1991–92	66
103rd	1993–94	70
104th	1995–96	54
105th	1997–98	60
106th	1999–00	59
107th	2001–02	68
108th	2003–04	77

*Rules for initial consideration of legislation, except rules on appropriations bills which only waive points of order. Restrictive rules are those that limit the germane amendments which can be offered and include so-called modified open and modified closed, as well as completely closed rules and rules providing for consideration in the House as opposed to the Committee of the Whole.

Source: Compiled by Donald Wolfensberger, formerly minority and then majority counsel, Committee on Rules, now Director of the Congress Project of the Wilson Center, from the Rules Committee calendars and surveys of activities.

As Table 6.4 shows, as late as 1977–1978 most special rules were still open rules; only 15 percent restricted amendments in some way. As Democratic members began to comprehend the costs of the wide-open amending process fostered by the reforms and to demand that their leaders do something about these costs, the frequency of restrictive rules increased. In the hostile climate of the 1980s and early 1990s, restrictive rules were used more and more often. Holding together compromises and protecting members from political heat became more difficult and more essential, and leaders, in response to their members' demands, developed special rules into powerful devices for shaping the choices members face on the floor. By 1993–1994, 70 percent of special rules restricted amendments to some extent.

The new Republican majority in the 104th Congress had promised during the campaign to pass an ambitious agenda, much of it in the first one hundred days. Before the election, however, House Republicans, including their leadership, had vehemently denounced restrictive rules and also had promised not to use them. And the proportion of all rules that were restrictive did go down in the 104th, although Democrats claimed that Republicans manipulated the figures by considering under open rules

TABLE 6.5   Substantially Restrictive Rules on Major Legislation,
Selected Congresses, 89th–108th

Congress	Years	Percentage structured, modified closed, or closed
89th, 91st, 94th	1965–66, 69–70, 75–76	12*
95th	1979–80	21
97th	1981–82	18
100th	1987–88	42
101st	1989–90	42
103rd	1993–94	60
104th	1995–96	63
105th	1997–98	72
107th	2001–02	73
108th	2003–04	87

*Mean percentage for these three Congresses.
Source: Compiled by the author.

some uncontroversial legislation that should have been considered under the suspension procedure. In the next Congress, the use of restrictive rules on all legislation rose, and it has continued to do so ever since, reaching an all-time high of 82 percent in the 109th Congress (2005–2006).

When only major measures are examined, the trend toward restrictive rules is even stronger. Table 6.5 displays the percent of major measures that were considered under substantially restrictive rules—that is, structured, modified closed, or closed rules (see Chapter 2 for definitions of these). These sorts of rules limit the amendments that may by offered on the floor to ones explicitly allowed by the Rules Committee.[6] The frequency of open or modified open rules dropped steeply between the 1970s and the late 1980s. In the 1990s and early 2000s, substantially restrictive rules become more and more frequent, rising from 60 percent in the last Democratic-controlled Congress of the early 1990s to 87 percent in the 108th Congress.

The power and flexibility of special rules make them a useful tool under a broad variety of circumstances. Both the uncertainty that the 1970s reforms begot and the problems that majority Democrats faced in

6. The percent is of those major measures that were considered under rules; usually a (very) few major measures come to the floor under suspension. In previous editions, I displayed the percent of major measures considered under any sort of restrictive rule, including a modified open rule, just as I do for all legislation. I have switched to substantially restrictive so that variation among the latter Congresses in the series is evident. Simple open rules have become an endangered species.

legislating during the adverse political climate of the 1980s and early 1990s stimulated an increase in the use of complex and restrictive rules (Bach and Smith 1988; Sinclair 1983, 1995). The election of a Democratic president in 1992 presented congressional Democrats with a great legislative opportunity, but it also put them under pressure to deliver under difficult circumstances. The Democratic leadership responded by intensifying its employment of restrictive rules during the 103rd Congress.

When Republicans won control of the House, they too found restrictive rules to be extraordinarily valuable tools and, on major legislation, increased their use. Even in the 104th Congress, their first, the usefulness of such rules for promoting the Republicans' legislative objectives outweighed any damage from the inevitable charges of hypocrisy that their use provoked. Narrow margins and, after the 2000 election, a president of their party with an ambitious agenda prompted Republican leaders to routinely employ highly restrictive rules.

The Senate Floor: Amending Activity and Extended Debate

The Senate, unlike the House, has not developed effective tools for coping with the consequences of alterations in its internal distribution of influence and challenges from its political environment. The attractiveness to modern senators of rules that give the individual so much power and the difficulty of changing Senate rules make developing such tools extraordinarily difficult. Since a two-thirds vote is required to cut off debate on a proposal to change Senate rules, an oversized coalition for change must be constructed. To be effective, the tools would have to give more control to the majority party leadership as they did in the House, but minority party senators certainly have no reason to do so, and even many majority party senators are likely to be ambivalent.

The rules changes the Senate was able to make were modest. Perhaps most important, the Budget Act imposed limits on debate on budget resolutions and reconciliation bills, preventing filibusters on these measures. In 1975 the number of votes required to invoke cloture was lowered from two-thirds of those present and voting to three-fifths of the full membership—usually sixty. (Cloture on changes in Senate rules was exempted and still requires a two-thirds vote.) In response to the postcloture filibuster developed in the late 1970s, rules concerning delaying tactics in order after cloture were tightened. In 1986 floor consideration after cloture was limited to a total of thirty hours.

Although no rules restricted senators' amending activity in the 1950s and 1960s, amending marathons (ten or more amendments offered and pushed to a roll call vote) were nevertheless infrequent. For example, on

TABLE 6.6   The Increasing Frequency of Extended Debate–Related Problems, Selected Congresses, 87th–108th

Congress	Years	Percentage filibuster problem
87th	1961–62	8
89th	1965–66	7
91st	1969–70	10
94th	1975–76	31
95th	1977–78	24
97th	1981–82	22
100th	1987–88	28
101st	1989–90	30
103rd	1993–94	51
104th	1995–96	50
105th	1997–98	55
107th	2001–02	55
108th	2003–04	43

Source: Compiled by the author.

average, slightly less than 10 percent of major measures were subject to an amending marathon in the 87th, 89th, and 91st Congresses.

Thereafter, however, an average of 30 percent of major measures considered on the Senate floor encountered such a barrage of floor amendments.

In the 1970s senators often pursued their individual policy interests by offering amendments on the floor. A senator's right to offer unlimited amendments to almost any bill proved as useful to senators in the 1980s, the 1990s, and beyond. The political climate of the 1970s may have been more conducive to policy entrepreneurship, and floor amendments may have been more frequently used as tools toward that end, but amendments also proved to be useful tools in the more ideological and partisan struggles of the 1980s, 1990s, and 2000s.

In the 1960s and before, filibusters were rare, although important because of their targets, especially civil rights legislation. Most legislation, however, was unlikely to encounter any sort of extended debate–related problem. As Table 6.6 shows, 10 percent or less of major measures in the 1960s Congresses for which I have data encountered any such difficulties. In the 1970s, senators made much more use of extended debate, and they continued to increase their use during the 1980s, the 1990s, and into the 2000s. Rules changes may have made imposing cloture easier, but they did not reduce the incentives to use extended debate. Rampant individualism combined with the highly charged political climate to put an increasing share of major legislation under at least a threat of a filibuster.

In the 1990s, the filibuster increasingly became a partisan tool. In the 103rd, the first Congress of the Clinton presidency, half of major measures confronted an extended debate–related problem. In that Congress, the filibuster was used as a partisan tool to an extent unprecedented in the twentieth century. A Republican filibuster killed Clinton's economic stimulus package, and Republicans used the filibuster or the threat thereof to extract concessions on major legislation—voter registration legislation ("motor voter") and the national service program, for example. Republican attempts to kill or water down legislation via a filibuster were not always successful, of course. For example, the Republican filibuster of the Brady bill, which imposes a seven-day waiting period for buying a gun, collapsed when a number of Republican senators began to fear the political price of their participation.

Time pressure makes extended debate an especially effective weapon of obstruction at the end of a Congress, and the greater the backlog of significant legislation, the more potent any threat of delay is. At the end of the 103rd Congress, Republican filibusters killed campaign finance and lobbying reform bills. Although unsuccessful in the end, Republicans filibustered and tried to prevent passage of a massive crime bill, the California Desert Protection Act, and a comprehensive education bill. In some cases filibusters were waged to prevent legislation from being sent to conference or, more frequently, to prevent approval of the conference report. Republican threats of obstructionist floor tactics contributed to the death of bills revamping the Superfund program, revising clean drinking water regulations, overhauling outdated telecommunications law, and applying federal labor laws to Congress. Succeeding Congresses maintained similar high levels of filibuster-related problems on major measures (see Table 6.6). Passing major legislation in the Senate has come to require sixty votes.

Omnibus Legislation and the Budget Process

Omnibus legislation—legislation of great substantive scope that often involves many committees—increased as a proportion of the congressional agenda of major legislation from none in the Congresses of the 1960s to a mean of 7 percent in the 1970s Congresses, and a mean of 13 percent in the 1980s. In the 1990s and early 2000s, an average of 14 percent of major measures were omnibus.[7]

During the 1980s, the Democratic majority party leadership sometimes decided to package legislation into omnibus measures as part of a strategy

---

7. In each case, figures are based on those Congresses for which I have data. For a list with dates, see Table 6.3.

to counter ideologically hostile Republican presidents, especially Ronald Reagan, who was so skillful at using the media to his advantage. Measures the president very much wanted could sometimes be packaged with others that congressional Democrats favored but the president opposed, thus forcing the president to accept legislative provisions that, were they sent to him in freestanding form, he would veto. By packaging disparate and individually modest provisions on salient issues such as trade, drugs, or crime into an omnibus bill, Democrats sought to compete with the White House for media attention and public credit. During the 103rd Congress, congressional leaders no longer needed to coerce the president into signing their legislation, but omnibus measures remained useful for raising the visibility of popular legislation, and the device continued to be employed in that way. When the Republicans took control of Congress, they used omnibus legislation for similar purposes.

Many omnibus measures are budget related. Budget resolutions, reconciliation bills, and massive omnibus appropriations bills have constituted the preponderance of omnibus measures since the passage of the Budget Act in 1974. In both the 94th and the 101st Congresses, for example, all of the omnibus measures were budget related. Budget-related measures, however, were much more important pieces of legislation in the 101st than in the 94th. The Budget Act made omnibus measures a regular part of the congressional agenda, but changes in the political environment made budget measures the focus of controversy. During the 1970s, budget resolutions did not include reconciliation instructions, that is, instructions to committees to make changes in law. The budget process, by and large, accommodated what the committees wanted to do rather than constrained them.

In 1980, as I discussed earlier, the president and congressional Democratic leaders, in response to an economic crisis, used the budget process to make spending cuts, and reconciliation instructions were included in the budget resolution for the first time. Then in 1981, the Reagan administration and its congressional allies not only used the budget process to make significant changes in domestic programs so as to cut spending; they also enacted a huge tax cut. With that, the budget process moved to the center of the legislative process and has remained there ever since. The Reagan administration's use of the budget process to redirect government policy made its potential clear; since then it has remained the tool of choice for comprehensive policy change and was used for that purpose by the Clinton administration in 1993, the new Republican majority in 1995, and the George W. Bush administration in 2001 and 2003.

The budget process's centrality also stemmed from the impact of the big budget deficits of the 1980s and 1990s. The deficits that resulted from the Reagan tax cut powerfully shaped American politics. From the mid-1980s to the late 1990s, efforts to do something about the deficit dominated political debate, if not legislative enactments. The decisions made in the budget resolution and in the reconciliation bill that it usually required became crucial. Decisions on other legislative issues were made within the context of scarce resources and, as discretionary domestic spending shrank, the trade-offs that had to be made among programs became increasingly tough. The Gramm-Rudman legislation, the stated aim of which was to force Congress to balance the budget, complicated the process by adding targets and deadlines that, if missed, would result in substantial, automatic spending cuts.[8]

The politics of big deficits thus made unpalatable policy decisions necessary. The deep policy divisions first between Republican presidents and congressional Democrats and, after 1994, between President Clinton and congressional Republicans made reaching agreement between the branches on such decisions excruciatingly difficult. The 1980s and 1990s saw a succession of high-visibility, high-stakes showdowns between the branches and the parties on budget measures. Reconciliation bills, like other omnibus measures, were sometimes used to try to force provisions on an opposition party president that he opposed; such attempts, of course, raised the level of conflict. The existence of the budget process at least made it possible to wrap unpopular spending cuts and, sometimes, tax increases into one big package—often sweetened with provisions that members wanted—and get a single vote on the package as a whole. The congressional leadership frequently could persuade its members to pass such a package because defeating it would be devastating for the party's reputation. Passing the components individually would have been impossible.

Even after deficits briefly turned into surpluses in the late 1990s, partisan and interbranch battles over priorities continued to be fought in the context of the budget process. High partisan polarization and narrow margins of control have assured the continued centrality of the budget process, because budget rules in the Senate protect budget resolutions and reconciliation bills from filibusters. In the contemporary climate, the sort of legislative changes made via the budget process in the early 2000s certainly would have provoked filibusters had they been possible, and quite likely these filibusters would have been successful. With the return of big deficits, House leaders also find it useful to package many, not necessarily palatable, changes in law into one bill "too big to fail."

---

8. The Gramm-Rudman law was superseded by the Budget Enforcement Act of 1990, which included a "pay as you go" (PAYGO) provision requiring that any tax cuts or increases in entitlement programs had to be offset by either revenue increases or spending cuts of equal total magnitude (see Oleszek 2004, 70–71). PAYGO expired in 2002 and was not renewed until the beginning of the 110th Congress.

Summits

In the 1980s and 1990s the sharp differences in policy preferences between presidents and opposition party majorities in the Congress and the tough decisions that had to be made sometimes stalemated normal processes. When normal processes, even supplemented by the increasingly active role of majority party leaders, were incapable of producing legislation, the president and Congress had to find another way—the costs of failing to reach an agreement on budget issues were just too high, especially after Gramm-Rudman, with its automatic spending cuts, went into effect in the mid-1980s. The new device of choice was the summit, relatively formal negotiations between congressional leaders and high-ranking administration officials representing the president. Because summits take place only when the stakes are very high, congressional party leaders have always represented their members in such talks; members are not willing to rely on committee leaders to make such decisions on behalf of the party membership as a whole.

Actually, the first instance of major legislation emerging from a process similar in some respects to the summits of the late 1980s and 1990s was the 1980 (FY1981) budget resolution and reconciliation bill during the Carter administration. The announcement on February 22, 1980, that the consumer price index had increased at an 18 percent annual rate in January created a crisis atmosphere. In early March an unprecedented series of meetings between the Carter administration and the Democratic congressional leadership took place for the purpose of discussing budget cuts. The budget resolution approved by Congress closely followed the agreement that had been reached in those meetings (Sinclair 1983).

The 1983 deal to reestablish the fiscal soundness of the Social Security system emerged from a process that showed some similarities to a summit (Gilmour 1990, 248–250). A commission had been appointed to develop a solution, but the deal was really worked out behind the scenes by a few commission members who directly spoke for President Reagan and Speaker Thomas "Tip" O'Neill, D-Mass. In the mid-1980s attempts at summit negotiations on budget issues were made several times but with limited success.

During the 100th and 101st Congresses (1987–1990), four summits took place, three of which concerned budget issues. In the fall of 1987, the stock market crashed; in response, Reagan administration officials met with the congressional leadership and worked out a deal that shaped the 1987 reconciliation bill and the full-year continuing resolution. The deal also determined the major outlines of the following year's budget resolution (FY1989). In the spring of 1989, the new Bush administration and the congressional leadership worked out a more modest deal to avert Gramm-Rudman across-the-board cuts; this agreement shaped the 1989 (FY1990) budget resolution and the 1989 reconciliation bill, although it by no means settled all the major issues, especially on reconciliation. The need for action and the inability of normal processes to produce agreement again led to a summit on budget issues in 1990. The highly contentious issue of aid to the Nicaraguan contras was the subject of the fourth summit. In 1989 the Democratic leadership met with Bush administration representatives to work out a final agreement on contra aid. (For details on these cases, see Sinclair 1995.)

An emergency and severe time pressure may create the conditions for a summit as they did in 1980, but when the congressional majority and the president are of the same party, normal processes supplemented by informal consultation and negotiations almost always seem to suffice. In fact, since that one instance, no summits have occurred when the president and Congress have been controlled by the same party. Thus, there were no summits during the first two years of the Clinton presidency or during George W. Bush's first six years in office. (Democrats controlled the Senate during much of the 107th Congress, but they did not gain control until after the budget resolution and the big tax cut bill of 2001 passed.)

Not surprisingly, normal processes are more likely to fail when the president's and the congressional majority's policy and electoral goals are in conflict, as they tend to be under divided government, when the presidency is controlled by one party and the Congress by another. In fact, the increase in partisan polarization and in congressional leadership strength make it less likely that a president can circumvent opposition House majority party leadership and pick off enough majority party members to pass administration priorities. Presidents frequently are forced to deal with opposition majority party leadership directly. So when Republicans won control of Congress in the 1994 elections, President Clinton and congressional Republicans found they had to resort to summits. The budget summit of 1995–1996 failed to produce an agreement; however, in 1997, Clinton and the congressional Republicans did manage to work out a deal to balance the budget. Differences on appropriations bills also increasingly came to be negotiated in an end-of-the-fiscal-year summit between Clinton administration officials and congressional leaders.

Unorthodox Lawmaking in the Republican Congress

The 1994 elections brought enormous and unexpected political change to Congress, especially to the House of Representatives. Republicans won majorities in both chambers, taking control of the House for the first time in forty years by picking up fifty-three seats. During the campaign, House Republicans had promised to change the way Congress works if the voters would give them control. In fact, the rules changes that constitute the reforms of the 1970s were in many cases changes in Democratic Party rules, not changes in the rules of the House itself. Much of the weakening of committees and their chairs and the strengthening of the party leadership was the result of new Democratic Caucus rules concerning committee assignments and the designation of committee and subcommittee chairs.

One might thus expect that a change in party control would have brought with it major alterations in how the House functions. In fact, the Republican House did operate differently than its Democratic predecessor. However, as the data on special procedures and practices presented in this chapter suggest, Republican control resulted not in a change in direction but rather in an amplification of preexisting trends. An analysis of why this is so illuminates the relationship between the congressional process and the broader political process in which it is embedded.

On the first day of the 104th Congress, House Republicans made some significant but far from revolutionary changes in House rules. Modest committee jurisdiction reform was accomplished by shifting some of the Energy and Commerce Committee's immense jurisdiction to other committees; three minor committees were eliminated; and committee staffs were cut by a third. Proxy votes, which absent committee members could give to any other committee member to cast for them but most often gave to the chair, were banned; and sunshine rules were modestly strengthened, making it harder to close a committee meeting. Committee chairs were subjected to a limit of three terms, a rules change that ultimately would have a major impact on the distribution of legislative influence in the House.

Term limits, staff cuts, and the abolition of proxy voting potentially weakened committee chairs. However, because Republican Party rules pertained, the new Republican committee chairs were in some ways actually stronger than their Democratic predecessors. They controlled the entire majority staff of the committee and had more control over the choice of subcommittee chairs and over the assignment of members to subcommittees.

During the 1980s and early 1990s, House Republicans had in many instances imitated House Democrats by adopting party rules that decreased the autonomy of their committee leaders and strengthened their party leadership. Their committee leaders (ranking minority members when the party was in the minority, committee chairs when Republicans became the majority), after being nominated by the committee on committees, had been made subject to a secret ballot ratification vote in the Republican Conference, the organization of all House Republicans; the Republicans' top leader had been given the power to nominate Republican members of Rules and more say on the party committee that makes committee assignments. Thus, rules strengthening Republican Party leaders were, by and large, not new at the beginning of the 104th Congress, nor did they give Republican leaders powers that Democratic Party leaders had not possessed.

Political circumstances, not rules changes, made Newt Gingrich a powerful Speaker. Gingrich, in the eyes of most Republicans and the media, was the miracle maker, as he was seen as responsible for the unexpected Republican victory in 1994. Gingrich had worked and schemed to build a majority for many years (Connelly and Pitney 1994); he had recruited many of the House challengers who won and had helped them with fund raising and campaign advice. The Contract with America, the policy agenda on which most House Republicans had run, was Gingrich's idea, and he had orchestrated its realization.

Consequently, the 1994 election results gave Gingrich enormous prestige. They also provided him with a membership that was ideologically homogeneous and determined to enact major policy change. The huge freshman class—seventy-three strong—consisted largely of true believers deeply committed to cutting the size and scope of government and to balancing the budget. Freshmen and sophomores, who were similar ideologically, made up more than half of the Republican House membership. These members and a considerable number of more senior Republicans believed themselves mandated to make policy change. Even moderate Republicans strongly agreed that, for the party to maintain its majority, Republicans had to deliver on the promises they had made in the Contract.

The combination of an extraordinarily ambitious agenda, a new majority united behind the agenda, and a leader with enormous stature made the exercise of strong leadership both necessary and possible. Without strong central direction, passing the agenda would have been impossible. Without a membership united in its commitment to swift and sweeping policy change, no Speaker could have exercised such strong, central direction of the legislative process.

Relying on his immense prestige with House Republicans, Gingrich, in the days after the 1994 elections, exercised power well beyond that specified in Republican Conference rules. He designated Republicans to serve as committee chairs, bypassing seniority in several instances. According to the rules, the party committee on committees nominates chairs and the Conference approves them. Gingrich preempted that process, assuming correctly that his stature would prevent anyone from challenging his choices.

The 104th Congress saw enormous party leadership involvement and oversight on major legislation; committee leaders were clearly subordinate to party leaders on Contract with America bills and on much of the major legislation that went into the Republicans' attempt to balance the budget (see Chapter 11). Because most senior Republicans had signed the Contract, Gingrich had a powerful tool for persuading committee leaders to report legislation without making major changes and to do so quickly; he simply reminded them: "We promised to do it in 100 days; we must deliver." In early 1995, and later when balancing the budget was at issue, the chairs knew that the leadership was buttressed by the freshmen's strong support.

The attempt to deliver on the ambitious promises House Republicans had made took the full set of procedural tools available to the majority party leadership. The need for speed and flexibility, and occasionally the political delicacy of the issues involved, dictated that the leaders sometimes bypass committee. The leadership made extensive use of member task forces on legislative issues ranging from agriculture policy to gun control to immigration reform. By and large, committees were not formally bypassed on the issues task forces worked on, but the task forces did have the purpose and the effect of keeping the pressure on committees to report legislation that was satisfactory to the party majority and to do so in a timely fashion.

Even though political circumstances made committee leaders unusually responsive to the wishes of the party leadership and the party membership, party leaders frequently found it necessary to make postcommittee adjustments in legislation. Multiple referral, the need for speed, and the ambitiousness of the agenda all contributed to producing circumstances in which the legislation as reported had to be altered in order to engineer passage in a form that would accomplish the party's objectives.

As developed by Democratic leaders in the 1980s and early 1990s, special rules had become powerful and flexible tools for the leadership. Given the task Republicans had set for themselves, their leaders could hardly eschew using restrictive rules, despite their pre-election promise to use predominantly open rules. In working to pass their ambitious agenda, House Republican leaders continued to use substantially restrictive rules.

The extraordinary political circumstances that allowed such hyperaggressive use of the full set of leadership tools, including the tools of unorthodox lawmaking, waned even before the end of the 104th Congress. The 105th Congress saw leaders retreat a bit from the deep substantive involvement on almost all major legislation that had characterized their role in the 104th. The extremely high 48 percent rate of postcommittee adjustment in the 104th declined to a more "normal" 35 percent in the 105th Congress, and task forces were employed less frequently. The reversion, however, was to a legislative process still heavily characterized by the practices and procedures I have labeled unorthodox lawmaking. In their attempts to satisfy the party's members by passing the legislation they favored, House party leaders continued to make use of the tools of unorthodox lawmaking. Speaker Hastert, who promised a return to "regular order" when he assumed the speakership in 1999, found himself frequently drawn into legislative substance and having to either bypass committees or make postcommittee adjustments, and he routinely employed strategic restrictive rules.

If passing the Republicans' agenda in the majority-rule House of the 1990s was a task requiring extraordinary means, getting it through the Senate was a considerably more difficult, and sometimes impossible, endeavor.

Majority Leader Bob Dole of Kansas and his immediate successor Trent Lott of Mississippi used all the special procedures available to them. In the 104th Congress especially, committees were frequently bypassed, and great effort went into postcommittee adjustments to bills in an attempt to craft legislation that could amass the sixty votes Senate passage usually requires.

Having had the filibuster wielded against them so effectively in the 103rd Congress, Democrats, now in the minority, returned the favor and made full use of their prerogatives under Senate rules. In the 104th and 105th Congresses, about half of major legislation encountered extended debate–related problems; Democrats killed regulatory overhaul and property rights legislation and forced majority Republicans to make concessions on a number of major bills—product liability legislation, the Freedom to Farm bill, and telecommunications legislation, among others.

Minority Democrats became increasingly adept at using extended debate and the Senate's permissive amending rules in combination to get their issues onto the Senate agenda. By threatening or actually offering their bills as often nongermane amendments to whatever legislation the majority leader brought to the floor and using extended debate to block a quick end to debate, Democrats forced Republicans to consider a number of issues they would rather have avoided—most prominently the minimum wage, tobacco taxes, campaign finance reform, and the patients' bill of rights.

The Republican majority responded with procedural strategies of its own. Majority Leader Lott attempted to impose cloture immediately upon bringing a bill to the floor because after cloture all amendments must be germane. When cloture failed, he simply pulled the bill from the floor to deprive Democrats of an opportunity to debate and vote on their amendments. Lott also "filled the amendment tree," that is, he used his right of first recognition to offer amendments in all the parliamentarily permissible slots, thus barring Democrats from offering their amendments. Democratic cohesion on cloture votes, however, limited the effectiveness of such majority party strategies; so long as the minority party can muster forty-one votes, the majority party may be able to prevent the minority from getting votes on its bills but it cannot pass its own. The result was most often gridlock, and once George W. Bush became president, Senate leaders had to abandon that strategy if they wished to move his program.

Intense partisan polarization is the single most salient characteristic of contemporary politics and one that increasingly shapes the legislative process. Since the mid-1990s, when Republicans won control of both chambers of Congress, the majority parties' margins of control have been narrow—sometimes extremely so; yet the ideological gulf between the parties has made bipartisan compromise costly. Even after the intense sense of mandate Republicans read into the 1994 elections waned, congressional

Republicans remained unusually ideologically homogeneous for an American party and continued to be dedicated to conservative policy change. In the 1990s, majority Republicans faced a politically adroit president hostile to their policy goals. After Bush became president in 2001, they enjoyed a like-minded ally in the White House but the pressure on them to produce intensified enormously. Bush offered an ambitious agenda, one that, by and large, Republicans—voters, activists, and members of Congress—supported strongly but, by the same token, one with limited bipartisan appeal.

Given these circumstances, the congressional Republicans' continued employment of the practices and procedures of unorthodox lawmaking is unsurprising. During the Clinton presidency, Republicans made use of omnibus bills to try to force the president to accept provisions he disliked by linking them to must-pass legislation or to provisions he favored, as Democrats had when facing a hostile Republican president. The strategy, however, produced mixed success at best (see Chapter 11). Often, the Republican leadership and President Clinton had to resort to summits to reach agreement. Leaders in both chambers frequently bypassed committee and engineered postcommittee changes in legislation during the Clinton and the George W. Bush administrations.

Republican House leaders gained additional leverage over committee leaders when the consequences of chair term limits became evident. In 2000, thirteen chairs became vacant simultaneously, mostly because of term limits, and the Republican Party leadership instituted a new procedure for the selection of committee chairs: chair aspirants were required to appear before the Steering Committee, the committee on committees which nominates chairs to the Conference. There they were put through rigorous interviews about their legislative and communication strategies and their proposed agendas. Given the leadership's influence on the Steering Committee as well as that committee's representative composition, the new procedure made the incentives to show responsiveness to the party and its leadership even stronger for committee chairs and those aspiring to these positions. House party leaders used the clout they gained thereby to ensure that legislation that got to the floor was acceptable to most Republican members and to President Bush.

Their narrow majorities and their determination to pass legislation without compromising with Democrats led House Republican leaders to accelerate their use of restrictive rules. The character of rules for major legislation most clearly distinguished the Republican House from its Democratic predecessor. By the 108th Congress (2003–2004), 87 percent of major measures brought up under rules were considered under a substantially restrictive rule—one that the Rules Committee itself classified as structured, modified closed, or closed; many of these rules were very restrictive, allowing at best one minority party substitute. The sort of free-wheeling, unscripted amending process that had still been common in the late 1980s became largely a thing of the past. The Republican leadership's tight control of the floor contributed enormously to the party's legislative success, but it also contributed greatly to the minority party's severe discontent with the legislative process and to the hostility between the parties.

High partisan polarization combined with the Senate's permissive rules spells trouble for the Senate as a legislative body. Contemporary majority leaders usually can count on a more cohesive party membership than could their predecessors of the 1970s and 1980s, but even a totally united party is not usually enough. The frequent bypassing of committees in recent Congresses was facilitated by partisan ideological homogeneity; usually the committee chair has to acquiesce, as Senate leaders lack the power over who holds committee leadership positions that their House counterparts now have.

However, while Republican House leaders were able to use their tools to craft and pass legislation that most of their members and President Bush truly supported, Republican Senate leaders usually were just trying to get something minimally acceptable onto the floor, passed, and into conference. Given the Senate's supermajority rules, that often requires a Herculean effort. About half of major legislation now typically runs into an extended debate–related problem in the Senate. And with the minority party now usually highly cohesive on cloture votes, getting the sixty votes to close debate often requires substantial concessions. Senate rules as they are now employed often lead to legislative stalemate, yet they also exert pressure toward bipartisan compromise even in this highly polarized era when little else does.

Neither the change in party control of Congress in 1995 nor the return of unified control of government with the George W. Bush presidency in 2001 disrupted the trend toward unorthodox lawmaking. In fact, as the case studies illustrate, House Republican leaders added innovations of their own. In part, continuity, and often acceleration, in the use of unorthodox practices and procedures can be attributed to the persistence of key conditions: internal rules were not altered very much and certainly not in a way as to resurrect strong, autonomous committees; the budget process continued to dominate congressional decision making; during the 1990s, the new congressional majority faced a hostile, opposition-party president; and in the early 2000s, that congressional majority confronted the high expectations that the first unified Republican government in a half century produced. Perhaps even more important, the frequent employment of these special procedures and practices continued because, whatever their origins, they have become flexible tools useful to members and leaders under a variety of circumstances. For that reason, we should not expect a return to what once was the regular order, at least not in the foreseeable future. Democratic majorities may use the tools of unorthodox lawmaking somewhat differently, but use them they will. House Democratic leaders bypassed committee on the bills constituting the party's "Hundred Hours" agenda and brought them to the floor under closed rules.

The case studies in the following chapters illustrate both how the broader political environment shapes the context in which the legislative process occurs and how legislative leaders—and sometimes rank-and-file members—use the various tools of unorthodox lawmaking to take advantage of the opportunities and to handle the problems that particular political contexts create. They show how House leaders now can tailor the legislative process to the problems that a particular bill raises in ways not available in the past, whereas Senate leaders frequently are confronted with problems derived from the tools being used by opponents to thwart their legislative aims. The cases also demonstrate how the practices and procedures of unorthodox lawmaking combine and interact and thereby illustrate the multiple paths through which bills now do—and sometimes do not—become law.

chapter seven

The 2005 Energy Bill:
About as Orthodox as It Gets

AS THE 109TH CONGRESS BEGAN, energy policy was back at the top of the legislative agenda. Energy legislation that would promote domestic production had been a high priority for President George W. Bush and congressional Republicans during Bush's first term, but, despite great effort, success had eluded them. In 2001 the House had passed a bill emphasizing increasing domestic energy production that was close to what the administration had recommended. The bill passed by the Democratic-controlled Senate in 2002, however, had focused much more on conservation and renewable energy sources. The differences between the two chambers' bills were too great, and the legislation died in conference. A major bone of contention was the Senate's refusal to open the Arctic National Wildlife Refuge (ANWR) to oil drilling, a provision Bush strongly advocated and the House had approved.

In the 108th Congress, the House again passed a bill largely to the administration's liking, although its price tag was higher than Bush wanted. In the Senate, the legislation ran into one problem after another even though Republicans had won control of the body in the 2002 elections. Opening ANWR to oil drilling was defeated in a Senate floor vote on the budget resolution, indicating that the chamber's view on that issue had not changed even if the majority party had. Unable to pass their energy bill on the floor, Senate Republican leaders agreed to abandon their draft and substitute language from the 2002 version that Democrats had written. This was the only way to get a bill to conference.

Hoping to reach a deal quickly, Sen. Pete Domenici, R-N.M., who chaired the House-Senate conference on the bill, and Billy Tauzin, R-La., chair of the Energy and Commerce Committee and the lead House negotiator, excluded Democrats from the conference. This infuriated Democrats without leading to the hoped-for resolution. Differences among Republicans, many constituency-based, held up the conference for weeks. Finally, Vice President Dick Cheney; Senate Majority Leader Bill Frist, R-Tenn.; and House Speaker Dennis Hastert, R-Ill., stepped in and settled the disputes. The House adopted the conference report on November 18, 2003.

However, even though Republican leaders had agreed to drop the House's ANWR drilling provision from the bill, Frist could not muster the sixty votes necessary to approve the conference report over intense opposition in the Senate. A number of provisions raised opposition, but most serious was a liability waiver for producers of MTBE (methyl tertiary butyl ether), a fuel additive that had been designed to make gasoline burn more cleanly but had been found to contaminate groundwater. House Majority Leader Tom DeLay, whose state of Texas was a major manufacturer of MTBE, insisted the liability waiver be included. A number of senators balked, fearing that the result would be their taxpayers getting stuck with the cost of cleanup.

Majority Leader Frist attempted to impose cloture on the conference report but failed on a 58–39 vote. Six Republican senators, all but one from the Northeast where the contamination problem was greatest, voted to support a Democratic-led filibuster. Last-minute intervention by Bush failed to persuade DeLay to drop the MTBE waiver. Frist was never able to find the two additional votes he needed, and the conference report died with the end of the 108th Congress. Now, in 2005, with President Bush reelected and Republican congressional majorities increased, they intended to try again.

The process by which the energy bill did indeed become law in 2005 was both less unorthodox and less partisan than the failed attempts in the previous two Congresses, indicating that more traditional practices and procedures sometimes work better. The biggest differences in process on the successful 2005 legislation when compared to the failed 108th Congress bill were in the Senate and in conference. The conference was a fairly traditional one in which both parties participated in negotiating the final bill. In committee Senate action was bipartisan, and on the floor it was cooperative.

Still, as this account shows, this was not your grandpa's legislative process. In the House, many committees took part in drafting the legislation and that in itself required party leadership involvement. The Senate made many of the big decisions on the floor through a lengthy amending process and imposed cloture to end debate, albeit by a bipartisan vote. This case illustrates as well how different the legislative processes in the House and Senate are. Both in committee and on the floor, the process in the House is now tightly controlled and scripted, with the party leadership providing oversight and ultimately in charge at every stage. In the Senate, the process is much less formal and predictable—senators are much less constrained in their participation, and no one is really in charge.

House Committee Action

A comprehensive energy policy encompasses myriad complex policy questions that fall under the jurisdiction of a number of committees in the House. In 2005, however, the problems inherent in this substantive and jurisdictional complexity were tempered by the fact that the House had passed such legislation in both of the previous two Congresses and that the committees had worked together to do so. Furthermore, having gone through the process before, the party leadership and the committee chairs were unlikely to be caught unawares by the multiple political pitfalls the issue raised. The rising price of oil and gas did alter the political context of legislative decision making; the cost of a barrel of oil had more than doubled between 2002 and early 2005. So, on the one hand, public concern about rising prices provided proponents of a production-based bill with a strong argument; on the other, with oil companies making record profits, the case for subsidies was weakened. Bush's concerns about the high price tag of the 2004 bill would carry added weight.

Energy and Commerce is the lead House committee on energy policy. In early February 2005, Joe Barton, R-Tex., the committee's chair, let it be known that the draft energy bill he would ask his committee to mark up would largely resemble the conference report of the bill that had died in the Senate in 2004. Lobbyists for the fossil fuels industries and many Republicans were disappointed that the starting point would not be the more generous House-passed version from the previous Congress. Barton, however, wanted to finally get a bill enacted and the party leadership supported him in that.

In contrast, House Resources Committee Chair Richard Pombo, R-Calif., announced he would revert to the language his committee and the House had approved previously. Most notably, Pombo's draft would allow oil drilling in ANWR, a proposal removed in conference in 2003 because of Senate opposition. Barton; Ways and Means Committee Chair Bill Thomas, R-Calif.; and Budget Committee Chair Jim Nussle, R-Iowa, began talks on the size of the tax incentives to be included in the bill, trying to mesh the president's bottom line with their own and their committee colleagues' preferences.

By early April four committees were ready for mark-up. The Science Committee had already marked up its part of the bill. The research and development title under its jurisdiction was relatively noncontroversial and a version quite similar to that reported in the 108th Congress was again approved on a bipartisan basis. Similarly, the main issue under the jurisdiction of the House Government Reform Committee—the setting of new standards for federal agencies to reduce energy consumption in government buildings—aroused no controversy and, on April 13, the committee approved by voice vote HR1533, which contained the committee's language.

Mark-ups in the other three committees were considerably more contentious. When Energy and Commerce met to mark up its bill on April 6, partisan lines were quickly drawn. Republicans praised the draft as forward thinking, balanced, and effective at reducing U.S. dependence on foreign oil. Chairman Barton described the legislation as an engine of "economic growth and jobs for working people. It means food on their tables, clothes on the back and college for their kids." The bill, he added, would "promote innovation, new conservation requirements and new domestic energy sources" (*CongressDaily,* April 6, 2005). Democrats objected that it harmed the environment, did nothing to reduce the price of gas, and was a give-away to fossil fuel producers. "Quite simply," said Energy and Commerce ranking member John Dingell, D-Mich., "it will harm the environment, hurt consumers and cost taxpayers a bundle" (*Daily,* April 6, 2005).

The mark-up stretched over three days, during which the committee considered dozens of amendments. A number of major amendments split the committee along ideological and partisan lines. Democrats unsuccessfully sought to remove the MTBE liability waiver provision that Barton had again included in the bill at DeLay's urging, to strip language that gave the Federal Energy Regulatory Commission ultimate jurisdiction over the siting of liquid natural gas (LNG) import facilities and thus the power to override state and local officials in this area, and to eliminate provisions on hydroelectric dam relicensing that favored dam operators over other stakeholders, such as farmers, Indian tribes, and conservation groups.

Constituency interests always play an important role in energy policy debates, and many amendments split the committee along regional lines. Gene Green, D-Texas, and Charles W. "Chip" Pickering Jr., R-Miss., proposed to change the formula for allocating Low Income Home Energy Assistance Program (LIHEAP) funds so as to make more money available for cooling for individuals in these two hot, and often humid, states. Their amendment was defeated 22–30 with mean district temperature, not party or ideology, determining a member's vote. The committee did approve an increase in overall funding for LIHEAP. The vote on an amendment increasing fuel efficiency standards for autos broke along both party and constituency lines, as it had in the past. Thus, although many Democrats supported the unsuccessful amendment, ranking Democrat John Dingell, who represents Detroit, Michigan, the nation's automotive capital, opposed it. An amendment lengthening daylight savings time won bipartisan support. Finally, after 11 p.m. on April 13, the mark-up concluded and the committee approved the bill by a vote of 39 to 16; 9 Democrats joined all the Republicans in voting for the bill.

On the same day, the House Resources Committee approved its part of the comprehensive energy bill. After a day-long debate on two dozen amendments and eleven roll call votes, the measure passed by voice vote. Ranking Democrat Nick Rahall, D-W.Va., offered a Democratic substitute to eliminate the ANWR drilling language and other provisions that Democrats believed threatened the environment and gave subsidies to the oil industry at the expense of taxpayers. It was defeated 27–11. As in the Energy and Commerce Committee, both party/ideology and constituency interest/region influenced members' votes.

Tax subsidies fall within the jurisdiction of the Ways and Means Committee, and all of the Republicans' energy bills had included generous subsidies to encourage energy production. On April 13, the committee approved more than $8 billion in tax breaks. The bill was heavily skewed toward production and traditional fossil fuels. Chair Bill Thomas, R-Calif., resisting conservation and alternate fuel amendments, explained that, because such provisions would be in the Senate bill, leaving them out of the House bill would give him extra bargaining leverage in conference. (Iowa Republican Jim Nussle withdrew his amendment after Thomas explained the strategy but complained, "try to explain this to the guy pumping gas in Manchester, Iowa, who is not interested in your legislative strategy" [*Markup Report* HR1541, April 13, 2005].) Members again divided along both ideological/partisan lines and constituency/regional lines. The committee voted for the bill 26 to 11; 21 of the 22 Republicans present supported the bill (Nussle voted no); 10 Democrats opposed the bill and 5 supported it.

At a news conference on April 14, the committee chairs touted their legislation, explaining its substantive virtues and assuring their audience that, this time, the bill would become law. Pombo, Thomas, and Barton each insisted that their committee's bill had bipartisan support and that this would strengthen their hand in conference with the Senate. Barton also talked about the MTBE provision that had caused so much trouble in the 108th Congress. He expressed confidence that he would be able to work out a satisfactory compromise and explained that he was already engaged in talks to do so.

House Minority Leader Nancy Pelosi of California, in the meantime, criticized the energy bill as a "boondoggle for the energy industry," and contested GOP claims that the bill would lower the cost of gasoline (*Daily*, April 14, 2005).

Preparing the Bill for the Floor

Although five committees had marked up and reported legislative language, the task of putting together a bill to take to the floor was far from over. The committees had, in fact, reported separate bills.[1] The pieces had to be assembled into a coherent measure, and doing so required leadership involvement. Policy aides from the majority leader's and the Speaker's offices had been keeping tabs on the progress of the bill. Now their task was melding the components into a coherent bill acceptable to most House Republicans and passable on the House floor. A participant explained:

> The committees will report their separate parts. Then the first thing is to decide who has jurisdiction over what, and that's really what the Parliamentarian does. But then there will be areas where there is joint jurisdiction, where there is in fact an overlap in language, where basically two committees have written language on the same parts of a bill. Fairly often the committees will be able to settle it themselves. We'll tell them, "look, you've got to take care of this." But it also may require sitting down with the committee staff and working out the language of where there were two committees doing the same bill. . . . [I]f you get to the point where you have to have a bill, you have to have language, then the Leadership will do it itself. And that puts pressure on the committees to come to an agreement. Eventually then we will come up with a shared text that will be the base bill for the purpose of amendment, and that will be what the Rules Committee will give the rule for.

HR6, the energy bill that would go to the floor, was the product of this process. It was, in fact, not formally introduced until April 18. This new bill was then multiply referred but, since the committees had already done their work, they did not report.

The House Rules Committee met on April 19 to consider a rule for the energy bill. House members had submitted more than eighty amendments that they wished to offer. The committee is an arm of the majority party leadership, and party leaders are deeply involved in the construction of rules on such major legislation as the energy bill. Top leadership staff and the chair of Rules and his staff sit down together before the committee meets to decide which amendments to allow. The committee refused to allow a number of key Democratic amendments, including one stripping out the MTBE liability waiver. The Rules Committee took roll calls on allowing eight amendments; in each case the motion to allow the amendment, offered by a Rules Committee Democrat, was rejected on a straight party line vote. Not all of the rejected amendments were by Democrats, however; one was by Maryland Republican Wayne Gilchrest and required

---

1. These bills had themselves been multiply referred but, in each case, only one committee had reported the bill.

the development of a National Climate Change Strategy, with the goal of stabilizing greenhouse gas concentrations in the atmosphere.

The rule reported was a structured rule. The committee's summary of the provisions of H.Res. 219 reads as follows:

> The resolution provides for consideration of H.R. 6, the Energy Policy Act of 2005, under a structured rule. The rule provides one hour and 30 minutes of general debate with 30 minutes equally divided and controlled by the chairman and ranking minority member of the Committee on Energy and Commerce and 20 minutes equally divided and controlled by the chairmen and ranking minority members of each of the following Committees: Science, Resources, and Ways and Means. The rule waives all points of order against consideration of the bill. The rule makes in order only those amendments printed in this report, and provides that those amendments may be offered only in the order printed in this report, may be offered only by a Member designated in this report, shall be considered as read, shall be debatable for the time specified in this report equally divided and controlled by the proponent and an opponent, shall not be subject to amendment except as specified in the report, and shall not be subject to a demand for a division of the question in the House or in the Committee of the Whole. The rule waives all points of order against the amendments printed in this report. The rule also provides one motion to recommit with or without instructions (www.rules.house.gov).

The rule made in order thirty amendments, five Republican amendments, including a manager's amendment, twenty-two Democratic amendments, and three bipartisan amendments. Democrats were allowed to offer an amendment striking drilling in ANWR and an amendment by Dingell

> to tighten enforcement of electric reliability standards, provide legal standing for states to contest price gouging by power companies, preserve electric consumer protections, and give all interested parties an equal say in contesting the relicensing of hydroelectric dams (*Daily PM,* April 21, 2005).

A bipartisan group of members was allowed to offer an amendment raising fuel efficiency standards, and an amendment striking the provision on LNG siting was given to a moderate Republican. Because Democrats split along regional lines on energy policy, there was no official Democratic substitute, but Tim Bishop of New York and Ed Markey of Massachusetts proposed and were allowed to offer a substitute that they billed as a Democratic alternative energy policy.

The majority leadership's aim in crafting the rule was to allow their own members to offer amendments that they felt strongly about for policy or reelection reasons and to let members of the other party offer enough amendments that the process would seem fair so that potential Democratic supporters would not consider that their party had been treated shabbily, while at the same time not permitting amendments that most Republicans opposed yet were likely to pass.

House Floor Action

Debate on the rule, H.Res.219, began on the House floor on April 20. Republicans were caught by surprise when Rules Committee Democrat James McGovern of Massachusetts raised a point of order against the rule on the grounds that it waived points of order against an unfunded mandate in the bill in violation of the Budget Act. The Democrats argued that the MTBE provision of the legislation constituted an unfunded mandate on the states and were supported in that view by a report from the Congressional Budget Office. The Republican leadership had barred any amendments stripping the MTBE provision; such an amendment might win and, even if the leadership could defeat it, some Republicans would have to be pressured into taking a tough vote. The leadership had not foreseen the Democratic tactic, but because the vote was on a procedural motion, not on the issue directly, they were advantaged. Every Republican voting supported the party position, and the House decided to consider the rule notwithstanding the point of order by 231 to 193, with 7 Democrats joining 224 Republicans. The rule itself was then approved by voice vote.

Debate on the energy bill began in the Committee of the Whole with time divided among the chairs and ranking minority members of four committees. Energy and Commerce Chair Barton began debate:

> Mr. Chairman, I rise in strong support of H.R. 6, the Energy Policy Act of 2005. Passage of this comprehensive bill will ensure a more affordable, environmentally friendly energy supply. America's prosperity and national security are at stake. The bill before us today is a balanced bill and it is a bipartisan bill. It will have lower energy prices over time for consumers, it will help spur our economy, create hundreds of thousands of jobs, and take unprecedented steps to promote greater energy conservation and efficiency.... (*Congressional Record*, April 20, 2005, H2193).

Ranking Minority Member Dingell's statement called into question Barton's claim of bipartisanship, arguing that HR6 was "a bad bill" that neither reduced gasoline costs nor protected the environment. The two floor leaders then yielded time to other members to speak.

After the Energy Committee's thirty minutes of general debate time was exhausted, the three other committees followed. Minority Leader Nancy Pelosi summed up the Democrats' case toward the end of general debate:

> The Republican bill is anti-consumer, anti-taxpayer, anti-environment, and with its MTBE provisions, it is harmful to children and other living things. The Republican bill was conceived in secrecy. It was written with the influence of the energy lobbyists, and it shows. It should be rejected by this Congress (*CR*, April 20, 2005, H2207).

With general debate concluded, the House moved on to debate and vote on the amendments allowed by the rule. Considering all the amendments took until late afternoon on April 21. The score: nineteen relatively minor amendments won, most on voice votes. The major amendments that the Republican leadership opposed were all defeated, although some of the votes were close. The amendment House Science Committee Chair Sherwood Boehlert, R-N.Y., proposed regarding corporate average fuel economy (CAFE) standards went down 177–254. Delaware Republican Michael Castle's amendment on LNG siting lost 195–237; the Markey amendment striking drilling in ANWR failed 200–231; and the Dingell amendment on electricity market reform failed 188–243. The Bishop amendment that had been billed as an unofficial Democratic substitute was defeated 170–259, but Democrats split in favor by 165 to 33.

The votes on all of these amendments as well as on all the other defeated amendments pitted a majority of Republicans against a majority of Democrats and, in most cases, the majorities were large ones. Although regional and constituency concerns do split both parties on energy policy, they do so unevenly. By far the closest vote came on a motion by Democrat Lois Capps of California to strike the MTBE provision; although the Rules Committee had denied them the right to offer such an amendment, Democrats were able to get a vote by invoking the House rule on unfunded mandates. Republicans defeated the Democratic move 219–213, but 25 Republicans joined all but 14 Democrats in opposition to the MTBE provisions.

The vote on passage was something of an anticlimax. At 4:38 p.m., the bill was declared passed. The vote was 249 to 183: 208 Republicans and 41 Democrats had voted for it; 160 Democrats, 22 Republicans, and the one independent had voted against it.

Senate Committee Action

Meanwhile, Pete Domenici, R-N.M., chair of the Senate Energy and Natural Resources Committee, was attempting to assure bipartisan support for any energy bill the Senate passed. His committee had primary jurisdiction over energy policy in the Senate although the Finance Committee would write the tax provisions. Domenici was all too aware that the Senate had killed the bill in the previous Congress and that only a real bipartisan effort was likely to result in enactment.

To that end, he and his ranking minority member, Jeff Bingaman, D-N.M., worked together from the beginning. By mid-April, joint draft language on research and development, coal, and other energy titles in the bill, including nuclear, had been worked out and passed around among committee members. On April 20, Domenici reported that talks were moving along "very, very well." And Bingaman agreed that the two sides were "making good progress." Domenici said that in ten to twelve days, he and

Bingaman would offer a presentation to senators on both sides detailing what they have agreed to so far (*Daily*, April 20, 2005).

In fact, the committee mark-up did not begin until May 17. Although much preliminary work had been done and many compromises reached, the complexity and importance of the subject matter led to the mark-up stretching over two weeks. All the pre–mark-up negotiations did pay off. The committee approved nine of thirteen sections of the legislation during the first week. Only the repeal of the 1935 Public Utility Holding Company Act created intense controversy. Democrats praised Domenici for his efforts to address their concerns in areas such as energy efficiency and electricity market reform and called the bill an improvement over previous Senate Republican versions. On May 26, the committee approved the bill on a 21 to 1 vote. A real bipartisan coalition had been assembled. However, as is common in the Senate, the committee put off a number of the most contentious issues to be decided on the floor. On lifting existing bans on new oil and gas leases in most federal waters, pre-empting state authority over the location of liquefied natural gas terminals, revising clean fuel rules, and updating electricity utility merger regulations, the committee punted.

On June 14 Senate Finance Chair Charles Grassley, R-Iowa, released a chairman's mark of the energy tax provisions. That he had effectively negotiated a bipartisan bill became evident two days later when the committee approved the bill on a voice vote without amendment. In contrast to the House tax provisions, Finance's bill heavily favored renewable fuels and conservation over aiding oil and gas producers. "It will improve air quality, strengthen national security, reduce the trade deficit, decrease dependence on the Middle East for oil, and expand markets for agricultural products," Grassley said in a statement issued by the committee (*MR*, June 16, 2005). "The tax provisions [in the Senate bill] differ from those contained in this year's House bill," ranking Democrat Max Baucus of Montana emphasized. "The House bill heavily favors conventional sources of energy, such as oil, natural gas and electricity [generated from coal- and gas-fired steam boilers]. The House bill also ignores the important contributions of conservation efforts, improved energy efficiency and expanded use of alternative fuels" (*MR*, June 16, 2005).

Senate Floor Consideration

On June 9, Majority Leader Frist announced a unanimous consent agreement to begin floor consideration of the energy bill on June 14. On that date debate began with a characteristic Senate moment: Senator Domenici, the floor manager, having asked for and then vacated (called off) a quorum call, explained:

Mr. President, so the Senate will have an idea what we are trying to do, the first amendment we are trying to offer up is in the process of being completed in a bipartisan manner, the ethanol amendment. We don't know exactly when that will be ready. It looks as though they are working on the last clearances or clarification of words. I was told a while ago it may be an hour, it may be less (*CR,* June 14, 2005, S6440).

In other words, negotiations on ethanol provisions were still going on behind the scenes even as floor consideration of the bill began.

Domenici then made his opening statement, emphasizing the bipartisan support for the bill in committee. "I think the most important thing to start with here is that this bill before us cleared the Energy and Natural Resources Committee, after years of stalemate, by a rather incredible vote of 21 to 1." Domenici continued:

I think it means that, for once, Republicans and Democrats have seen an American problem of real significance and have tried very, very hard to see if they could cooperate at every level, with every amendment, and give everybody a chance to argue, present, win, lose, and produce a bill (*CR,* June 14, 2005, S6440).

He went on to extoll the bill as ". . . a jobs bill, a security bill, a clean air bill, and a clean energy bill. Add all of that up, it is a tremendous step forward for the United States" (*CR,* June 14, 2005, S6440).

When Bingaman, who had been engaged in the ethanol negotiations, made it to the floor to deliver his opening statement, he began by congratulating Domenici on successfully moving the bill through the committee and attaining a near unanimous vote. "That vote is a testament, not only to what is contained in the bill but also to the process [Domenici] followed when moving the bill to the Senate floor," the ranking Democrat praised, expressing thanks for the bipartisan process. He continued, however, on a more grounded note. "This bill is a good starting point, but there are several important issues with which we need to deal in the full Senate that we were not able to address in committee" (*CR,* June 14, 2005, S6442).

Over seven days of floor debate, the Senate considered dozens of amendments on myriad energy-related topics. More than one hundred amendments were submitted. During the first four days, the Senate debated eleven major amendments. The ethanol amendment being negotiated as the bill came to the floor was adopted on a 70–26 vote after two second-degree amendments (that is, amendments to the amendment) offered by liberal Democrats from urban states failed. The ethanol amendment, requiring refiners to use at least eight billion gallons of renewable fuel annually by 2012, was attractive to members from farm states, especially those in the Midwest, because ethanol was the renewable fuel most likely to be used and it is made from corn. An amendment offered by Maria

Cantwell, D-Wash., that called for reducing the U.S.'s projected oil imports by 40 percent by 2025 lost on a 47 to 53 vote that fell almost completely along party lines. But Jeff Bingaman's amendment mandating that at least 10 percent of the electricity sold by electric utilities by 2020 be produced from renewable energy sources won 52 to 48 when 9 Republicans joined all but 2 Democrats and independent Jim Jeffords of Vermont in support.

On June 20, the Senate adopted the Finance Committee's tax provisions, which were offered as an amendment rather than having been incorporated in the bill before it went to the floor. Then debate began on an amendment offered by Florida's senators to strike the bill's section providing for a comprehensive inventory of Outer Continental Shelf oil and natural gas resources. The senators feared such an inventory would be a first step toward drilling off the Florida coast, which most Floridians strongly opposed.

By the end of the day, the first restrictions on debate were agreed to. The majority leader announced that a unanimous-consent agreement had been reached

> providing for further consideration of the bill at 9:45 a.m., on Tuesday, June 21, 2005; that there be 80 minutes of debate on Martinez (for Nelson (FL)) Amendment . . . and the Senate then vote on, or in relation to the amendment with no second-degree amendments in order prior to the vote (*Congressional Digest,* June 20, 2005).

The next morning, after the specified debate, the Floridians' amendment was defeated 44 to 52, with the vote falling along party and constituency interest lines. Thus, Louisiana senator Mary Landrieu, although a Democrat, was a strong proponent of the inventory provision and spoke and voted against the effort to strike it. Louisiana allowed drilling, and the state's elected officials believed the provision would benefit their state.

Emphasis then shifted to the highly controversial issue of climate change. Three amendments representing alternative approaches to the problem had been submitted. Nebraska Republican Chuck Hagel's amendment, which reflected the Bush administration's approach, proposed offering economic incentives for businesses to reduce emissions of carbon dioxide and other greenhouse gases voluntarily. The much tougher amendment by Joseph Lieberman, D-Conn., and John McCain, R-Ariz., would place a mandatory cap on greenhouse gas emissions at 2000 levels by 2010. Jeff Bingaman's amendment would express the sense of the Senate that "Congress should enact a national program of mandatory, market-based limits and incentives on greenhouse gas emissions that slow, stop and reverse their growth at a rate that would not harm the economy, and would encourage comparable action by other nations" (*Roll Call,* June 22, 2005). Senators concerned about global warming squared off against those worried about the impact of controls on the economy and the dwindling number unconvinced that global warming was actually occurring. The Hagel amendment came to a vote by afternoon and was easily adopted 66 to 29.

By the evening of June 21 another unanimous consent agreement had been reached. It specified that Sen. Dianne Feinstein, D-Calif., would be recognized the following morning to offer an amendment relating to liquefied natural gas, with sixty minutes of debate allowed; then Sen. Robert Byrd, D-W.Va., would be recognized to offer an amendment related to rural gas prices; finally, when debate resumed on the McCain-Lieberman amendment, there would be three additional hours for debate "with Senator McCain, or his designee, in control of 90 minutes, Senator Domenici in control of 30 minutes, and Senator [James] Inhofe [R-Okla.] in control of the remaining 60 minutes" (*CD*, June 21, 2005). Inhofe was given debate time because he chaired the Environment and Public Works Committee, which had jurisdiction over the climate change issue. No second-degree amendments were allowed to either the Feinstein or the McCain-Lieberman amendment.

Also on June 21 a cloture petition was filed. The majority leader and the minority leader agreed that the Senate needed to finish the energy bill by the end of the week and move on to other legislation.

On the 22nd, Feinstein's amendment requiring the state governor's approval before a LNG facility could be sited in a state was debated; Domenici then moved to table the amendment, a motion that, if successful, kills an amendment without an up-or-down vote on the amendment itself. This provides those voting against a popular amendment a bit of a procedural fig leaf, but not much of one. The motion to table passed 52 to 45, with Republicans voting 44 to 10 to table and Democrats splitting 34 to 8 against tabling. Independent senator Jim Jeffords joined the seven Democratic senators in voting to table.

In the afternoon, the Senate returned to the climate change issue. The McCain-Lieberman amendment lost 38 to 60; 31 Democrats, Senator Jeffords, and 6 Republicans supported the amendment, 49 Republicans and 11 Democrats opposed it. Environmentalists scored a middling victory two hours later when the Bingaman amendment was adopted. Inhofe's motion to table lost on a 44 to 53 vote, when 12 Republicans joined 40 Democrats and Jeffords to beat back the attempt to kill the amendment. Once the motion to table failed, the Senate adopted the amendment by voice vote, as it often does. Although the Bingaman amendment was nonbinding, environmentalists considered its adoption a victory because it carried an acknowledgment that global warming was a real problem about which the U.S. government should do something.

The day ended with Majority Leader Frist proposing twenty-four amendments, all of which quickly passed by unanimous consent. In each case the amendment was offered for another senator and passage had been negotiated with the committee chair and the majority leader and his staff. As a Senate staffer involved in the process explained: "At this point they're [committee leaders] willing to take just about anything.... And that's okay because they will go to conference with it where they can get rid of a lot of it." Accepting the amendments is the price for getting the UCAs (unanimous consent agreements) and then cloture that make possible passing a bill that affects so many interests.

On the morning of June 23, after defeating an amendment raising fuel economy standards, the Senate considered the cloture motion. Domenici and Bingaman advocated a vote for cloture. As Bingaman explained:

> I join [Chairman Domenici] in urging that we go ahead and invoke cloture on the bill. I do believe we have had a good debate on the Senate floor. We have had a good opportunity for amendments to be offered. The process has been open. I have supported some amendments that have been offered to the bill; I have opposed others. I note my colleague has done the same.... That is exactly how the Senate is intended to operate.
>
> Obviously, there are Senators who still have amendments they would like to offer. Some of those amendments will be germane after the cloture vote occurs even if cloture is invoked. Those amendments can be considered by the Senate and disposed of at that time. That is appropriate.
>
> But I understand the scheduling problems the majority leader has and the Democratic leader has as well. They believe they need to move to other legislation early next week... (*CR*, June 23, 2005, S7209).

The Senate voted cloture on the energy bill by 92 to 4; three liberal Democrats and John McCain opposed limiting debate.

Cloture does not cut off debate and amending activity immediately. A number of other amendments still were debated and voted on. The day ended with another wrap-up session during which eighteen or so amendments were proposed and passed by unanimous consent. Sen. Larry Craig, R-Idaho, acting for the majority leader, explained: "Mr. President, we have a series of managers' amendments that have been cleared on both sides. Therefore, I now ask unanimous consent that the series of amendments at the desk be considered and agreed upon en bloc" (*CR*, June 23, 2005, S7267). The bill was essentially finished but senators were eager to leave for the weekend, so no passage vote was taken. A unanimous consent agreement was reached providing for the vote on final passage of the bill to occur at 9:45 a.m. on Tuesday, June 28, 2005.

When the vote was taken the bill passed 85 to 12, with only 5 Republicans and 7 Democrats in opposition. Senate proponents of an energy bill had managed to produce a true bipartisan measure. To be sure, most environmental interest groups were unhappy with many of the bill's provisions and a number of Democrats supported it with limited enthusiasm as the best they could expect to get from a Senate with fifty-five Republicans. Still, most Democrats and environmental groups saw the bill as much better than previous Republican energy bills and, for Senate Democrats, the open, bipartisan process on the bill was a big plus.

The Conference

Reaching agreement between the House and Senate promised to be difficult. To avoid bitter partisan battles, Domenici had kept both the ANWR drilling and the MTBE liability protection provisions out of his bill, essentially leaving them to be settled in conference. The Senate bill emphasized tax breaks for renewable energy and conservation, whereas the House bill focused on traditional fossil fuels. The Senate bill had a global warming provision, albeit a weak one, and a mandate that at least 10 percent of the electricity sold by electric utilities by 2020 be produced from renewable energy sources; the House had neither. The Senate required the use of much more ethanol than the House did. And the administration, although pleased that an energy bill had passed both chambers, opposed the high price tag and wanted it reduced.

On July 1, the Senate asked for a conference with the House and appointed its conferees: eleven from the Committee on Energy and Natural Resources, six Republicans and five Democrats; and three members of the Finance Committee; Chairman Grassley; Orrin Hatch of Utah, the next most senior Republican; and ranking minority member Baucus. On July 13 the House agreed to go to conference, and the next day the Speaker appointed conferees: eleven Republicans and seven Democrats from the Energy and Commerce Committee were made conferees for the entire bill, and three conferees from each of the other four committees that had taken part in drafting the bill were appointed for the specific provisions in their committee's jurisdiction. In addition, three conferees from each of seven other committees were included, also with specifically delineated jurisdiction. Whip Roy Blunt, R-Mo., was appointed one of the Energy Committee conferees although he was a fairly junior member of that committee.

Two of the most contentious issues seemed less likely to stymie the conference than they had in the past. The Senate had agreed to include drilling in ANWR in the budget reconciliation bill, which cannot be filibustered, so the House was less likely to insist that it be included in the energy bill, which could be filibustered. Chairman Barton had been working assiduously to negotiate a deal on MTBE with Charles Bass, R-N.H., as towns in New Hampshire have been at the forefront of defective product litigation against producers of MTBE and New England Republicans had been instrumental in killing the energy bill over that issue in the previous Congress. If they could be satisfied, the bill's prospects improved greatly.

Also portending well for success was a pledge made in June at a closed-door meeting of Barton, Dingell, Domenici, and Bingaman, who would be the top negotiators on the bill. Barton promised to have open discussions and allow input from Democrats. In exchange, the Democrats agreed not to stall the deliberations (*CQ Weekly,* July 29, 2005, 2108).

On July 12, President Bush met with the top energy bill conferees at the White House and pressed them to have a bill on his desk by the beginning of the August recess. The administration formally laid out its position in a letter from Energy Secretary Samuel Bodman to Barton, the conference chair. The administration expressed strong opposition to House and Senate language that gave some revenues generated from states that produce oil and natural gas in the Outer Continental Shelf to those states for broader uses. It also opposed the nonbinding sense of the Senate language that called for Congress to draft legislation mandating reductions in greenhouse gas emissions as a way to combat global warming. Furthermore, the letter continued, the administration "is concerned that the House and Senate bills contain tax provisions whose total cost significantly exceeds [the administration's $6.7 billion] proposal and provide unnecessary subsidies" (*Daily,* July 12, 2005). Bodman's letter did not, however, contain any veto threats.

The first open meeting of the conference occurred on Thursday, July 14. During opening statements, which consumed most of the time, Barton pledged to "do everything I can as chairman to actually have a bipartisan, bicameral open process" (*Daily,* July 15, 2005). The second open meeting, on July 19, revealed how much work had gone on behind the scenes. Staff-recommended language for seven mainly noncontroversial sections of the bill was formally presented and debated. House and Senate Democratic conferees offered several amendments, including attempts to increase federal fuel efficiency standards for cars and light trucks, but none passed. Barton announced that, at the next meeting, conferees would take up a renewables section, including debate over a renewable electricity mandate. Behind-the-scenes talks on Senate-approved language that would require 10 percent of electricity to be produced from renewable energy sources by 2020 were ongoing, Barton said.

Over the next few days, through staff work, high-level negotiations, and long open conference meetings, a compromise energy bill came together. The Republican and Democratic Energy Committee leaders met on Friday and Saturday to discuss compromise language. The full conference met Sunday afternoon. On Monday the top four energy conferees released text for several remaining sections of the energy bill conference report, making them open to amendments during the evening's open conference meeting. That session lasted for nine hours—till 3 a.m.

Key to getting an agreement was Barton's abandoning of the MTBE liability waiver language. After repeatedly assuring all and sundry that a deal was almost finished, Barton and Bass finally unveiled their plan on July 22. It proposed to grant the liability waiver in return for the industry setting up an $11.4 billion cleanup fund. Neither the industry nor state and local governments liked the plan, and Senate conferees refused to accept it. So, on July 24, Barton bowed to the inevitable and agreed to drop the liability waiver.

While the main energy conference was holding free-wheeling open sessions in which members debated and amended the bill, the Ways and Means and Finance conferees were meeting behind closed doors to work out the tax sections. Democrats objected, but to no avail. By July 27, the conferees had a deal. The package of tax breaks totaled $14.6 billion for 2005 through 2015, with the net cost after revenue-raising offsets being $11.5 billion over eleven years.

Overall, the bill negotiated by the conference balanced the House's focus on oil and gas production with the Senate's greater emphasis on renewable energy and conservation. It included an overhaul of the nation's electricity markets, repealing the 1935 Public Utility Holding Company Act (PUHCA), but replacing it with provisions designed to provide disclosure of power company finances. Some provisions to encourage the use of renewable fuels and more energy-efficient products were included, but the requirement that utilities use renewable energy, such as wind or solar energy, to generate 10 percent of their electricity by 2020 was not. The final bill required that the annual average volume of ethanol and other renewable fuel additives used increase, starting at 4 billion gallons in 2006 and climbing to 7.5 billion gallons in 2012, a win for the Senate position. The inventory of gas and oil supplies on the Outer Continental Shelf was included, as was federal control over LNG siting.

Barton filed the conference report on July 27. All Republican conferees from both chambers signed the report, as did all but one Senate Democrat. House Democrats were split; a number of the stronger environmentalists—Markey and Californian Henry Waxman, for example—did not sign, signaling their disapproval of the bill. Environmental groups argued that the bill failed to make truly significant strides toward conservation and the use of renewable fuels and thus opposed it. A majority of House Democratic conferees did sign the conference report, expressing themselves satisfied on balance. "I voted against the measure in April, because it hurt consumers, taxpayers and the environment," said John Dingell. "Now consumer protections in electricity and natural gas markets will be strengthened, taxpayers are no longer on the hook for MTBE cleanups, and the environmental risk has been reduced" (*CQW,* July 29, 2005, 2108). Although the bill was more expensive than Bush had wanted, Energy Secretary Bodman said that the Bush administration was "extremely enthused about this bill in its totality. We think this is a terrific product" (*Daily,* June 27, 2005).

The House approved the conference report on July 28 by 275–156; 200 Republicans and 75 Democrats voted for the bill; the independent, 124 Democrats, and 31 Republicans opposed it. Of the Republicans voting against the bill, fourteen were Floridians, the rest were mostly moderates from the Northeast. The next day the Senate approved the bill 74 to 26, with 49 Republicans and 25 Democrats supporting it and 6 Republicans, 19 Democrats, and Jeffords voting against. On August 8, President Bush signed the bill into law.

About as Orthodox as It Gets: Enacting Energy Legislation in 2005

The legislative process on the 2005 energy bill was indeed about as close to the old standard process as major contentious legislation is now likely to get. Certainly, the process on energy legislation in the two previous Congresses was far more unorthodox. Yet the process on the 2005 bill deviated in many ways from the simple, linear process that used to be the orthodoxy. The bill was the product of a number of committees in the House. The committees had gone through the process before and had developed working relationships, yet, after the committees reported, party leadership involvement to put together a bill to take to the floor was still required. The bill was considered under a complex, structured rule. In the Senate, one committee did most of the drafting; the Finance Committee's tax provisions were added as an amendment on the floor. The Energy Committee did leave a number of major controversies to be decided on the floor, and a large number of amendments were offered. Floor consideration was governed by a series of piecemeal unanimous consent agreements. After a lengthy debate, cloture was invoked, but the leadership's move to terminate debate was not contentious. Most senators agreed the time to finish the bill had arrived, and only four opposed cloture.

Why did energy legislation become law in 2005 when it had failed in both the 107th and 108th Congresses? Both process and substance contributed to changing the outcome. In brief, in the Senate and in conference, bipartisanship replaced hard-edged partisanship and the resulting legislation was a true compromise. Republican and Democratic Senate Energy Committee leaders worked together to draft the legislation that went to the Senate floor, and Democrats were included in the conference negotiations.

This switch in approach was not without cost to majority Republicans. "It's hard to sit there and negotiate when you know you have the votes [to win without the support of minority party members of the conference]," House Energy Committee Chair Joe Barton said. "But if you do that, at the end when it comes to the floor, everybody has a stake in it" (*CQW*, July 29, 2005, 2108). The result was a quite different bill than the one that had emerged from the Republican-only conference in the previous Congress. "The only way we got the energy bill was to pick a lot of the meat out of it," Republican senator Trent Lott of Mississippi bemoaned. "This is not a particularly impressive bill" (*Washington Post*, June 30, 2005).

In a division of powers system, some compromises are almost always necessary to pass legislation of any importance, and policymakers—and those who attempt to influence them—often have to weigh whether the compromise bill that can pass is better than no bill at all.

TABLE 7.1 2005 Energy Bill: A Chronology

Date	House Action	Date	Senate Action	Date	Postpassage Action
4/6	Energy and Commerce Committee begins mark-up.				
4/13	Energy and Commerce approves a bill 39–16. House Government Reform Committee marks up HR1533 and approves it by voice vote. Committee on Resources marks up a bill and approves it by voice vote. Ways and Means Committee marks up HR1541 (tax provisions) and approves it 26–11.				
	Republican Party leadership and the committee chairs put together a composite bill.				
4/18	HR6 introduced and referred to the Committee on Energy and Commerce, and in addition to the Committees on Education and the Workforce, Financial Services, Agriculture, Resources, Science, Ways and Means, and Transportation and Infrastructure, for a period to be subsequently determined by the Speaker; in each case for consideration of such provisions as fall within the jurisdiction of the committee concerned.				
4/19	Rules Committee meets and grants restrictive rule.				
4/20	House floor consideration: rule approved, bill debated, and amendments voted on.				

4/21	Floor consideration continues; House passes bill.
	Domenici, chair of the Energy and Resources Committee, and Bingaman, ranking member, engage in informal bipartisan negotiations on the provisions of an energy bill.
5/17	Energy and Resources Committee begins mark-up of an energy bill.
5/26	Committee approves bill.
6/9	Majority Leader Bill Frist announces a unanimous consent agreement to begin floor consideration of the energy bill on June 14.
6/14	Measure laid before Senate by unanimous consent.
6/15	Senate begins floor consideration.
6/16	Finance Committee marks up and approves tax sections of an energy bill.
6/16, 20–23, 28	Senate continues consideration.
6/20	Senate adopts Finance Committee's tax provisions as an amendment.
6/23	Senate votes for cloture.
6/28	Senate passes HR6.
7/1	Senate asks for a conference and appoints conferees.
7/13	House agrees to conference.
7/14	Speaker appoints conferees.
7/14, 19, 21, 24, 26	Conference meets.

TABLE 7.1 (*Continued*)

Date	House Action	Date	Senate Action	Date	Postpassage Action
				7/26	Conferees agree to file conference report.
				7/27	Conference report filed.
				7/28	House agrees to conference report.
				7/29	Senate agrees to conference report.
				8/8	President signs bill, and it becomes law.

Note: Official actions are in roman type; behind-the-scenes, unofficial actions are in italics.

Medicare/Prescription Drug Legislation: Making Sweeping Policy Change in a Highly Partisan Environment

ADDING PRESCRIPTION DRUG COVERAGE TO MEDICARE had been on the agenda since at least the late 1990s. When Medicare was designed in the 1960s, prescription drug costs accounted for only a small part of medical expenses; by the 1990s they were a major expense, and many senior citizens struggled to pay for the drugs essential to their health. In the late 1990s, President Bill Clinton had proposed a plan that would make it possible for the government to negotiate discounts on prescription drugs for the elderly, but the pharmaceutical industry shot it down before it ever got off the ground. House Republicans passed a bill based on private insurance in 2000, but it got no further and was interpreted by many political analysts as "preventative medicine" for the GOP in the upcoming elections. The issue remained salient enough that both 2000 presidential candidates promised seniors help with prescription drug costs.

At the same time other problems with Medicare were gaining policymakers' attention. Costs had been rising steeply, and some analysts believed that when the baby boomers retired the program's costs would become unsustainable. Conservatives believed that only by bringing the private sector into the provision of health care for the elderly could costs be controlled.

The 107th Congress failed to enact legislation. The House did pass a bill; however, the Democratic-controlled (but narrowly divided) Senate could not amass sixty votes for any of the plans proposed. The 2002 elections switched control of the Senate back to the Republicans, and President

George W. Bush and Republican congressional leaders were determined to succeed in the 108th.

Bush and congressional Republicans saw both policy and political opportunities in the issue. It offered them the chance to inject private sector competition into the Medicare program, which they believed would serve to control costs. Health care had long been an issue favoring Democrats, the party that had enacted Medicare. This battle might allow Republicans to appropriate one of the Democrats' primary issues and make it their own.

This account shows that to pass the Medicare/prescription drug bill, House and Senate party leaders used all sorts of unorthodox practices and procedures. Enacting sweeping policy change is always difficult in the American system, and high partisan polarization and narrow partisan majorities compound the problem. The House Republican leadership aggressively used the now familiar tools of unorthodox lawmaking: party leaders, for example, engineered postcommittee adjustments to pick up support; they designed a strategic restrictive rule for floor consideration, which even brought to the floor (right before the prescription drug bill) an unrelated bill never considered by committee; the leaders had agreed to do this to pick up the support of some conservatives opposed to a new entitlement.

In addition, the House Republican leaders came up with some unorthodox practices of their own; for example, when they found they lacked the votes to pass the bill, they stretched the usual fifteen-minute vote to an hour so as to give them time to persuade a sufficient number of their members to change their votes. The Senate majority leader lacks these kinds of mechanisms of control; yet he too was deeply and continuously involved in the process. The case illustrates just how big a role the party leaders now play in the legislative process, especially on legislation at the center of their party's agenda.

The Bush Proposal and the Congressional Response

In his State of the Union address, President Bush proposed to spend $400 billion over the next decade "to reform and strengthen Medicare." That reform would include a drug benefit. "All seniors," he asserted, "should have the choice of a health care plan that provides prescription drugs" (*CQ Weekly*, February 1, 2003, 268). Although Bush provided no details, that wording suggested and leaks confirmed that the administration was working on a proposal that would require seniors to join some sort of managed care plan in order to get the drug benefit. Bush already had made clear that he wanted significant cost savings through adding private sector competition.

However, the notion of forcing seniors to leave traditional fee-for-service Medicare to get the drug benefit raised a storm of protest on Capitol Hill—from Republicans as well as Democrats. "Instead of updating Medicare to include prescription drugs, the president is requiring seniors to join an H.M.O. to get the help they need paying for their medicine," charged Sen. Debbie Stabenow, D-Mich. More ominously for the White House, Iowa Republican Charles Grassley, chair of the Finance Committee that would write the Senate bill, also expressed opposition. "All of our changes should be voluntary," he said in a statement. "If you like what you have now, you should be able to keep it. All seniors should have access to affordable prescription drug coverage, regardless of the choice they make." Republicans representing rural constituencies were especially upset because managed care plans often are not available in rural areas.

Republicans' anxiety about what they were hearing about the Bush proposal intensified their complaints that the administration was not consulting enough with congressional Republicans; the chairs of the committees that would do the heavy lifting grumbled that even they were not really in the loop. However, White House spokesman Scott McClellan assured them, "We are only beginning the consultation phase with lawmakers over how we improve Medicare based on the principles we outlined" (all quotes from *New York Times,* February 2, 2003).

On February 6, Tommy G. Thompson, Secretary of Health and Human Services (HHS), testified before the Ways and Means Committee, one of the committees with jurisdiction over the issue. Although he assured members that seniors would not be forced to join HMOs in order to get prescription drug benefits, he refused to guarantee that those in the traditional fee-for-service program would be eligible. "The final decisions have not been made," Mr. Thompson said over and over again. Committee members, especially Democrats, pushed him for a commitment, but he refused, replying, "The proposal is still being worked on" (*NYT,* February 6, 2003). The administration sent officials to the Hill to try to reassure Congress but did not actually release a plan. However, as constituents and interest groups representing seniors weighed in, the notion of requiring seniors to join a private plan got more and more unpopular. In mid-February, Speaker Dennis Hastert, R-Ill., told the *Chicago Tribune* that such a requirement was a nonstarter and that he had told President Bush as much. "I don't think you can do it humanely," he recalled telling Mr. Bush. "I don't think you can do it politically" (*NYT,* February 17, 2003).

On March 4, Bush finally unveiled his proposal. In response to the intense criticism, the administration abandoned the notion of making any drug benefits dependent on seniors' joining a private health plan. The proposal still set up a two-tiered system: those who joined a private health plan would get comprehensive drug benefits; for those who remained in traditional fee-for-service Medicare, the new drug benefits would be modest. Furthermore, rather than releasing a detailed plan, Bush only set forth a conceptual "framework"; the details would be worked out with Congress, administration spokespersons said. The administration, it seems, wanted to avoid giving its critics too much to shoot at.

Nevertheless, the reception of the revised plan was not much more friendly than that of the first. Democrats denounced it as still essentially privatizing Medicare. "This is not a compromise," stated Sen. Edward (Ted) M. Kennedy, D-Mass. "It's a hoax. It still forces seniors to abandon their family doctors to join H.M.O.'s to get the drug benefit they deserve" (*NYT*, February 28, 2003). Senator Stabenow asserted, "The president talks about Medicare reform, but those are code words. What he really wants to do is to privatize Medicare" (*NYT*, March 4, 2003). "The president's new plan still privatizes Medicare," Senate Minority Leader Tom Daschle of South Dakota charged. "It still requires seniors to leave the traditional Medicare program if they want insurance coverage that helps them with the routine costs for medications" (*NYT*, March 4, 2003).

Republicans were more guarded but also expressed concern. Senator Grassley said the drug benefits available in traditional Medicare and in private plans had to be "of equal value," although not "exactly the same" (*NYT*, February 28, 2003). Sen. Olympia Snowe, a moderate Republican from Maine and often a swing vote on the Finance Committee, and Billy Tauzin, a Republican from Louisiana and chair of the House Energy and Commerce Committee, both declared that the Bush proposal did not guarantee adequate drug benefits for people in the traditional fee-for-service Medicare program. "You couldn't move my mother out of Medicare with a bulldozer," Tauzin said. "She trusts it, believes in it. It's served her well." His committee, Tauzin added, "almost certainly will want a strong and adequate prescription drug benefit within fee-for-service Medicare" (*NYT*, March 5, 2003). Speaker Dennis Hastert and Senate Majority Leader Bill Frist of Tennessee welcomed the president's proposal, but emphasized that it was just one step in what would be a long and complicated legislative process.

Pre-Floor Action in the Senate

Majority Leader Frist personally preferred a plan that injected a considerable component of private sector competition into Medicare. Yet he knew that to get the sixty votes necessary to pass a bill in the Senate, Republicans would have to overcome the divisions they had displayed in 2002 as well as solicit some support from Democrats. As the only medical doctor in the Senate and an aspiring presidential candidate, Frist had a great deal riding on success. This, more than any other major bill, was one that Frist and his senior staff would track "from cradle to grave." To try to bridge the differences among Republicans, Frist and Grassley held weekly meetings with Finance Committee Republicans on the issue. Just before Easter, they met with Montana senator Max Baucus, ranking Democrat on the committee (*CongressDaily*, May 3, 2003). Frist also met periodically with Ted Kennedy, who had long been the Senate Democrats' lead person on health issues.

On June 5, Grassley and Baucus announced that they and some other members of the committee had reached a bipartisan compromise on a Medicare drug bill. Reaching the deal had taken so long in part because the Finance Committee had been busy with Bush's tax proposal but also because the issue was such a difficult one. On the hot button issue of differential benefits, the deal crafted by the two senators, both from rural states, was unequivocal. "Our agreement adds a comprehensive prescription drug benefit for all seniors in Medicare," Grassley affirmed. "The benefit is equal for everyone, both in traditional Medicare and in the enhanced Medicare we're setting up" (*NYT*, June 6, 2003). The drug benefit would be provided by private insurance firms but, should private plans not enter a particular Medicare market, the government would provide drug benefits through a contractor. Given the $400 billion cap on spending, the proposal was not a generous one, and it contained what was to become known as the infamous doughnut hole—after spending a certain amount for drugs, for which they would get assistance, beneficiaries would be responsible for the entire amount up to a very high level, when aid would kick in again.

Conservative Republicans expressed concern, saying the plan did not do enough to encourage the growth of private plans, whereas some liberal Democrats denounced it as a move to privatize Medicare. Ted Kennedy, however, called the Grassley-Baucus package "a major breakthrough in our effort to give senior citizens the prescription drug coverage under Medicare they need and deserve" (*CQW*, June 7, 2003, 1358).

The White House said the administration was pleased that progress had been made and did not comment on the substance. On June 10, White House aides let it be known that the administration would accept, at least for now, a bill with equal benefits (*NYT*, June 10, 2003).

The bill was introduced as S1 on June 11 with Majority Leader Frist as sponsor. On June 12, the Senate Finance Committee marked up and approved the Grassley-Baucus legislation with only minor changes. Four amendments were rejected on roll call votes, including a Daschle amendment limiting premiums and one from Oklahoma Republican Don Nickles to block subsidies for the health care of certain alien minority children. The latter unrelated provision had been inserted so as to pick up some Democratic support. The committee approved the bill by a vote of 16 to 5.

Three Democrats—Jay Rockefeller of West Virginia, John Kerry of Massachusetts, and Bob Graham of Florida—and two Republicans—Don Nickles and Trent Lott of Mississippi—voted against the bill. Although he had been a severe critic of the draft, Daschle voted for the bill, promising to "improve it on the floor" (*Markup Report,* June 12, 2003).

House Committee Action

Meanwhile, in the House the two committees with major jurisdiction over health care, Ways and Means and Energy and Commerce, held hearings to, as the committee report would later state, "examine all aspects of the Medicare program" and heard "expert testimony from academic, beneficiary and provider representatives." Ways and Means or its Health subcommittee held six days of hearings between February 6 and May 1; the Health subcommittee of the Energy Committee held two days in April.

Despite pressure from the party leadership to move toward mark-up, progress was slow. Ways and Means, like its counterpart Finance in the Senate, was preoccupied with the tax bill; but turf competition between the two committee chairs was also a barrier. California Republican Bill Thomas, chair of Ways and Means, and Billy Tauzin, chair of Energy and Commerce, were both strong-minded, aggressive leaders who protected their own committee's turf jealously and worked to expand it zealously. To encourage the chairmen to pick up the pace, Speaker Hastert appointed a cross-committee task force on the legislation. It was, however, the top Republican committee leaders who, by June 10, reached an "agreement in principle" on a proposal similar to but "more workable" than the bill the House had passed the previous year. No Democrats were included in the negotiations (*Daily,* June 11, 2003).

A bill reflecting the agreement in principle was introduced by Thomas and Tauzin on June 16 and referred to the two committees the same day. Ways and Means approved its version on June 17; Energy and Commerce took a little longer, approving its version on June 19. In both committees, the mark-up sessions to consider and amend the legislation were contentious and highly partisan.

The Ways and Means mark-up began with a demonstration by seniors shouting, "Don't privatize Medicare!" (*CQW,* June 21, 2003, 1537). Committee Democrats attempted to alter the bill. They offered amendments to guarantee a $35 monthly premium; to eliminate the provision that, after 2010, traditional Medicare would have to compete with private plans in a bidding process; and to encourage lower drug prices. They also offered a full substitute that was more generous and also more costly. Committee Republicans were completely united in voting down the four key Democratic amendments and approving the bill. Every Democrat supported three of the four amendments and, on the other and on passage, one Democrat broke off to join the Republicans. The committee approved the bill 25 to 15. The bill would "move Medicare into the 21st century," Connecticut Republican Nancy Johnson, chair of the Health subcommittee, argued. Pete Stark of California, the second ranking Democrat on the committee, countered, "It's a rotten deal for seniors—the first step toward privatizing Medicare" (*MR,* June 17, 2003).

The Energy and Commerce Committee mark-up lasted three days and was characterized by "ferocious debate" (*MR,* June 19, 2003). "The heart of our bill," Tauzin said, "is a competition-driven approach that not only causes Medicare to compete but offers seniors a choice of [health care] plans that might better fit their circumstances." Competition would drive down costs, Republicans maintained. "This is an ideological experiment with seniors as guinea pigs," ranking minority member John Dingell of Michigan charged (*MR,* June 19, 2003). "Under this bill," Ohio Democrat Sherrod Brown explained,

> seniors who want to stay in traditional Medicare would invariably pay more for that privilege . . . they would pay more because private plans would be able to customize their benefits and cost-sharing to attract the youngest, healthiest beneficiaries, leaving Medicare with the oldest and sickest [and] leaving those who stay in Medicare to bear the full weight for the increased costs (*MR,* June 17, 2003).

Democrats offered twenty-six amendments, including a substitute without the competition provision and with more generous benefits; an amendment authorizing the government to negotiate drug prices with pharmaceutical companies as it does in the Department of Veterans Affairs and the Medicaid program; and an amendment to close the doughnut hole. These and all the others failed. Of the 26 Democratic amendments, 18 were voted down on straight party-line votes; on 7 others, an average of 1.4 Democrats and .7 Republicans crossed party lines. The only Democratic amendment that received a bipartisan "negative" vote was one to adopt the Senate bill; on that, fourteen of the twenty-three Democrats voting joined all Republicans in opposition. Energy and Commerce approved its bill on a 29 to 20 vote, with one Democrat and no Republicans crossing party lines.[1]

Senate Floor Consideration

The Senate agreed by unanimous consent to begin debate on S1 on June 16. Despite the strong bipartisan vote in the Finance Committee,

---

1. Data are from *National Journal's CongressDaily* Mark-up Reports.

many senators on both ends of the ideological spectrum were unhappy with the bill. Conservatives complained that the bill did not inject enough private sector competition into Medicare and that costs might well sky-rocket. Pennsylvanian Rick Santorum, chair of the Senate Republican Conference, said, "There are those who are suspicious that Senator Kennedy wouldn't be for something that wasn't in the direction of a government-run health care system" (*NYT*, June 22, 2003).

Some believed that in their eagerness to preempt a Democratic issue, Bush and Senate leaders had given much too much ground on the basic issue of reforming Medicare. Some liberals, on the other hand, argued that the drug benefit was too stingy and worried that the bill was a step toward privatizing Medicare. That passage might deprive Democrats of a good reelection issue was a concern as well. Kennedy's endorsement of the bill upset many Democrats. At the regular weekly lunch meeting of Democratic senators on June 10, Kennedy was subjected to sharp criticism; some liberals charged that his support cut the ground out from under other Democrats who wanted to oppose the plan as inadequate.

Dissatisfaction with the bill as well as its complexity meant that senators would want to offer large numbers of amendments. In fact, debate stretched out over nine days and more than two hundred amendments were submitted. Democrats offered amendments to make drug coverage more generous, to ensure that drug coverage would be available to all seniors, and to control the cost of drugs. Conservative Republicans attempted to inject more competition and to charge higher-income beneficiaries more. Ultimately, almost every senator offered narrowly targeted amendments to tweak some aspect of the committee bill. No significant curbs on debate or amendments were ever agreed to. The Senate took roll call votes on thirty-four amendments and disposed of many others by voice votes or unanimous consent.

All of the Democrats' most significant amendments were defeated, most on largely party-line votes. For example, Debbie Stabenow's amendment to create a prescription drug benefit under the traditional Medicare program available to all eligible recipients lost 37–58 and Illinois Democrat Richard Durbin's amendment to create a prescription drug coverage plan within Medicare with no deductible was defeated 39–56. Tom Daschle's amendment to limit any increase in prescription drug premiums to 10 percent of the national average monthly prescription drug premium also lost 39–56. The conservatives' amendments lost as well. A proposal by John Ensign, R-Nev., and Chuck Hagel, R-Neb., to limit coverage to a discount card rather than a prescription drug benefit was killed on a 21–75 vote.

Some significant amendments did win. A bipartisan amendment by Judd Gregg, R-N.H., and Charles E. Schumer, D-N.Y., designed to bring cheaper generic drugs to market faster by making it harder for the makers of brand-name drugs to extend their patents was approved 94–1. The Senate also approved, 62–28, an amendment by Byron L. Dorgan, D-N.D., to allow the reimportation of drugs from Canada, but not before requiring that the U.S. government certify their safety. A big manager's amendment that included many less significant amendments was offered by Grassley and Baucus and adopted by unanimous consent.

Just before 1 a.m. on June 27, the Senate passed S1 by 76 to 21. Forty Republicans, thirty-five Democrats, and independent Jim Jeffords of Vermont voted for the bill; ten Republicans and eleven Democrats voted against it. The Finance Committee leaders and Majority Leader Frist hailed passage as a major milestone and an historic accomplishment. As Frist expressed it:

> . . . the bill we have just passed is nothing less than historic. By dramatically expanding opportunities for private sector innovation, it offers genuine reform that will dramatically improve the quality of health care for all seniors. At the same time, the legislation preserves traditional Medicare so that those who wish can remain in traditional Medicare and keep exactly what they have today. This bill combines the best of the public and private sectors and positions Medicare to evolve with the medical treatments of the future. It is entirely voluntary.
>
> I am very pleased by the overwhelming majority of this body who tonight voted to move this legislation towards a more competitive private model but a partnership between the public and private sector (*Congressional Record,* June 27, 2003, S8707).

The Republicans who voted against the bill, conservatives all, faulted it as not containing enough private sector competition. And even many who voted for it had the same concern. Frist spoke to their concerns: "As many people have stated, it is not a perfect bill, but we will continue to move this legislation forward now to conference, we will have the opportunity to make the private sector provisions more flexible, indeed more competitive. . ." (*CR,* June 27, 2003, S8707).

Many Democrats, both those who voted against the bill and the larger number who voted for it, worried that the Senate bill, which many found only minimally acceptable, indeed would be changed for the worst in conference. Sen. Barbara Mikulski of Maryland expressed a broadly held view:

> I tried to improve the bill. I voted for amendments to improve the bill. For example: For the Durbin substitute which would have created a stronger, more comprehensive benefit at a lower cost to seniors.
>
> For an amendment to get rid of the coverage gap. . . .
>
> For an amendment to provide seniors with a guaranteed prescription plan that is under Medicare. . . .
>
> I am sorry all these amendments failed on party line votes.
>
> This legislation is a beginning. It is something we can build on. . .

So I will vote for this bill. It is not the bill I want. Yet we can't let the perfect be the enemy of the good. We can't do nothing—as seniors struggle to pay for the drugs they need.

But let me be very clear, this is as far as I will go. If this bill comes back from conference and it is a benefit for insurance companies—say goodbye to my vote. If it increases costs for seniors, say goodbye to my vote. If it cuts benefits, say goodbye to my vote.

So I will vote for this legislation tonight because I don't want to say goodbye to this opportunity to provide a Medicare prescription drug benefit for seniors (*CR,* June 27, 2003, S8698–S8699).

House Pre-Floor Decisions

Although both of the House committees with jurisdiction had approved their bills by June 19, decisions about how to handle the legislation on the floor had to be made before floor consideration could begin. The agreement between the chairs had yielded one bill that they jointly introduced, but both chairs had made some changes in the vehicle—the chairman's mark—that their committees marked up. Thomas had added a rural health care package and Tauzin had added several provisions of the proposal championed by the so-called rump group of conservative Republicans. These members favored a "defined contribution" approach to drug benefits because that would contain costs, as well as encourage private sector participation. Tauzin had agreed to include their provision for means-testing the drug benefit—that is, requiring better-off seniors to pay more—and a provision for a limited drug debit card (*Daily,* June 18 and 23, 2003). In addition, some amendments, although not major ones, had been adopted during mark-up.

The committee chairs got together with Speaker Hastert and other Republican Party leaders to work out a final bill to take to the floor (*Daily,* June 25, 2003). Their aim was not just to meld the two committees' bills into one but also to make changes that would pick up the support of various groups of disgruntled Republicans. Over the course of several days, the party leaders met with small groups of members in an attempt to persuade them to vote for the bill and, when necessary, they negotiated changes to get those votes. At the same time, the Republican whip system was in high gear, "educating" and persuading Republicans and reaching out to the more conservative Blue Dog Democrats.

President Bush also got into the act, inviting groups of members to the White House to urge them to support the bill, as it was a top White House priority and would be a huge GOP win if passed, the president emphasized (*Daily,* June 25, 2003). Those conservatives worried about setting up a new entitlement or about there not being enough private sector competition in the bill were an especially problematic group to woo. "I trust and love my president," said John Culberson, R-Texas. "But I have tremendous concern about creating what I am confident will become one of the largest, most expensive entitlements in the nation's history" (*NYT*, June 26, 2003). Bush urged the conservatives to be pragmatic; the bill would be improved in conference.

On Wednesday, June 25, 2003, Speaker Hastert formally introduced the bill as HR1; he had been saving that symbolically important number. The Rules Committee met just after midnight and at 6:20 a.m. reported the special rule to govern floor consideration of the bill. Although House members had requested the opportunity to offer dozens of amendments, the rule allowed only one—an amendment in the nature of a substitute if offered by Charles Rangel of New York and John Dingell, the ranking Democrats on the Ways and Means and Commerce Committees, respectively.

The rule also included a provision that brought up right before HR1 a bill that expanded private medical savings accounts. The rule further specified that, if both this bill and HR1 passed, the medical savings account bill would be added to HR1, and they would be sent to the Senate as a package. The medical savings account bill, which would cost $174 billion over ten years, had not been considered and reported by a committee. Hastert agreed to bring it up and include it in the rule in return for the votes of a number of conservatives unhappy with a new entitlement.

House Floor Consideration

Floor consideration on the rule began at midday on the 26th. Deborah Pryce, R-Ohio, managing the rule for the Rules Committee majority, argued that the modified closed rule was "an appropriate rule for such a delicate, complex, and historic piece of legislation" (*CR*, June 26, 2003, H5952). Louise Slaughter, D-N.Y., managing the rule for the Democrats, responded:

> Mr. Speaker, this rule is an affront to the democratic process. The underlying bill will harm every single one of the 40 million Americans served by Medicare. At 1 a.m. this morning, with absolutely no meaningful opportunity to review the almost 700-page prescription drug legislation, the Committee on Rules met to consider the resolution now before us. By now I should be used to it, but we cannot tolerate these continual attacks on democracy. When you refuse to allow half this House to speak and to give their amendments, you are cutting out half of the population of the United States from any participation in the legislation that goes on here. It defies reason and it defies common sense that political expediency and newspaper headlines could force this monumental legislation, probably the most monumental that any of us will do in

our tenure in the Congress of the United States, to force it through the Chamber with little more than cursory consideration (*CR,* June 26, 2003, H5952).

The rule was approved over fierce Democratic opposition; Republicans split 219 to 4 in favor of the rule; 198 Democrats voted against the rule and 2 voted for it.

As the rule stipulated, HR2596, the bill expanding personal medical savings accounts, was considered first. An hour of general debate and no amendments were permitted. Republicans argued that allowing people to put away more pretax money for their health care would foster responsibility and sensible frugality in the use of health services; Democrats responded that it was simply a giveaway to the "wealthy and healthy" and would encourage some employers to drop health care for their employees. The bill passed on a vote of 237 to 191; 222 Republicans and 15 Democrats voted for the bill; 188 Democrats, 2 Republicans and independent Bernie Sanders voted against it.

Floor consideration of HR1, the Medicare/prescription drug bill, began at 6:55 p.m. The rule provided for three hours of debate equally divided among and controlled by the chairs and ranking minority members of the Committee on Energy and Commerce and the Committee on Ways and Means. Republicans hailed the bill for finally delivering on the promise to seniors of a prescription drug benefit and also for beginning the process of modernizing an antiquated program. What Republicans saw as "modernization," Democrats saw as demolition. Sander M. Levin, D-Mich., denounced the bill as "a radical effort to dismantle Medicare." Jim McGovern, D-Mass., charged, "This bill ends Medicare as we know it and turns it into a convoluted, complicated voucher program" (*NYT,* June 27, 2003).

After general debate, Democrats offered their substitute, a more expensive defined-benefits plan under Medicare without a doughnut hole and with a provision that specifically authorized that which the Republican bill specifically prohibited—government negotiation of drug prices with the pharmaceutical companies. Coming up with an alternative that united Democrats had not been easy and was not completely successful. When the roll call came, 174 Democrats supported the substitute, but all 226 Republicans and 29 Democrats voted against it.

Not long thereafter the vote on passage of the Republican version began. When the fifteen minutes allotted for a recorded vote ran out, the bill was losing by two votes. Holding the vote open, Hastert and other Republican leaders descended en masse on Republicans who had voted against the party position. Jo Ann Emerson, R-Mo., switched her vote for a promise that the leaders would strip out in conference a provision making the importation of drugs from Canada harder and a pledge to schedule a separate House vote on her drug importation bill.

Vice President Dick Cheney had met with reluctant conservatives earlier in the day. The leadership now went after those who had not been won over and finally persuaded Butch Otter, R-Idaho, to change his vote. Eventually, they managed to persuade just enough Republicans to switch their votes to pass the bill 216–215 (*Los Angeles Times,* June 28, 2003). The fifteen-minute vote had stretched to almost an hour but, at 2:32 a.m., the bill was declared passed. Despite serious misgivings by many conservatives, only nineteen Republicans voted against the bill. Democrats had whipped the vote intensively as well, and only nine Democrats voted for the bill.

Reconciling the House and Senate Bills

Bush hailed passage of the legislation in both houses and called on Congress to send him a bill to sign by the August recess. Reconciling the two bills would not, however, be easy, congressional leaders knew. The bills differed in a number of important ways, as summed up in the June 28, 2003, edition of the *New York Times*:

- The House bill would create two types of tax-free personal savings accounts for medical expenses. The Senate bill has no such provision.
- The Senate bill offers more generous assistance to some people with low incomes. But the House bill would require high-income people to spend more of their own money before they could qualify for certain types of drug coverage.
- The Senate bill would require the government to deliver drug benefits if private plans showed no interest in a particular region. The House bill has no such backup mechanism.
- The House bill tilts more toward the private sector. It would increase Medicare payments to health maintenance organizations and set up direct competition between private plans and traditional Medicare starting in 2010. The Senate bill has no similar provisions.

The House provision forcing traditional Medicare to compete with private plans was the single most controversial provision and the most likely to lead to a breakdown in negotiations. In the House forty-two Republicans had told their leadership that, were this provision removed in conference, they would not vote for the resulting bill. For Senate Democrats this provision was also a deal breaker. In early July, Ted Kennedy drafted a letter to President Bush that was signed off on by thirty-six Democrats, including Minority Leader Tom Daschle; the letter stated their bottom line: "We will oppose a conference report that forces seniors to choose between giving up their doctor or facing higher premiums to stay in the current Medicare program," they wrote (*Roll Call*, July 7, 2003). Daschle warned Republicans not to be fooled by the big passage margin. Conservative Republicans responded with a letter of their own; seventy-six signed a letter to Bush urging more rather than less private sector involvement.

The Senate named its conferees on July 7, all from the Finance Committee: Chairman Grassley and ranking Democrat Baucus; Majority Leader Frist and Minority Leader Daschle; Republicans Don Nickles, Orrin Hatch of Utah, and Jon Kyl of Arizona; and Democrats John Breaux of Louisiana and John D. Rockefeller IV of West Virginia. Nickles and Rockefeller had voted against the bill, but a number of the other conferees also had doubts about it. A week later the House named as conferees Majority Leader DeLay; Ways and Means Committee Chair Thomas; Energy and Commerce Chair Tauzin; Ways and Means Health Subcommittee Chair Johnson; and Florida Republican Michael Bilirakis, chair of the Energy Committee Health Subcommittee. Democrats named as conferees were Charles Rangel and John Dingell, ranking minority members of the Ways and Means and Energy and Commerce Committees, respectively, and Marion Berry, a licensed pharmacist from Arkansas and co-chair of the House Democratic Health Care task force.

Conferees began meeting in July. On July 23, Bush met with the entire conference membership, urging a speedy resolution. After one of the early meetings, conference chair Bill Thomas questioned whether Democratic conferees were serious about a bipartisan resolution, a comment that suggested trouble ahead. Most of the Democratic conferees soon found themselves excluded from the real negotiations over the bill.

The August recess, which most members normally spend in their districts, saw an intensification of lobbying on the bill. The AARP (formerly, American Association of Retired Persons), the largest interest group representing seniors, and labor groups and drug companies all revved up their campaigns to influence constituents' opinions and thereby the votes of members. AARP held town hall meetings, discussions with lawmakers in their districts, and meetings with editorial boards. The organization also ran ads advocating a more generous drug benefit. The Alliance of Retired Americans, a group of retired labor activists affiliated with the AFL-CIO, held rallies across the country, warning that the bill could undermine the traditional Medicare program. Drug industry officials traveled the country calling for more private sector competition in Medicare, and the United Seniors Association, a group with ties to the drug industry, urged members of Congress to pass a Medicare bill that focuses on "dynamic, competitive markets, not bureaucracies" (*CQW*, August 2, 2003).

Both parties sent their House members home for the August recess with instructions to talk about the legislation. In July the Democratic leadership had urged its members to begin organizing town hall meetings on the bill in their districts. "While we lost a vote on June 27, the fight continues," the leaders wrote in their "Dear Colleague" letter to their members. They went on to stress:

> [I]t's our strong belief that Democrats must take this debate directly to our seniors.... The best way to do that is through the give-and-take of town hall meetings that individually generate favorable media coverage in your District and collectively generate a pro-active, positive message about House Democrats in the national media (*RC*, July 9, 2003).

In July as well, the Democratic Congressional Campaign Committee (DCCC) had run TV ads in the districts of eight Republican House members "chosen because they were judged to be vulnerable by the party in the upcoming elections and had large numbers of older voters in their districts" (*NYT*, July 12, 2003). According to the DCCC e-mail newsletter, "The ads inform voters in eight Republican-held Congressional districts that their Representatives recently voted in support of a bill that would 'end Medicare as we know it.' The bill they just passed:

- Pushes seniors into HMOs;
- Has huge gaps in [drug] coverage and provides no guaranteed coverage;
- Shortchanges rural seniors; and,
- Prevents Medicare from negotiating the best prices for prescription drugs" (July 14, 2003).

During the recess, congressional staff continued to work, attempting to negotiate agreements on the lesser differences between the two bill versions. When Congress returned to Washington in early September, conferees accepted much of what the staff had done, but the big issues remained. High-level negotiations resumed, but again only two Democratic conferees—moderates Max Baucus and John Breaux—were included. In late September, Speaker Hastert and Majority Leader Frist set a target date of October 17 for an agreement, and Bush met with the conferees again. Still, the big issues—especially, but not only, the matter of forcing traditional Medicare to compete with private plans—were so divisive—and not just between Republicans and Democrats but also within the Republican Party—that little progress on them was made. The deadline was missed.

Conferees were being pressured from all sides. In late October, Minority Leader Daschle and forty other senators, including Republican Olympia Snowe and independent Jim Jeffords, sent Bush a letter objecting to language on the competition issue and asking him to intervene in the talks. Bush had taken a largely hands-off approach to the negotiations, leaving it to HHS Secretary Thompson to represent the administration

(*CQW*, October 25, 2003, 2621). Although neither Breaux nor Baucus signed the letter, Baucus warned that the competition language might doom the bill. Yet conservatives repeatedly warned that they would vote against any bill without strong competition provisions.

By early November, time was running short. Most participants believed that a bill had to be passed before Congress adjourned for the holidays because, were the process to go into an election year, the chances of success would be slim. With President Bush and the congressional Republican Party having staked their reputations on enacting a prescription drug benefit for seniors, failure could have severe electoral consequences.

Frist and Hastert, who had been increasing their participation in the negotiations, now took over. On November 12, over Thomas's objections, they cut a deal with Breaux and Baucus on the competition issue. The full-fledged House competition proposal that Thomas championed was cut back to a temporary experiment instead. "In Conference it was really threading a needle between what the House needed, so that the conservatives would vote for the bill, and what we needed in the Senate, so we could get our 60 votes," a Senate leadership aide explained. For getting the sixty votes, he explained, "Baucus and Breaux were key; so what Baucus and Breaux needed, they got. . . . It was Frist who insisted that Breaux and Baucus be kept on board." At a news conference on November 13, Frist assured, "We're 95 percent there in producing a bill we will be able to take to the floor next week" (*CQW*, November 15, 2003, 2827). In fact, it took until November 21 to finalize the conference report. *Congressional Quarterly* described the conference agreement:

> Beginning in 2006, prescription coverage would be available through private insurers to seniors paying a monthly premium estimated at $35 in 2006. Those enrolled in the plan would cover the first $250 of annual drug costs themselves and 25 percent of all drug costs up to $2,250. Benefits would then stop until out-of-pocket drug costs exceeded $3,600, after which a beneficiary would cover 5 percent of all costs. Low-income seniors would be eligible for discounts on premiums, deductibles and co-payments. If no private plans bid in a region, the government would offer a fallback prescription drug plan. In 2004 and 2005, beneficiaries would be able to use drug discount cards to reduce prices by up to 25 percent. Medicare payments to managed care plans would increase by $14.2 billion over 10 years. A pilot project would begin in 2010 in which Medicare would compete with private insurers to provide coverage for hospital and doctor costs in six metropolitan areas for six years. Drugs from Canada would be eligible for importation only if the Health and Human Services Department determines there is no safety risk and the move would save consumers money. Beginning in 2007, Part B premiums would increase for some higher-income recipients. Certain individuals under 65 years of age, as well as Medicare recipients, would be able to establish health-savings accounts to pay for health care services not covered by their insurance policy.

Democrats believed the compromise jettisoned much of what they had won in the Senate; conservative Republicans, many of whom thought the original House bill was not strong enough, judged the compromise considerably worse. On the other hand, the scaling back of the competition provision induced the AARP to support the bill. "We would have opposed the bill instead of supporting it" had the compromise failed, John C. Rother, policy director at AARP, said. Convinced that the support of this huge and highly influential senior lobby was crucial, the Republican leaderships had done what it took to get the AARP on board.

Passing the Conference Report

Once the conference agreement was reached, the House Republican Party apparatus went to work to pass it. Since House Democrats had been completely excluded from the negotiations, Hastert knew he could not count on many Democratic votes. In the House, passage would depend on Republicans, as Hastert preferred anyway, and that meant persuading conservatives to support a conference report about which they had serious substantive doubts.

The leaders brought former Speaker and Georgia Republican Newt Gingrich in to speak to a Republican Conference meeting and vigorously defend the bill from a conservative perspective. The House Republican whip system went into overdrive to produce an accurate count of Republicans' voting intentions. At a whip meeting, the chairs of Ways and Means and Energy and Commerce explained the complex bill's provisions and countered arguments against it. They emphasized, as the party leaders did also, that the addition of a prescription drug benefit to Medicare was inevitable and that, if this bill failed, Democrats would eventually do it in a way conservatives found a great deal more distasteful. According to Commerce Committee Chair Tauzen, it was "a not too subtle message: this is the best you are ever going to get" (*LAT*, November 23, 2003). The whips fanned out to do their count. Whip Roy Blunt of Missouri met with his assistant whips and with the leaders of the coalition of interest groups supporting the bill to coordinate strategy. That the lobbying efforts of the coalition of several hundred groups was headed by Susan B. Hirschmann, a former chief of staff to Majority Leader DeLay, facilitated cooperation between the Republican leadership and the interest groups. The GOP had scored a major coup when the leaders had persuaded the AARP to endorse the bill, and the AARP played an important role in the lobbying effort.

When a whip found a member who was either opposed or undecided, the member was asked for a list of specific objections to the bill. Blunt and the chief deputy whip then met with small groups of members with similar complaints, attempting to address their problems. Bush telephoned a number of holdouts from Air Force One as he returned from Britain. At a Republican Conference meeting the evening of floor consideration, Republican leaders promised concerned members that payment rates for oncologists would be revisited in six months if the doctors were unhappy with the provision; by doing this, supporters picked up several votes.

The vote on the Medicare prescription drug bill conference report posed a major test for House Democrats. If significant numbers of Democrats voted for the final bill, the party's argument that the bill represented a bad deal for seniors would ring hollow. Yet, especially considering the AARP's backing, voting against the bill struck some Democrats as electorally risky. The House Democratic Party leaders believed a maximum effort to hold down defections was essential. At her Leader's Lunch the week of the vote, Nancy Pelosi told members "there will be no passes" on this issue; "this is a party vote." Other members backed her up; Marion Berry, a conservative Democrat and excluded conferee, avowed, "We must not give them a single vote.... If you go with this, you do not belong in this party." Emphasizing the legislation's flaws, Whip Steny Hoyer of Maryland argued, "This is not about party, but about policy" (*RC,* November 19, 2003).

As the vote approached, Pelosi and Hoyer met continuously with members in groups and individually trying to persuade them to vote "no." Hoyer held more than a dozen whip meetings. Because the bill was more than one thousand pages long and Democrats were given little time to study the final version, providing information and clearing up confusion were important functions of the meetings. The Democratic message was: this is a bad bill that does little for seniors in terms of prescription drug coverage, but it does endanger Medicare. Despite the AARP, you can sell that message to your constituents.

Consideration began on the evening of November 21, 2003. When the normal fifteen minutes allotted to a recorded vote expired at 3:15 a.m., the bill was losing, with 219 votes cast against the conference report. The Democratic effort had continued on the floor, and not a single Democrat had voted for the bill. David Wu of Oregon, the only member who had not cast a vote, was surrounded by Pelosi and many of the whips. Wu wanted to vote for the bill but, out of party loyalty, did not want to be the one who pushed the measure over the top (*CQW,* November 29, 2003, 2959).

Democratic cohesion intensified the Republicans' problem with their conservatives. Speaker Hastert held the vote open; GOP leaders had posted "door men" at the exits from the floor to make sure that Republicans who voted "no" could not escape into the night (*The Hill,* November 16, 2005). The leaders and HHS Secretary Thompson who had been working on members all evening redoubled their efforts. Speaker Hastert even allowed Thompson onto the floor of the House chamber to lobby members, a highly unorthodox move as ordinarily only members of Congress and selected congressional staff are allowed on the floor when the House is in session. "Knots of senior House Republicans and Health and Human Services Secretary Tommy G. Thompson huddled repeatedly around several of the two dozen skeptical members who had initially voted against the bill," reported the *Washington Post* on November 22, 2003. Ernest Istook of Oklahoma, chair of an Appropriations Committee subcommittee, a position now subject to a Steering Committee vote, changed his vote from nay to yea. Nick Smith, a Michigan conservative who was retiring, refused to switch, although he later said he was offered inducements to do so.

The vote stretched on and on with no change in the tally. Bush was awakened at 5 a.m. and set to calling recalcitrant conservatives on their cell phones to argue for a "yes" vote. The party leaders met off the House floor with a group of seven conservatives. These conservatives would later say that they were told that if the Republican bill failed, House Democrats intended to bring to the floor through a discharge petition the Senate version of the Medicare prescription drug bill, a version the conservatives found even more objectionable. Although the success of such a strategy was far from assured, the argument allowed a few of the conservatives to switch their vote. Just before 6 a.m., C. L. "Butch" Otter of Idaho and Trent Franks of Arizona changed their votes; then a few other members followed suit. Only after the two Republicans switched their votes and changed the outcome, did Wu cast his vote for the bill.

The count stood at 220–215 when the presiding officer, after almost three hours, gaveled the vote to a close. The conference report had passed. "It's nicer if you can win easy, but this was an absolute have-to," remarked House Republican Conference Chair Deborah Pryce.[2]

The Senate began debate on the conference report on November 22. Ted Kennedy, now a strong opponent, argued that the bill was "a first step toward a total dismantling of Medicare" (*NYT,* November 24, 2003). He indicated he would filibuster the bill, and Frist moved to file for cloture. On November 24, cloture was invoked on a 70 to 29 vote; forty-seven Republicans were joined by independent Jeffords and twenty-two Democrats in voting for cloture, whereas twenty-six Democrats and three Republicans opposed it. Majority Leader Daschle voted against cutting off debate but made no attempt to persuade other Democrats to join him. Especially with the AARP supporting the bill, killing it would have been a high-risk strategy. Democrats would be blamed for depriving seniors of a prescription

---

2. Quote from *Congressional Quarterly Weekly,* November 29, 2003, 2962; this account is also based on *Congressional Quarterly Weekly,* November 22, 2003, 2879–2882; November 29, 2003, 2956–2963; *Washington Post,* November 22, 2003; *Roll Call,* November 19, 2003; and *Los Angeles Times,* November 23, 2003.

drug benefit that might seem more attractive in the abstract than it would in reality.

Daschle did raise a budget point of order against the bill, arguing that, were it to prevail, there would be another chance to negotiate a good bill. Frist and Senate Republicans had to scramble to find the sixty votes needed to waive all budget points of order, but won on a 61 to 39 vote. Two Republicans and thirty-seven Democrats voted against waiving. The Senate then passed the conference report 54–44, a considerably closer tally than on the initial passage vote; the number of Democrats supporting the bill had shrunk from thirty-five to eleven. Nine Republicans also voted against the bill.

Aftermath

"With the theatrics of a campaign kickoff rally," in the words of the *New York Times*, President Bush signed the bill on December 8 at an elaborate celebratory ceremony (December 9, 2003). "We show our respect for seniors by giving them more choices and more control over their decision-making," the president told an invited audience of about two thousand at the bill-signing ceremony at Daughters of the American Revolution Constitution Hall (*Washington Times*, December 9, 2003). Bush was surrounded by more than a dozen members of Congress, almost all Republicans; over his head was a blue banner with a large "Rx" and the words "Keeping Our Promise to Seniors." In the audience, in addition to lobbyists, campaign donors, and politicians, were seniors flown in by the White House from across the country and seated in bleachers directly behind the president, in full view of the television cameras (*NYT*, December 9, 2003).

Democrats had lost the legislative fight but they did not consider the war over. As they saw it, the problems with the bill were simply too great. It opened the door to forcing traditional Medicare to compete with private programs and gave the private sector large subsidies to entice just that; it prevented the government from bargaining with pharmaceutical companies on drug prices; it provided $174 billion in tax breaks for health savings accounts, which would mostly benefit the well-off; and all this for a stingy and confusing drug benefit. On the day Bush signed the bill, Ted Kennedy and other congressional Democrats lambasted it at a Capitol Hill rally. "We have only just begun to fight," Kennedy told a cheering crowd of several hundred retirees—some wearing T-shirts reading "Drug Companies Make Me Sick"—who jammed a large Senate hearing room to protest the bill's enactment (*Washington Post*, December 8, 2003). Along with their labor, senior, and consumer group allies, Democrats continued to blast

Bush and congressional Republicans for passing a bill that helps drug companies and HMOs at the expense of the elderly.

The legislative battle may have been over, but the PR war will continue until the public or at least the voters have rendered a decisive verdict on the program.

Making Sweeping Policy Change in a Highly Partisan Environment

With the enactment of the Medicare/prescription drug bill in 2003, sweeping policy change was accomplished by a narrow partisan majority. To be sure, Republicans had to make some compromises, especially to keep a few key Senate Democrats on board. Yet, most Democrats strongly opposed the final bill. In the end, Republicans did it largely on their own. How was that accomplished?

The tools of unorthodox lawmaking that have been developed in recent decades, plus some newer ones, were essential to the bill's success. In both chambers, party leaders superintended the legislative process from the beginning, helping committee leaders put together a passable package and leaning on them to move the process along. In the House, the party leadership oversaw the melding of the bills from the two committees with jurisdiction. Postcommittee adjustments to pick up votes from skeptical Republicans also were negotiated by the leadership. The resulting combined bill was then brought to the floor under a strategically designed restrictive rule. When they found that they did not have the votes necessary for passage, the House Republican Party leaders held the vote open for about an hour until they could turn the tally around. All the minority party conferees from the House and most from the Senate were excluded from the conference negotiations that produced the final bill. The remaining conferees and the top party leaders produced a bill acceptable, if sometimes barely, to most Republicans but unacceptable to most Democrats. To pass the conference report in the House, the leadership had to hold the vote open for three hours.

If such tools of unorthodox lawmaking as postcommittee adjustments and restrictive rules were essential to enacting this legislation, a signature component of unorthodox lawmaking in the Senate was essential by its absence. Even when the bill that the conference committee produced was totally unacceptable to most Democrats, they did not attempt to mount a serious filibuster. Whether they could have done so successfully is unclear, since the forty-four "no" votes on the conference report included nine Republicans. What is clear is that they did not seriously consider doing so.

And this makes an important point about the use of the filibuster as a tool of minority obstruction. The minority must always consider the potential political cost of using the tool. In this case, the issue was extremely salient, and the bill was a top priority of the president; a highly influential interest group—the AARP—had endorsed the bill. Minority Democrats feared voter punishment if they killed the bill.

More generally, although the tools of unorthodox lawmaking can be extremely useful, they are just tools. The political context determines how aggressively they can be employed and, beyond that, the likelihood of legislative success. The Republican accomplishment of enacting sweeping policy change largely on their own is unusual and the more so given their narrow margins in both the House and the Senate. Most domestic legislation of comparable scope has required considerably more bipartisanship to enact. The Republicans' success would not have been possible without some conducive factors in the political context. The national government was unified, with both houses of Congress and the presidency under Republican control, and this was the first full Congress in fifty years of unified Republican government. Republican members of Congress were unusually ideological homogeneous, and they firmly believed that their own electoral fate depended on President Bush's success; this belief enabled them to maintain high cohesion and allowed their leaders to employ the tools of unorthodox lawmaking aggressively to ram the bill through.

Although under the political conditions in effect in the early part of the twenty-first century narrow partisan majorities sometimes have been able to effect sweeping policy change, there are costs to their doing so. Republicans were able to force enactment of sweeping policy change in the case of the Medicare/prescription drug bill without compromising enough to mollify substantial chunks of the minority, but they have not been able to build a true consensus on their program among the citizenry. This and a number of other major policy departures that were similarly enacted by Republicans during the Bush administration remain contested. It is only when major policy departures have become broadly accepted that the task can really be considered accomplished.

TABLE 8.1 The Medicare/Prescription Drug Bill of 2003: A Chronology

Date	House Action	Date	Senate Action	Date	Postpassage Action
Feb.–May	Ways and Means and Energy and Commerce health subcommittees hold 8 days of hearings.	Winter/ spring 2003	*Majority Leader Frist meets with Finance Committee Chair Grassley, Republican members of committee, and selected Democrats to work toward a compromise. Grassley and ranking minority member Baucus negotiate.*		
6/10	*Ways and Means Committee Chair Bill Thomas and Energy and Commerce Committee Chair Billy Tauzin reach an "agreement in principle" on a bill.*	6/5	Grassley and Baucus announce a bipartisan compromise bill.		
		6/11	S1 introduced by Majority Leader Frist.		
		6/12	Senate Finance Committee marks up and approves S1.		
6/16	HR2473 introduced by Thomas and Tauzin referred to the Committee on Energy and Commerce and in addition to the Committee on Ways and Means.	6/16	Senate agreed to consider S1 by unanimous consent.		
6/17	Ways and Means marks up and approves HR2473.				

TABLE 8.1 (Continued)

Date	House Action	Date	Senate Action	Date	Postpassage Action
6/17–19	Energy and Commerce marks up and approves HR2473. *Thomas, Tauzin, and Republican Party leaders negotiate a bill to take to the floor.*	6/17–20, 23–27	Senate considers and amends S1.		
6/25	HR1 introduced by Speaker of the House Dennis Hastert. Referred to the Committee on Energy and Commerce, and in addition to the Committee on Ways and Means, for a period to be subsequently determined by the Speaker; in each case for consideration of such provisions as fall within the jurisdiction of the committee concerned.				
6/26 6:20 a.m.	Rules Committee reports restrictive rule for the consideration of HR1 and HR2596.				
6/26–27 early morning	House approves rule, considers bills, passes them.	6/27	Senate passes S1.		

Date	Action
7/7	Senate asks for a conference and names its conferees.
7/14	House agrees to conference and names its conferees.
Mid-July	Conference meetings begin.
Late September	*Speaker Hastert and Majority Leader Frist set target date of October 17 for an agreement.*
November	*Hastert and Frist take over lead negotiation role.*
11/21	Conferees reach agreement and agree to file conference report. House considers conference report.
11/22	House approves conference report in the early morning. Senate begins consideration of the conference report. Frist files cloture motion.
11/23	Senate consideration continues.
11/24	Senate votes for cloture.
11/25	Senate approves conference report.
12/8	President signs bill, and it becomes law.

Note: Official actions are in roman type; behind-the-scenes, unofficial actions are in italics.

Medical Malpractice Caps: Senate Rules and Unorthodox Lawmaking—or Not

LIMITING MEDICAL MALPRACTICE AWARDS has long been on the Republican agenda. Party members argue that extraordinarily high malpractice awards contribute significantly to the high cost of health care and drive some doctors out of medicine altogether. Seldom stated publicly but nevertheless a consideration, severely curtailing large malpractice awards also would reduce trial lawyers' income, and trial lawyers are major campaign contributors to Democrats.

Between 1995, when Republicans took control of Congress, and 2000, the House passed bills capping malpractice awards five times. Republicans knew, however, that even were a bill to pass the Senate, President Bill Clinton would veto the legislation and an override would be impossible. Democrats believed that rising malpractice insurance rates for doctors largely were caused by insurance companies attempting to recoup investment shortfalls, not by big payouts in malpractice suits, and that limiting such suits would hurt deserving plaintiffs and remove an important guarantor of accountability from health care providers and insurance companies. With the election of President George W. Bush, for whom the issue was also a priority, Republican prospects of success brightened. However, the bill failed again in the 107th Congress. The House passed legislation, but the Senate rejected it. With the Senate controlled by Democrats, Republicans offered their bill as a nongermane amendment to a generic drug bill; the Senate tabled and thus killed the amendment by a vote of 57 to 42.

The 108th Congress offered new opportunities. Republicans again controlled the Senate, and the issue had become more highly salient. In several well-covered instances, doctors staged walkouts to protest soaring malpractice insurance premiums. Bush highlighted the issue in his 2003 State of the Union address, saying,

> To improve our health care system we must address one of the prime causes of higher cost: the constant threat that physicians and hospitals will be unfairly sued. Because of excessive litigation, everybody pays more for health care, and many parts of America are losing fine doctors. No one has ever been healed by a frivolous lawsuit (*CQ Weekly*, March 1, 2003, 485).

What happened on this issue in the 108th Congress highlights the differences in the legislative processes in House and Senate. Unorthodox practices and procedures facilitate lawmaking in the House because they are tools the majority can use to work its will; in the Senate, they enhance the influence of the minority and as such may impede lawmaking.

House Action

A bill "[t]o improve patient access to health care services and provide improved medical care by reducing the excessive burden the liability system places on the health care delivery system" was introduced by James C. Greenwood, R-Pa., on February 5, 2003, and assigned the symbolic low number of HR5 to signal that it was a top priority of House Republicans. Speaker Dennis Hastert, R-Ill., reinforced the message by endorsing the bill. "With medical costs rising and doctors and hospitals shuttering their doors, it's obvious that America's health care system is in critical condition," said Hastert. "One of my goals for this new Congress is to expand access to affordable health care and stem this growing medical crisis" (*CQW*, February 8, 2003, 355).

The Greenwood bill, similar to the one that had passed the House in the 107th Congress, would cap noneconomic damages at $250,000 and would limit punitive damages against providers and insurers to twice the economic damages or $250,000, whichever amount was greater. It would cap lawyers' fees, and would shield drug or medical device manufacturers from punitive damages if their products were approved by the Food and Drug Administration (FDA) (*CQW*, February 8, 2003, 355).

HR5 was referred to the Committee on the Judiciary, and in addition to the Committee on Energy and Commerce. Subcommittees of the Commerce Committee already had held hearings. The Subcommittee on Oversight and Investigations held a field hearing (that is, one outside of Washington, D.C.) on "The Medical Liability Insurance Crisis: A Review of the Situation in Pennsylvania" on February 10, 2003. On February 27, the Subcommittee on Health held a hearing on "Assessing the Need to Enact Medical Liability Reform." Democrats countered with a Democratic Forum on

Malpractice on February 11. Testifying at this unofficial hearing were experts and victims of malpractice.

Republicans and Democrats saw the issue very differently, and both wanted to persuade the public to buy their point of view. Hearings often are aimed at raising the visibility of an issue and framing it to the majority's advantage. Field hearings, which are frequently held in the district of the subcommittee chair, also are intended to burnish that member's reputation with constituents. As in this case, the minority may respond with an event of its own aimed at generating media coverage of its perspective.

On March 4, the Health Subcommittee of the Energy and Commerce Committee marked up HR5. A Democratic substitute offered by full committee ranking member John Dingell of Michigan was defeated on a straight party-line vote. The substitute would have deleted the caps; instituted other barriers to frivolous lawsuits; and removed liability protections from HMOs, insurance companies, and drug and device manufacturers. Another Democratic amendment simply deleted language that shielded HMOs and drug and medical device companies from liability; it also went down on a party-line vote. The subcommittee approved the bill on a voice vote. "H.R. 5 ensures that injured patients are justly compensated without permitting ambulance-chasing attorneys to run doctors out of town," declared Billy Tauzin, R-La., chair of the full Energy and Commerce Committee. Democrats saw it differently. The cap "would disproportionately hurt women, seniors, and low-income families" and "will shield HMOs, insurance companies, drug and device manufacturers from liability," Dingell argued (*Markup Report*, March 4, 2003).

The mark-up in the full Energy and Commerce Committee was similar but longer. During a full-day session, Republicans defeated one Democratic amendment after another. Nine such amendments, including again the Dingell substitute and a number of narrower amendments, were decided by recorded votes; the votes fell overwhelmingly along party lines. The bill was approved by voice vote.

In the meantime, the House Judiciary Committee also was working on the bill. On March 4, the committee held hearings and on the following day, it marked up the bill. Eight Democratic amendments were defeated on recorded votes; on most, voting was strictly along party lines but, on a few, a handful of Republicans defected and voted with Democrats. Thus, three Republicans voted for an amendment indexing to inflation the cap on noneconomic damages. The Republican defections were never enough to pass any of the Democratic amendments, however. The committee approved the bill 15–13 on a straight party-line vote.

The two bills, which were largely similar, were melded together by the committee chairs. The Rules Committee substituted the new product for the bills reported by the committees and, by a self-executing provision, stipulated that adoption of the rule entailed adoption of the chairs' new language:

> In lieu of the amendments recommended by the Committees on the Judiciary and on Energy and Commerce now printed in the bill, the amendment in the nature of a substitute printed in the report of the Committee on Rules accompanying this resolution shall be considered as adopted (H.Res.139, thomas. loc.gov).

House members asked the Rules Committee to make thirty-one amendments in order, twenty-nine of which were proposed by Democrats. Yet, at its now-typical late-night session the day before floor consideration, the committee reported out a rule that specified the bill be considered in the House—not in the Committee of the Whole—and that "the previous question shall be considered as ordered on the bill." This meant that no amendments were in order. The rule did allow

> two hours of debate . . . with 80 minutes equally divided and controlled by the chairman and ranking minority member of the Committee on the Judiciary and 40 minutes equally divided and controlled by the chairman and ranking minority member of the Committee on Energy and Commerce; and one motion to recommit with or without instructions (H.Res.139, thomas.loc.gov).

The closed rule infuriated Democrats. "[O]nce again today the Republican leadership is employing outrageous tactics that trample the rights of the minority and rig the rules of this debate," Democratic Whip Steny Hoyer of Maryland charged (*Congressional Record*, March 13, 2003, H1821). "I say to my colleagues, vote down this iniquitous rule. It is unfair. It is demeaning. It strikes at the heart of the parliamentary practices that are the proud tradition of this body," John Dingell declared. "It also tears at the throat of honorable and open and fair debate. It denies every Member, not just Democrats, the right to offer amendments to the bill. Mr. Speaker, 31 amendments were requested of the Committee on Rules last night; not a one was given" (*CR*, March 13, 2003, H1823). Republicans defended the rule as fair, although the Rules Committee chair also said, "I believe that we should have as open and as fair a process as we can . . . I also know that we have a responsibility to move our agenda" (*CR*, March 13, 2003, H1824). On identical votes of 225 to 201, with only one Democrat and no Republicans crossing party lines, the previous question was ordered and the rule was adopted.

The debate on the bill itself showed that Democrats and Republicans disagreed not just on the remedy but on the facts as well. Republicans continued to argue that malpractice awards were a major cause of rising health care costs, whereas Democrats touted studies that showed they had little impact. Republicans talked about doctors being driven out of medicine;

Democrats offered tragic stories of malpractice victims who would get little compensation under the Republican bill. Under the closed rule, Democrats were forced to offer their substitute as a motion to recommit with instructions. It was defeated by a vote of 191 to 234; 1 Republican and 12 Democrats crossed party lines. The House then passed the bill 229 to 196, with 9 Republicans and 16 Democrats crossing party lines.

Senate Stalemate

On July 7, 2003, Majority Leader Bill Frist, R-Tenn., took the floor and the following exchange occurred:

> MR. FRIST. Mr. President, I ask unanimous consent that the Senate now proceed to the consideration of Calendar No. 186, S. 11, the Patients First Act of 2003.
> THE PRESIDING OFFICER. Is there objection?
> MR. DURBIN. Mr. President, I object.
> THE PRESIDING OFFICER. Objection is heard.
> MR. FRIST. Mr. President, with that objection, I now move to proceed to S. 11. I understand that Members on the other side of the aisle are prepared to debate the motion itself. The majority whip, Senator McConnell, is prepared to open our debate on this issue as well. It would be my intent later today to file a cloture motion on the motion to proceed to this medical liabilities reform bill. This vote would then occur on Wednesday of this week. I look forward to the very important debate on this truly national crisis, and I encourage Members who want to speak to come to the floor today. We will be debating this legislation today as well as tomorrow. We encourage Members to come to the floor today (*CR*, July 3, 2003, S8871).

Republicans had known all along that the Senate was the likely stumbling block for medical malpractice legislation. After all, when the House passed HR5 in 2003, it was the seventh time since 1995 that the House had passed such a bill. In each case, the Senate balked at following suit. Earlier in 2003, Kentuckian Mitch McConnell, the Senate Republican whip, had negotiated with moderate Democrat Dianne Feinstein of California, attempting to come to a compromise, but the talks had failed. Feinstein was open to some caps on malpractice awards against doctors, but Republicans were unwilling to go far enough to satisfy her. On February 11 the Senate Judiciary Committee and the Senate Labor Committee held joint hearings on the "patient access crisis," but neither committee marked up a bill. As the bill's sponsor later admitted, Republicans did not have the necessary votes in committee.

Thus, Majority Leader Frist bypassed committee when he attempted to bring S11 to the Senate floor. S11, a bill very similar to HR5, had been introduced by John Ensign, R-Nev., on June 27 and placed directly on the legislative calendar. Frist knew, of course, that Democrats would object to his unanimous consent request, as they did.

The motion to proceed is a debatable motion, and Frist's motion to proceed to consider S11 set the stage for a prolonged debate on the issue. Whip Mitch McConnell and Dick Durbin of Illinois, assistant Democratic floor leader, managed the debate for their parties. Democrats objected to the bill being brought up without committee consideration first. Explaining his objections to Frist's request, Durbin said, "The most revolutionary and dramatic reform of tort law in America, in modern memory, will come to the floor without the normal hearings, witnesses, opportunities to amend, opportunity to work out compromises and negotiate, all part of the legislative process" (*CR*, July 7, 2003, S8876). No real attempt to negotiate a true bipartisan compromise had been made, Democrats complained. "Jamming this in the Senate, overriding the committee, and filing cloture on the motion to proceed is not the way to achieve some bipartisan consensus on a very legitimate issue," Minority Leader Tom Daschle of South Dakota protested. "So we will vote in opposition to the motion to proceed, not because we do not want to address the issue but because there is a better model if we are ultimately going to find a solution" (*CR*, July 7, 2003, S8889).

Most of the debate focused on the issue itself. Both Republicans and Democrats largely reiterated the arguments made by their House counterparts. With debate time less constrained, senators on both sides of the issue described horror stories, sometimes in gory detail. Tony, critically injured in a car accident, suffered permanent brain damage because no specialist was available to treat him, McConnell recounted; the specialists had been driven out of the area by the medical liability crisis. Durbin responded with the tale of six-year-old David, left a quadriplegic and unable to communicate after delayed and mistaken treatment; he would be limited to a $250,000 award for pain and suffering if S11 were to become law.

Democrats also touted a bill that Durbin and Republican Lindsay Graham, S.C., were co-sponsoring as an alternative to S11. In the tradition of Senate mavericks, Graham criticized his GOP colleagues for offering legislation that is a "political product, not a solution to a problem" (*CQW*, July 12, 2003, 1745).

Debate continued on July 8 and 9. Since the cloture motion had been filed on July 7, Senate rules specified that the vote would come on July 9. On July 8, Senate leaders had reached a unanimous consent agreement to govern consideration the next day. It provided

> that at 9:30 a.m. on Wednesday, July 9, 2003, Senate continue consideration of the motion to proceed to the consideration of S. 11, Patients First Act, and that the time until 11:30 a.m. be equally divided between the Majority Leader and the Democratic Leader or their designees; that at 11:30 a.m., Senate vote on the motion to close further debate on the motion to proceed to consideration of S. 11 (*Daily Digest*, July 8, 2003).

At 11:30 July 9, the cloture process proceeded:

> The PRESIDING OFFICER. All time having expired, under the previous order, the clerk will report the motion to invoke cloture.
> The bill clerk read as follows:
> Cloture Motion
> We the undersigned Senators, in accordance with the provisions of rule XXII of the Standing Rules of the Senate, do hereby move to bring to a close debate on the motion to proceed to the consideration of Calendar No. 186, S. 11, the Patients First Act of 2003.
> Bill Frist, Mitch McConnell, John Ensign, Craig Thomas, Rick Santorum, Larry E. Craig, George V. Voinovich, John Cornyn, Trent Lott, Ted Stevens, Michael B. Enzi, James Inhofe, Chuck Hagel, Jon Kyl, Judd Gregg, Pat Roberts, John E. Sununu.
> The PRESIDING OFFICER. By unanimous consent, the mandatory quorum call has been waived.
> The question is, Is it the sense of the Senate that debate on the motion to proceed to S. 11, the Patients First Act, shall be brought to a close?
> The yeas and nays are ordered under the rule. The clerk will call the roll.
> The legislative clerk called the roll.
> The PRESIDING OFFICER. On this vote, the yeas are 49, the nays are 48. Three-fifths of the Senators duly chosen and sworn not having voted in the affirmative, the motion is rejected (*CR*, July 9, 2003, S9083).

Graham and fellow Republican Richard Shelby of Alabama voted with all the Democrats present against cutting off debate and so against considering S11.

The Senate Republican leadership knew before Frist attempted to bring the legislation to the floor that they lacked the votes to cut off debate. Senate Republicans nevertheless proceeded because they believed that they could make Democrats pay a political price for their opposition. "It was an important issue to get a vote on, to let people know where [senators] stand," explained GOP Conference Committee Chair Rick Santorum of Pennsylvania (*CQW*, July 9, 2003, 1744). Doctors groups, insurance companies, and other provider organizations who strongly supported malpractice caps and were generous campaign contributors, would express their disappointment with Democrats, Republicans believed. Republicans also hoped to increase the issue's salience among the broader public and so make it a voting issue. In the meantime, President Bush expressed his disappointment at the Senate's action and said, "Access to quality health care for Americans is endangered by frivolous and abusive lawsuits. The medical liability crisis is driving good doctors out of medicine, and leaving patients in many communities without access to both basic and specialty medical services" (*CQW*, July 9, 2003, 1744).

To further their political aims, Senate Republicans decided to bring other malpractice capping legislation to the floor. In February 2004, Frist again asked unanimous consent and, when Democrats objected, again moved to proceed to consider the legislation, S2061. The bill was similar to S11 except that its protections were limited to obstetricians, gynecologists, and nurse midwives. The cloture motion failed on a 48 to 45 vote. In April, Republicans tried once again with S2207, a bill that covered trauma doctors and emergency room personnel as well as obstetricians and gynecologists. The cloture motion on that bill went down on a 49 to 48 vote. Republicans had hoped these bills—targeted at particularly sympathetic medical personnel—would peel off some Democrats, but the strategy was unsuccessful. The three cloture votes were nearly identical, with no more than one Democrat ever voting for cloture. The "malpractice crisis" did not seem to be catching on as a voting issue either, so Republicans abandoned their plan to bring up more narrowly tailored bills. The issue was dead for the 108th Congress.

The Impact of Senate Rules

The fate of malpractice capping legislation in the 108th Congress and in the Republican-controlled Congresses proceeding it highlights the differences between the legislative processes in the two chambers. A cohesive majority party, even if its margin of control is narrow, can work its will in the House; it need pay little regard to the policy preferences of the minority party. In the Senate, legislating successfully almost always requires compromise. Sometimes, public opinion forces senators to accept—or at least not attempt to stop by filibuster—legislation they detest. Attempts to create or amplify favorable public opinion are ubiquitous in Washington policy battles, but full success is elusive. In this case, Bush and his Republican congressional allies were not successful in creating enough public pressure on Democrats to induce them to capitulate. When a minority of forty-one senators or greater is willing to use the powers granted by Senate rules, the majority must compromise if it wishes to pass legislation.

The intensified partisan polarization of recent years has accentuated the legislative effects of the differences in the House and the Senate. The House majority party, employing the practices and procedures of unorthodox lawmaking, is almost always able to pass major legislation on its own. The Senate minority party is often cohesive enough to fully use the prerogatives inherent in Senate rules and thereby force the majority to compromise or, if the majority is unwilling, to block legislation altogether.

TABLE 9.1 Medical Malpractice Award Caps: A Chronology (all dates 2003)

Date	House Action	Date	Senate Action	Date	Postpassage Action
2/5	HR5, a bill capping medical malpractice awards, is introduced. *Speaker Dennis Hastert endorses HR5.*				
	HR5 referred to the Committee on the Judiciary, and in addition to the Committee on Energy and Commerce, for a period to be subsequently determined by the Speaker; in each case for consideration of such provisions as fall within the jurisdiction of the committee concerned.				
3/5	Judiciary considers, marks up, and orders HR5 to be reported (amended) by 15–13.				
3/6	Energy and Commerce Committee considers, marks up, and orders HR5 to be reported (amended) by voice vote. *The chairs of the Judiciary and Energy Committees informally negotiate a composite bill.*				
3/12	Rules Committee approves a closed rule that self-executes the chairs' composite bill.				

3/13	House approves rule, debates HR5, and passes it.
6/27	S11 introduced, read the first time, and placed on the Senate legislative calendar.
	Read the second time and placed on Senate legislative calendar under General Orders.
7/7	Majority Leader Frist asks unanimous consent that the Senate now proceed to the consideration S11. Objection is made. Frist makes motion to proceed to consideration of measure. Cloture motion on the motion to proceed to the measure is made.
7/8–9	Motion to proceed to measure considered.
7/9	Cloture on the motion to proceed to the measure not invoked by vote of 49–48.
	Bill dies.

Note: Official actions are in roman type; behind-the-scenes, unofficial actions are in italics.

The Budget Process as an Instrument for Policy Change: Clinton's Economic Program

DURING THE 1992 CAMPAIGN, Democratic presidential candidate Bill Clinton advocated making major changes in the direction and priorities of the federal government. In 1993 the problem confronting President Clinton and the congressional Democratic leadership was how to get such comprehensive—and sometimes painful—policy change through Congress. The usual difficulties of enacting major policy change would be exacerbated, they knew, by the highly charged partisan atmosphere and the growing ideological gulf between the parties.

Two years later the new Republican congressional majorities faced the same problem in even starker terms. In their Contract with America, House Republicans were advocating considerably more far-reaching changes in policy direction, they confronted an opposition-party president, their margins were narrower, and the atmosphere had become even more intensely partisan. When George W. Bush became president in 2001, he also wanted to make sweeping changes in the direction and priorities of the national government, with huge tax cuts his highest priority. Yet he entered the White House without a policy mandate and with very narrow majorities in Congress.

In each of these cases, as this and the next two chapters show, the procedural solution to the problem was the congressional budget process. Through the budget process many changes in policy can be made in one piece of legislation rather than in a number of separate bills; fewer battles have to be won. By custom, budget measures are considered on the House floor under tight rules restricting the number of amendments that may be offered, thus further reducing the number of fights that must be waged. Senate rules prohibit extended debate on budget measures, a huge advantage to those endeavoring to enact legislation. The deadlines in the Congressional Budget and Impoundment Control Act of 1974 (hereafter the Budget Act) exert a pressure to action that can also work to the advantage of those attempting to pass a bill.

However, the congressional budget process is complex, even when it is not being used to attempt to enact comprehensive policy change. Its deadlines can present problems as well as exert salutary pressure for action. Successful completion of the budget process depends on supervision and coordination by the congressional majority party leadership, and when the process is used to make major policy change, leadership involvement must be continuous and intense. Adroit use of the full set of procedural strategies that the new legislative process makes available to leaders is necessary but, as the next chapter shows, still does not guarantee success.

To understand the contemporary policy process and its politics, one must understand the budget process, which is so often central to the legislative strategies of presidents and congressional leaders. The simplest way to gain such an understanding is by following the process step by step as it actually unfolded in real-life cases. That is what this and the following chapters do. These chapters also provide a brief history of budget politics since the early 1990s, which is key to understanding current political debate.

Budget Policy Making and Politics: The Context in 1993

Because the economy was the 1992 campaign's dominant issue, the success of Bill Clinton and the Democratic Congress in enacting an effective economic program became a key test of whether the Democratic Party could govern.[1] Democrats had been out of the White House for twelve years, and Jimmy Carter, the last Democratic president, was remembered as ineffective. Could a Democratic president provide effective leadership, and would congressional Democrats, accustomed to going it alone, work cooperatively with the new president?

As a newly elected president who had run on the issue, Clinton set the economic policy agenda. The approach Clinton had outlined during the campaign was complex: it involved an immediate stimulus to jump-start a sluggish economy, major long-term investment spending in such areas as education and infrastructure, and deficit reduction through tax increases on the wealthy and spending cuts in less essential programs. The news media, however, painted the election as primarily a public call for deficit

---

1. At the beginning of the 103rd Congress, there were 258 Democrats, 176 Republicans, and 1 independent in the House; the Senate consisted of 57 Democrats and 43 Republicans.

reduction, in part because of Ross Perot's surprisingly strong showing in the 1992 presidential election. A sizable number of congressional Democrats, including many of the large freshman class, believed they would be judged in terms of how much they cut spending and reduced the deficit. In contrast, Democrats from core Democratic districts tended to emphasize the economic stimulus and investment spending.

On February 17, in his first address to a joint session of Congress, Clinton outlined an economic program containing three basic elements: economic stimulus, investment spending, and deficit reduction. In response to the political climate and strong economic growth in the fourth quarter of 1992, the direct spending part of the stimulus program was reduced to $16.3 billion. The revenue component included tax increases for corporations, the wealthy, and upper-income Social Security recipients, and it contained a broad-based energy tax (the Btu tax).

Congressional Democrats, by and large, reacted favorably, although they knew passing the package would not be easy given its ambitiousness. Republicans immediately went on the attack, blasting the proposal for being tax heavy (*CQ Weekly*, February 20, 1993, 355–359). Opposition to any new taxes by then had become a core tenet of Republican ideology, and many congressional Republicans believed George H. W. Bush's reneging on his "no new taxes" campaign pledge had cost him reelection to the presidency in 1992. Understandably, the public never wants to pay more taxes, and, in a period of pervasive distrust of government, politicians will not damage their reelection prospects by opposing taxes.

The lack of incentives for Republicans to support Clinton's economic program made it clear from the beginning that Democrats would have to pass it on their own. Dick Armey of Texas, a Republican leader in the House, expressed his party's hard-line opposition: "They wanted to lead, now they've got to live with the accountability. Why should we give them cover?" (*CQW*, February 20, 1993, 380).

Although the stimulus package would be enacted as a supplemental appropriations bill, most of the rest of the program would be enacted through the budget process. That would require Congress to pass a budget resolution with instructions to the substantive committees to bring law in their areas of jurisdiction into conformity with the budget resolution and then enact a massive reconciliation bill incorporating all the necessary changes.

Committing to the Clinton Plan: Crafting and Passing the Budget Resolution

On March 10 the House Budget Committee approved a budget resolution that closely followed Clinton's plan. However, the Congressional Budget Office's estimate of how much deficit reduction the Clinton plan would accomplish had showed a shortfall of about $66 billion from the administration's estimate and, to get the support of "deficit hawk" Democrats, Democratic Budget Committee leaders had had to add $63 billion in spending cuts to the resolution. With this change committee Democrats held firm and voted down every Republican amendment, frequently on straight party-line votes. The committee approved the resolution on a vote of 27 to 16 with every Democrat supporting it and every Republican opposed.

Two days later the Senate Budget Committee approved a similar resolution on a 12–9 party-line vote. Despite the Senate committee's much narrower partisan margin, Senate Democrats maintained sufficient unity to vote down every Republican attempt to alter the resolution.

The House Democratic leadership brought the budget resolution to the floor on March 17. Such early consideration was the result of a problem that had developed with the stimulus package. Republicans' attacks made many Democrats nervous about voting for spending increases before they voted for spending cuts. To alleviate those members' concerns and ensure their votes, Clinton and the congressional leadership decided on a schedule change: action on the budget resolution would be accelerated, and it would be brought to the floor before the stimulus package.

On March 17 a rule for general debate on the budget resolution was approved. This rule, which provided for ten hours of general debate, allowed the House to begin consideration while the rule covering the amending process was still being worked out. The next day the second rule was brought to the floor and approved by a strictly party-line vote. That rule allowed votes only on four comprehensive substitutes; crucially, no narrow amendments aimed at particular unpopular provisions were allowed. The substitutes were not amendable and were to be voted on in the order specified using the king-of-the-hill procedure under which the last one approved prevails.

A substitute by Rep. John R. Kasich, R-Ohio, then ranking minority member on the Budget Committee, was placed first; it proposed deeper spending cuts and no tax increases. Another Republican substitute, offered by Gerald B. H. Solomon of New York, was placed second; the Solomon substitute added to the spending cuts in the Kasich proposal some of the tax increases in the Democrats' plan so as to achieve much deeper deficit reduction. The Black Caucus substitute, placed third in order, was a liberal plan that increased taxes more and made greater cuts in defense spending in order to make fewer domestic spending cuts. Last, in the advantaged position, was the "substitute consisting of the text of the concurrent resolution as reported by the Budget Committee"—that is, the Democratic leadership's proposal.

The House voted down all three substitutes by wide margins. Even the Kasich substitute garnered only 135 votes; about a quarter of Republicans voted against it. Only nineteen Republicans (and one Democrat) voted for the Solomon substitute, showing again the central place that opposition to all new taxes had come to occupy in Republican Party doctrine. The Black Caucus substitute attracted eighty-seven votes. The budget resolution was then approved by a vote of 243 to 183; no Republicans voted for it, and only 11 Democrats voted in opposition.

In the Senate Democratic leaders had to pass the budget resolution without the help of a restrictive rule to protect their members from tough votes. To keep the plan intact, Democrats had to vote down a plethora of amendments, most offered by Republicans to cause Democrats maximum pain. Thus, Republicans forced votes on amendments to delete the tax increase on high-income Social Security recipients, to reduce or delete the new energy taxes, to exempt certain small businesses from the increase in corporate taxes, and to cut Congress's own operating funds by 25 percent. Democrats stuck together and voted down every substantive change Republicans attempted to make.

To make it a little easier on their members, Democratic leaders offered a number of "sense of the Senate" resolutions, which allow senators to go on the record but have no binding effect. Senator Edward (Ted) Kennedy of Massachusetts, for example, offered an amendment to express the sense of the Senate that the Btu tax should not apply to fuel used for home heating. On March 25, after six days of floor debate and forty-five roll calls, the Senate approved by a 54–45 vote a budget resolution very similar to the one that passed the House. No Republican supported the economic blueprint, and all but two Democrats voted for it. Because budget resolutions are considered under special Budget Act rules that limit debate, Republicans could stretch out the process and make Democrats take a series of tough votes, but they could not block action.

The differences between the House and Senate versions were not large, and the conference committee quickly came to an agreement. The House on March 31 and the Senate on April 1 approved the conference report. The votes were largely along party lines and almost identical to the initial passage votes. (See Table 10.1 for a chronology of action on the budget resolution and on the reconciliation bill that followed.)

Delivering on Promised Policy Change: Reconciliation

Passing a budget resolution that reflected Clinton's priorities was an important first step; the crucial next step of enacting a reconciliation bill would, Democrats knew, be much harder. The budget resolution is a blueprint for future congressional decisions. It does not become law and does not actually make any changes in policy; the detail about policy that it, or the report accompanying it, may contain is just advice to committees. To enact into law policy changes meeting the budget resolution's deficit reduction targets, Congress must pass a reconciliation bill. In the Senate particularly, Democratic leaders had persuaded some of their members to vote for the resolution and against Republicans' attempts to change it by reminding them that the policy detail in the resolution was not binding. Once work on the reconciliation bill began, that argument could no longer be made. As Minority Leader Bob Dole of Kansas put it, "We start shooting with real bullets from here on" (*Congressional Quarterly Almanac* 1993, 106).

The political climate had also become more difficult for Democrats. Although the scheduling change had facilitated easy passage of the stimulus package in the House, a Republican filibuster in the Senate eventually killed it. Republicans had won the media battle, successfully portraying the stimulus bill as wasteful spending on pork barrel projects. The consequent lack of public demand for the bill allowed Republicans to kill it without great fear that they would pay an electoral price (Sinclair 1996).

Reconciliation in the House

The 1993 budget resolution contained instructions to thirteen House committees and twelve Senate committees to make changes in law under their jurisdiction so as to meet specific deficit reduction targets assigned to them. By Budget Act rules the committees are free to ignore any specific recommendations for policy change contained in the budget resolution or the report accompanying it, but they are bound to meet the total amount of savings assigned to them. For example, the tax-writing committees could ignore any budget resolution recommendations about what sorts of taxes to raise; they were only required to make changes in law sufficient to produce their deficit reduction figure.

The Btu tax that the president had proposed was shaping up as a particular problem. The administration favored it because it was a broad-based tax on all energy sources and thus seemed fair; in addition, it would improve air quality by promoting more efficient use of energy. The tax's broad reach, however, proved to be a serious problem as a correspondingly broad range of interests were roused to lobby against the tax. The big umbrella business organizations, such as the National Association of Manufacturers and the U.S. Chamber of Commerce, opposed it; many affected industries—for example, the oil industry, which was taxed especially heavily by the plan, and the aluminum industry, which is a heavy energy user—worked feverishly to get changes or kill the Btu tax altogether.

The House Ways and Means Committee and the Senate Finance Committee were responsible for by far the single biggest chunk of deficit reduction; not only do these committees write tax legislation, but they also have jurisdiction over Medicare, from which the Clinton plan proposed extracting a significant amount of savings. Because the Constitution specifies that tax legislation must originate in the House, the Ways and Means Committee began work first. Its chair, Rep. Dan Rostenkowski, D-Ill., vowed to produce legislation close to Clinton's proposal. To put together a coalition that could withstand Republicans' continuing attacks on the Clinton plan, he met behind closed doors with committee Democrats, working out agreements that brought them on board. Much of the negotiation concerned the Btu tax; members sought to protect their regions and crucial industries in their districts. A number of exemptions were written into the legislation. Rostenkowski made it clear that Democrats who were accommodated were then expected to support the bill actively. On May 6, when committee mark-up began, Democrats immediately voted to work on the bill in closed session; Rostenkowski knew that holding his coalition together would be easier away from the press and the legion of interested lobbyists. Democrats voted down every Republican amendment and, on May 13, approved the legislation on a 24–14 party-line vote.

The legislation that Rostenkowski had put together and that the committee approved largely followed Clinton's blueprint. It raised income taxes on the rich and on high-income Social Security recipients, included a Btu tax (although one with some exemptions), increased the earned-income tax credit for the working poor, and extracted significant savings from Medicare. To lessen the opposition of business and thus gain the votes of conservative Democrats, Rostenkowski significantly cut the increase in the corporate tax rate that Clinton had proposed.

All thirteen House committees met their May 14 deadline for reporting and met the deficit reduction targets assigned to them; although a multitude of smaller compromises were made to get the necessary majorities, the major features of Clinton's economic program were preserved. The Budget Committee packaged the provisions from all the committees into one bill and ordered it reported on May 20.

Clinton and the Democratic leadership faced a formidable task in passing the bill. Ambitious deficit reduction targets had been met, which meant that inevitably many committees had made unpopular decisions. Not only would Democrats have to pass the legislation without any help from Republicans, they would have to contend with the Republicans' loud and repeated charge that the program consisted mostly of taxes on the middle class.

The job of passing the bill in the House became immeasurably harder when, on May 20, Sen. David Boren, D-Okla., an ally of his home state's gas and oil interests, and three colleagues (two moderate Republicans and another conservative oil-state Democrat) proposed an alternative reconciliation package that eliminated the Btu tax and imposed a cap on entitlement spending. A few days later Boren formally announced that he would vote against the Btu tax in the Senate Finance Committee, which would have to approve the tax law changes. Since the party ratio on the committee was only eleven Democrats to nine Republicans, his opposition made the survival of the Btu tax, and even of the broader package, appear doubtful. House Democrats were leery of voting for the unpopular Btu tax only to see it die in the Senate. "We don't want to be in a position of walking the plank and then have them go over and make a compromise in the Senate," Rep. Charles Wilson, D-Tex., explained (*CQW*, May 22, 1993, 1278). Boren's high-profile opposition also gave impetus to a push by conservative House Democrats for a cap on entitlement spending, which was in Boren's plan as well.

A deal on the entitlement cap, intimations of changes in the Btu tax in the Senate, adept procedural strategy, and an intense lobbying campaign by the House Democratic leadership and the administration produced a close win on the House floor.

Majority Leader Richard A. Gephardt of Missouri brokered a compromise on entitlements that satisfied conservatives without alienating liberals. Throughout the budget process two deficit hawk Democrats—Charles W. Stenholm of Texas and Timothy J. Penny of Minnesota—had advocated placing a tight cap on entitlement spending; they wanted a mechanism by which, if such spending exceeded the cap, cuts would automatically occur. This was a proposal that neither the White House nor Democratic leaders liked. Stenholm had been pressuring the Speaker to allow him to offer such an amendment on the floor, threatening to lead a revolt by conservative Democrats against the rule if his amendment were barred. When Democrats still lacked enough votes to pass the rule shortly before floor action was planned, the Speaker instructed the majority leader to try to work out a deal. Less than twenty-four hours before the floor vote, an agreement was reached: rather than automatic cuts if the entitlement cap were exceeded, either the president would have to propose a way of paying for the overspending or he would have to raise the cap. Congress would have to vote on whatever the president proposed.

The administration got some energy-state Democrats back on board by acknowledging what was becoming inevitable: the Btu tax would be altered in the Senate.

The House leadership brought the bill to the floor under a rule that allowed only a vote on a comprehensive Republican substitute; amendments to delete various unpopular elements of the package—the Btu tax and the tax on Social Security payments to high-income recipients—were barred. The rule also prohibited the minority from offering a motion to recommit with instructions, which is another way of amending the bill. The rule thus gave Republicans an opportunity to offer a comprehensive alternative to the Democratic plan, and it gave the whole House a choice between two distinct approaches. However it also made it impossible for Republicans to use the amendment process to unravel the Democratic package by narrowly targeting the least palatable provisions, and it protected Democrats from having to cast some excruciatingly difficult votes. A vote for a deficit reduction package would be easier for Democrats to explain to their constituents than would a stand-alone vote for higher taxes.

In addition to these provisions, the rule contained what is called a "self-executing" provision by which adoption of the rule simultaneously results in adoption of certain legislative language. In this case the deal on the entitlement cap, as well as some other language about enforcement of the budget agreement that was worked out after the bill was reported from committee, was thereby incorporated into the bill without requiring a separate vote.

Democratic Whip David Bonior of Michigan personally headed the whip task force set up to pass the bill. Starting work several weeks before the bill got to the floor, members of the task force, and later the top leaders, unrelentingly pursued every House Democrat. Anyone who might have influence with an undecided or recalcitrant member—state party chairs, governors, union officials, personal friends—was enlisted to help in the persuasion effort.

The administration was very much engaged in the drive to build support for the bill. Cabinet secretaries called and visited Democrats; Secretary of the Treasury Lloyd Bentsen, for example, attended the Texas delegation's regular lunch meeting to sell the bill. Two days before the vote, President Clinton invited about seventy-five House members to the White House; he personally called close to sixty members—some of them repeatedly.

Given the level of effort, Democrats could not fail to understand that how they voted on the bill would affect their future in the House. As Rep. Barney Frank, D-Mass., said, "Nobody got a pass on this" (*CQW*, May 29, 1993, 1341). At a Democratic caucus meeting the day before the vote, some members made clear that this was a litmus-test vote, that future decisions on committee and subcommittee chairmanships would be influenced by how members voted. Just before the vote, freshmen circulated a petition demanding that any committee or subcommittee chair who voted against the party be stripped of his or her position by the caucus. Within hours, more than eighty Democrats, including several influential committee chairs, had signed.

The rule was adopted by a vote of 236 to 194, with all but 19 Democrats and no Republicans supporting it. Republicans were much less united on their substitute; as with the budget resolution, many Republicans believed attacking the Democratic plan without giving Democrats anything on which to attack them was the politically smarter course. The Kasich substitute received only 138 votes, with 40 Republicans opposing it.

Because of the character of the rule, the key vote would be on passage. The Speaker himself closed floor debate for his party, acknowledging that this was indeed a tough vote: "We seldom do important, valuable and lasting things by taking easy votes, comfortable votes, politically popular votes." He challenged members, saying, "This is a time to stand and deliver; this is a time to justify your election" (*CQW*, May 29, 1993, 1341). On May 27 the House passed the legislation, 219–213. Again, not a single Republican voted in support; thirty-eight Democrats opposed their party's position.

Reconciliation in the Senate

Although twelve Senate committees were under instructions to report reconciliation provisions, the Finance Committee had by far the most formidable task. Boren's opposition to the Btu tax and the committee's narrow partisan margin meant that significant changes would have to be made. Some strategists suggested that the Democratic leadership bypass the Finance Committee altogether and bring the tax and other provisions within its jurisdiction to the floor directly. Majority Leader George Mitchell of Maine decided not to do so, evidently convinced that such a course would only make a hard job harder.

Finance Committee Chair Daniel Patrick Moynihan of New York and Mitchell, who was a member of Finance, took on the task of putting together a package that could pass the committee and the chamber. Given the hardening of the Republicans' antitax position, they knew they had to form their majority from Democrats only. It took "two weeks of grinding negotiations" to craft a compromise package (*CQW*, June 19, 1993, 1542). As had been expected from the beginning of the negotiations, the Btu tax was jettisoned; that, however, produced a huge revenue shortfall. Eventually, a gas tax, sharper cuts in Medicare, and a host of minor changes were agreed to. Republicans offered a multitude of amendments during mark-up, but once the deal was struck, Democrats held together and defeated them all.

On June 18 the Finance Committee reported its crucial part of the reconciliation bill on a straight party-line vote of 11 to 9. The other committees already had complied with their instructions and reported their provisions. On June 22 the Budget Committee ordered the reconciliation bill reported.

On June 23 Tennessee Democrat James Sasser, chair of the Senate Budget Committee, began floor debate on the reconciliation bill by reminding his colleagues what was at stake and thanking the committees for doing their job:

> Mr. President, the Senate today begins consideration of the budget reconciliation bill. The reconciliation bill is really the centerpiece of the President's economic proposal and economic plan ... deficit reduction is something

everybody likes to talk about but no one really wants to do much about it. I think literally hundreds of Academy Awards would be in order for some of the posturing and play acting that I have witnessed over the past few years. . . .

So, the President of the United States and the committees of the U.S. Senate looked the deficit squarely in the eye and they made some very difficult, some very tough, and some very painful choices in developing this reconciliation bill. The fruits of their labor are before us today (*Congressional Record,* June 23, 1993, S7662).

Republicans responded by calling the bill "the largest tax increase in history" and charging that it was a "job killer." As Texas senator Phil Gramm expressed it:

I oppose this bill because you cannot create more investment by taxing investors. You cannot create more savings by taxing savers. You cannot create more jobs by taxing job creators. Hundreds of thousands of Americans will lose their job because of this bill. Bill Clinton will be one of those Americans, but he will deserve to lose his job (*CR,* June 23, 1993, S7672).

Democrats argued that, while the bill did raise taxes, most of the new taxes would be paid by the very well-off. Yes, it was a tough bill, but a fair and responsible one; it really cut the deficit and did so in a way that spread the pain according to citizens' capacity to pay.

Budget Act rules protected the bill against a filibuster and made successfully amending it more difficult than with other legislation. Republicans, however, were free to offer all sorts of amendments that would put Democrats in a difficult political position. And that they did. Republicans forced Democrats to vote on each of the tough provisions by offering amendments to strike them. Some of the votes were agonizingly close— the amendment to strike the gas tax increase failed by only two votes—but Democrats held together and defeated every significant change.

In the wee hours of June 25, after two long and intense days of floor consideration, the time for the vote came. The majority and minority leaders closed debate. Senator Dole said:

The choice tonight could not be more clear. Senators can vote for President Clinton's record-breaking tax increase or they can cast a vote for America's taxpayers and send a wake-up call to the White House and to the Congress. The President has tried to make this a defining moment of his Presidency. He is right. It is and will be for years to come. He has already earned his place on Mount Taxmore (*CR,* June 25, 1993, S7986).

Senator Mitchell closed:

For 12 years we have laughed as the national debt has gone up. We have had jokes, not deeds. We have had talk, not action. It is now time for action.

> This Chamber has been filled to overflowing with speeches about the need to reduce the deficit and there is only one way to reduce the deficit and that is to vote for this package. There is no other alternative. No other serious or credible alternative has been presented in either Chamber. If you mean to reduce the deficit you must vote for this package.
>
> Mr. President, I ask for the yeas and nays (*CR*, June 25, 1993, S7986).

At about 3 a.m., the Senate passed the bill on a 50–49 vote, with Vice President Al Gore, as president of the Senate, casting the deciding vote. Every Republican and six Democrats opposed passage.

Resolving House-Senate Differences

Changes made to pass the bill in the Senate and the narrowness of the vote to pass the bill in both chambers guaranteed that reaching a conference agreement on a version passable in both houses would be a delicate and difficult task. House liberals—especially members of the Black Caucus—were dismayed with the cuts in benefits for the poor and for cities made to compensate for the revenue lost when the Btu tax was replaced by a gas tax. Many deficit hawk Democrats in the Senate had voted for the package without enthusiasm, believing it did not do enough; they might well defect if significant changes were made. A number of western Democrats refused to support a gas tax higher than the 4.3 cents in the Senate bill.

Because so many committees had played a role in drafting the bill, the conference committee was huge: 164 House members from 16 committees and 53 senators from 13 committees. The House delegation was formally composed of twenty-seven subgroups, each with specifically delineated jurisdiction. Although the Senate designated no formal subgroups, it was understood that Senate conferees would also work on the provisions from their own committees. Most of the work of crafting a compromise proceeded in subconferences made up of members from the committee that had drafted the legislation and of Budget Committee members; Budget Committee leaders, including House Majority Leader Gephardt, the leadership's representative on Budget, took part in all of the subconferences.

The most crucial decisions fell within the jurisdiction of the taxing committees. As other subconferences worked out their differences outside the media's glare, Chairs Rostenkowski and Moynihan, under intense pressure and scrutiny, began their negotiations. Democratic Party leaders and representatives of the Clinton administration also participated. Although the conflicting priorities of the various groups of Democrats who had voted for the bill often made it seem impossible, a compromise package was worked out.

Out of the media's spotlight, Democratic staff worked to protect the bill from Byrd rule attacks. Before the bill had passed the Senate, Pete Domenici, N.M., ranking minority member on the Budget Committee, had put Democrats on notice. If and when the bill returned from conference, he would invoke the Byrd rule to try to knock many provisions out of the bill as "extraneous matter." Any senator can make a point of order that a provision violates the Byrd rule; if the parliamentarian agrees, sixty votes are required to waive the rule and save the provision. With solid Republican opposition, Democrats knew they could not muster the sixty votes. Therefore, as the conference proceeded, they tried to persuade the parliamentarian that their provisions did not violate the rule, or they tried to work out language that would pass the test. In many cases Democrats were forced to remove provisions; the review mechanism for entitlement spending that had been instrumental in getting deficit hawk Democrats to support the bill in the House fell victim to the Byrd rule.

Already tense relations between House and Senate Democrats were made even worse by the dictates of the Byrd rule. Senate Democrats' individualism, the willingness of many to pursue their own interests and agendas at the expense of those of their party, and Senate rules that encouraged such behavior had infuriated House Democrats all year; they had done the responsible thing and taken the hard votes and then someone like Senator Boren negated their efforts for narrow selfish gain, they believed. Now, with the Byrd rule, Senate rules were forcing decisions on the House and making House Democrats jettison policy changes dear to their hearts. The animosity of House Democrats toward the other body would make the difficult task of passing the conference report even harder, as a House Democrat's complaints about "the insidious influence of the so-called Byrd rule on the conference agreement" made clear (*CR*, August 5, 1993, H6251).

The End Game: Passing the Conference Report

With a conference agreement in hand, the task of selling it, already under way, intensified. Methodically and relentlessly, the House leadership pursued every Democrat. "There was whip meeting after whip meeting," a participant explained. "Members were getting really sick of being beat on, they would run when we came. But we kept after them." Clinton met personally with almost every organized group of Democrats—from the Black Caucus to the Conservative Democratic Forum. He also met with women, freshmen, and even gym users. Many senators and some House members were courted individually as well (*CQW*, July 31, 1993, 2023–2028).

The president and the Democratic leadership argued that the reconciliation bill should be approved because it was good public policy and because Democrats needed to show they could govern. When essential to pick up needed votes, they made deals. Liberals had been mollified by the conference restoring a significant part of the social spending the Senate had cut. On August 4 Clinton by executive order set up an entitlement review process similar to that deleted from the bill because of Byrd rule problems. A last-minute agreement to allow a vote on further spending cuts in the fall satisfied some deficit hawks.

When the mercurial Boren announced he would switch and vote against the conference report, a replacement "yes" vote had to be found. "After four days of feverish wooing" by the administration and Senate leaders, Dennis DeConcini, D-Ariz., agreed to switch his vote; in return he received several policy concessions, including a lessening of the tax bite on Social Security recipients (*CQW,* August 7, 1993, 2122–2129). With every vote essential in the Senate, some erstwhile supporters took advantage of their bargaining position to extract benefits for their constituents; freshman senator Russell D. Feingold, D-Wis., cut a deal on regulation of bovine growth hormone. A tête-à-tête at the White House and a promise of a commission on entitlements finally induced Sen. Bob Kerrey, D-Neb., to declare his support after he had very publicly criticized the package and indicated he might defect.

On August 5 the House began consideration of the reconciliation bill conference report under a rule that allowed six hours of debate. Through a self-executing provision, the rule made the entitlement review process a part of standing House rules; this was done to mollify deficit hawk Democrats.

The debate was highly charged, even for the partisan House. "We oppose this plan because it's a giant tax on the American dream and on America's future," Republican Dick Armey said. "This plan is . . . a recipe for disaster. Democrats may give your President a political victory today, but it's a defeat for our economy and the well-being of the American people." A California Republican charged that "the Clinton tax bill will drive a stake into the heart of California's economy," and another Republican called it "a ship of fools" and urged the House to "sink it." Georgia Republican Newt Gingrich, then the minority whip, predicted the plan would cause "a job-killing recession" (*CR,* August 5, 1993, H6267–H6269).

Democrats defended the plan and accused Republicans of being unwilling to make the hard choices. "Let me tell you what a 'no' vote on this budget means," said a freshman Democrat bluntly: "no action; no growth; no hope; no guts" (*CR,* August 5, 1993, H6229).

Closing debate for the Republicans, Minority Leader Bob Michel of Illinois said:

> The differences here are philosophical, they are real, profound, differences over fundamentals that transcend partisanship.
> ... [T]his package will not create any new jobs ... because you are taxing away the incentives of the small entrepreneurs who create three-fourths of all the new jobs...
> Mr. Speaker, I strongly urge a vote against this harmful, ill-conceived conference report... (*CR,* August 5, 1993, H6270).

Speaker Tom Foley of Washington State closed debate:

> This is not an easy bill. We have all noted that. . . . The Republican Party will march in lockstep, so we on this side of the aisle must bear the burden of responsibility. We are ready to do it. We are anxious to do it, and we will do it.
>
> The Bible says that there is a time for everything. Tonight is the time to decide. Tonight is the time for courage. Tonight is the time to put away the old easy ways. Tonight is the time for responsibility. Tonight is the night to vote.
>
> Let us not break faith with our people. Let us pass this plan. Let us move forward to a better day for our country (*CR*, August 5, 1993, H6271).

At the end of an exhausting day of feverish, one-on-one lobbying and combative floor rhetoric, the House passed the conference report by a vote of 218 to 216; only a vote switch by Rep. Marjorie Margolies-Mezvinsky, D-Pa., saved the package. When working to put together a majority on a high-profile, contentious bill, congressional party leaders often accumulate "pocket," or "if you need me," votes; these are promises of votes from members who would rather not support the legislation, usually for reelection-related reasons, but who do not want to be responsible for its demise. Margolies-Mezvinsky, a freshman from a Republican district, had promised her constituents she would vote against any tax increase and had opposed the reconciliation bill initially; she was not willing, however, to grievously wound the new Clinton presidency, so she switched her vote.[2]

The next day, August 6, the Senate passed the conference report— also by a hair. The vote was 51 to 50, with Vice President Gore casting the deciding ballot, as he had on passage of the reconciliation bill. No Republican in either chamber voted for the legislation. Speaker Foley had been right. The Republicans had marched in lockstep, but the Democrats had held together enough to prevail.

Unified Government, Procedural Control, and Policy Success

Passing the economic program represented a major legislative victory for President Clinton and congressional Democrats. Although many alterations and compromises were made during the long, complex process, the final product followed the outlines of the plan Clinton had laid out in February 1993 and, within the severe constraints imposed by the deficit, reoriented economic policy in a direction Democrats favored. The most

---

2. Representative Margolies-Mezvinsky was defeated in 1994. Given how badly Democrats did in that election, it is unlikely that voting differently on the conference report would have saved her.

significant deviation from the initial proposal and the biggest compromise necessary for passage was substituting a modest gas tax hike for the more ambitious Btu tax.

Democrats accomplished this legislative success by working together across the institutional divide. Throughout the process, Clinton maintained an enormous amount of personal contact with congressional Democrats, and the Democratic congressional leadership worked closely and loyally with the administration.

As important as cooperation between the president and the congressional majority was to success, the president's program would never have passed were it not for the special procedures the leadership had available and used to maximum effect. In both chambers the leaders worked out postcommittee adjustments to the legislation in order to build majority coalitions. In the House, restrictive special rules were crucial to keeping the supportive coalition together.

Most important, of course, was the budget process and the packaging it makes possible. Despite voters' professed desire for deficit reduction in the abstract, a real deficit-cutting package will unavoidably contain some unpalatable provisions, and it is unlikely to be popular. Had it been procedurally necessary to bring up those elements as separate bills, few of the provisions would have survived. Packaging allows popular and less popular elements to be combined and reduces the number of fights that need to be won. It also raises the stakes so high that members are faced with repudiating and severely weakening their leaders if they desert them; that makes it high risk for leaders but also gives them leverage. Budget rules give the budget resolution and the reconciliation bill protection against a filibuster and amendments in the Senate that is enormously advantageous.

The budget process makes comprehensive policy change possible; it makes it a bit less difficult for the Congress to make hard choices and unpopular decisions. However, as shown by the saga of Clinton's economic program in 1993 and even more by the Republicans' attempt in 1995 to enact nonincremental policy change, it certainly does not make either comprehensive policy change or hard choices easy.

Success also requires favorable political circumstances. Without a Democratic Congress, President Clinton's economic program would have had no chance at all. With stronger public support, the compromises necessary to pass it would have been less extensive.

TABLE 10.1   1993 Budget Process: A Chronology

		Budget Resolution			
Date	House Action	Date	Senate Action	Date	Postpassage Action
	President Clinton outlines economic program in an address to a joint session of Congress on February 17, 1993.				
2/23–3/5	House Budget Committee holds hearings.				
3/10	House Budget Committee marks up the budget resolution, H.Con.Res. 64, and orders it reported.				
3/12	*House Democratic leadership negotiates postcommittee adjustments.*	3/12	Senate Budget Committee marks up the budget resolution, S.Con.Res. 18, and orders it reported.		
3/16	Rules Committee grants rule for general debate only.				
3/17	House approves rule and completes general debate. Rules Committee grants second rule allowing votes on four substitutes.				
3/18	House approves rule, considers resolution for amendments, and passes resolution, 243–183.				
		3/25	Senate passes budget resolution, 54–45.	3/25	House and Senate name conferees.
				3/31	Conferees agree to file a conference report. House approves conference report, 240–184.
				4/1	Senate approves conference report, 55–45. Budget resolution, having been approved by both chambers, is now in effect.

3/31–5/13	House committees instructed by reconciliation instructions in budget resolution hold hearings and mark up their recommendations.
5/6	Budget reconciliation recommendations are ordered reported by the Banking, Finance, and Urban Affairs Committee.
5/11	Budget reconciliation recommendations are ordered reported by the Energy and Commerce Committee and the Veterans' Affairs Committee.
5/12	Budget reconciliation recommendations are ordered reported by the Armed Services, Education and Labor, Merchant Marine and Fisheries, and Natural Resources committees.
5/13	Budget reconciliation recommendations are ordered reported by the Agriculture, Ways and Means, Post Office and Civil Service (with a provision approved by Foreign Affairs), and Public Works and Transportation committees.
5/20	Budget Committee marks up reconciliation bill, HR2264, and orders it reported. *Majority Leader negotiates postcommittee changes in bill to pick up support.*
5/26	Rules Committee grants rule with self-executing provision and allows only the Kasich substitute.
5/27	House adopts rule. House considers and passes reconciliation bill, 219–213.

TABLE 10.1 (*Continued*)

		Reconciliation Bill			
Date	House Action	Date	Senate Action	Date	Postpassage Action
		6/9–6/18	Senate committees instructed by reconciliation instructions in budget resolution consider and mark up their recommendations.		
		6/9	Budget reconciliation recommendations are ordered reported by the Energy and Natural Resources, Banking, Housing and Urban Affairs, and Governmental Affairs committees.		
		6/10	Budget reconciliation recommendations are ordered reported by the Armed Services, Veterans' Affairs, Judiciary, Foreign Relations, Environment and Public Works, and Labor and Human Resources committees.	6/24	Senate conferees are named.
				7/14	House conferees are named.
		6/15	Budget reconciliation recommendations are ordered reported by the Commerce, Science and Transportation Committee.	7/15	Additional House conferees are named.
		6/18	Budget reconciliation recommendations are ordered reported by the Finance Committee.	8/3	Conferees agree to file conference report.
		6/22–6/24	Budget Committee orders reported the reconciliation bill, S1134. Senate begins consideration of bill.	8/5	House considers and approves conference report, 218–216.
		6/25	Senate considers and passes bill, 50–49 (with the vice president voting 'yea').	8/6	Senate considers and approves conference report, 51–50 (with the vice president voting 'yea').
				8/10	President Clinton signs HR2264, the Omnibus Budget Act of 1993, and it becomes law.

Note: Official actions are in roman type; behind-the-scenes, unofficial actions are in italics.

c h a p t e r   e l e v e n

Republican Majorities, Divided Government, and Budget Politics

DURING THE 1994 ELECTIONS Republicans promised that, were the voters to make them the congressional majority, they would balance the budget in seven years and enact a host of specific, major policy changes. Using all of their considerable political resources and all of the procedural tools at their command, they tried but failed. Two years later, in different circumstances, congressional Republicans and President Bill Clinton came to an agreement to balance the budget. Yet despite a strong economy, budget surpluses, and the budget agreement, the last years of the Clinton administration saw continuing intense conflict over budgetary issues. Congress had to resort to extraordinary procedures just to get done the essential legislative work of passing the spending bills.

An examination of budget policy making and politics during the second half of the 1990s, when Republicans controlled Congress and Democrats held the White House, illustrates how political conditions and structural features of the U.S. system of government interact to affect the opportunities for and the barriers to lawmaking. The course of the legislation surveyed in this chapter further shows how many of the procedures and practices of unorthodox lawmaking can contribute to legislative success, but it also makes clear that they are only tools and cannot be expected to engineer legislative success when critical political conditions are adverse.

The Republican Revolution and the Budget Process, 1995–1996

In early January 1995, the new Republican majorities in the House and Senate confronted a monumental task in delivering on their promises. House Republicans had formalized a number of their promises in their

Contract with America, which they had pledged to bring to a vote within the first one hundred days of the Congress. Balancing the budget (without touching Social Security or reducing defense spending, as they had also promised) would require restructuring and making big reductions in such large, complex federal programs as Medicare, Medicaid, and farm programs. House Republicans had included a big tax cut in the Contract; fulfilling that promise would, of course, make balancing the budget that much harder. The Contract committed House Republicans to revamping federal welfare programs, especially Aid to Families with Dependent Children (AFDC), and Senate Republicans also were dedicated to that task.

Thus Republicans faced making a host of highly significant and extraordinarily complex policy decisions—many of which would inflict pain on constituents and as such be extremely controversial—in a limited period of time. House Republicans believed they had to bring all the Contract items to the floor within the promised one hundred days, but even the full two years of a Congress is not much time to thoroughly overhaul large numbers of programs developed over decades.

Furthermore, Republicans faced enacting such far-reaching policy change with narrow margins of control in both chambers and a hostile president in the White House. The radical character of the Republicans' agenda assured that the battle over its enactment would be hard fought and that opponents would attempt to stop passage using all available tools. Certainly opponents would appeal to the court of public opinion and attempt to make voting for the components of the program prohibitively expensive in reelection terms for many Republicans. Given the ideological gulf between President Clinton and congressional Republicans, the president, with his veto and his bully pulpit, would be a chief opponent.

The budget process provided the primary procedural tool through which Republicans would attempt to enact their agenda. Without it, the "Republican revolution" of a balanced budget in seven years would have had no chance whatsoever; the Republican congressional leaders knew that getting a large number of major and often painful changes through both chambers and past the president as separate bills was a hopeless task. The budget process allowed the packaging of many policy changes into one piece of legislation; it provided protection against the Senate filibuster; and, combined with an adept strategy, it might make it possible to force Clinton to sign the legislation. (See Table 11.1 for a chronology of the budget process.)

Committing to a Balanced Budget: The Budget Resolution

On May 18, 1995, the House approved the budget resolution its Budget Committee had reported by a vote of 238 to 193; only 1 Republican opposed it and only 8 Democrats supported it. The resolution proposed balancing the budget in seven years and called for a $353 billion tax cut and deep spending cuts; entitlements such as Medicare and Medicaid and domestic discretionary programs were slated to be severely slashed, with spending for programs to aid the poor hit especially hard (*CQ Weekly,* May 13, 1995, 1302).

The Republican Party leadership brought the budget resolution to the House floor under a highly restrictive rule to prevent Democrats from forcing votes on narrow amendments targeting unpopular features of the measure. Anticipating difficulty in getting Clinton to accept legislation enacting the major policy changes required by the budget resolution, the Republican leadership also inserted a special provision in the rule: it suspended a House budget process rule that automatically raised the debt limit by providing for the automatic adoption of a debt limit identical to the level contained in the conference report on the budget resolution. Republican House leaders wanted to keep in reserve the need to increase the debt limit as a weapon in the confrontation with the president that they knew would eventually come.

On May 25, the Senate passed its budget resolution by a vote of 57 to 42, with every Republican and 3 Democrats supporting it. The Senate resolution called for a smaller tax cut and made it contingent on the passage of a balanced budget plan certified as valid by the Congressional Budget Office (CBO). A number of Senate Republicans were less enthusiastic about a huge tax cut than were their House colleagues. However, others such as Phil Gramm of Texas, who was challenging Senate Majority Leader Bob Dole of Kansas for the Republican presidential nomination, wanted at least as big a cut as the House had approved.

Senate Republican leaders, lacking an instrument like restrictive rules, had to beat back a barrage of amendments, not all of them offered by opposition party members. Nevertheless, budget process rules aided them in passing their resolution. Those rules restrict total debate time and so prohibit a filibuster by opponents. They also require that an amendment increasing spending in one area must be paid for with cuts in another, which tends to work against major changes.

The budget resolution then went to a conference committee. After two weeks of tough bargaining among congressional Republicans (Democrats having been relegated to the sidelines), Speaker Newt Gingrich of Georgia and Dole reached an agreement on taxes, the remaining and most contentious issue separating the chambers. To a very considerable extent, the House won. The House Republicans' iron commitment to a big tax cut, the Senate's eagerness to get a budget resolution because chamber rules prevented movement on appropriations bills until then, and

Bob Dole's presidential ambitions worked to the advantage of the House position.[1]

On June 29, both chambers approved the conference report on largely party-line votes. Republicans were ecstatic about what they had accomplished. "We are changing directions," said elated Senate Budget Committee Chair Pete Domenici of New Mexico. "It is the framework to change the fiscal policy of America and to change the way the federal government operates" (*Los Angeles Times,* June 30, 1995). They were determined to finish the job, Republicans said, no matter how recalcitrant Clinton was. "This is a revolution," declared moderate Chris Shays of Connecticut, vowing to refuse to raise the debt ceiling if Clinton did not agree to a balanced budget. "We are prepared to shut the government down in order to solve this problem," proclaimed Budget Committee Chair John Kasich of Ohio (*CQW,* July 1, 1995, 1905).

Shooting with Real Bullets: Reconciliation

As difficult as passing the budget resolution had been, a bigger and more politically difficult task lay ahead—passing the reconciliation bill that actually enacts the policy changes into law. The budget resolution is a blueprint; by its passage Congress had promised to make the changes in law necessary to reach balance in the federal budget by fiscal 2002. Now Republicans had to deliver. As Bob Dole had said at the same stage in 1993, "From now on we're shooting with real bullets."

The budget resolution committed Congress to making savings of $894 billion over seven years. It instructed twelve House and eleven Senate committees to change law under their jurisdictions so as to meet spending targets. Much of the savings was slated to come from entitlement programs: $270 billion from Medicare, $182 billion from Medicaid, and $175 billion from a number of other mandatory spending programs such as food stamps, farm subsidies, welfare, and federal pensions. The committees of jurisdiction were free to decide just how to reach these targets, but the magnitude of the required savings dictated a major restructuring of the programs.

The budget resolution also prescribed $190 billion in savings in nondefense discretionary spending, which funds all those government activities—from the federal courts to Head Start to national park maintenance—that are not entitlements. The Budget Committees' reports accompanying the

---

1. The rule against the Senate's considering appropriations bills before final agreement on a budget resolution mattered because of another departure from orthodox lawmaking. The Senate had started moving appropriations bills before the House passed them. In the past, the Senate had always waited for the House to pass an appropriations bill before it did so.

budget resolution contained numerous suggestions for how these cuts could be made; the committees had proposed closing down whole departments, agencies, and programs. Such specifics just provide guidance, however; they are not binding. The Appropriations Committees would be responsible for deciding how to make the cuts; but again, given the magnitude of the cuts—about 10 percent in the first year—drastic changes would be required.[2]

About the only pleasant task mandated by the reconciliation instructions was for the tax writing committees to cut taxes by $245 billion; however, given the disagreements within the Republican Party about whether a sizable tax cut made political and policy sense, even that task promised to be difficult. And finally, all this had to be done in a very short period of time. The thirteen appropriations bills are supposed to be enacted by October 1, the beginning of the federal government's fiscal year. There is no such statutory deadline for the passage of the reconciliation bill, but the budget resolution instructed the committees to report their provisions for the bill by September 22.

Congress returned to work in early September after an August recess that had been filled with heated rhetoric in members' districts and on the airwaves. Democrats accused Republicans of sacrificing the elderly's health care to pay for huge tax cuts for the wealthy; Republicans claimed they were restructuring Medicare to save it from bankruptcy and that Democrats were acting irresponsibly. Returning members from both parties reported that their constituents supported their positions; Republicans, thus, were fortified to proceed with the difficult task ahead.

By the end of September the pieces were coming together. Ten House committees had reported their provisions. In the Senate, all except Finance had reported. The tough political decisions to be made assured that the process would not be smooth; lawmakers often were forced to use unorthodox processes. The politically delicate Medicare provisions were put together by a Gingrich-led "design team." Responding to their constituents' interests, enough Republicans on the Agriculture Committee resisted their chair's plan to drastically change and reduce the cost of farm policy to prevent the bill from being approved in the committee, despite threats from the party leaders. In Senate Finance, moderate Rhode Island Republican John Chafee forced his fellow Republicans to temper their Medicaid overhaul legislation to get his vote; but then, responding to complaints from Republican governors, Senate Republicans changed the language after the committee had reported.

---

2. The authorizing committees with jurisdiction would be in charge of making major changes in or abolishing programs; however, by cutting funding drastically, Appropriations can achieve the same effect.

On October 12 the House Budget Committee approved on a single 24–16 vote the approximately $562 billion in spending cuts made by the authorizing committees. The bill that went to the floor would, however, include in addition the Medicare cuts, the welfare bill, tax cuts, and cuts in agriculture subsidies and federal pensions. The Agriculture Committee and the Government Reform Committee, which have jurisdiction over farm subsidies and federal pension legislation, respectively, had not been able to report those provisions; too many committee members believed they hurt their constituents. Nevertheless, at the instructions of the party leadership and under authority provided by the budget resolution, the agriculture and pension provisions were to be included in the bill. The leadership's plan to dismantle the Commerce Department also would be incorporated in the package (*CQW,* October 14, 1995, 3119).

The House Republican leadership devoted the week preceding floor consideration to last-minute bargaining and intense persuasion. The bill's enormous scope and its importance to the Republican Party made it hard for Republicans to oppose, but the same characteristics also ensured that many members would strongly dislike some provisions and would be tempted to extract a price for their vote. The party leaders had been centrally involved in the budget process from its beginning; now they became the preeminent players. Speaker Gingrich agreed to restore $12 billion in Medicaid spending and to distribute the money to states particularly hard hit by the committee's plan; he thereby assuaged the concerns of some moderates and members from fast-growing states. Although the agricultural provisions were not altered, disgruntled farm-state members were brought back on board with implied promises that, since the Senate provisions were less radical, changes to their liking would be made in conference. Moderates upset by environmental provisions were not given any concessions on that issue, but the leadership did agree to drop the repeal of the Davis-Bacon Act, which requires federal contractors to pay the prevailing wage, a move aimed at moderates (*LAT,* October 21, 1995).

These and other changes to which the leadership agreed either were included in the revised bill, HR2517, that Kasich put together and unveiled on October 20 or, in the case of the many last-minute deals, were incorporated into the bill taken to the floor by the rule. The rule granted by the Rules Committee on October 25 contained a self-executing provision specifying that when the House approved the rule it thereby approved HR2517 as modified by the last-minute leadership amendments as a substitute for the bill the Budget Committee had reported. This procedure allowed the leadership to avoid having to offer their changes and additions to the bill reported by the Budget Committee as amendments on the floor. The rule allowed only one amendment, a minority party substitute. The Democratic leadership did not draft its own alternative; the leaders knew a Democratic substitute would have no chance and feared it would only distract media attention from the Republican plan just when public opinion seemed to be turning against it.

The Republican leaders' combination of fervent, high-minded exhortation and nitty-gritty deal making paid off. The biggest and most ambitious reconciliation bill ever passed the House on a 227–203 vote, with only 10 Republicans defecting.

To engineer passage in the Senate, Majority Leader Dole had to placate Republican moderates who had serious concerns about a number of the bill's provisions. The bill passed on a 52–47 vote; no Democrat voted for it, but all but 1 Republican did. Dole's concessions as well as a few additional victories on the floor brought all the other Republican moderates on board. Ironically, Clinton's vow to veto the bill made it easier for moderate Republicans to vote for passage. "We know this isn't the last station," Chafee said (*CQW*, October 28, 1995, 3290).

Summitry: Struggling to Reconcile Irreconcilable Differences

Politics and procedure had relegated President Clinton to the sidelines during much of the budget process. Clinton had, of course, submitted a budget in February as law requires the president to do. In June he had unveiled a new budget that reached balance in ten years. Republicans, however, insisted that any plan balance the budget in seven years according to conservative CBO figures. Convinced that the 1994 elections had given them a mandate that superseded any Clinton may have had and finding nothing of value in either of Clinton's budget plans, Republicans had proceeded on their own. Since the budget resolution does not require the president's signature, Republicans were not forced to take Clinton's preferences into account. However, the president can veto the reconciliation bill, and Republicans knew they could not muster the votes to override.

As Republicans were crafting their bill, President Clinton made clear that he strongly opposed many of its provisions. The bill, Clinton argued, cut much too deeply into Medicaid, Medicare, welfare, education, and the environment. That it ended poor people's entitlement to health care under Medicaid and slashed the earned income tax credit for the working poor while providing huge tax cuts to the well-off was unacceptable.

If, as he had repeatedly threatened, Clinton vetoed the reconciliation bill, Republicans would have to bargain with him; otherwise the legislation on which they had spent so much of their first year in power would die. They hoped that public opinion—which, they were convinced, strongly supported a balanced budget—would force Clinton to sign the bill or at least to agree to a deal to their liking. However, they had from early in the year contemplated the use of additional weapons. To provide the funds necessary to keep the government functioning, appropriations legislation has to be passed every year; otherwise, large chunks of the government must shut down. Perhaps even more of a weapon was legislation raising the debt ceiling. Congress must periodically pass such legislation so that the federal government can borrow the funds necessary to pay its debts; if borrowing authority were to run out, the federal government would have to default on its obligations, a course potentially disastrous for the economy and the credibility of the United States. Republicans believed they could use the threat of shutting down the federal government or of bringing it to the brink of default as bargaining tools.

All thirteen appropriations bills are supposed to be enacted by the October 1 beginning of the new fiscal year. In 1995, the process was far behind schedule, slowed by the time the House had spent on the Contract, the big cuts that the Appropriations Committees were required to make, and legislative riders. With the party leadership orchestrating the effort, House Republicans, eager to make changes in law quickly, attached numerous controversial legislative provisions—known as riders—to appropriations bills. Intended to protect the provisions from a presidential veto, the strategy in many cases made House-Senate agreement on the bills excruciatingly difficult to reach. Moderate Senate Republicans were much less enthusiastic about hobbling the Environmental Protection Agency, imposing new restrictions on abortion, or effectively barring liberal interest groups from lobbying than hard-line House Republicans were.

By late September, only two of thirteen appropriations bills had been cleared for the president. Not wanting to call attention to their inability to meet deadlines, congressional Republicans agreed with the president on a continuing (appropriations) resolution to fund government programs for forty-four days. This was a "clean" continuing resolution (CR) in that it contained no extraneous provisions and was not controversial.

The early rounds and the first government shutdown. Both sides knew that they would have to talk. On November 1, President Clinton and the Republican leadership met for two hours at the White House to discuss budget issues, including the debt limit, but no agreements were reached.

Implementing their strategy of using must-pass legislation to pressure the president into an agreement, congressional Republicans passed a CR and a debt ceiling increase, including in both pieces of legislation provisions the president strongly opposed. On November 13 Clinton vetoed both bills, as he had said he would.

In a final attempt to avert a government shutdown, Clinton sent Leon Panetta, White House chief of staff, to the Hill to confer with Gingrich and Dole; however, when Panetta insisted that congressional Democrats be included in the talks, the Republican leaders refused and no negotiations took place. On November 14 the federal government shut down. At that point, only two of the regular appropriations bills had been signed into law by the president.

Under law, "essential" government services—law enforcement, for example—continue even if appropriations bills are not passed; but all other services and programs not yet funded have to close down. About eight hundred thousand federal employees were sent home all across the country. National parks were closed, and the Small Business Administration stopped processing loan requests. New applicants for Social Security were out of luck, although the checks (an entitlement and therefore not funded by appropriations) continued to go out.

On November 15, with no debt limit bill having passed, Treasury Secretary Robert Rubin made use of an extraordinary procedure to prevent default. Two days later both chambers passed the reconciliation bill conference report. Resolving the differences between the House and Senate bills had been a huge task. The bills, after all, dealt with hundreds of issues and programs. Agriculture, Medicare, Medicaid, welfare, and taxes presented the trickiest problems. In addition to being faced with many tough issues, the negotiators were constrained by the numerous promises that had been made during the effort to pass the bill. In both chambers the leaders had over and over again promised members concerned with some provision that "we'll fix it in conference."

Countering this formidable set of problems was the momentum created by the passage of the legislation in both chambers; members had made a host of difficult decisions. They had put their careers on the line; if no agreement were reached it would all be for naught. And, given that important deadlines already had been missed, more long delay was likely to hurt the Republican Party's image. The leaders were determined to get a bill to the president before Thanksgiving.

The conference committee consisted of forty-three senators divided into twelve subgroups and seventy-one House members divided into fourteen subgroups. Had Gingrich not assertively exercised the Speaker's discretion in the appointment of conferees, the House delegation easily could have been much larger. Fearing that sheer numbers would delay resolution, Gingrich chose, whenever possible, members who could do double duty because they served on the Budget Committee and another concerned committee; in this and other ways he kept the number of conferees down.

A subgroup of eight House members had authority over the entire bill and included, in addition to high-ranking Budget Committee members, a number of party leaders—Majority Leader Dick Armey of Texas, Whip Tom DeLay, also of Texas, and conference chair John A. Boehner of Ohio on the Republican side and Whip David Bonior of Michigan on the

Democratic side. In the Senate, the group of three that had authority over the entire bill was confined to the Budget Committee leaders. The other subgroups consisted of members from the committees with provisions in the bill and had authority over the relevant provisions only. The Republican members of these subgroups made most of the many decisions that a bill of such broad scope required. On the big, tough issues, however, the party leaders were centrally involved. Gingrich and Dole, working with shifting groups of committee leaders, depending on the issue, hammered out agreements on the most sensitive issues.

The agreement on agriculture provides an example of the power of conferees; much of the fairly radical House language was adopted, even though the House Agriculture Committee had turned it down and the Senate version entailed less drastic change. The chair of the House Agriculture Committee, who was the author of the "freedom to farm" version, headed the House conferees and the top House party leaders supported him; the chair of the Senate Agriculture Committee also liked much of the House version even though his committee had reported a more moderate bill.

The conferees approved the conference report on November 15, and on November 17 both houses approved the report on largely party-line votes. Democrats in the Senate used the Byrd rule to force deletion of a number of extraneous provisions, as they had during initial floor consideration. Again Republicans could not muster the sixty votes needed to waive the rule. Since the House had already approved the conference report with the offending provisions, the legislation had to go back to the House for approval in altered form. When on November 20 the House concurred in the Senate amendment, both chambers had passed the bill in identical form.

Agreements, disagreements, and the second government shutdown. On November 19 President Clinton and Republican leaders announced an agreement to end the six-day shutdown. To their surprise, Republicans found the public blaming them rather than the president by a 2-to-1 margin. Threats of defection by significant numbers of congressional Democrats put Clinton under pressure as well. The deal, which was incorporated in a CR passed the next day, funded the government until December 15 and bound the president and Congress to enacting a budget that the CBO certified as balanced by 2002 and that, at the same time, protected future generations; ensured Medicare solvency; reformed welfare; and provided adequate funding for Medicaid, education, agriculture, national defense, veterans, and the environment (*CQW,* November 25, 1995, 3598).

To carry out the face-to-face negotiations, a group of sixteen was chosen, eight from each side. The Republican group consisted of a combination of party and Budget Committee leaders from each chamber: House Republicans were represented by Majority Leader Dick Armey, Whip Tom

DeLay, Budget Committee Chair John Kasich, and Robert Walker of Pennsylvania, a high-ranking member of the Budget Committee and a confidant of the Speaker; the Senate Republican contingent was made up of Whip Trent Lott of Mississippi, Budget Committee Chair Pete Domenici, and the two next most senior members of the Budget Committee, Charles Grassley of Iowa and Oklahoman Don Nickles. The administration was represented by White House Chief of Staff Leon Panetta, Treasury Secretary Robert Rubin, and Office of Management and Budget (OMB) Director Alice Rivlin.

Republicans had wanted to limit participants to representatives of the administration and congressional Republicans; the White House, however, had insisted that congressional Democrats be included. The difficult political environment for Democrats since the 1994 elections had strained relations between the White House and congressional Democrats; excluding them from the talks was a prescription for disaster. Therefore, Rep. Martin Sabo of Minnesota and Sen. Jim Exon of Nebraska, ranking members of the House and Senate Budget Committees, respectively; House Democratic Whip David Bonior; Texan Charles Stenholm, a senior member of the House Budget Committee and a leader of the Coalition, a group of conservative Democrats; and Byron Dorgan of North Dakota, representing the Senate Democratic leadership, were included (*CQW*, December 2, 1995, 3640). In the background would be Speaker Gingrich, Senate Majority Leader Dole and the president, all of whom would have to sign off on any deal.

The negotiators met for the first time on November 28 in the Capitol. On November 30, after three bargaining sessions of a few hours each, the talks stalled. Each side accused the other of bad faith. Republicans charged that Clinton still had not proposed a detailed alternative plan; the White House responded that Republicans refused to follow a previously agreed-upon agenda for the meetings.

On December 6 the president vetoed the reconciliation bill, using the pen with which President Lyndon B. Johnson had signed the Medicare/Medicaid bill into law in 1965. At the same time he announced that he would unveil a seven-year alternative budget. Clinton's new budget did not rely on the more pessimistic CBO numbers (which required deeper cuts), as the Republicans had demanded, and they dismissed it out of hand. Still another White House proposal met with the same reception on December 14 (*CQW*, December 16, 1995, 3789).

With the talks stalled once more, Republicans refused to approve another short-term CR and the government shut down again. Many were convinced that the president did not really want a balanced budget deal and that they would have to play hardball to force him to agree. Treasury Secretary Rubin's extraordinary but legal financial maneuvering had, at least temporarily, removed the debt limit as a lever. Appropriations remained their best weapon. Vowing that the House would not pass another CR, Gingrich confidante Bob Walker of Pennsylvania said, "We will politically endure as much pain as it takes to get a [balanced-budget] deal" (*CQW*, December 23, 1995, 3876).

Peak-level summitry and the longest shutdown. On December 19 President Clinton called Gingrich and Dole; that afternoon, after a two-hour meeting at the White House, the Republican leaders announced a breakthrough—Clinton had agreed to negotiate a seven-year budget deal starting from CBO numbers by the end of the year. Furthermore, Clinton had promised to participate personally in the negotiations.

Republican leaders had promised that once good faith talks were underway Congress would pass a CR. However, House Republicans absolutely refused. A statement by Vice President Gore, seeming to dispute that Clinton had agreed to CBO numbers, although quickly contradicted by the White House, fed already suspicious Republicans' distrust and hardened their inclination to hold fast. By a near-unanimous vote, the House Republican Conference voted to hold out until Clinton agreed to a balanced budget deal. The freshmen, many of whom lacked political experience and disdained compromise, were especially adamant. "This government is going to remain shut down until he [President Clinton] realizes that we are not going to compromise on a balanced budget," said Mark W. Neumann, R-Wis. (*LAT*, December 21, 1995).

When Congress returned in early January, the government shutdown had lasted far longer than any before. Although several more appropriations bills had become law before the second shutdown started, six were still outstanding. The press was full of articles about the harm the shutdown might cause—the preparation of the next year's flu vaccine was being hindered, for example—and about the suffering of federal employees. The public was blaming Republicans far more than the president for the impasse. Never enthusiastic about the strategy of closing the government down and concerned that the focus had shifted from budget balancing to the shutdown, Majority Leader Dole on January 2 pushed through the Senate a condition-free CR to fund the government until January 12 while budget talks proceeded. To move the legislation so quickly, Dole took up a most-favored-nation bill for Bulgaria and offered the CR as a substitute amendment to it, a maneuver which the Senate's loose rules on germaneness made possible. When the Senate adopted the "amendment," the CR was substituted for the original bill.

The House Republican leadership decided that House Republicans were in a politically untenable position; a change in strategy was needed. The leaders proposed a CR that would run through March 15, but at a contentious party conference the membership refused to go along. "I am vehemently and steadfastly opposed to this . . . defeatist strategy, which is going to blur the differences between the parties," said Frank Riggs of California, reflecting the views of many of his fellow freshmen (*LAT*, January 5, 1996). Republican leaders regrouped, came up with another plan, and, at a conference the next morning, pressed their members to support it. House Republicans had been so successful in 1995 because they had acted as a team, Gingrich told his members. If they wanted to stay a part of the team, they would vote for the CR, he added pointedly. Later in the day, the leadership-supported measures were approved by the House; fifteen Republicans refused to vote in favor of reopening the government.

Clinton responded by putting forth his own plan to balance the budget in seven years according to CBO numbers; since Clinton had thereby finally met what Republicans said was their one "nonnegotiable" demand, this initially seemed like a breakthrough. But the talks soon stalled again. It was becoming increasingly clear that the policy differences between the president and congressional Republicans were too great to bridge. Even as negotiations narrowed the dollar amount differences between the sides, Republicans found the ways in which the administration proposed balancing the budget unacceptable because they did not include the sort of basic restructuring of entitlement programs to which Republicans were committed. The president and congressional Democrats, although they had conceded on balancing the budget, deemed the Republicans' means of doing so unacceptable because they weakened or destroyed government programs Democrats considered essential. "It's not a debate about numbers, it's a debate about policies," Majority Leader Dole succinctly summarized (*CQW* 1996, 89).

With the prospects of an agreement dimming but with neither side wanting to throw in the towel and reap the blame for failure, negotiations spluttered along, more frequently in neutral than at full throttle. In late January, congressional Republicans and the White House worked out a mutually agreeable CR that extended funding until mid-March.

Raising the debt limit. Not long into the new year the debt limit re-emerged as a front-burner issue; Treasury Secretary Rubin was running out of stopgap measures to ward off default. The Republican House leadership no longer talked blithely about preferring default to compromise; the government shutdown had cost the Republican Party dearly with the public, and Republicans could not afford another such debacle. Yet the leaders desperately wanted to be able to claim if not a victory at least not a total defeat, and they, of course, had to amass a majority vote for the debt limit increase. Both considerations dictated adding provisions favored by Republicans to the debt limit bill.

The Republican leaders negotiated a deal with the Clinton administration to include language in the bill providing for a long-term increase in the debt ceiling, some regulatory relief for small business, an increase in the earnings limit for Social Security recipients, and the line-item veto. These "sweeteners," especially the line-item veto, were sufficient to enable most Republicans, even the hard-line House freshmen, to vote for the debt limit increase and to give the Republican Party something to brag about. Essentially, Republican leaders made the best of a weak hand.

Both chambers passed HR3136 on March 28, and Clinton signed it the next day, thereby ending the threat of default but also depriving Republicans of the lever they had hoped to use to force the president to accept their policy proposals.

With a whimper. The curtain finally came down on the 1995 budget battle in late April, when Congress passed and Clinton signed an omnibus appropriations bill to fund the nine departments and the dozens of agencies covered by the five regular appropriations bills that had not been enacted by that point. Six months late, after fourteen continuing resolutions and two government shutdowns, the government was finally funded for the fiscal year that ended September 30, 1996.

Both chambers had passed their own versions of the omnibus appropriations bill in March, but reaching a final agreement had required weeks of negotiations between House and Senate Republicans and with the White House. Both funding levels and policy riders were at issue. Hard-line House Republicans were resistant to increasing funding, especially for programs such as AmeriCorps (the national service program) and Goals 2000 dearest to Clinton's heart, and to dropping policy riders on such hot-button topics as abortion and the environment. Clinton, buoyed by his increasing popularity, also had hung tough, and Senate Republicans often found themselves in between. There was much less support for the policy riders in the Senate than in the House, and the Senate bill included more money than the House bill—although not as much as Clinton wanted.

Extensive negotiations between House and Senate appropriators in small groups, in which a multitude of compromises were reached, were followed by a series of high-level talks. Finally, on Wednesday, April 24, the core negotiating group of White House Chief of Staff Leon Panetta and the chairs and ranking minority members of the House and Senate Appropriations Committees reached agreement. House Republicans were forced to make major concessions on both funding levels and policy riders; considerable money for Clinton's priorities in the areas of education and the environment was restored, and most of the riders were dropped or the president was given the authority to waive them. "We got rolled," House freshman Mark Souder of Indiana complained (*LAT*, April 25, 1996). Despite much grumbling by House Republicans, the House as well as the

Senate overwhelmingly approved the conference report that contained the agreement. As senior House Republican and appropriator Bill Young of Florida summed up, "At this stage, we've got to get it settled" (*LAT,* April 25, 1996).

The Budget Process and "Revolutionary" Policy Change: Possibilities and Limits

Using the budget process, the new Republican majorities managed to cut domestic appropriations by 9 percent over the previous year, a very considerable achievement from their perspective (*CQW,* April 27, 1996, 1156). They failed in their much more ambitious attempt to cut spending in and to fundamentally restructure the big entitlement programs, especially Medicare and Medicaid.

A number of the procedures and practices of unorthodox lawmaking were essential tools in the Republicans' strategy to accomplish their ambitious goal; without the packaging the budget process allowed and the protection from filibusters it afforded the legislation in the Senate, passing such nonincremental policy change would not have been possible. Had the minority Democrats in the Senate been able to filibuster the reconciliation bill, they certainly would have done so, just as the minority Republicans would have filibustered the Clinton economic program in the 103rd Congress. Other tools of unorthodox lawmaking were instrumental at a number of stages in the process as well. To ensure that the bill would pass the chamber and satisfy most Republicans, the Republican leadership used task forces, negotiated postcommittee adjustments, and, in some instances, bypassed committees altogether. As employed by an activist party leadership, special rules were critically important to Republican strategy; such rules were used to hold the package together at a number of crucial stages.

The procedures and practices of unorthodox lawmaking are, however, just tools and are by no means sufficient to produce nonincremental policy change. Summits are, in fact, a procedure of last resort; the president and Congress agree to try to settle their differences through a summit when more orthodox procedures have failed. The U.S. governmental system of separate institutions sharing power has a status quo bias; making major policy changes is difficult and usually requires compromise.

When the philosophical differences between the president and the congressional majority are so great that what one considers a reasonable compromise the other regards as selling out, significant policy change is unlikely unless the actor advocating such change can marshal strong public support and thereby make holding out too costly in electoral terms for the other actor. In fact, in summer 1996, Republicans scored a major victory when President Clinton signed a welfare overhaul bill. Although Clinton had extracted a number of significant compromises, the legislation ended

TABLE 11.1 1995 Budget Process: A Chronology

	Budget Resolution and Reconciliation			Senate Action	Appropriations and Debt Limit Legislation
	House Action				
			1/26, 2/1	Budget Committee holds hearings.	
3/21, 3/22, 3/30, 4/4	Budget Committee holds hearings.				
			5/8, 5/9, 5/10	Budget Committee considers and marks up budget resolution.	
5/10, 5/11	Budget Committee considers, marks up, and approves budget resolution.				
5/16	Rules Committee grants modified closed rule allowing votes on four substitutes and suspending the automatic adoption of an increase in the debt limit.		5/11	Budget Committee completes mark-up and approves budget resolution.	
5/17	House adopts rule.		5/18, 5/19, 5/22, 5/23, 5/24	Senate considers budget resolution.	
5/18	House considers and adopts budget resolution, H.Con.Res. 67, by a 238–193 vote.				
6/8	House conferees named.		5/25	Senate completes consideration and approves budget resolution, S.Con.Res. 13, by a 57–42 vote.	
			6/7	Senate conferees named.	
	6/8	Conference begins.			
		Gingrich and Dole negotiate an agreement on taxes.			
	6/22	Conferees reach agreement.			
	6/29	House and Senate approve conference report by votes of 239 to 194 and 54 to 46.			
		Budget resolution, having been approved by both chambers, is now in effect.			

House		Senate	
7/19–10/11	House committees, under instructions by the budget resolution, hold hearings. They then consider and mark up their recommendations.	7/11–10/19	Senate committees, under instructions by the budget resolution, hold hearings. They then consider and mark up their recommendations.
8/1	Budget reconciliation recommendations are ordered reported by the National Security Committee.		
9/12	Budget reconciliation recommendations are ordered reported by the Judiciary Committee.	9/18	Budget reconciliation recommendations are ordered reported by the Armed Services Committee.
9/19	Budget reconciliation recommendations are ordered reported by the Banking and Financial Services Committee and the Resources Committee.	9/19	Budget reconciliation recommendations are ordered reported by the Environment and Public Works Committee.
		9/20	Budget reconciliation recommendations are ordered reported by the Banking, Housing and Urban Affairs Committee and Veterans' Affairs Committee.
9/21	Budget reconciliation recommendations are ordered reported by the Ways and Means Committee.	9/21	Budget reconciliation recommendations are ordered reported by the Energy and Natural Resources Committee and the Judiciary Committee.
9/22	Budget reconciliation recommendations are ordered reported by the Commerce Committee.	9/22	Budget reconciliation recommendations are ordered reported by the Labor and Human Resources Committee.
9/27	Budget reconciliation recommendations are ordered reported by the International Relations Committee.		
9/28	Budget reconciliation recommendations are ordered reported by the Economic and Educational Opportunities, Transportation and Infrastructure, and Veterans' Affairs committees.		

TABLE 11.1 (Continued)

	Budget Resolution and Reconciliation			Appropriations and Debt Limit Legislation
	House Action		Senate Action	
10/12	Budget Committee marks up and orders reported the reconciliation bill, HR2491. *Republican party leaders engage in intense bargaining and agree on postcommittee adjustments.*	9/28	Budget reconciliation recommendations are ordered reported by the Agriculture Committee and the Commerce, Science and Transportation Committee.	10/1 1997 fiscal year begins; FY 1996 appropriations run out; continuing resolution (CR) extending funding through November 13 in effect.
		10/19	Budget reconciliation recommendations are ordered reported by the Finance Committee. *Dole negotiates with moderates.*	
10/20	Budget chair Kasich unveils the omnibus reconciliation bill, HR2517. (It includes Medicare, welfare, and tax cut bills passed separately earlier and cuts in agricultural subsidies and in federal pensions that the committees of jurisdiction refused to report.) *Republican party leaders continue their negotiations and agree on more postcommittee adjustments.*	10/20	Budget Committee marks up reconciliation bill. *Dole and moderates and other holdouts agree on postcommittee adjustments to be offered as amendments on the floor.*	
		10/23	Budget Committee completes markup and orders reconciliation bill reported.	
10/25	Rules Committee grants rule allowing a vote on one substitute and including a self-executing provision incorporating last-minute deals into the bill.	10/25, 10/26, 10/27	Senate considers reconciliation bill.	

Date	Event		Date	Event
10/26	House approves rule and debates and approves the reconciliation bill, HR2491, which incorporated HR2517. The vote was 227–203.		11/1	*Clinton and Republican congressional leaders meet to discuss budget issues.*
10/27	Senate passes reconciliation bill, S1357, by a 52–47 vote.		11/9, 11/10	House and Senate pass and clear for president a short-term debt limit increase with "strings."
10/30	House conferees named.		11/8, 11/13	House and Senate pass and clear for president a CR with extraneous matter that Clinton opposes.
11/13	Senate conferees named.		11/13	Clinton vetoes CR and debt limit increase; old CR runs out.
11/15	Conferees agree to file conference report.		11/14	Federal government shuts down.
11/17	House agrees to conference report, 237–189. Portions of bill stricken in Senate as violations of the Byrd rule. Senate agrees, 52–47, to conference report without stricken provision. (Amendments between the chambers used.)		11/19	*Clinton and Republican congressional leaders reach agreement to open the government and to hold high-level talks; group of sixteen chosen to negotiate deal.*
11/20	House agrees to conference report as altered in the Senate, 235–192.		11/19, 11/20	Senate and House pass and clear for president a CR funding government until December 15.
11/30	Bill presented to the president.		11/28	*Negotiations begin.*
12/6	President Clinton vetoes reconciliation bill, HR2491.			*Negotiations continue in fits and starts.*
			12/6	Clinton vetoes reconciliation bill.

TABLE 11.1 (*Continued*)

Budget Resolution and Reconciliation		Appropriations and Debt Limit Legislation
	12/15	CR runs out and federal government shuts down again.
	12/19	*Clinton and Republican congressional leaders agree to peak-level summit with Clinton participating.*
	12/22	*Clinton, Dole, and Gingrich meet at White House.*
		Talks continue intermittently.
	1/2/96	Senate passes "clean" CR.
	1/5/96	House passes CR, ending the longest government shutdown ever.
		More talks, maneuvering, and negotiations; short-term CRs keep government open. Republican leaders and Clinton administration negotiate deal on debt limit increase.
	3/28/96	Long-term debt limit extension passes.
		Congressional party leaders and appropriators and administration negotiate deal on remaining appropriations.
	4/24/96, 4/25/96	House and Senate pass and clear for president omnibus appropriations bill funding government for the rest of FY 97.
	4/26/96	Clinton signs omnibus appropriations bill, HR3019.

Note: Official actions are in roman type; behind-the-scenes, unofficial actions are in italics.

welfare as an entitlement and bore a clear Republican stamp. This was a case in which the Republicans were backed by a strong public desire for policy change; Clinton and many other Democrats feared the electoral consequences of killing the legislation.

On the budget, Republicans had hoped that public support for a balanced budget in the abstract would translate into strong public pressure on Clinton to make a deal on their terms. Instead, the Democrats' warnings that the Republicans' plan would cut Medicare, education, and environmental protection proved more persuasive. When Clinton won the battle for public opinion, Republicans lost their chance of winning the policy war.

Balancing the Budget, 1997

By 1997 the political context offered new opportunities for a balanced budget deal. Having been reelected, President Clinton clearly wanted a budget deal to burnish his legacy. The hard experiences of 1995 and 1996—the government shutdown for which they were blamed and the "near death" experience of the 1996 elections, in which they only narrowly maintained control of the House—had made Republicans more realistic about what they could accomplish under conditions of divided government and had made them more willing to deal.

Furthermore, Republicans knew they would have real difficulty proceeding on their own. After the public pounding they had taken from Democrats, many Republicans were unwilling to take the lead on making the unpopular decisions on programs like Medicare; the only way of making those choices less draconian was to scale back substantially their tax cut proposals, a course of action anathema to many Republicans. Since House Republicans could count on no Democratic votes for a partisan budget resolution and thus had to hold all but a handful of their own members, they probably could not pass such a budget resolution.

Getting a Deal

On February 6, President Clinton unveiled a budget that balanced by fiscal 2002; contained significant tax cuts, including a $500 per child tax credit; and cut projected Medicare spending. Clinton's meetings with Republican Party and committee leaders immediately following the elections and then this proposal signaled his desire for a budget deal. Yet, although the president had accepted a number of the Republicans' proposals, his priorities and theirs were still far apart. Clinton's budget was based on the more optimistic OMB numbers, not on the CBO numbers Republicans insisted on; his net tax decrease was much more modest than theirs and differently distributed, much of it targeted at education; and he proposed spending more money on selected domestic programs, including education and a restoration of some welfare benefits for legal aliens.

Low-key talks between White House officials and congressional budget leaders began in early February. In public, both sides jockeyed for advantage. The Budget Committees held hearings on the president's budget, with Republicans criticizing it as not credible. In March, House Republicans passed a nonbinding resolution calling on the president to submit a new budget that was balanced using CBO numbers. As negotiations proceeded, members not involved in the talks pressured their fellow partisans to hang tough on matters of special interest to them. House Democrats had been unenthusiastic about negotiations, believing that Republicans should have been forced to come up with their own proposal before talks. When liberal Democrats heard that the negotiators were seriously considering a downward adjustment in the Consumer Price Index (CPI) to save money on entitlement spending increases tied to the CPI, they pressured their leaders and the White House to drop the idea. When Speaker Gingrich raised the possibility of postponing the tax cuts until deficit reduction had taken place, conservative Republicans reacted with horror and disbelief, and the Republican leadership quickly disavowed the idea.

With the mid-April deadline for the budget resolution quickly approaching, negotiations became intense during the week of April 7. Representing the While House were OMB Director Franklin Raines, legislative liaison John Hilley, and director of the president's National Economic Council Gene Sperling; House Budget Committee Chair John Kasich and Senate Budget Committee Chair Pete Domenici spoke for the Republicans. The ranking minority members of the Budget Committees, Rep. John Spratt of South Carolina and Sen. Frank R. Lautenberg of New Jersey, represented congressional Democrats. Each of the negotiators consulted regularly with his congressional party leadership or, in the case of the White House representatives, with the president. No deal could be final until the congressional majority party leaders and the president signed off on it.

Pressure from liberal Democrats and conservative Republicans intensified, and negotiators realized that an agreement had to be reached soon if it were to receive the majority approval that it needed. As secret talks proceeded, members not in the room were becoming increasingly suspicious and were beginning to lock themselves into hard positions. White House representatives met with Republican budget leaders, and although congressional Democrats were outraged about their exclusion, a deal was coming together. The hostile reception the tentative deal received from congressional Democrats when White House officials presented it suggested serious problems ahead. However, a last-minute change in CBO projections saved the day. The unexpectedly strong economy had made the original deal possible by limiting how much had to be cut; now the CBO estimated that, with the economy even stronger than it had projected earlier in the year, the cuts could be scaled back further. Negotiators agreed to drop some of the politically more problematic cuts, making the deal more acceptable to congressional Democrats.

President Clinton and congressional Republicans announced the deal at separate news conferences on May 2. Yet, at this point, the deal was primarily an oral one, and it quickly became apparent that Republicans and Democrats understood what had been agreed on differently in many important respects. Congressional Democrats and the White House wanted a written agreement in as much detail as possible so as to constrain the Republicans when they actually drafted the legislation that would turn the deal into law. Republicans, of course, wanted as much discretion as possible, and Republican committee leaders not directly involved in the negotiations bridled at being instructed in detail about matters under their jurisdiction. Nevertheless, after two more weeks of negotiations in which Speaker Gingrich and Senate Majority Leader Lott took a lead role, a final, written agreement was worked out.

Passing the Budget Resolution

The House Budget Committee quickly approved by a 31–7 vote a budget resolution incorporating the deal. Even though Democratic attempts to write still more specifics into the resolution failed on a series of votes in committee, a majority of Democrats, as well as all Republicans, supported the resolution. A few days later, the Senate Budget Committee approved an almost identical resolution on a 14–4 vote, with 2 conservative Republicans and 2 Democrats dissenting.

In the House, the leadership brought the resolution to the floor under a rule that allowed votes on five substitutes. Bud Shuster, R-Pa., and James L. Oberstar, D-Minn., chair and ranking minority member of the House Transportation and Infrastructure Committee, proposed a budget substitute that increased transportation funding and paid for it by an across-the-board cut in spending and smaller tax cuts. The Shuster-Oberstar proposal offered members much-prized projects for their districts. Yet, for the Republican Party leadership and the White House, the substitute was a deal breaker; it made cuts both groups opposed and, perhaps worse, it reopened negotiations on the fragile agreement and might well lead to its unraveling.

As the leadership had feared, the Shuster-Oberstar substitute proved to be the greatest threat to the bipartisan deal. (The leaders allowed a vote on this substitute only because they realized they could not pass a rule that barred such a vote.) Although White House officials made their opposition to Shuster-Oberstar clear to House Democrats, the Republican leadership had to do the heavy lifting to defeat it. The Republican leaders worked their members hard, warning that the deal would probably come undone if the substitute won. The Shuster-Oberstar substitute was defeated on a 214–216 vote; Republicans voted 58–168 against, Democrats 155–48 for.

The passage vote was anticlimactic; the budget resolution passed 333–99. Even many hard-core conservatives and liberals—the majority of the firebrand 1994 Republican class and Democratic Whip David Bonior among them—voted for the resolution. During the eleven hours of debate, many supporters had made clear that there was much about the deal they did not like but that, given divided government, this was the best that was attainable. Opposing the resolution were twenty-six Republicans, mostly rigid conservatives, and seventy-two Democrats, mostly liberals.

After four days of debate and more than fifty amendments, the Senate approved a budget resolution little changed from that reported by its Budget Committee. Lacking the procedural tools for limiting amendments, leaders had to beat them back by other means. Most problematic was an amendment jointly sponsored by Orrin Hatch of Utah and Ted Kennedy of Massachusetts to raise the tax on cigarettes by 43 cents a pack and use the money to provide additional health insurance for uninsured children and to reduce the deficit. Portrayed in posters and newspaper ads as a choice between Joe Camel (the tobacco companies) and a cute little boy named Joey, this was a hard amendment for many senators to oppose.

Yet, like the Shuster-Oberstar substitute, it was a deal breaker; if the amendment passed, Republican support for the deal would bleed away. Majority Leader Lott insisted that the president give Republicans cover for voting against the amendment by coming out against it. Clinton had White House spokesman Mike McCurry explain that, if this were a freestanding amendment, Clinton would support it; but that was not the case here, and Clinton did not want to see the deal unravel. The amendment was tabled, that is, killed, on a 55–45 vote, with 8 Democrats opposing it and 8 Republicans voting in favor. As in the House, the final vote was anticlimactic; on May 23, the resolution passed 78–22, with only 14 Republicans and 8 Democrats voting against it.

After the Memorial Day recess, conferees quickly worked out the minor differences between the House and Senate versions, and the two chambers approved the final resolution by big votes. Since this agreement was a concurrent resolution and would not become law, it did not need to go to the president for his signature.

The Tough Road to Reconciliation

By approving the resolution the House and Senate had bound themselves to pass legislation that would reduce the deficit by $204.3 billion over five years, including a $115 billion savings from Medicare; make $85 billion net in tax cuts; institute a child health initiative costing $16 billion;

and restore various benefits to legal aliens (*Congressional Quarterly Almanac* 1997, 2–23). The resolution specified that two separate reconciliation bills would be enacted, one with the spending cuts and the other with the tax cuts. Packaging the changes into two bills rather than one would allow for the building of somewhat different coalitions on the two bills, a possibility given that this was a bipartisan deal, and would let members vote for one of the bills if, for policy or reelection reasons, they could not vote for both.

By June 5, when the budget resolution conference report received final approval, the committees that would make the changes in law had already started their work. On June 9, House Ways and Means Committee Chair Bill Archer, R-Tex., released his draft proposal (called the chairman's mark) of the tax bill. Congressional Democrats and the White House immediately cried foul; Archer had skewed the tax cuts so as to benefit the well-off at the expense of low-income people. Even many Republicans were worried about the message sent by the large corporate tax breaks Archer's proposal contained. Especially problematic for Republicans was his proposal to abolish the alternative minimum tax for corporations and pay for that by phasing in the cut in estate (inheritance) taxes more slowly. Small business and farm groups, representing core Republican constituencies, objected strenuously to the estate tax provisions and, under intense pressure from the Republican leadership, Archer revised that part of his bill before he took it to mark-up.

The mark-up in Ways and Means began June 12 and was rancorous and highly partisan. Republicans turned down the Democratic substitute, which reflected Clinton administration priorities, on a strict party-line vote. The bill was then approved on an almost straight party-line vote of 22–16, with only Jim Nussle, R-Iowa, defecting because Archer's bill ended the tax credit for ethanol, a fuel made from corn.

On June 19 Senate Finance approved its bill on a bipartisan 18–2 vote, with 2 conservative Republicans opposing it. Members of the committee had closed their mark-up and, after a freewheeling eight-hour session, had emerged with a deal that garnered broad support. It included a smaller net tax cut than the House bill, an increase in the cigarette tax, a child tax credit that was more generous to lower-income families than that in the House bill, and more money for children's health care.

In staged news events, television interviews, and floor speeches, House Democrats amplified their criticism of the Ways and Means bill, decrying it as unfair to the average American family. Lobbyists for interests unhappy with how they were treated in the Archer bill stepped up their campaign for changes; many of them were GOP allies and conveyed their complaints to the Republican Party leadership either directly or through Republican members whose districts were adversely affected.

The Republican leadership used all the tools at its command to pass the bill. Speaker Gringrich insisted on a number of postcommittee adjustments to the bill; thus the ethanol provision was dropped and the child tax credit made a bit more generous to lower-income families. Interest group allies were mobilized to lobby members for support; the leaders mounted a media campaign, and the whip system engaged in intensive one-on-one persuasion.

The postcommittee adjustments were incorporated into the Ways and Means bill through a self-executing rule, thereby making separate votes on those provisions unnecessary. After a sharply partisan debate, the Democratic substitute was defeated on a 197–235 vote, with no Republicans and only 8 Democrats crossing party lines. No other amendments were allowed under the rule, and the bill passed 253–179; 1 Republican voted against the bill, and 27 Democrats supported it.

One day later, on June 27, the Senate passed its tax bill by an 80–18 vote. Fifty-one Republicans and twenty-nine Democrats supported the bill; four Republicans and fourteen Democrats opposed it. Both Democratic and Republican supporters criticized provisions of the bill; Majority Leader Lott vowed that the tobacco tax would be dropped, and the net tax cut increased in conference. Nevertheless, although a multitude of amendments were offered and about thirty pushed to a roll call vote, the bill emerged from the process little changed.

As the tax bill wound its way through the process, so did the companion spending cut bill. The budget resolution called for more than $260 billion in gross spending cuts over five years, with $140 billion to come from discretionary spending controlled by the appropriations process and $122 billion to come from entitlement programs, $115 of that from Medicare. The resolution, following the budget deal, also stipulated increases in spending for specific purposes, most notably for a new child health initiative and the restoration of some welfare benefits for legal aliens. Eight committees in each chamber had jurisdiction over the programs at issue and were instructed to report legislation making the savings. The biggest burden fell on the Ways and Means and Commerce Committees in the House and the Finance Committee in the Senate because those committees have jurisdiction over the Medicare program.

House Ways and Means managed to produce a bipartisan Medicare bill, making most of its savings by reducing payment rates to health care providers and adding a preventative-care benefits package. The Commerce Committee, in contrast, split along partisan lines on both its Medicare and its Medicaid bills and, on the latter, also failed to comply with the budget resolution. On the welfare provisions, both the Ways and Means Committee and the Education and the Workforce Committee, which shared jurisdiction, produced Republican bills that congressional Democrats and the White House strongly opposed.

By mid-June, the House committees had reported their reconciliation recommendations to the Budget Committee. The Budget Committee cannot change those recommendations, yet at this point considerable bargaining frequently takes place. In several cases, committees with joint jurisdiction had reported conflicting provisions; in others, committees' provisions did not comply with the budget resolution; and, in still others, the White House adamantly opposed what committees had done. Clearly the bill needed some adjustment before it was ready for the floor. Budget Committee Chair Kasich undertook negotiations with Republican committee chairs, John Spratt (the ranking Democrat on the Budget Committee), and White House officials. Under the supervision of and with guidance from Speaker Gingrich, Kasich worked out a number of deals; although Democrats were far from satisfied, the deals were good enough to move the process along.

Under instructions from the Speaker, the Rules Committee drafted a rule that included a self-executing provision by which approval of the rule would also incorporate these postcommittee adjustments into the bill. The rule allowed no Democratic amendments.

Despite the adjustments, most Democrats were still unhappy with the bill and believed it violated in numerous important ways the budget deal. The White House agreed but urged that the bill be passed so that changes could be made in conference. After a heated debate, the House on June 25 passed the spending cut bill 270–162, with 51 Democrats joining all but 7 Republicans in support.

In the Senate, almost all the major issues fell under the jurisdiction of the Finance Committee. Under the leadership of its chair, William Roth, the committee drafted its Medicare, Medicaid, and welfare provisions through a bipartisan process. Aided by the composition of its membership, which included a number of proponents of entitlement reform among its Democrats, the committee went well beyond the budget deal and approved means-testing Medicare, increasing the Medicare eligibility age, and instituting a $5 copayment for home health care visits. An ideological fight did erupt on the child health care initiative; a conservative proposal sponsored by Phil Gramm defeated a more liberal proposal co-sponsored by Jay Rockefeller, D-W.V., and John Chafee and supported by the White House. Finance approved its bill by a 20–0 vote on June 18 and sent it to Senate Budget, which packaged it with the recommendations of the other committees and approved the resulting bill on June 20.

The Senate debated the spending cut bill for two days. Liberals tried to knock out the home health care copayment, the increase in the Medicare eligibility age, and the means-testing of Medicare but failed on a series of votes. The Senate did approve amendments liberalizing somewhat the welfare provisions and the child health care initiative. The body then passed the bill by a vote of 73–27; Democrats split 21–24.

By late June, both the House and the Senate had passed two reconciliation bills—a tax bill and a spending cut bill—that turned the recommendations in the budget resolution into law. However, the House and Senate bills differed substantially; on both taxes and spending cuts, the House had produced its bills through a more partisan process than had the Senate, and the outcomes reflected the process. Furthermore, President Clinton strongly objected to many provisions in all the bills. If congressional Republicans wanted the president to sign the bills, they would have to address his concerns.

Negotiating the Final Deal

The conference committee met and broke down into thirteen subconferences to negotiate on the myriad issues that had to be reconciled. After a week, Republicans concluded that the normal process would not work; to negotiate from a position of strength with Clinton, they needed a unified position. From July 18 to July 23, key House and Senate Republicans met in Speaker Gingrich's office to develop a unified Republican position. House party leaders immediately insisted that the structural changes in Medicare the Senate had approved (means-testing, a rise in the eligibility age) be dropped; their members were not willing to take the heat such changes were likely to generate from senior citizens. On most other issues, Republicans agreed to take the more conservative of the House or Senate positions into negotiations with Clinton. They believed this would give them maximum bargaining leverage.

Serious negotiations with the White House began July 24; on July 25, the negotiation group was pared down to Republican leaders Lott and Gingrich and three White House Representatives, Chief of Staff Erskine Bowles, Legislative Liaison John Hilley, and Treasury Secretary Rubin. Over the next several days, in fits and starts, they and a few other key players—Chairman Archer on taxes, for example—worked out a series of compromises. On July 28 an overall agreement was reached, and on July 29 Republicans and Democrats touted the deal at separate rallies.

The final deal represented a compromise between the parties' very different positions and philosophies. Republicans got a balanced budget by fiscal 2002; cuts in projected entitlement spending, mostly from Medicare; and substantial tax cuts. Included was a cut in the capital gains tax and in estate taxes. Clinton and congressional Democrats got the education tax credit provisions Clinton wanted; a child health initiative larger than that specified in the original deal, funded in part by an increase in the cigarette tax; and the restoration of some welfare benefits for legal aliens. They also had cut down the size of the tax cut from what Republicans originally wanted and had made many of the tax provisions more progressive.

Both House and Senate approved the conference reports easily, and on August 5 President Clinton signed the two reconciliation bills into law. (See Table 11.2 for a chronology of the budget process.)

Why a Balanced Budget Deal in 1997?

Why were congressional Republicans and President Clinton able to reach an agreement to balance the budget in 1997 when they could not in 1995 and 1996? Certainly the booming economy was critical because it made the task much easier. Also important was the Republican majority's growing policy and political realism. By 1997 most Republicans had come to terms with the imperatives of the U.S. political system; if they were to accomplish any policy change, compromise would be required. Furthermore, keeping their majority dictated working with Clinton so as to have something to show for their tenure. Many hard-line conservatives outside Congress blasted the deal as timid and minimalist; but, within Congress, even the firebrands of the 1994 class mostly held their fire. They might have grumbled in private, but they realized that the deal was the best that could be gotten so long as the president, with his bully pulpit and his veto, was a Democrat.

The differences in policy preferences and electoral needs between the congressional Republicans and President Clinton were great enough that ordinary processes could not produce legislation. A summit—a direct and relatively formal negotiation at a high level—was required to reach the initial budget agreement and then to work out the actual legislation. The budget process by which large numbers of often-difficult policy decisions could be packaged and protected from Senate obstructionism was essential to the successful transformation of the initial deal into legislation. Along the way, leaders used other "unorthodox process" tools to aid the legislation, most notably restrictive and self-executing rules in the House.

Budget Politics after the Balanced Budget Deal, 1998–2000

More than half of the spending cuts the budget deal required were to come from discretionary spending, which is under the purview of the Appropriations Committees. The deal imposed caps on such spending, ones that became tighter each year. Some liberal Democrats had argued that the spending caps were highly unrealistic for the later years of the budget deal. The caps certainly made the budget and appropriations processes extremely difficult for Republicans starting in 1998.

In 1998, for the first time, Congress failed to agree on a budget resolution. The Senate passed a resolution that basically rubber-stamped the 1997 budget deal; but the House, after a long and arduous process, passed a more ambitious resolution calling for big tax cuts and even bigger spending cuts. Senate Budget Committee Chair Domenici considered the House budget resolution totally unrealistic and refused to negotiate a compromise.

Failing to pass a budget resolution makes Congress look bad; failing to pass appropriations is not an option—as Republicans had learned so painfully in 1995. Because of the policy differences between Democrats and Republicans accentuated by the need to make painful spending decisions, the majority Republicans attempted to pass their appropriations bills on a partisan basis; with their narrow seat margin in the House, that too proved to be difficult, and the Republicans found themselves far behind schedule in the fall of 1998. An election was looming, and Republicans knew that shutting down the government was a prescription for electoral disaster. They were, therefore, forced into negotiations with the administration.

In mid-October, White House officials, led by Chief of Staff Erskine Bowles and OMB Director Jack Lew, met with Republican leaders, often in the office of Speaker Gingrich, to hammer out an agreement on the hundreds of items in dispute on the eight appropriations bills not yet finished. Clinton emerged the clear winner in the negotiations; he obtained funding for his priority programs and succeeded in having many of the legislative riders Democrats opposed dropped from the omnibus appropriations bill in which the deal was incorporated. Deficit hawk Republicans were outraged because the deal busted the spending caps and funded many programs they opposed, but in the end enough voted for it to pass it. The alternative was unthinkable.

Although vowing to avoid a similar scenario in 1999, Republicans were again forced into end-of-the-session negotiations with Clinton on unfinished appropriations bills. Republicans had managed to pass a budget resolution and a big reconciliation bill that consisted mostly of huge tax cuts. They had done so on a strictly partisan basis, however. Before actually sending the tax bill to President Clinton, who had threatened all along to veto it, the Republican Party mounted a major PR campaign aimed at mobilizing the public to demand the tax cuts. This failed, Clinton vetoed the bill, and Republicans did not even attempt to override his veto.

The struggle then turned to appropriations bills. New Speaker Dennis Hastert of Illinois was determined to pass all the bills in the House, despite the problem created by the caps. All but the most committed deficit hawks acknowledged that staying under the caps would be impossible, but "busting the caps" was obviously politically perilous. House Republicans almost achieved their aim; they passed all but one of the appropriations bills as freestanding bills. Lacking the votes to pass it on its own, the leadership wrapped the Health and Human Services-Labor-Education bill into the conference report of another appropriations bill.

Many of the bills were unacceptable to Clinton and under veto threat. So in the end, to get a complete agreement, negotiations between the White House and Republican leaders were again required. OMB Director Jack Lew and Senate Budget Chair Pete Domenici took the lead, but several phone conversations between Speaker Hastert and President Clinton, who was abroad, were required to get agreement on the final sticking points.

To speed action, the leaders inserted all the bills into the conference report for the District of Columbia appropriations bill—a most unorthodox procedure! Because conference reports cannot be amended, this procedure also protected the deal from being unraveled on the floor. The deal had been reached Wednesday night, November 17. House leaders called a meeting of the Rules Committee in the middle of the night to get a rule, then took the bill to the floor the next day—Thursday, November 18—and passed it without difficulty. The Senate approved the bill on Friday, but only after placating a number of disgruntled senators (see Chapter 3). The bill was flown to Turkey for President Clinton to sign before the last of several temporary CRs ran out.

Since "only" five appropriations bills were at issue, Republicans believed they had narrowed Clinton's bargaining room, yet Clinton once again got much of what he wanted, both in terms of money and in terms of the deletion of legislative riders. The caps had been breached again, but neither side had any interest in highlighting that fact.

In 2000, the same scenario played out, but with a somewhat different ending. In addition to the policy differences between the Republican congressional majorities and Clinton that made agreement difficult, the upcoming elections and the subsequently undecided presidential election gave all the participants incentives to delay. The winning party would gain considerable leverage in the negotiations. On December 15, after twenty CRs, a deal was reached. The ordinarily huge Health and Human Services-Labor-Education appropriations bill served as the base bill; rolled into it were two other unfinished appropriations bills and a number of nonappropriations provisions dealing with Medicare, Medicaid, tax breaks for distressed areas, and immigration regulations, among other subjects. The Republican presidential victory reduced Clinton's bargaining power, so he had to compromise more than in previous years (*CQW,* December 16, 2000, 2857).

Clearly, the 1997 balanced budget deal did not end controversy on budgetary matters. A budget deal sets the framework for later spending and taxing decisions, but leaves many particulars to be decided later. Furthermore, because the 1997 agreement was a compromise between bitter antagonists with very different notions of good public policy and diametrically opposed electoral interests, neither side was fully satisfied with the deal. When opportunities later arose, each attempted to achieve policy goals that they had not accomplished in 1997. Thus, in both 1998 and 1999, Republicans pushed hard, if unsuccessfully, for big tax cuts. Even within the context of a budget deal, key actors differed enough in legislative preferences to require a resort to summits and omnibus legislation to get the essential appropriations bills enacted.

TABLE 11.2   1997 Budget Process: A Chronology

	House Action		Senate Action		Postpassage Action
		2/6	President Clinton unveils a budget that balances by 2002.		
Feb.	*Talks between White House and Congress begin.*				
4/7	*Talks intensify.*				
5/2	*President Clinton and congressional Republicans announce a deal.*				
5/2–5/15	*Two weeks of negotiation transform oral deal into agreed-upon written terms.*				

Budget Resolution

	House Action		Senate Action		Postpassage Action
5/18	Budget Committee reports budget resolution.	5/19	Budget Committee reports budget resolution.		
5/20	Budget resolution debated on House floor.	5/20, 21, 22	Budget resolution debated on the Senate floor.		
5/21	Budget resolution debated and passed by House, 333–99.	5/23	Budget resolution passed by the Senate.		
				6/3	House and Senate appoint conferees and conference begins.
				6/4	Conferees reach agreement and file conference report.
				6/5	House and Senate agree to conference report.

Reconciliation Bills

Date	Action	Date	Action
6/12	Ways and Means Committee approves tax provisions.	6/19	Finance reports tax provisions as S949.
June	House committees draft and then send their reconciliation provisions to the Budget Committee.	June	Senate committees draft and then send their other reconciliation provisions to the Budget Committee.
6/24	Budget Committee reports HR2014 (containing tax provisions) and HR2015 (containing spending cuts).	6/20	Budget Committee reports S947 (spending cuts).
6/25	House debates and passes HR2015.	6/23, 6/24	Senate debates S947 (spending cuts).
6/26	House debates and passes HR2014.	6/25	Senate passes S947 and begins debate on S949 (tax bill).
		6/26	Senate debates S949.
		6/27	Senate debates and passes S949 (tax bill).
		6/27	Senate appoints conferees for both bills.
		7/10	House appoints conferees for both bills and spending bill conference begins.
		7/11	Tax bill conference begins.
		7/18–7/23	*Key House and Senate Republicans meet to develop a unified Republican position.*
		7/24	*Serious negotiations between White House and congressional Republicans begin.*
		7/28	*An overall agreement is reached.*
		7/30	Conference reports filed on spending cut bill and on tax bill.
		7/30	House approves spending cut bill conference report.
		7/31	House approves tax bill conference report and Senate approves both spending cut bill and tax bill conference reports.
		8/5	President Clinton signs both bills.

Note: Official actions are in roman type; behind-the-scenes, unofficial actions are in italics.

The Republican Tax-Cutting Agenda and the Budget Process: The Bush Tax Cuts of 2001 and 2003

GEORGE W. BUSH MADE big tax cuts a centerpiece of his 2000 presidential campaign. However, any claim that the voters had given Bush a mandate for his program ran up against the murky outcome of the 2000 elections. Bush received fewer popular votes than his chief opponent, Democratic nominee Albert Gore; his narrow electoral college majority depended on questionable counts in the state governed by his brother and on a 5–4 decision by an ideologically split U.S. Supreme Court. His party lost seats in both chambers of Congress. Republicans held on to control of the House of Representatives by a razor-thin majority of 221 to 211;[1] the Senate, which before the elections was 54–46 Republican, emerged from the 2000 elections with an even split.

After barely squeaking into office, Bush was advised by most Democrats, many unaffiliated commentators, and even some Republicans to cut back the size of his proposal so as to make it more broadly acceptable. A majority of Democrats had opposed much of the tax cutting agenda in the past. Getting their support would probably require considerable compromise.

Yet despite the weakness of any mandate claim, other political circumstances were more favorable. Bush enjoyed unified partisan control of both chambers of Congress, something no Republican president since Eisenhower in 1953–1954 had had. And big tax cuts were the number one priority of a great many Republicans; congressional Republicans had passed large tax cut packages several times in the late 1990s, only to see them

---

1. There was one vacancy and two independents, who usually split their votes between the parties.

vetoed by Clinton. Furthermore, the budget surplus seemed likely to make selling a sizeable tax cut easier.

Bush and his political advisors decided that paring down his proposal would be seen as an admission of weakness and would alienate his core supporters. Bush therefore determined to stick with his full package of across-the-board income tax rate cuts, repeal of the estate tax, alleviation of the "marriage penalty," new charitable giving deductions, and some lesser provisions estimated to cost in total $1.6 trillion over ten years.

Everyone took for granted that the budget process would be used. Although the big deficits of the 1980s and much of the 1990s had led many casual observers to associate the budget process with spending cuts and tax increases, the process itself is neutral and reconciliation instructions can dictate tax cuts. Republicans knew that in the Senate the protection from filibusters that the budget process afforded would be indispensable to enacting the Bush tax cut.

In fact, as this account shows, the budget process and some of the other practices and procedures of unorthodox lawmaking—restrictive rules and close and continuous leadership involvement in the process, for example—were essential; in order to get Republican tax cut legislation through Congress in 2001 and again in 2003, Republican House leaders even extended the boundaries of unorthodox lawmaking.

Delivering: Cutting Taxes in 2001

Before Bush even formally presented his proposal, congressional Republicans began pushing for quick action, and they and business lobbyists began to lay out their own preferences for possible add-ons to the package. In a January 9 memo to all House Republicans, Majority Leader Dick Armey, R-Tex., wrote that Congress should push Bush's entire plan, plus a few additions, and should make the cuts retroactive to January 1, 2001. Senate Majority Leader Trent Lott, R.- Miss., endorsed making the cuts retroactive and urged Bush to settle soon on a proposal—and a timetable for selling it (*CQ Weekly,* January 13, 2001, 100). Lobbyists swarmed across Capitol Hill touting their clients' preferred tax breaks. A coalition of business and trade associations, whose formation was announced February 6, said it aimed to amend Bush's plan to benefit "all U.S. taxpayers" by adding tax breaks for business (*CQW,* February 10, 2001, 318).

Concerned that the package could get out of hand, the administration responded. "Some in Congress view this as an opportunity to load up the relief plan with their own vision," Bush said at the White House on February 5. "I want the members of Congress and the American people to hear loud and clear: This is the right-size plan, it is the right approach, and I'm going to defend it mightily" (*CQW,* February 10, 2001, 318).

On February 8, Bush formally sent Congress his tax cut proposal and, on February 13, Treasury Secretary Paul O'Neill testified before the Ways and Means Committee, urging its swift adoption. The Bush camp, which had been arguing that the large budget surplus made their tax cut not just possible but necessary, now argued that it was the best response to a slowing economy.

The softening economy had led Democratic congressional leaders to signal that they were willing to accept a tax cut, but not such a huge one and not one so heavily targeted to the well-off. Democrats faulted Bush's proposal as unfair to working people. To make their point in dramatic fashion, House Minority Leader Richard Gephardt of Missouri and Senate Minority Leader Tom Daschle of South Dakota appeared with a black Lexus sedan and a battered replacement muffler. The car, Daschle charged, was "just like the Bush tax cut—fully loaded. If you're a millionaire, under the Bush tax cut, you get a $46,000 tax cut, more than enough to pay for this Lexus. But if you're a typical working person, you get $227, and that's enough to buy this muffler" (*New York Times*, February 9, 2001). Democrats also argued that such a big tax cut would endanger Medicare and Social Security by using up too much of the surplus.

Early Action in the House

The normal budget process requires that first both chambers pass a budget resolution to set guidelines for future legislative action, including any tax cut. Then the chambers would be expected to pass a reconciliation bill that actually enacts into law the instructions included in the budget resolution. Bush and House Republican leaders, however, decided to pass the first and biggest part of the Bush tax cut—the across-the-board cut in income tax rates—in the House before the budget resolution was passed. They wanted to establish momentum and feared the budget resolution might highlight less popular elements of Bush's budget plan, such as spending cuts.

On February 27, in his first address to a joint session of Congress, Bush promoted his agenda to members of Congress and to a large television audience. Although he also discussed his spending priorities, the tax cut was front and center. Bush then undertook a campaign-style tour across the country to sell the tax cut, but the effort seemed to have little impact on Democrats. "When members were home last week, they were feeling no pressure on tax cuts," an aide to a Blue Dog (conservative) Democrat reported. A Gallup poll showed that Democrats in the electorate opposed the Bush plan by more than 2 to 1 (*CQW*, March 3, 2001, 466).

On March 1, the House Ways and Means Committee approved HR3, the Economic Growth and Tax Relief Act, a bill cutting income taxes across the board, on a 23–15 party-line vote. The chairman's mark had been put together through a strictly partisan process, and the committee turned down two major Democratic amendments (one a substitute) on party votes. Bush had talked about bipartisanship, but Democrats claimed little was in evidence. "At no time were the Blue Dogs consulted about these things," said Charlie Stenholm of Texas, a senior leader of the group of conservative Democrats. "We weren't even consulted. What's bipartisan about that?" (*CQW,* March 10, 2001, 530).

On March 8 the House took up the bill, and debate was sharply partisan. The Republican leadership had brought up the bill under a rule that allowed only one Democratic substitute and no other amendments. In the debate on the rule, Republicans focused on the bill's substance as a majority that knows it can pass its rule often does.

Democrats discussed their objections to the contents of the bill, but they focused more on the timing. It is against the rules—and worse, it is irresponsible—to pass a tax cut before agreeing on a budget resolution, Democrats argued. A special rule can waive all points of order against the bill, including the relevant Budget Act provisions, as this one did, but that does not make it either right or sensible. A rule can be amended if (and only if) the motion to call the previous question is first defeated. The ranking Democrat on the Rules Committee explained, "Mr. Speaker, I urge defeat of the previous question so that I may offer an amendment to the rule. My amendment would require Congress to adopt the budget resolution before the House takes up the tax bill" (*Congressional Record,* March 8, 2001, H748).

The tactic failed as everyone knew it would. The previous question was ordered, thus precluding any attempt to amend the rule, on a 220–204 vote; every Republican voted for the rule; only 4 Democrats did. The rule itself passed 220–204. To make their point as strongly as possible, Democrats in both cases forced recorded votes on motions to reconsider the vote.

In the hour of general debate and the additional hour of debate on the Democratic substitute that the rule allowed, Republicans continued to emphasize that the bill would stimulate a lagging economy and would lift the yoke of a cruelly and unnecessarily heavy tax burden off the backs of the American people. "Today we say to the American people, you earned it, you will get to keep more of it," a Republican declared (*CR,* March 8, 2001, H767). Democrats argued that the bill gave thousands to the well-off and very little or nothing to struggling working families; and they repeated that a budget resolution should be approved first. Charlie Rangel of New York, ranking Democrat on Ways and Means, offered the Democratic substitute, which was less costly and differently distributed, with much more going to the less well-off. It was defeated on a 155 to 273 vote; all Republicans and 53 Democrats voted against it. Many of the Democratic opponents were simply unwilling to vote for any tax cut prior to a budget resolution being approved.

Democrats showed their disapproval of the Republicans' strategy one last time by the content of their motion to recommit with instructions. This is a motion that the minority can make that, if approved, essentially amends the bill. Charlie Stenholm moved "to recommit the bill to the House Ways and Means Committee with instructions not to report the bill back until April 15, 2001, unless Congress has completed action on the concurrent budget resolution for fiscal 2002" (*Roll Call,* April 15, 2001). The motion was defeated 204 to 221, with every Republican and 2 Democrats voting against it. Minority Leader Dick Gephardt and Speaker Dennis Hastert of Illinois closed debate for the minority and the majority, respectively, signaling the importance both parties placed on the bill. HR3 passed on a vote of 230–198. On the eight roll calls on the bill or the rule, not a single Republican defected, whereas only ten Democrats voted for the bill.

Although many conservative Republicans would have preferred an even bigger tax cut, all voted for the bill. The administration had by this point convinced the many Republican interest groups to support the Bush bill even if it did not include their favorite provisions. The groups worked in coalition with the Republican White House and the congressional leadership throughout the tax cut battles.

Passing a Budget Resolution

A much rockier road lay ahead in the Senate. Unless the tax cut was passed as part of the budget process, it could be filibustered. With the Senate split 50–50, the prospects of getting the sixty votes to end a filibuster seemed dim. Bush's campaigning for his tax plan in the states of electorally marginal Democratic senators had produced no results. Democrat Zell Miller of Georgia had come out in support of the tax cut early in the year, but no other Democrats followed. Republican Lincoln Chafee of Rhode Island was on record as opposed, and a number of other moderate Republicans were expressing anxiety about the size of the cut and proposing tying reductions to continuing budget surpluses, a notion Bush and most other Republicans rejected. Passing the Bush plan in the Senate would certainly require the protections afforded a reconciliation bill, which cannot be filibustered. And that required passing a budget resolution.

On March 11, after a 12-hour mark-up, the House Budget Committee approved a budget resolution on a 23–19 party-line vote. In his February 27 speech to Congress, Bush had called for holding the overall spending increase to 4 percent, in addition to proposing $1.6 billion in tax cuts; the budget resolution in general terms followed Bush's proposals. It did give the chair of the House Budget Committee unusual authority to raise the resolution's proposed ceilings on discretionary spending later in the year, with agriculture and the military mentioned as possible areas meriting more funding, and to accommodate a refundable tax credit if the Ways and Means Committee were to approve such legislation. The resolution also stated that the tax cuts could go higher than Bush's request if surplus projections improved during the year. Ways and Means was instructed to write four reconciliation bills cutting taxes with deadlines of May 2, May 23, June 20, and September 11. It called for a fifth reconciliation measure—to be reported by the Ways and Means and Energy and Commerce Committees by July 24—to alter Medicare and to add a limited prescription drug benefit.

Democrats complained about the unusual flexibility in the resolution and the consequent unprecedented power it gave the chair, and they objected that some important domestic priorities were shortchanged. Despite offering more than thirty amendments in committee, however, they were unable to alter the Republican-drafted resolution significantly.

The House began consideration of H.Con.Res.83, the fiscal 2002 budget resolution, on March 27. The rule allowed votes on four comprehensive substitutes: a Blue Dog Democratic proposal that cut taxes less and increased defense spending more, a conservative Republican Study Committee version that increased the size of the tax cut and more strictly limited the growth in spending, a Progressive Caucus proposal that cut taxes less and increased domestic spending more, and a Democratic leadership version similar in thrust to—but more moderate in amounts than—the Progressive Caucus plan. All four were defeated, with the Blue Dog plan doing best, loosing 204 to 221 on a largely party-line vote. On March 28, the House adopted the budget resolution 222–205, with only 3 Democrats and 2 Republicans defecting from their respective party's position.

Meanwhile, as the economy worsened, a proposal for an immediate tax rebate to stimulate the economy gained traction in the Senate. Budget Committee Chair Pete Domenici, R-N.M., suggested a $60 billion tax cut as an immediate stimulus, and Democrats endorsed the idea and began promoting it as a substitute for the Bush tax cut.

With the president unable to induce any Senate Democrats other than Miller to support his tax proposal, it became clear that the evenly split Senate Budget Committee would be unable to report a budget resolution. The 50–50 Senate split had forced Republicans to enter into a power-sharing agreement with Democrats that specified equal numbers of members on every committee. Republicans would, however, chair committees. (Because Dick Cheney as vice president was president of the Senate and cast the deciding vote, the Republicans were the nominal majority in the chamber; their leader was the majority leader.) Budget Chair Domenici drafted a resolution that largely followed Bush's proposal, except for the $60 billion stimulus tax cut in 2001; Majority Leader Lott bypassed the committee and brought it directly to the floor.

Although Budget Act rules protect the budget resolution from a fili-buster and from nongermane amendments, senators can and do offer ger-mane amendments. On the second full day of debate, liberal Democrat Tom Harkin of Iowa offered an amendment reducing the tax cut by $488 billion and shifting the money to education and debt relief. When three Republican moderates—Chafee; Jim Jeffords, Vt.; and Arlen Specter, Penn.—deserted their party, the amendment passed 53 to 47. Every Demo-crat except Zell Miller voted for the Harkin amendment. At the end of the roll call, Majority Leader Lott changed his vote from nay to yea because that would allow him to move to reconsider the vote later.

Vice President Dick Chaney, Office of Management and Budget (OMB) head Mitch Daniels, and other White House officials scurried around trying to figure out how to reverse the setback. However, the vote just broke the dam, and a number of other amendments altering the presi-dent's program also passed. The Senate took roll call votes on twenty-one amendments, and while Republicans defeated a number of Democratic amendments, in many cases they did so only by offering slightly less gener-ous versions of those amendments themselves. The budget resolution as amended called for a tax cut of $1.18 trillion over ten years, an immediate $82 billion stimulus tax cut, and a cap on discretionarily spending of $678 billion, which was a 7 percent increase over fiscal 2001. Money had been shifted from tax cuts to spending on agriculture, education, the National Institutes of Health, defense, and veterans programs. The resolution passed the Senate 65 to 35, with all the Republicans and 15 Democrats voting for it.

Republicans hoped to recoup some of their losses in conference with the House. When Democrats complained about being excluded from the negotiations, Domenici baldly replied, "We don't expect you to sign [the conference report], so we don't expect you to be needed" (*CQW,* April 28, 2001, 904). The administration focused on getting the support of just enough moderate Senate Democrats to pass the conference report in the Senate, so only they were included in the negotiations.

Maintaining the support of Senate moderates required not substan-tially increasing the Senate's tax cut figure but did allow other changes, including cutting the Senate's figure for discretionary spending back to Bush's requested 4 percent increase, which pleased conservative House Republicans. Conferees reached an agreement and filed the conference report calling for $1.35 trillion in tax cuts on May 3. However, in the rush, two very important pages were missing from the conference report as filed, so votes had to be put off until the next week.

Bush hailed the agreement as a bipartisan triumph, but most Demo-crats objected to that characterization. "When he gets up and talks about

Democrats and Republicans working together, I'd like to know who the hell he's talking about," said John Spratt, South Carolina representative and the ranking Democrat on the House Budget Committee.

On May 9, the budget resolution conference report passed the House on a 221 to 207 vote, with 6 Democrats and 3 Republicans crossing party lines. The Senate vote the next day was 53–47. Whereas fifteen Democrats had supported the budget resolution as amended on the Senate floor, only five supported the conference report. This was enough, however, to offset the two Republican defections.

Reconciliation

With a budget resolution calling for tax cuts in place, the Senate could now proceed to write a tax bill, assured it would be protected by budget rules from a filibuster. The resolution called for one tax cutting reconciliation bill; the Senate parliamentarian, a nonpartisan expert on Senate rules, had ruled that the Budget Act allowed only one.

The Senate Finance Committee has jurisdiction over tax legislation, and Chair Charles Grassley, R-Iowa, and ranking Democrat Max Baucus, D-Mont., very much wanted the committee to take the lead role in drafting the tax bill. As the tax issue had become key in defining the difference between the parties during the 1990s, party leaders had increasingly usurped the committee's role. In addition to his desire to reestablish the committee's prestige, Baucus was concerned about his own upcoming reelection battle in a state that Bush had won handily. But Grassley and Baucus could maintain control over the legislation only if they worked together and crafted a plan with bipartisan support in the committee.

Grassley and Baucus began talking well before the budget resolution was approved but, once the conference report cleared, they were under pressure to produce a proposal. The budget resolution set a May 18 deadline for the committee to report. Senators in both parties looked on the collaboration with suspicion and were not shy about letting the committee leaders know: at a May 9 meeting of Republican Finance members, Grassley received "long lectures" from several of his more conservative colleagues, and when Baucus briefed the full Democratic membership, he "got an earful of dissent" (*CQW*, May 12, 2001, 1069). Lott attempted to talk Grassley out of drafting a bipartisan bill, and Daschle tried to discourage Baucus from working with Grassley. Both party leaders believed that reaching a bipartisan deal would require giving away too much. John Breaux, a moderate Democrat from Louisiana who supported the committee leaders' efforts, told Baucus not to worry about the heat. "The only good thing is they're jumping on Grassley just as much, so we must be headed in the right direction," Breaux quipped (*CQW*, May 12, 2001, 1069).

On May 11, Grassley and Baucus unveiled a rough draft of their compromise and set the mark-up for May 15. Their plan included the same components as Bush's proposal: a reduction in income tax rates, mitigation of the marriage penalty, a doubling of the $500-per-child tax credit, and a phasing out of the estate tax. To appeal to Democrats, the plan changed the distribution of tax benefits so that more went to lower- and middle-income people and less to the wealthy. It also made the $1,000-per-child tax credit available even to those who earned too little to owe income taxes. To abide by Senate budget rules, they were forced to include a provision that "sunsetted," or repealed, the entire bill after ten years, when the revenue set aside under the budget resolution would no longer be available. Without that provision, the bill would have lost the Budget Act protections and would have been subject to a point of order requiring an impossible-to-attain sixty votes to waive (*CQW*, May 19, 2001, 1145).

Led by Minority Leader Daschle, a member of the Finance Committee, dissatisfied Democrats attempted to alter the Grassley-Baucus draft during mark-up, but all their amendments failed. Many Finance Republicans were also unhappy with the draft, but they wanted to get a bill to the floor so they held their fire. Grassley and Baucus steered their compromise through Finance without significant change, winning approval on a 14 to 6 vote, with all Republicans and 4 of the 10 Democrats voting for it.

Before the budget resolution conference report passed, the House had already approved four different tax cutting bills that contained all the components of the Bush request, although in somewhat rewritten form. Now, in order to give their tax legislation Budget Act protections, House Republicans repassed the income tax rate cut. HR1836 was identical to HR3, but it was officially designated a reconciliation bill. Only a bill passed after the budget resolution is in effect and pursuant to reconciliation instructions can be so designated.

House Republicans were especially concerned that, were the conference to adopt the House's 33 percent top income tax rate rather than the Senate's 36 percent figure, the House figure have reconciliation protection in the Senate and so not be subject to a sixty-vote requirement. As Ways and Means Democrat Ben Cardin of Maryland succinctly explained, the reason for repassing the bill in the House was "so we can pass a single tax bill in the other body, not by a bipartisan vote, but along very partisan lines. That is what this bill is allowing us to do. I urge my colleagues to vote against it" (*CR*, May 19, 2001, H2210).

The Republican leadership brought up HR1836 under a modified closed rule that allowed one Democratic substitute—if offered by Ways and Means ranking Democrat Charlie Rangel—and one motion to recommit with or without instructions. The substitute amendment, which would provide a one-time, retroactive tax rebate; reduce the lowest income tax bracket rate to 12 percent; and increase the amount of income that one can earn and still qualify for the Earned Income Tax Credit, was defeated on a 188 to 239 vote, and the bill was passed by a vote of 230 to 197. All three recorded votes—these two and the vote on the rule—were highly partisan, with not a single Republican crossing party lines.

The Senate began floor debate on May 17 and continued it on May 21, 22, and 23. More than fifty amendments were offered and pushed to a roll call vote. Budget Act rules require that amendments to reconciliation bills be germane and specify that sixty votes are needed to waive that requirement. So, in many cases, the vote was not directly on the amendment itself but on a motion to waive the Budget Act with respect to a point of order against the amendment. Many of the Democratic amendments sought to shift money from top bracket tax cuts to Medicare, education, or other social programs and were killed by a point of order that they were not germane. Both Republicans and Democrats offered amendments, but Democrats seemed intent on delaying passage of the bill. Budget Act rules limit debate on reconciliation bills to twenty hours, but time spent in roll calls is not counted. Therefore, an almost unlimited number of amendments could be offered, "debated" for a minute or less, and then put to a vote, one after another in what is known as a "vote-a-rama."

On the evening of May 22, word that Jim Jeffords, R-Vt., was considering leaving the Republican Party to caucus with the Democrats, thus shifting Senate control to the Democratic Party, began to leak out; the next day it was confirmed. Jeffords said he would leave the Republican Party the day the tax bill reached Bush's desk. Democrats no longer had an incentive to delay, and Republicans realized they had better settle for what they could get.

On May 23, 12 Senate Democrats joined all 50 Republicans to pass the legislation on a 62 to 38 vote. Despite the barrage of amendments on the floor, the bill passed largely intact. Grassley and Baucus had put together a package that could pass; neither liberal Democrats nor conservative Republicans had the votes to move the bill significantly in their preferred direction. To ease passage, Grassley and Baucus did put together a manager's amendment that made $65.7 billion worth of changes in the bill. The managers had negotiated behind the scenes with many senators who wanted changes; these senators agreed to refrain from offering their amendments on the floor in return for the managers including versions of their proposals in the manager's amendment.

The Senate had substituted its own bill for HR1836 and as soon as it passed the bill, it insisted on its amendment, asked for a conference, and appointed conferees. The conferees were all from the Finance Committee and comprised Republicans Grassley, Phil Gramm of Texas, Orrin Hatch of Utah, Frank Murkowski of Alaska, and Don Nickles of Oklahoma, and Democrats Baucus, Breaux, Daschle, and Jay Rockefeller IV of West Virginia. On the evening of May 23, the House agreed to a conference, and the Speaker appointed as conferees Ways and Means Chair Bill Thomas of California, Majority Leader Dick Armey, and Ways and Means ranking Democrat Charlie Rangel.

Bush publicly called on the conferees for a quick resolution and, despite the complexity of the issues, the conference committee moved with unusual speed to approve a compromise bill. And as much as conservative House Republicans hated to admit it, the Republican leadership of both chambers, the experienced Republican conferees, and the Bush administration all recognized that the final legislation would have to largely track the Senate bill. The Grassley-Baucus bill had passed the Senate with a substantial vote, but the underlying coalition was fragile. Moderates, who were the key to victory, had to be kept on board. Fifteen Senate moderates, led by John Breaux and Olympia Snowe, R-Maine, signed a letter threatening to oppose any conference report that did not "closely reflect the delicate compromise that was reached in the Senate" (*CQW,* May 26, 2001, 1251).

After three days of negotiations, the conferees agreed on a bill that cut taxes $1.35 trillion through 2011, considerably less than Bush's initial request and the House figure. It also distributed that tax cut somewhat differently, giving more to those in the lower income brackets, and it provided immediate tax rebates to act as a stimulus; finally, it sunsetted the entire bill at the end of 2010 (*CQW,* May 26, 2001, 1251–1254). In addition, it phased out the estate tax and alleviated the marriage penalty, both high Republican priorities. One possible reason for the rapid wrap-up was the fact that the majority of the Democratic conferees were excluded from the negotiations; "as soon as I was appointed, I waited and I waited and I waited for an invitation to the meeting," Charlie Rangel recounted. "But the invitation never came" (*CR,* May 26, 2001, H2832).

The conference report was filed in the House at 5:17 a.m. on May 26. Because House members were eager to go home for the Memorial Day weekend, the Rules Committee reported the rule for consideration at 6:54 a.m. and consideration began at 8:24 a.m. The House adopted the conference report on the bill by a 240–154 vote shortly after 10 a.m. Every Republican voted for the conference report; Democrats split 153 to 28 against it. Republicans extolled the bill as fair and as delivering on a campaign promise:

> The real issue here today is who should spend the money. Do we believe that individuals and families make the best decisions about how to spend their money, or do we believe government is in the best position to do so? The special interests that we heard from the minority leader are in this bill. Want to hear what they are? People who are married, people who have children, people who are worried about the education of those kids, people who are worried about their small business and farms, and people who are worried about more and more money that goes to Washington that is not available to pay for

higher energy bills, higher college costs and higher expenses (*CR*, May 26, 2001, H2837).

The Senate cleared the measure, 58–33, later the same day; two Republicans—Chafee and John McCain of Arizona voted against it; 12 Democrats supported the bill. Senator Gramm praised Bush's role in the passing of the legislation, "Elections have consequences. Leadership makes a difference." Enactment did indeed represent a big victory for President Bush and for congressional Republicans. The largest tax cut since Ronald Reagan's first year in office became law, and it included many of the provisions—across-the-board rate cuts, alleviation of the marriage penalty, and the eventual ending of the estate tax—that Bush had advocated and that the Republican base had long desired.

Once More with Feeling: The 2003 Tax Cut

The 2003 tax cuts again illustrate how crucial the budget process is to the enactment of major policy change in the contemporary Congress. It also shows the ability of the House as currently structured to pass important legislation quickly and with slim partisan majorities and the effects of the Senate's permissive rules, as currently employed by partisan minorities and individuals, on legislative outcomes.

The 2002 elections were a triumph for Bush. He had campaigned hard for Republicans in congressional elections and was rewarded with a highly unusual gain in seats by the president's party in midterm elections. Republicans regained control of the Senate, albeit by the narrow margin of 51–49.

As a top priority, Bush asked Congress for a tax cut of $726 billion over eleven years, with an elimination of the tax on stock dividends as its centerpiece. He justified the tax cut as a necessary stimulus for an economy in the doldrums since the 9/11 attacks; throughout the process, Republicans labeled the proposal a jobs and economic growth plan. Most congressional Republicans strongly supported further big tax cuts, although their views on what form the cuts should take were diverse. Democratic opposition made it clear that the budget process would again have to be used so that the bill would be protected from a Senate filibuster.

Passing the Budget Resolution

After a "lengthy round of 'listening sessions' with rank-and-file Republicans," Budget Committee Chair Jim Nussle of Iowa drafted a budget resolution that included the full $726 billion in tax cuts but otherwise was very austere, calling for spending cuts in Medicare, Medicaid, and most other entitlement programs (except Social Security)—for a total savings of $467 billion over ten years (*CQW,* January 3, 2004, 25). The Budget Committee approved Nussle's draft on a party-line vote, but it soon became clear that it could not pass the House. Republican moderates rebelled, forcing majority party leaders to rewrite the measure significantly. The resolution that went to the floor did not include the tougher spending cuts, but did include the $726 billion for tax cuts. Even so, passing the resolution proved to be difficult and took a "full court press" by the leadership and Vice President Cheney. The resolution passed 215 to 212, with only 1 Democrat voting for it and 12 Republicans voting against.

As usual, the process was even more difficult in the Senate. Don Nickles, the new chair of the Budget Committee, produced a resolution that included the same tax cut figure but lacked the steep cuts in mandatory spending. The committee approved it on a 12 to 11 party-line vote. Floor debate was long and contentious. On March 19, the Senate adopted an amendment by Barbara Boxer, D-Calif., to strike language that would have allowed oil drilling in the Arctic National Wildlife Refuge (ANWR) to be included in the reconciliation bill.

Much more troubling for the Republican leaders, on March 25 Democrat John Breaux offered an amendment that would limit the tax cut to $350 billion. A group of Senate centrists, which included Republicans George Voinovich of Ohio and Olympia Snowe, as well as Breaux, had been working on this alternative that they believed would be more defensible given the likely cost of the Iraq war and the soaring deficits. When the senators who opposed new tax cuts—most of the Democrats and Republican Lincoln Chafee—decided to vote for the Breaux proposal, it passed on a largely party-line vote of 51 to 48, with 47 Democrats, 3 Republicans, and independent Jeffords supporting it.

With most House Republicans passionately committed to big tax cuts, the adoption of the Breaux amendment assured that the conference would be excruciatingly difficult. When, after much cajoling and pressuring, Senate Republican leaders could not find more than forty-eight votes for a budget resolution with a tax cut of more than $350 billion, Majority Leader Bill Frist of Tennessee began advocating that the resolution contain different reconciliation instructions for the House and the Senate, something that had never been done before.

The first version of the strategy did not pass muster with the Senate parliamentarian, but a second version was cleared. The reconciliation instructions would allow the tax committees in both chambers to draft bills that cut taxes by up to $550 billion. However, any bill with more than a $350 billion tax cut would be subject to a sixty-vote point of order on the Senate floor that, everyone knew, proponents could not possibly waive. So, in effect, the Senate would not initially be able to pass a tax bill more expensive than $350 billion. The strategic element that made this approach attractive to proponents of a bigger tax cut was that a conference report that contained a tax cut as big as $550 billion would have reconciliation protections and so would only require a simple majority to pass the Senate.

The House passed the conference report on a tight 216 to 211 vote almost completely along party lines. The Senate moderates, however, refused to go along with the ploy. Voinovich and Snowe agreed to vote for the conference report only after extracting a promise from Majority Leader Frist and Finance Committee Chair Charles Grassley that the tax cut would not exceed $350 billion. The promise made possible the 51 to 50 approval of the budget resolution conference report with Vice President Cheney casting the tie-breaking vote. Republicans Chafee and John McCain voted against it. Only one Democrat—Zell Miller—voted for it.

House Republicans were furious; Frist had reneged on an agreement, they contended. House Majority Leader Tom DeLay of Texas insisted that $550 billion was the binding ceiling. "As far as we're concerned, that's the deal. We expect the Senate leadership to honor the deal," he said (*CQW*, April 12, 2003). Many Senate Republicans were themselves unhappy about the figure and hoped to increase it in the bill itself. "Obviously the House has expressed its feelings, and we have to respect that," said Rick Santorum of Pennsylvania, chair of the Senate Republican Conference. "We are going to do our best to repair it where it matters, and that is to get a bigger tax bill" (*NYT*, April 17, 2003).

Reconciliation

Ways and Means reported a $550 billion tax cut bill on May 6 on a 24–15 party-line vote. Committee Chair Bill Thomas, after ascertaining that Bush's proposal could not garner sufficient Republican votes to pass, came up with a plan that would reduce but not eliminate tax rates on both dividends and capital gains; accelerate the 2001 tax cuts for individuals, as Bush had requested; and provide other tax cuts for business. The House considered the bill under a closed rule allowing no amendments. This meant that Democrats were forced to offer their substitute through a motion to recommit with instructions, the sort of procedural vote that is difficult to exploit electorally and, when Rangel did attempt to offer his substitute in the motion to recommit with instructions, the chair ruled it nongermane and the Democrats' appeal of the ruling of the chair was tabled (i.e., killed) on a party-line vote. The bill passed May 9 by 222 to 203, with only 3 Republicans and 4 Democrats crossing party lines.

Senate Finance Committee Chair Grassley was faced with what proved to be an impossible task. He was under intense pressure from the administration and his leadership to include in his bill a version of Bush's proposal to eliminate the tax on dividends. Conservative Republicans wanted bigger tax breaks. Moderates were insisting that he not exceed $350 billion and that he make the cuts at least a bit more progressive. A number of senators also wanted him to include significant aid to the states, which were suffering because of the recession.

To get the crucial vote of moderate Snowe in the Finance Committee, Grassley reworked his original draft. To stay under $350 billion, Grassley had relied on manipulating the dates when the dividend tax cuts were to go into effect and expire, a method that Snowe considered a "gimmick" (*CQW,* March 10, 2003). Grassley replace his initial plan with a dividend proposal that for each individual taxpayer would exclude the first $500 of dividend income from taxes and give a 10 percent exemption on dividend income over $500. In 2008, the additional exemption would go up to 20 percent.

Conservative Republicans dislike that plan, but it picked up Snowe's vote on the closely divided Finance Committee. Grassley also added $20 billion in aid to the states, which helped him get the vote of Blanche Lincoln of Arkansas, the only Democrat he won. To keep the net cost of his plan down to $350 billion, Grassley also included nearly $90 billion in "offsets," primarily changes in tax law that would increase taxes on businesses. Finance approved the bill 12 to 9. Many committee Republicans voted for the bill only to get it out of committee.

The Republican leadership in both chambers; most Republicans, espeally conservatives; and Republicans' business allies disliked the bill intensely and immediately vowed to change it on the floor. A Republican House member from Florida expressed the sentiment most colorfully:

> Some Republicans in the Senate are making it very difficult to abide by [President] Ronald Reagan's 11th Commandment [thou shalt not criticize fellow Republicans], because they're not acting like Republicans. I think the Capitol Police better check to see if someone's slipped something into the water over there (*CQW,* May 10, 2003, 1087).

Senate consideration began on May 14. Over the course of the two days of debate, the Senate took recorded votes on thirty amendments.[2] Don Nickles, Budget Committee Chair and a conservative member of the Finance Committee, proposed an amendment that would change the dividend provision in a direction more acceptable to the president and most Republicans. The amendment exempted 50 percent of dividend payments from taxation in 2003 and increased that to 100 percent from 2004 through 2006. Dividend tax rates would return to their present levels in 2007.

To adhere to budget rules, offsets also were included to pay for the extra costs. The amendment passed on 51 to 50 vote, with Cheney casting the tie-breaking vote. Two Democrats voted for the amendment—Zell Miller, who had supported the Bush tax cutting agenda since 2001, and Ben Nelson of Nebraska won over by the lure of money for the states. Three Republicans opposed it—John McCain and Lincoln Chafee, who

---

2. Some were not votes on the amendments directly but votes to waive the Budget Act to make the amendment in order.

had opposed tax cuts all year because of concern about the deficit, and Olympia Snowe, who disliked the sunset gimmicks in the amendment. The vote on passage was almost identical, with only Evan Bayh, D-Ind., switching to vote in favor. Although the Nickles amendment made the Senate bill more acceptable to many Republicans, it still included $101 billion in off-setting revenue increases, much of which would fall on businesses. Not only were business groups strongly opposed to these provisions, many House Republicans unalterably opposed tax increases of any sort.

Bush urged a quick resolution to the differences between the chambers' bills and, to effectuate that, the administration threw its weight behind the Thomas plan on dividends. If, as seemed clear, the compromise could not exceed the Senate's figure of $350 billion, Thomas asserted the House should have the greater say on how the tax cut was structured. Grassley objected, but to no avail. The conference agreement included the Thomas provisions on dividends and capital gains; a number of other tax cuts, includ-ing acceleration of the individual income tax rate cuts of 2001 and more gen-erous first-year write-offs for business investment; and $20 billion in aid to the states. The offsets the Senate had included were dropped. To fit the total into the $350 billion total, conferees phased in some tax cuts and set early expiration dates for others. Majority Leader DeLay served as a conferee, but it was Vice President Cheney who played a crucial role in brokering the major deals that made an agreement possible (*CQW*, May 31, 2003, 1306).

On May 23, just before their Memorial Day recess, both the House and the Senate approved the conference report on largely party-line votes. In the House one Republican and seven Democrats crossed party lines. In the Senate, three Republicans—Chafee, McCain, and Snowe—voted against the final bill; two Democrats—Ben Nelson and Zell Miller—voted for it. Again, passage depended on Vice President Cheney's tie-breaking vote.

Cutting Taxes via Unorthodox Lawmaking

When Congress and the White House are controlled by the same party, the budget process offers an extremely useful tool for making sweeping pol-icy change. This is even more true in the early twenty-first century than it was in the early 1990s because the parties have continued to become more ideologically homogeneous and more polarized. Thus, Republicans were able to enact huge tax cuts in 2001 and in 2003 over intense Democratic opposition and despite their narrow margins of control.

The budget process and some of the other tools of unorthodox law-making were indispensable to the majority Republicans' legislative success. Most crucial were the protections from filibusters and nongermane amend-ments that the budget process affords the reconciliation bill. Absent those protections, Senate passage without much more extensive compromise would have been unlikely. The Republican leadership in the House used the now ordinary tools of unorthodox lawmaking, such as highly restrictive rules, to facilitate passage. Republican leaders also extended the boundaries of unorthodox lawmaking, in this case by crafting a budget resolution in 2001 that gave the Budget Committee chair formally—and actually the leadership itself—extraordinary flexibility to adjust the resolution's contents after passage if necessary.

The design of the tax cut bills in itself represents another form of unorthodox lawmaking. By adjusting the dates when tax provisions went into effect and when they expired, Republicans fit a much bigger tax cut into the amounts specified by the budget resolution than would otherwise have been allowed. The sunsets on a number of provisions would never go into effect, most Republicans believed; when they became imminent, political pressure would force extensions of the tax cuts (Hacker and Pierson 2005). Proponents of the tax cuts called the strategy clever; opponents labeled it dishonest and charged it was intended to fool the public. It does seem likely that the strategy could not have been successfully carried out without the tight majority party leadership control over the process in the House and in conference that has become an integral part of unorthodox lawmaking in the twenty-first century.

Budget Policy and Politics since the Early 1990s: A Final Word

This and the preceding two chapters illustrate how much of the major policy and political battles are now fought out through the budget process. Partisanship, already high in the early 1990s, has intensified and strongly shapes these battles. Over this period the political context varied widely— unified Democratic control of government gave way to a new Republican congressional majority with a strong sense of mandate and a seemingly weakened president and this gave way to a revived president and a period of divided control, which gave way to unified Republican government for the first time in half a century.

The budget process and many of the other tools of unorthodox lawmaking proved to be useful in all these contexts. They have made it possible for Congress to legislate successfully in some extremely difficult contexts—when unpalatable decisions needed to be made and when partisan disagreements were intense and margins of control were narrow. By the same token, however, they have made possible enacting major legislation with almost no participation by or support from the minority party. And House Republican leaders' use of the tools of unorthodox lawmaking greatly intensified the partisan hostility in that chamber.

TABLE 12.1 The George W. Bush Tax Cuts of 2001

President George W. Bush formally sends Congress his tax cut proposal on February 8, 2001.

Date	House Action	Date	Senate Action	Date	Postpassage Action
2/13	Treasury Secretary Paul O'Neill testifies before the Ways and Means Committee.				
2/28	HR3 is introduced.				
3/1	Ways and Means Committee marks up and approves HR3, the Economic Growth and Tax Relief Act, a bill cutting income taxes across the board.				
3/8	House approves restrictive rule, debates HR3, and passes it.				
3/11	Budget Committee approves budget resolution calling for four tax cut reconciliation bills.				
3/27–28	House approves structured rule, debates and passes budget resolution, H.Con.Res.83.				
		4/2	Budget Committee discharged. (Majority Leader Trent Lott bypasses Budget Committee and brings budget resolution directly to the floor.) Motion to proceed to consideration of measure agreed to by unanimous consent.		
		4/3–6	Senate considers and passes budget resolution.		

TABLE 12.1 *(Continued)*

Date	House Action	Date	Senate Action	Date	Postpassage Action
		4/4	Harkin amendment reducing the tax cut by $488 billion passes.		
		5/11	*Finance Committee Chair Grassley and Ranking Minority Member Baucus unveil a rough draft of their compromise tax bill.*		
5/15	HR1836, the Economic Growth and Tax Relief Reconciliation Act, introduced. (HR1836 includes major provisions from HR3, the Economic Growth and Tax Relief Act; from HR6, the Marriage Penalty and Family Tax Relief Act; from HR8, the Death Tax Elimination Act; from HR10, the Comprehensive Retirement Security and Pension Reform Act; from HR622, the Adoption Tax Credits bill; and from S896, the Senate budget reconciliation bill.) Bill is referred to Ways and Means. Rules Committee reports rule providing for consideration of HR1836.	5/15	Finance Committee marks up and approves Grassley-Baucus bill.		
5/16	House approves rule; considers and passes HR1836.	5/17, 21–23	Senate debates tax bill.		
		5/23	Senate passes tax bill.		

Date	Action
4/23	Senate asks for conference on budget resolution and names conferees.
4/24	House agrees to conference and names conferees.
4/25	Conference held.
5/3	Conference report filed.
5/9	House considers and agrees to conference report. Senate considers conference report.
5/10 5/23	Senate agrees to conference report. Senate asks for a conference on tax bill and appoints conferees. House agrees to conference and appoints conferees.
5/23–26	Conference meets.
5/26	Conference report filed. House approves conference report. Senate approves conference report.
6/7	President signs, and it becomes law.

Note: Official actions are in roman type; behind-the-scenes, unofficial actions are in italics.

The Consequences
of Unorthodox Lawmaking

UNORTHODOX LAWMAKING has become standard operating procedure in the U.S. Congress—one might almost say it is unorthodox no more. Not only does the textbook model no longer describe how most major legislation becomes—or fails to become—law, no single model has replaced it. Some previously unusual practices, such as significant leadership involvement at the prefloor stage, have become standard but, overall, variety, not uniformity, characterizes the contemporary legislative process. After briefly reviewing the contours of unorthodox lawmaking, this chapter examines its consequences. Do the procedures and practices that constitute unorthodox lawmaking as here defined enhance or hinder a bill's chances of becoming law? Are there other, less measurable costs and benefits of unorthodox lawmaking? Overall, how should observers of Congress assess unorthodox lawmaking?

Lawmaking in the Contemporary Congress

Most major legislation used to follow a single, well-defined process; the question at each stage was simply whether the bill would survive (and in what form) to go on to the next. These days, bills and other important measures confront a series of decision points where more complex choices are at issue, including if the bill will be referred to more than one committee. In the House, rules of committee jurisdiction dictate which committees receive referral, but beyond that, the Speaker also has some discretion.

Usually, the Speaker designates one lead committee; the other committees with jurisdiction may be given additional initial referrals, and the

Speaker likely will impose time limits for action, which may be generous or tight. When a number of committees work on a bill, many perspectives and interests are represented in the bill-drafting process. If the committees come to an agreement among themselves, the supportive coalition for the bill becomes formidable. But the more committees involved, the longer the process is likely to take and the more difficult working out disagreements among the committees is likely to be.

In the Senate, committee leaders usually work out problems of conflicting jurisdiction among themselves, sometimes by agreeing to multiple referral, more often informally; the majority leader lacks the procedural powers of the Speaker and is less likely to take a hand. Fairly frequently, several Senate committees work on different bills that deal with the same subject; such instances can raise many of the same questions and problems as multiple referral does in the House.

Although in both chambers most legislation is referred to committee, the option of bypassing the committee stage altogether does exist; most of the time, it is one that only the party leaders can exercise. Bypassing committee can speed up the process significantly. For that reason, committee leaders sometimes agree wholeheartedly to the strategy, particularly if the committee reported the bill or a very similar one in the previous Congress. Party leaders occasionally bypass committee and draft the legislation themselves or delegate the drafting to a special task force because they believe the committee will not do a satisfactory job. They fear that, because of its membership or the political delicacy of the issue, the committee will not be able to come to an agreement in a reasonable period of time or that it will produce a bill that cannot pass the chamber or is unsatisfactory to significant numbers of majority party members. Frequent bypassing of committees, however, is likely to engender considerable hostility from the membership, majority as well as minority, and leaders who need their party members' votes for reelection to their positions are reluctant to take this action except under extraordinary circumstances.

Once a bill has been reported from committee, the majority party leadership must decide if the bill as reported is ready for floor consideration. That decision depends on the answers to a series of questions: If the bill has been reported from several committees, are there major outstanding differences between the committees' versions? Does the bill as reported command enough support to pass the chamber? Is it satisfactory to most majority party members? If the answer to any of these questions is "no," postcommittee changes to the legislation will have to be negotiated. If the president is a fellow partisan, his views also are likely to be taken into account; provisions he opposes also may occasion postcommittee negotiations.

Once leaders decide postcommittee adjustments are necessary, they are faced with a host of choices about the form such changes should take.

In the House the next decision centers on the type of special rule under which to bring the legislation to the floor. Are there special problems that confront the legislation as a result of multiple referral? Do special provisions have to be made for incorporating a postcommittee compromise into the bill? Are there amendments that members very much do or do not want to vote on? The majority party leadership, in consultation with the Rules Committee majority, designs a rule intended to give the legislation its best chance on the floor. Whereas in the past most rules were simple open rules, and the rest were simple closed rules, now only leaders' creativity and the need for House approval limit the form of rules. More and more the choice is a highly restrictive rule. A majority of the House membership can defeat a rule, but because leaders are sensitive to their party members' preferences, this seldom happens.

In the Senate the majority leader has no such powerful tool at his command. He will often try to work out one or a series of unanimous consent agreements for expeditious and orderly consideration of the legislation on the floor; for success, however, he is dependent on the acquiescence of all senators.

The prerogatives individual senators and the minority party possess give them choices to make at this stage. If they dislike the legislation, should they try to block it from being brought to the floor by putting a hold on it? Should they explicitly threaten to filibuster it? Should they make known to the bill's supporters that they are willing to negotiate? Whatever their sentiments about the bill, if it does come to the floor, what amendments will they offer to the legislation? Should they offer measures not related to the bill's subject matter as nongermane amendments— either to load down the legislation and hurt its chances of enactment or to piggyback their own pet ideas on a popular bill? Should the minority party use the bill as a vehicle to get votes on its agenda? If a bill they strongly dislike passes the chamber, should they try to prevent it from going to conference or filibuster the conference report?

These are the sorts of choices confronting actors in the legislative process on more-or-less ordinary major bills—the kind of legislation discussed in Chapters 7 and 9. Legislative actors also can choose (or be faced with) complex types of legislation and processes that either did not exist at all or were rarely used several decades ago. For example, leaders can decide to package a broad array of provisions into an omnibus bill to raise the visibility of individually modest measures on a popular issue or to make possible the passing of unpalatable but necessary provisions by bundling them with more popular ones. The budget process makes omnibus measures a regular part of the legislative process and forces majority party leaders regularly to deal with the problems passing such broad measures creates.

Central leaders—the majority party leaders but also the president— can use the budget process as a mechanism for attempting to make comprehensive policy change, something that the legislative process as it functioned before the 1974 Congressional Budget and Impoundment Control Act made extremely difficult. When the president and the congressional majority cannot come to an agreement on major legislation through normal processes, they may decide to try a summit—formal negotiations between congressional leaders and high-level representatives of the president or even the president himself. Summits are unlikely to be required when the president and the congressional majority are fellow partisans, but high partisan polarization has made them increasingly necessary when the branches are controlled by different parties.

Congressional actors—especially congressional majority party leaders but also individual senators and the Senate minority party—now have more choices, and the alternatives they choose lead to different legislative processes. Majority party leaders make most of their choices with the aim of facilitating the passage of legislation; individual senators and the Senate minority party may have quite different aims in mind. When, as they often do, congressional actors make choices that produce a legislative process that is unorthodox by the standards of the old textbook model, what is the effect on whether the bill becomes a law?

Unorthodox Lawmaking and Legislative Outcomes

I have argued that changes in the legislative process can be seen as the responses of members to the problems and opportunities that the institutional structure and the political environment present as members individually or collectively pursue their goals of reelection, influence in the chamber, and good public policy. Specifically, I have contended that a number of the innovations and modifications were driven by the difficulties in legislating that internal reforms and a hostile political climate created for majority Democrats in the 1980s. When Republicans won control of Congress in the mid-1990s and a Republican president took office in 2001, Republicans adapted the process to the problem they faced: passing an ambitious agenda with narrow margins. If the aim was to facilitate successful lawmaking, does unorthodox lawmaking, in fact, do so?

Most bills do not become law. The House has been passing an average of 14 percent of the bills introduced by its members in recent Congresses (100th through 106th) and the Senate slightly more than 24 percent; and of course, passage in one chamber does not ensure enactment (Ornstein, Mann, and Malbin 2002, 146–147). Thousands of bills are introduced in each chamber during each Congress; neither chamber could possibly consider each one, so most are referred to committee and die there without any further action. Members introduce legislation for a variety of reasons, ranging from placating an interest group in their home state or district to

TABLE 13.1   The Fate of Major Legislation, 1989–1990, 1993–1998, 2001–2004

	Percentage of major measures	Number of major measures
Total measures	100	300
Reached House floor	93	278
Reached Senate floor	83	248
Passed House	88	265
Passed Senate	72	217
Passed House and Senate	71	212
Became law*	59	178

*Or otherwise successfully completed the legislative process. This means approval of the conference report in both chambers in the case of budget resolutions and approval by two-thirds vote in each chamber in the case of constitutional amendments.

Source: Computed by the author.

publicizing a little-recognized problem or an innovative approach to an acknowledged problem. Members may not expect certain of their bills to pass and, sometimes, may not even want them to.

Major legislation is different; by definition, it is significant legislation that has made it on to the congressional agenda where it is being seriously considered. As Table 13.1 shows, its prospects are considerably brighter than that of all legislation. Most major measures get to the floor of at least one chamber, and those that do usually pass—although the likelihood is considerably greater in the House than in the Senate. About seven of ten major measures pass both chambers, and about six out of ten become law or otherwise successfully finish the process.[1] Thus, measures that have attained the status of being considered major legislation on the congressional agenda do tend to become law, but it is no sure thing.

How do the special procedures and practices that often characterize the legislative process on these major bills affect their probability of successful enactment? An examination of the relationship between the number of special procedures and practices used and legislative success provides at least a partial answer. The cumulative indexes introduced in Chapter 5 are used. For each of the major bills in seven recent Congresses (the 100th, 101st, 103rd, 104th, 105th, 107th, and 108th), the House measure counts the number of the following special procedures and practices that the legislation encountered as it worked its way through that chamber: multiple referral, omnibus, the result of a summit, committee bypassed, postcommit-

1. Legislative success is defined as enactment in the case of bills, as approval of the conference report in both chambers in the case of budget resolutions, and as approval by two-thirds vote in each chamber in the case of constitutional amendments.

TABLE 13.2   The Effect of Unorthodox Lawmaking on Legislative Success, by Chamber, 1987–1990, 1993–1998, 2001–2004

	Number of special practices and procedures*	All major measures	
		Percentage that passed chamber	Percentage enacted
House	0	75	54
	1	85	63
	2	93	59
	3 or more	97	73
Senate	0	66	56
	1	80	62
	2 or more	89	79

*The number of the following special procedures and practices that the legislation encountered as it worked its way through the chamber: for the House, multiple referral, omnibus legislation, legislation was the result of a legislative-executive branch summit, the bypassing of committees, postcommittee adjustments, and consideration under a complex or closed rule; for the Senate, all of the above except consideration under a complex or closed rule.

Source: Computed by the author.

tee adjustments, and consideration under a restrictive rule. The Senate measure is identical, except that it does not include consideration under a restrictive rule.

The likelihood that a bill will pass the House increases with the number of special procedures and practices employed and the same is true for the Senate. When the legislative process on a bill in the House includes at least one special procedure or practice, that legislation is considerably more likely to become law than if it includes none and, if it includes three or more, it is still more likely to successfully complete the legislative process (see Table 13.2). Again, the relationship is similar for the Senate.

Because becoming law requires that both chambers pass the legislation, the combination of special procedures and practices in the two chambers should make a difference. As Table 13.3 shows, it does. Of measures subject to two or more special procedures and practices in both chambers, 79 percent were successful; at the other extreme, if subject to none in either chamber, only 58 percent were successful.

Of course, other things being equal, leaders are more likely to use these procedures and practices on the most important legislation—legislation they believe really must pass for the good of country or party. Yet leaders are unlikely to employ the special procedures and practices under their control unless they expect passing the bill in satisfactory form will be problematic. Negotiating postcommittee adjustments and crafting and

TABLE 13.3   The Cumulative Effect of Unorthodox Lawmaking on Legislative
Success, 1987–1990, 1993–1998, 2001–2004

Number of special procedures and practices*	Percentage of all major measures enacted
None in either chamber	58
None in one chamber, one in the other chamber, or one in each chamber	58
All other combinations except two or more in both chambers	62
Two or more in both chambers	79

*The number of the following special procedures and practices that the legislation encountered as it worked its way through the chamber: for the House, multiple referral, omnibus legislation, legislation was the result of a legislative-executive branch summit, the bypassing of committees, postcommittee adjustments, and consideration under a complex or closed rule; for the Senate, all of the above except consideration under a complex or closed rule.

Source: Computed by the author.

passing restrictive rules, not to mention bypassing committee, take time and resources; if the legislation is going to pass without trouble, why expend either? Therefore, when the legislative process displays several special procedures and practices, the chances are that the bill was in some trouble and that, without intervention, its chances of legislative success were lower than those of other legislation. Since the data show a higher frequency of legislative success, these special procedures and practices do appear to accomplish their purpose.

The special practices stemming from the Senate's unique rules can be used by individual senators and by the minority party and may well be employed for different purposes and have different consequences than those that are primarily leadership tools. What impact do amending marathons and filibusters have on legislative outcomes? Amending marathons are associated with legislative success. Bills subject to ten or more Senate amendments decided by roll call votes are as likely to pass the Senate and more likely to become law than are other measures (see Table 13.4).

The adoption of floor amendments may enhance a bill's chances of ultimate legislative success as amendments may make a bill more broadly attractive or at least give the sponsors of successful amendments a greater stake in the legislation's enactment. However, the substantial differences in success rates between bills subject to high amending activity and those subject to low amending activity (regardless of whether the amendments that were offered passed) strongly suggest that senators engage in amending marathons on bills highly likely to become law. Senators sometimes use the Senate's permissive amending rules to try to kill legislation, but

TABLE 13.4   Amending Marathons, Filibusters, and Legislative Outcomes
for Major Measures, 1987–1990, 1993–1998, 2001–2004
(in percentages)

Outcome	Amending marathon*		Filibuster problem	
	Yes	No	Yes	No
Passed Senate	91	87	72	84
Enacted	79	69	57	70

*An amending marathon is defined as ten or more amendments offered and pushed to a roll call vote. Only measures that reached the Senate floor are included.

Source: Computed by the author.

that is not their primary use; they primarily use such bills as vehicles for lawmaking.

The uses senators make of extended debate are much less benign in purpose and in effect, and extended debate has its most severe impact on legislative outputs when employed as a partisan tool. Legislation subject to a filibuster problem (a hold, a threatened filibuster, or a filibuster) is less likely to pass the Senate and less likely to become law than is other legislation (see Table 13.4). In recent Congresses 84 percent of legislation that did not encounter any extended debate–related problem passed the Senate and 70 percent became law; in contrast, only 72 percent of measures that ran into a filibuster–related problem passed the Senate and 57 percent became law. Almost half of the major measures that failed to pass the Senate (48 percent) encountered a filibuster problem. Of all measures that failed to complete the entire process, 49 percent encountered a filibuster problem.

Extended debate–related problems have had quite different effects on legislative success in different Congresses. In the 101st Congress, whether a measure ran into a filibuster problem had little impact on its chances of enactment, and the same is true for the 97th Congress, for which data are also available. In these Congresses, the filibuster had not yet become a predominantly partisan tool. In the 103rd through 105th and in the 108th Congresses the impact was major. In the 103rd, minority party Republicans pursued a strategy heavily based on the filibuster; in the 104th, 105th, and 108th Congresses, the minority Democrats pursued a filibuster-based strategy.[2] Only 67 percent of major measures that encountered an extended debate–related problem in these Congresses passed the Senate, whereas 83 percent of major bills that did not encounter a filibuster problem passed.

2. In the 107th Congress, in which Senate control switched from Republicans to Democrats, there is no relationship between either Senate passage or enactment and whether a major measure encountered a filibuster problem.

Fifty percent of those with a filibuster problem were enacted compared to 66 percent of those without such a problem. Since about half of all major measures in these Congresses were subject to a filibuster problem, the impact on enactment was substantial.

Of course, filibusters, actual and threatened, can influence outcomes without killing the legislation at issue. The perpetrators' aim, in fact, may be to extort substantive concessions from the bill's supporters rather than to kill the bill altogether. Those measures that became law despite a filibuster problem show a high incidence of postcommittee adjustments (about 45 percent for the 101st, 103rd–105th, and 107th–108th), suggesting that substantive alterations were required to overcome the filibuster problem.

Other Costs and Benefits

What effect does unorthodox lawmaking have beyond its impact on legislative outcomes? Scholars know that even planned changes in complex organizations and processes are likely to have unintended consequences; many of the changes examined here were not planned but evolved out of ad hoc responses to pressing problems.

Deliberation and Inclusion in the House

Congress has long done its serious substantive work on legislation in committees. A number of the procedures and practices that constitute unorthodox lawmaking were a response to the decline in the committees' autonomy and power; however, procedures and practices such as multiple referral, postcommittee adjustments, and the bypassing of committees have further eroded the committees' influence, at least to some extent. Has the result been less expertly crafted legislation and less deliberation at the pre-floor stage of the process? If so, this would be a serious negative byproduct of unorthodox lawmaking, since this is when real deliberation takes place, if it takes place at all.

At least before the 104th Congress, pre-floor deliberation had not, by and large, been sacrificed. It is when committees are bypassed that the possibility that deliberation will be truncated is greatest. Yet in many cases, when a committee was bypassed in a particular Congress, the committee had, in fact, reported the legislation in a previous Congress. In those instances when Democratic House leaders used task forces rather than committees to draft legislation, they chose as task force leaders members who brought great substantive as well as political expertise to bear on the issue (Sinclair 1995, 188–192).

During the 104th Congress, House Republican leaders put extraordinary pressure on committees to report legislation quickly. Hearings, if they were held at all, were perfunctory; mark-ups often were hurried and were held before most members had had an opportunity to study the legislative language at issue; they were, in effect, pro forma. Party leaders and task forces on which inexperienced freshmen predominated exercised considerable influence on the substance of legislation in committee or through postcommittee adjustments; committees were frequently bypassed both to move legislation more quickly and for substantive reasons. Deliberation and the quality of legislation did suffer. Many Republicans, members and staff alike, concede privately that the legislation brought to the floor was sloppy at best; the careful substantive work had not been done.

The power of Congress, especially that of the House, in the political system depends on its specialized, expert committees. The issues and problems with which the federal government deals are too numerous, diverse, and complex for any one person to master. For a relatively small body such as Congress to hold its own vis-à-vis the executive branch and outside interests, it must divide labor and rely on its members' expertise in their area of specialization. Has unorthodox lawmaking decreased the incentives for members to specialize and gain expertise?

In the 104th House, especially during 1995, substantive expertise and hard work on one's committee had relatively little payoff in influence. The modes of decision making prevalent during that Congress arose out of highly unusual circumstances—a new House majority after forty years and the attendant sense of mandate. Committees began to regain influence in 1996 and, in the 105th and 106th Congresses, committee processes were in many ways similar to those before the Republican takeover. To be sure, the parties remained polarized, and the Republican seat margin was narrow, which led to the persistence of somewhat greater centralization. The difficulties of legislating under these circumstances forced the majority party leadership to involve itself in all phases of the legislative process.

With the accession of George W. Bush to the presidency, however, the House Republican leadership, determined to deliver for their president, again dominated legislative decision making on top priority legislation, effectively subordinating the committees. Committee chairs and other senior majority party members might play important roles, but most other committee members, majority as well as minority, were cut out of the action. And, if they were not sufficiently responsive to White House wishes, even committee chairs could find themselves relegated to the sidelines, their committee bypassed or legislation reported by committee replaced with an administration-approved version. If this mode of decision making were to persist, the incentives for members of the House to develop committee expertise would likely weaken severely.

Senators specialize less than they used to, but this is not a recent phenomenon, dating back to the 1970s. Even now notable specialists still exist. Effective senators must develop some expertise; they must know what they are talking about to be taken seriously. To some extent, senators can substitute staff expertise for personal expertise, and it was the increase in staff, especially in the 1970s, that made it possible for senators to involve themselves effectively in more issues than once was possible.

Ensuring that the broadest possible range of interests is heard and considered is as important as expertise to an effective legislative process. What effect has unorthodox lawmaking had on the likelihood that the full range of views and interests will find a hearing? From that perspective, unorthodox lawmaking as practiced in the 104th House was problematic. When, as was common during the Contract with America period in early 1995, committees do not hold meaningful hearings, an important forum for the expression of a diversity of views is unavailable. To an unprecedented extent, the minority party was excluded from decision making at the pre-floor stage; committee procedures made meaningful participation impossible. The real decisions often were made elsewhere, within Republican-only task forces or by the Republican leadership itself. Interest groups that the Republican Party considered hostile—environmental groups, for example—were not given access to make their case, whereas the party's business allies participated in drafting legislation in which they had a direct interest.

Understandably, the first Republican House majority in forty years had a lot it wanted to accomplish; these extraordinary circumstances led to the truncated process. Furthermore, Republicans paid a price for their exclusionary procedures. Because neither the committees nor the leadership did the hard and often ideologically painful work of building a coalition broad enough to survive the entire process, much of the legislation passed by the House did not become law; excluded interests blocked it elsewhere.

The high costs of exclusion led the House Republicans to temper their ways in the late 1990s. When Bush became president, however, the tendency towards more inclusiveness and greater attempts at bipartisan compromise in committee was reversed. With narrow margins and an ambitious agenda, House Republicans regularly excluded Democrats from real participation in committee on major legislation. Decisions were often made in behind-the-scenes informal negotiation sessions that included only majority party members. Even when they won in committee, a rare occurrence, minority party members were likely to see their victory annulled by post-committee adjustments directed by the Republican leadership.

To be sure, Democrats, when they were the majority party before 1995, employed some of the practices and procedures of unorthodox lawmaking in ways that excluded the minority from effective decision making in the pre-floor legislative process in the House. In the 1980s and early 1990s, most (though not all) Democratic task forces consisted of Democrats only. When Democratic leaders negotiated postcommittee adjustments to bills, they were most likely to do so among Democrats. As a more diverse party and one accustomed to governing, Democrats did not exclude major interests from receiving a hearing, nor did they truncate the committee process.

Finally, in evaluating the effects of unorthodox lawmaking on the inclusiveness of the pre-floor legislative process in the House, one must remember that the orthodox process often could be highly exclusionary. One committee had a monopoly on legislative action in a given area and was not necessarily responsive to the wishes of the chamber or of the majority party. Decisions were made behind closed doors, and the membership of many committees was biased in a way that favored some interests and excluded others. Diffuse interests—consumer and environmental interests in particular, which are seldom represented by wealthy and well-connected organizations—had little access.

Have specially tailored and usually restrictive special rules for House floor consideration of legislation degraded floor deliberation, as both Republican and Democratic minorities have claimed? It is unrealistic, I would argue, to expect deliberation, as a great many people use the term, to take place on the floor of either chamber and certainly not in the House. If deliberation is defined as the process by which a group of people gets together and talks through a complex problem, maps the problem's contours, defines the alternatives, and figures out where the members stand, it is unrealistic to expect all of that to occur on the chamber floors. Deliberation is a nonlinear, free-form process that depends on strict limits on the size of the group; subcommittees, other small groups, and possibly, committees are the forums in which it might be fostered. Deliberation so defined certainly did not occur on the House floor before restrictive rules became prevalent.

What can and should be expected on the chamber floors is informed and informative debate and sound decision making. Restrictive rules can, in fact, contribute toward those goals. Rules can provide order and predictability to the floor consideration of complex and controversial legislation. They can be used to ensure that floor time is apportioned in a reasonably sensible way, both within a given bill and across legislation, and that debate focuses on the major alternatives, not on minor or side issues. In addition, through the use of restrictive rules, committee compromises can be protected from being picked apart on the floor.[3]

---

3. Formal theorists have shown that, for any bill of more than minimal complexity (technically, any bill involving more than one dimension of choice), there exists an alternative that can defeat it (and, of course, there then exists an alternative that can defeat that one, ad infinitum). This result means that the legislators' preferences are not and cannot be the sole determinant of the legislative outcome because there is no single choice that a majority prefers to all others; the legislative outcome is also a function of the body's rules. For an accessible review of this literature, see Krehbiel (1988).

One's conclusions about the appropriate form of special rules depend on what sorts of decisions one believes can and cannot be made well on the House floor. The membership as a whole can and should make the big decisions; it can and should choose among the major alternatives that have been proposed. A body of 435 should not, I believe, get involved in a detailed rewriting of legislation on the floor via multitudes of individual amendments; the chamber is too large and unwieldy, the necessary expertise often is lacking, and the time almost always is too short for full consideration of the impact of proposed changes. Restrictive rules, in and of themselves, need not damage the quality of House floor consideration.

Yet when committee processes do not allow real deliberation, and especially when the minority is excluded from meaningful participation at the prefloor stage, highly restrictive rules become much more problematic. Democrats, when in the majority, sometimes used rules that were unnecessarily restrictive. Republicans, however, made extremely restrictive floor procedures standard operating procedure, using closed rules much more frequently than Democrats ever did. Their regular employment of self-executing rules that incorporate language into the bill without a vote also was troubling because it obscured responsibility for legislation decisions.

Informed floor decision making requires that members not directly involved in the crafting of legislation nevertheless have available sufficient information to make a considered choice. When Congress legislates through large omnibus measures, the likelihood increases that members will not know about or understand all of the measures' provisions. When high-level summits make legislative decisions, members also are likely to face information problems. This is not a situation unique to such unorthodox processes of lawmaking; it also occurs with much other complex legislation.

Minority exclusion from the pre-floor legislative process exacerbates the information problem. If minority party committee members do not know what the bill contains they cannot serve as sources of information for their fellow partisans. The Republican leadership routinely had the Rules Committee meet in the evening—often late into the night—to grant a rule for a bill the language of which had just been finalized; the bill was then brought to the floor the next morning. Layover requirements were regularly waived, so that members and their aides were often physically unable to read the bill. The result was that even most majority party members lacked detailed information on the legislation they were being asked to vote on.

Republicans' tendency to exclude minority party members from participation in conference negotiations again presented the minority with a serious information problem. However, again the problem was not restricted to the minority and sometimes not even to rank and file majority members. Sometimes even most majority party conferees were unaware of what was being inserted into the conference report. In fact, formal meetings of conferences to approve reports often were not held. Rather, the necessary signatures were gathered by staff, and members signed without actually seeing the final language. The decisions had been made by a small group of majority party committee and party leaders. Although not a new practice by any means, the regular waiving of layover requirements for conference reports became increasingly problematic as the number of members with knowledge of what was in those reports shrank.

The way in which the Republican leadership ran the House floor led to members spending little time in Washington. The House typically considered only suspensions early in the week: either the House was not in session at all on Mondays or only suspensions were on the schedule. On Tuesdays, only suspensions were considered, and all recorded votes from both days were postponed until 6:30 p.m. At that time, the votes were stacked; that is, they were taken in succession with no legislative business in between. The first was a fifteen-minute vote, the succeeding ones were shortened to five minutes.

With major legislation being considered under highly restrictive rules, the floor time consumed was considerably less than in the past. Most members arrived just in time for the recorded votes that had been postponed until 6:30 p.m. on Tuesday and left after the last vote on Thursday. The House seldom had real legislative sessions on Friday. The 2006 House schedule, for example, called for votes during the day on only seventy-one days, with votes scheduled no earlier than 6:30 p.m. on an additional twenty-six days. In contrast, Congress was in session an average 140 days a year during the 1980s and 1990s (*Roll Call,* March 7, 2006).

This drastically truncated Washington work week made it hard for committees and subcommittees to get much serious work done, particularly as work groups or collective entities. For members, meetings conflicted, and committees and subcommittees had difficulty getting quorums. Even if committees had been inclined toward serious oversight hearings, time pressure militated against such activity. Congress expert Norman Ornstein reports a steep drop in the number of committee and subcommittee meetings: "the average Congress in the 1960s and '70s had 5,372 committee and subcommittee meetings; in the 1980s and 1990s, the average was 4,793. In the last Congress, the 108th, the number was 2,135" (*RC,* March 7, 2006). Committees used to be forums in which representatives got to know members of the other party; that has become much less so in recent years.

Decision Making in the Senate

In the Senate, the most striking manifestation of unorthodox lawmaking is senators' increasingly frequent exploitation of extended debate.

Does this trend in the Senate have consequences beyond the blocking of specific legislation? Are there benefits not otherwise attainable that outweigh the costs?

The habitual exploitation of extended debate by senators has a pervasive impact on the legislative process that extends far beyond its effect on specific legislation. By requiring a supermajority to pass legislation that is at all controversial, it makes the coalition-building process much more difficult and increases a status quo–oriented system's tendency toward gridlock. The costs of prolonged gridlock can be severe; a government that cannot act, that cannot respond satisfactorily to its citizens' demands, loses its legitimacy.

Supporters of the filibuster argue that it promotes deliberation; by slowing the legislative process, it provides an opportunity for second thoughts and perhaps for cooler heads to prevail. Furthermore, many argue, it gives extra weight to intensity in the process, allowing an intense minority to protect itself from a possibly tyrannical majority.

In reply one can argue that, quite apart from extended debate in the Senate, the legislative process advantages intensity. For example, the committee assignment process (in which members' preferences are given substantial weight) and members' considerable freedom in both chambers to choose the issues to which they will devote their time result in greater influence being exercised by those with the more intense preferences on an issue (Shepsle 1978; Hall 1987). Deliberation is promoted by ensuring that a minority has time to attempt to raise public opposition to a proposal it believes unwise, but guaranteeing the minority an opportunity to publicize its views need not require such a difficult cloture procedure. If Rule 22 were altered so that the longer a measure is debated on the floor, the smaller the supermajority needed for cloture, the minority would have the floor time to make its case but would not be able to block action on majority-supported legislation forever.

Individuals and small groups of senators frequently have used the Senate's permissive amending rules in combination with extended debate to highlight neglected issues and policy proposals. Their aim has been to get their issues on the public agenda, to push them to the center of debate, and perhaps to pressure the Senate into legislative action. Now the minority party regularly uses this strategy to force on to the agenda issues the majority party would rather not consider. The minority party's aim is to raise the visibility of the issues, to compel wide-ranging debate, and to pass legislation if possible. Yet within the current climate, the result more often than not is neither debate nor legislative action on either the minority's or the majority's agenda. The majority uses procedural devices to prevent debate and action on the minority's agenda, and the minority reciprocates by blocking the majority's agenda.

This state of affairs requires remedy if the Senate is to function adequately. A deal in which the minority party receives a right to full floor consideration of its issues in return for the majority party's eventually getting a simple majority vote on passing its bills might be to the advantage of both. However, as long as the House is so tightly controlled by the majority party and the minority is excluded from meaningful participation in the legislative process, any bipartisan agreement on reform in the Senate is inconceivable. The minority party sees the Senate as its only forum for influencing policy outcomes.

To have a positive effect on how the Senate functions, any change in Senate rules must be made through normal processes. In 2005, Republicans threatened to change the rules for presidential nominations through a highly controversial procedure that required only a simple majority. This "nuclear option" would have entailed the Senate's presiding officer ruling — against established Senate precedents — that cutting off debate on nominations only requires a simple majority. Democrats would, of course, have appealed the ruling, but only a simple majority is required to uphold a ruling of the chair. If such a rules change had been brought about through the nuclear option, the current partisan rancor would have been enormously exacerbated. The pressures toward bipartisanship on legislation not at the center of the parties' agendas that Senate rules now exert would certainly have been overwhelmed.

Assessing Unorthodox Lawmaking

Overall, then, how do we rate unorthodox lawmaking? A broader assessment requires some discussion of the appropriate criteria for judging Congress. Unless we are clear about what it is we want Congress to do, how are we to evaluate the impact of unorthodox lawmaking?

Certainly, we expect Congress to represent us; we expect members to bring into the legislative process the views, needs, and desires of their constituents, and we expect Congress as an institution to provide a forum in which the interests and demands of all segments of society are expressed. But beyond this, we also want Congress to make decisions — to pass laws.

This second criterion has sometimes been labeled lawmaking, but obviously not just any laws will do. In characterizing what sort of laws Congress is expected to pass, two criteria are frequently mentioned and often conflated. First, Congress should pass laws that reflect the will of the people; that is, Congress should be responsive to popular majorities. Second, Congress should pass laws that deal promptly and effectively with pressing national problems. These two criteria, which can be labeled responsiveness and responsibility, are distinct. Only in a perfect world would what the majority wants always accord with what policy experts deem most likely to be effective. Both responsiveness and responsibility are values we would like Congress to further in its lawmaking, yet at times they may come into conflict.

In popular and journalistic discourse, members of Congress are admonished to "do what's right, not what's popular." But do we really want Congress to regularly thwart popular majorities? Furthermore, and critically, uncertainty about the link between a specific policy choice and the societal outcome means that, in most major policy areas, legitimate differences of opinion as to what constitutes good public policy exist. Members of Congress also are told to pay attention to the people, not to special interests or out-of-touch experts; yet how should Congress respond when what the people want is based on faulty logic or incorrect information, a not infrequent occurrence given citizens' inattention to public policy problems? And what if the majority in question is a slim or relatively indifferent one and the minority passionately dissents?

Some tension among the values of representation, responsiveness, and responsibility is unavoidable. The institutional structures and processes most conducive to each are not necessarily the same. A decentralized, open, permeable body in which individual members have considerable resources and autonomy of action has great potential for representation— for articulating the broad variety of opinions and interests in our society. A more centralized, hierarchical body is more capable of expeditious decision making. Decision-making processes highly exposed to public scrutiny further responsiveness; those that are less visible may promote responsibility. Representation takes time, especially when there are a great variety of viewpoints; by definition, lawmaking requires closure, an end to debate, and, implicitly or explicitly, a choice among competing alternatives. Thus, it is logically impossible to maximize all three values simultaneously. It would require an institution and a legislative process that make decisions quickly and slowly at the same time, ones that both expose members to the full force of public opinion and also provide some insulation.

If we expect a Congress that gives all interests a full and fair hearing on each issue and then, in every case, expeditiously passes legislation that both satisfies a majority, preferably a large one, and effectively addresses the problem in question, we are doomed to disappointment. Congress has never been able to live up to that standard, and the environment in which the contemporary Congress functions makes that even less feasible than in the past. The problems facing the country are highly complex. On many, there is little consensus among the experts about the appropriate governmental response; on others, the experts' prescriptions are unpalatable. Citizens are divided, unclear, and often ambivalent in their views as to what they want government to do. Political elites, including the representatives citizens elect, are sharply divided with regard to what they believe constitutes good public policy.

If, as I have argued, it is logically impossible for Congress to be perfectly representative, responsive, and responsible at the same time, and if the climate in which it currently functions is a difficult one, how should we evaluate unorthodox lawmaking? I argued in previous editions of this book that so long as unorthodox lawmaking facilitates Congress's ability to make decisions without sacrificing deliberation or restricting significantly the range of interests with access to the process, it performs an extremely important function. My conclusion was that, through the mid-1990s, unorthodox lawmaking on balance made it possible for Congress to carry out its essential function of lawmaking during an exceedingly tough time and had done so without unacceptably sacrificing other core values.

However, in the period since Republicans won control and especially from 2001 through 2006, the balance between deliberation and inclusiveness on the one hand and expeditious lawmaking on the other tilted too far toward expeditiousness at the expense of the other values, particularly in the House. The combination of a severely truncated Washington schedule, committees that had neither the time nor the incentives to legislate or carry out oversight seriously, tightly controlled floor consideration and conference decision making, and minority exclusion from meaningful participation at any stage of the process produced a legislative process in which deliberation was slighted and representation and responsiveness were skewed. Thoughtful critics such as Thomas Mann and Norman Orenstein argued that the result was often "poor laws and flawed policy" (2006, 145–146).

Certainly, when a large minority of the House membership is excluded from participation in the legislative process, it is unclear whether the legislation passed is really responsive to the public's needs and wishes. By aggressively using unorthodox procedures for partisan ends, House Republican leaders made possible the enactment of legislation entailing sweeping domestic policy change despite their narrow margins. Yet President Bush's signature legislative achievements remain contested. The Medicare/prescription drug bill; many of the tax cuts, the termination of the estate tax in particular; and even the No Child Left Behind Act continue to excite great controversy, the latter because Democrats and many state officials claim Bush reneged on funding promises; these major policy departures have not become broadly accepted.

The 2006 elections brought in new majorities in both chambers. The new Democratic leaders promised to operate in a more bipartisan and fair manner. Senate majority leaders have little choice but to deal with the minority. The large Republican minority in the 110th Congress quickly began using its prerogatives under Senate rules to extract concessions from the majority. It also sought to block measures, such as the resolution opposing President Bush's troop surge in Iraq. As in the past, the majority leadership either compromises or the result is stalemate.

In the House, where the problems of minority exclusion and lack of information have been much greater, Democrats pledged themselves to some fairly specific changes during their campaign. They committed to giving members at least twenty-four hours to examine a bill before it is considered in committee, initially on the House floor or as a conference report; to "generally" considering bills on the floor under "a procedure that allows open, full and fair debate"; to restricting recorded votes to the customary seventeen minutes; and to requiring regular and open conference committee meetings in which all conferees are given an opportunity to vote on all amendments.[4] The rules package put together by the new majority and adopted by the House at the beginning of the 110th Congress prohibits the Speaker from holding open votes for "the sole purpose of changing the outcome," "requires House conferees to insist that conference committees operate in an open and fair manner and that House conferees sign the final conference papers at one time and in one place," and "prohibits the consideration of a conference report that has been altered after the time it was signed by conferees" (Summary of House Rule Package, Prepared by the House Rules Committee, January 2007). The package also contains strong language on making earmarks transparent and reinstitutes PAYGO.

The new Democratic majority has ample incentives to engage in oversight of an opposition-party administration, and committees began hearings on a variety of programs and policies immediately. During the campaign, Democrats promised to expand the workweek and spend more time in Washington attending to congressional duties. They delivered on that promise during their first weeks in control and, because Democrats have much they wish to accomplish, Congress is likely to continue holding to a longer Washington workweek. Democratic committee leaders and members are likely to insist on returning to a legislative process that gives committees a greater role. All these changes further deliberation.

The Democrats' pledge to include the minority in a more open legislative process will be harder to stick with. Whether chairs will be able to deliver on their vow to include the minority in committee decision making will depend more on the issue and on the role the minority decides to play than on good intentions. Despite their complaints about the Republican majority's use of closed rules, Democrats brought all of their "Hundred Hours" agenda legislation to the floor under highly restrictive rules, and none of the measures had gone through committee. The imperative of

---

4. "A New Direction for Democrats" at www.housedemocrats.gov.

keeping their legislative promises trumped their promises about an open process. Since then, the leadership's record on rule restrictiveness has been mixed.

Both polarization and narrow margins continue, so the temptation to use the tools the House majority party leadership possesses in a heavy-handed fashion often will be strong. However, House Democrats tend to be less ideologically homogeneous than the Republican majority they replaced, and many Republicans seemed chastened by the elections; so members of both parties may see more benefit in working together toward bipartisan compromises. The Democratic leadership, needing to establish a record of legislative productivity, also may have incentives to work with Republicans at least periodically, and that will require maintaining a more inclusive legislative process. It is unlikely that the Democratic leadership will eschew the tools of unorthodox lawmaking altogether, however; they are much too useful.

The development of what I have called unorthodox lawmaking is the latest chapter in an ongoing story of congressional adaptation and change. Confronted by a political and institutional environment that made lawmaking difficult, congressional leaders modified and sometimes transformed existing procedures and practices as they attempted to do their job of facilitating lawmaking. The result, unorthodox lawmaking, is often not neat and not pretty, especially on those highly salient and contentious issues most likely to lead the news. It is, however, highly flexible and so can be tailored to the problems—political, substantive, and procedural—that a particular major measure raises. To be sure, it can be used in ways that skew the balance between deliberation and expeditiousness, and I have argued House Republican leaders did, in fact, do so. The verdict on the Democratic majority in the 110th Congress is still out.

Even so, unorthodox lawmaking on balance represents successful adaptation to a tough environment. It need not lead to the sacrificing of deliberation or the restricting of the range of interests with access to the process. It has not made it possible for Congress consistently to make laws that both reflect the will of the people and deal promptly and effectively with pressing national problems. No process can ensure that. Unorthodox lawmaking tends to empower House majorities and Senate minorities but, on balance, it has made it possible for our most representative branch to continue to perform its essential function of lawmaking in a time of popular division and ambiguity; it has thereby given us all the opportunity to work toward a political system in which the branch closest to the people better performs the tough tasks we assign to it.

References

Bach, Stanley. 1994. "Legislating: Floor and Conference Procedures in Congress." In *Encyclopedia of the American Legislative System*, vol. 2, ed. Joel Silbey. New York: Scribner's.

Bach, Stanley, and Steven S. Smith. 1988. *Managing Uncertainty in the House of Representatives*. Washington, D.C.: Brookings Institution.

Beth, Richard. 1994. "Control of the House Floor Agenda: Implications from the Use of the Discharge Rule, 1931–1994." Paper presented at the annual meeting of the American Political Science Association, New York, September 1–4.

———. 1995. "What We Don't Know about Filibusters." Paper presented at the meeting of the Western Political Science Association, Portland, Oregon, March 15–18.

———. 2003. "Motions to Proceed to Consider in the Senate: Who Offers Them?" Congressional Research Service Report RS21255.

———. 2005. " 'Entrenchment' of Senate Procedure and the 'Nuclear Option' for Change: Possible Proceedings and the Implications." Congressional Research Service Report RL32843.

Beth, Richard, and Elizabeth Rybicki. 2003. "Sufficiency of Signatures on Conference Reports." Congressional Research Service Report RS21629.

Binder, Sarah. 1996. "The Partisan Basis of Procedural Choice: Parliamentary Rights in the House, 1798–1990." *American Political Science Review* (March): 8–20.

———. 1997. *Minority Rights, Majority Rule: Partisanship and the Development of Congress*. New York: Cambridge University Press.

Binder, Sarah, and Steven S. Smith. 1997. *Politics or Principle? Filibustering in the United States Senate.* Washington, D.C.: Brookings Institution.

Cohen, Richard E. 1992. *Washington at Work: Back Rooms and Clean Air.* New York: Macmillan.

Congress and the Nation. 1993. Washington, D.C.: CQ Press.

Congressional Quarterly Almanac. Various years. Washington, D.C.: CQ Press.

Connelly, William, and John Pitney. 1994. *Congress' Permanent Minority? Republicans in the U.S. House.* Lanham, Md.: Rowman and Littlefield.

Cooper, Joseph. 1981. "Organization and Innovation in the House of Representatives." In *The House at Work,* ed. Joseph Cooper and G. Calvin Mackenzie. Austin: University of Texas Press.

Cooper, Joseph, and Cheryl D. Young. 1989. "Bill Introduction in the Nineteenth Century: A Study of Institutional Change." *Legislative Studies Quarterly* (February): 67–106.

Davidson, Roger H. 1981. "Two Avenues of Change: House and Senate Committee Reorganization." In *Congress Reconsidered,* ed. Lawrence C. Dodd and Bruce I. Oppenheimer, 2d ed. Washington, D.C.: CQ Press.

———. 1989. "Multiple Referral of Legislation in the U.S. Senate." *Legislative Studies Quarterly* (August): 375–392.

Davidson, Roger H., and Walter Oleszek. 1977. *Congress Against Itself.* Bloomington: Indiana University Press.

———. 1992. "From Monopoly to Management: Changing Patterns of Committee Deliberation." In *The Postreform Congress,* ed. Roger H. Davidson. New York: St. Martin's.

Dodd, Lawrence C., and Bruce I. Oppenheimer. 1977. *Congress Reconsidered.* New York: Praeger.

DSG (Democratic Study Group). 1994. "A Look at the Senate Filibuster." *DSG Special Report,* June 13, 103–128, Appendix B (compiled by Congressional Research Service).

Ellwood, John W., and James A. Thurber. 1981. "The Politics of the Congressional Budget Process Re-examined." In *Congress Reconsidered,* ed. Lawrence C. Dodd and Bruce I. Oppenheimer, 2d ed. Washington, D.C.: CQ Press.

Epstein, Lee, and Jeffrey Segal. 2005. *Advice and Consent: The Politics of Judicial Appointments.* New York: Oxford University Press.

Evans, C. Lawrence, and Walter J. Oleszek. 1995. "Congressional Tsunami? Institutional Change in the 104th Congress." Paper presented at the annual meeting of the American Political Science Association, Chicago, August 31–September 3.

Fenno, Richard. 1973. *Congressmen in Committees.* Boston: Little, Brown.

Gamm, Gerald, and Kenneth Shepsle. 1989. "Emergence of Legislative Institutions: Standing Committees in the House and Senate, 1810–1825." *Legislative Studies Quarterly* (February): 39–66.

Gilmour, John B. 1990. *Reconcilable Differences?* Berkeley: University of California Press.

Gold, Martin, Michael Hugo, Hyde Murray, Peter Robinson, and A. L. "Pete" Singleton. 1992. *The Book on Congress: Process, Procedure and Structure.* Washington, D.C.: Big Eagle Publishing. Supplements published biannually.

Hacker, Jacob, and Paul Pierson. 2005. *Off Center.* New Haven: Yale University Press.

Hall, Richard L. 1987. "Participation and Purpose in Committee Decision Making." *American Political Science Review* (March): 105–127.

Hibbing, John, and Elizabeth Theiss-Morse. 1995. *Congress as Public Enemy.* New York: Cambridge University Press.

King, David. 1994. "The Nature of Congressional Committee Jurisdictions." *American Political Science Review* (March): 48–62.

Koger, Gregory. 2002. "Obstructionism in the House and Senate: A Comparative Analysis of Institutional Choice." Dissertation, University of California–Los Angeles.

Lilly, Scott. 2005. "How Congress Is Spending the $.18 a Gallon You Pay in Gasoline Tax." Center for American Progress Report, October.

Longley, Lawrence, and Walter Oleszek. 1989. *Bicameral Politics.* New Haven: Yale University Press.

Mann, Thomas, and Norman Ornstein. 2006. *The Broken Branch.* New York: Oxford University Press.

Matthews, Donald E. 1960. *U.S. Senators and Their World.* New York: Vintage Books.

Oleszek, Walter J. 2004. *Congressional Procedures and the Policy Process,* 6th ed. Washington, D.C.: CQ Press.

Oppenheimer, Bruce. 1994. "The Rules Committee: The House Traffic Cop." In *Encyclopedia of the American Legislative System,* vol. 2, ed. Joel Silbey. New York: Scribner's.

———. 2002. *Vital Statistics on Congress 2001–2002.* Washington, D.C.: CQ Press.

Risjord, Norman K. 1994. "Congress in the Federalist-Republican Era." In *Encyclopedia of the American Legislative System,* vol. 1, ed. Joel Silbey. New York: Scribner's.

Rohde, David. 1991. *Parties and Leaders in the Postreform House.* Chicago: University of Chicago Press.

Roust, Kevin. 2005. "Special Rules and the Motion to Recommit." Manuscript.

Rybicki, Elizabeth. 2003. "Unresolved Differences: Bicameral Negotiations in Congress, 1877–2002." Paper delivered at the History of Congress Conference, University of California–San Diego, December 5–6.

Schick, Allen. 1980. *Congress and Money.* Washington, D.C.: Urban Institute.

Shepsle, Kenneth. 1978. *The Giant Jigsaw Puzzle: Democratic Committee Assignments in the Modern House.* Chicago: University of Chicago Press.

Sinclair, Barbara. 1983. *Majority Leadership in the U.S. House.* Baltimore: Johns Hopkins University Press.

———. 1989. *The Transformation of the U.S. Senate.* Baltimore: Johns Hopkins University Press.

———. 1991. "Governing Unheroically (and Sometimes Unappetizingly): Bush and the 101st Congress." In *The Bush Presidency: First Appraisals,* ed. Colin Campbell and Bert Rockman. Chatham, N.J.: Chatham House.

———. 1995. *Legislators, Leaders and Lawmaking.* Baltimore: Johns Hopkins University Press.

———. 1996. "Trying to Govern Positively in a Negative Era: Clinton and the 103rd Congress." In *The Clinton Presidency: First Appraisals,* ed. Colin Campbell and Bert Rockman. Chatham, N.J.: Chatham House.

———. 1997. *Unorthodox Lawmaking: New Legislative Processes in the U.S. Congress,* 1st ed. Washington, D.C.: CQ Press.

———. 2000. *Unorthodox Lawmaking: New Legislative Processes in the U.S. Congress,* 2nd ed. Washington, D.C.: CQ Press.

———. 2006. *Party Wars: Polarization and the Politics of the Policy Process.* Julian Rothbaum Lecture Series. Norman: University of Oklahoma Press.

Smith, Steven S. 1989. *Call to Order: Floor Politics in the House and Senate.* Washington, D.C.: The Brookings Institution.

———. 1995. *The American Congress.* Boston: Houghton Mifflin.

Smith, Steven S., and Marcus Flathman. 1989. "Managing the Senate Floor: Complex Unanimous Consent Agreements since the 1950s." *Legislative Studies Quarterly* (August): 349–374.

Stockman, David Alan. 1986. *The Triumph of Politics.* London: Bodley Head.

Strom, Gerald, and Barry Rundquist. 1977. "A Revised Theory of Winning in House-Senate Conferences." *American Political Science Review* (June): 448–453.

Thurber, James, and Samantha Durst. 1993. "The 1990 Budget Enforcement Act: The Decline of Congressional Accountability." In *Congress Reconsidered,* 5th ed., ed. Lawrence C. Dodd and Bruce I. Oppenheimer. Washington, D.C.: CQ Press.

Tiefer, Charles. 1989. *Congressional Practice and Procedure.* Westport, Conn.: Greenwood Press.

Wolfensberger, Donald. 2002. "Suspended Partisanship in the House: How Most Laws Are Really Made." Paper delivered at the American Political Science Association meetings, August 29–September 1.

Useful Web Sites
for Congress Watchers

Central Congressional Sites:

http://thomas.loc.gov/: Library of Congress site that includes bill chronologies, the *Congressional Record*, and links to other congressional and governmental sites.

www.house.gov/: Official House of Representatives site that includes information on operations and schedule and links to committee and member sites.

www.senate.gov: Official Senate site that includes information on operations and schedule and links to committee and member sites.

Congressional Party Sites:

www.gop.gov: House Republicans

www.housedemocrats.gov: House Democrats

www.democrats.senate.gov: Senate Democrats

www.republican.senate.gov: Senate Republicans

House Republican Leadership:

http://minoritywhip.house.gov/

www.gop.gov/

www.speaker.gov/

House Democratic Leadership:

http://democraticleader.house.gov/

http://democraticwhip.house.gov/

http://majoritywhip.house.gov/

Senate Leadership:

http://reid.senate.gov/

www.senate.gov/~dpc/

www.senate.gov/~rpc/

Capitol Hill Media:

www.c-span.org/

www.hillnews.com/

www.rollcall.com/

Abbreviations of Commonly Used In-text Citations

CD	*Congressional Digest*
CQA	*Congressional Quarterly Almanac*
CQW	*Congressional Quarterly (CQ) Weekly*
CR	*Congressional Record*
Daily	*CongressDaily*
LAT	*Los Angeles Times*
MR	*National Journal's Markup Report*
NYT	*New York Times*
RC	*Roll Call*
WP	*Washington Post*

Index

AARP, 174, 177, 178, 182
Abortion
    appropriations bills and, 81, 222,
        228
    bankruptcy law and, 80, 88
    federal funding, 80
    "partial-birth" abortion bill, 48, 89
Acid rain, 3
Additional initial referral, 14
Advise and consent power, 54
Afghanistan, 18, 59, 96
AFL-CIO, 174
Agriculture. See Farm programs
Aid to Families with Dependent
    Children, 97 *n*5, 216
Air Force promotions, 56
Airline industry, 18–19, 85
Airport improvement projects, 24
Air quality. See Clean air entries
Alaskan lands bill, 74
Alexander, Lamar, 70
Aliens
    children's health benefits, 165
    welfare benefits, 236, 239, 240, 242
Alliance of Retired Americans, 174
Alternative minimum tax, 239
Aluminum industry, 201
Ambassador nominations, 54

Amendments. See Constitutional
    amendments; Legislative
    amendments
AmeriCorps (national service), 51,
    127, 228
Anti-drug legislation, 48, 75, 92
Appointment politics
    conferee appointments, 78–79
    presidential nominations, 54–56,
        69, 283
Appropriations bills
    authorizations distinguished from,
        94
    House, as originating chamber,
        10
    line-item veto, 80
    1995 budget politics, 87, 222
    omnibus bills, 65, 82
    reconciliation procedures, 88 *n*2
    role in budget process, 94–99
    Senate procedures, 63, 65, 69
    supplemental bills, 96
Archer, Bill, 239, 242
Arctic National Wildlife Refuge
    (ANWR), 23, 48, 139–141, 143, 145,
        147, 153, 260
Armey, Dick, 79, 81, 93
    Bush tax plan, 249, 258

Armey, Dick *(cont.)*
    Clinton budget politics, 100, 198, 209, 223, 224
Authorization process, distinguished from appropriations, 94
Automobiles, 1
    fuel efficiency standards, 142, 145, 147, 154
    MTBE fuel additive, 140, 142–144, 146, 147, 153, 155, 156
Ava Gardner Post Office Building Designation Act, 24

Balanced budget. *See* Budget process
Bankruptcy legislation, 14, 41, 80, 88
Barton, Joe, 141–143, 146, 153–155, 157
Base bill, 21
Bass, Charles, 153, 155
Baucus, Max, 69
    Bush tax plan, 255–257
    energy legislation, 148, 153
    prescription drug legislation, 165, 169, 174–176
Bayh, Evan, 263
Bentsen, Lloyd, 204
Berry, Marion, 174, 178
Biden, Joseph, 63
Bilirakis, Michael, 174
Bill
    legislative success, 272 *n*1
    term explained, 11 *n*2
Bill introduction
    House, 11
    Senate, 43–44
Bill referral
    House, 11–20, 268–269
    Senate, 44–49, 269
Bingaman, Jeff, 48
    energy legislation, 147–150, 152, 154
Bishop, Tim, 145
Black Caucus, 30, 199, 200, 207
Blue Dog Democrats, 30, 250, 251, 253
Blunt, Roy, 101, 153, 177
Bodman, Samuel, 154, 156
Boehlert, Sherwood, 147
Boehner, John A., 223
Bonior, David, 204, 223, 225, 238
Boren, David, 202–203, 205, 208, 209
Bovine growth hormone, 209

Bowles, Erskine, 242, 244
Boxer, Barbara, 63, 260
Brady bill, 127
Breaux, John
    Bush tax plan, 255, 257, 258, 260
    prescription drug legislation, 174–176
Broadcast Decency Enforcement Act of 2004, 30–31, 63
Brown, Sherrod, 167
Brownback, Sam, 63
Btu tax, 198, 200–203, 205, 207, 211
Budget Act
    debate rules, 98, 100, 125, 206, 254
    legislative politics, 66, 146, 196–197, 251, 255–257
    new budget process created by, 93, 112–113
    statutory requirements, 63, 97, 100, 128, 201
Budget deficit
    Clinton plan to reduce, 197–199, 201–202, 204, 211
    estimating methods, 97
    legislative politics, 22, 128–129
Budget Enforcement Act of 1990, 129 *n*8
Budget process, 83, 196–267
    appropriations and authorizations distinguished, 94
    appropriations process, 94–99
    constitutional amendment for balanced budget, 18, 50–51
    continuing resolutions, 95–96
    debate rules, 98, 100, 125, 254
    germane amendments required, 63, 100
    as instrument for policy change, 7–8, 101–102, 112–113, 128–129, 196–197, 210–211, 215–216, 248–249, 259, 270–271
    legislative amendment for balanced budget, 48, 79, 103, 129, 130
    1993 chronology, 197–214
    1995 chronology, 8, 215–235
    1997 chronology, 8, 32, 78, 235–243, 246–247
    1998–2000 politics, 243–245
    omnibus legislation, 22–23, 91–102, 270

statutory authorization, 93,
112–113
summit negotiations, 41, 130–131
2001 tax cuts, 48, 248–259,
265–267
2003 tax cuts, 259–263
2004 politics, 29–30, 42, 88
unorthodox practices, 263–264
Budget reconciliation bills
amending activity, 65, 66
conference negotiations, 100–101
debate rules, 100, 101, 125
"germane" amendments required,
63, 100
as instrument for policy decisions,
101–102, 129
omnibus legislation, 99–100
purpose and scope, 22–23, 99–100,
201
Budget resolutions
debate rules, 125
germane amendments required,
63
legislative politics, 32, 65, 98
legislative success, 272 *n*1
originating legislation, 10
purpose and scope, 22–23, 97–98,
200–201
reconciliation bill relationship,
99–100, 201
reconciliation instructions, 98–99,
113, 128, 249
Budget surplus, estimating methods,
97
Bulgaria, 226
Bush, George H. W.
budget politics, 104, 130–131
clean air legislation, 2, 3
legislative politics, 47, 55, 89, 114,
131
tax policy, 104, 198
veto bargaining, 84
Bush, George W., 7, 23
appointment politics, 55, 56, 69
budget politics, 87, 88, 96, 99, 101,
105, 128
energy legislation, 139–141, 154,
156
legislative politics, 23, 30, 41, 48,
64, 66, 70, 92, 93, 131, 136, 277,
286

medical malpractice caps, 186, 187,
192, 193
policies assessed, 285
prescription drug legislation,
162–164, 168, 170–171, 173–176,
178–180, 182
2001 tax cuts, 196, 248–255, 258,
265–267
2003 tax cuts, 259, 263
veto bargaining, 85–86
Bypassing committees, 5
House practice, 17–20
increased use, 120–122, 134, 135
reasons for, and effect on decision
making, 269, 276–277
Senate practice, 47–49
Byrd, Robert C., 67, 102, 151
Byrd rule, 102, 207–208, 224

Calendars, House, 23
California Desert Protection Act, 127
Calio, Nick, 86
Campaign finance reform, 18, 32, 33,
41, 64, 67, 70, 74, 127, 135
Canada, importation of drugs from,
169, 172, 176
Cantwell, Maria, 149–150
Capital gains taxation, 242, 261, 263
Capps, Lois, 147
Cardin, Ben, 256
Carter, Jimmy, 113, 130, 197
Castle, Michael, 147
Central American Fair Trade
Agreement, 41
Chafee, John, 219, 221, 241
Chafee, Lincoln, 252, 254, 259, 260,
262–263
Chairman's mark, 251
Charitable deductions, 249
Chemical Weapons Convention, 54
Cheney, Dick
appointment politics, 55
Bush tax cuts, 254, 260–263
energy legislation, 140
legislative politics, 85, 122, 253
prescription drug legislation, 173
Cheyenne, Wyoming, 24
Child care legislation, 15, 21, 50
Children, and health care, 165,
238–242
Child tax credit, 35, 239, 240, 256

Cigarette tax, 238, 239, 242
Civil rights legislation, 33
Civil Rights Restoration Act, 19
Class action lawsuits, 50, 51, 70
Clean Air Act of 1970, 1, 3, 4
Clean Air Act of 1990, 2–4, 50, 68, 92
Clean bills, 75–76
Clean drinking water regulations, 127
Climate change (global warming),
    150–151, 154
Clinton, Bill, 12, 49, 52, 54
    budget politics, in general, 55, 69,
        104, 127, 128, 131, 249
    legislative politics, 63, 131, 136
    medical malpractice caps, 186
    1993 budget politics, 7, 23, 92, 99,
        101, 196–214
    1995 budget politics, 99, 215–235
    1997 budget politics, 8, 235–243,
        246–247
    1998–2000 budget politics,
        243–245
    prescription drug legislation, 161
    recess appointments, 55
    veto bargaining, 84
    veto overrides, 90
Clinton, Hillary Rodham, 56
Closed rules, 25, 26, 122, 123n, 124,
    136, 138, 270
Cloture
    extended debate ended by, 6, 43
    germane amendments after, 63
    number of votes required, 6, 125
    Senate rules and practice, 5,
        67–72, 137
    suggested reform, 282
The Coalition, 225
Coast Guard, 83
Columbine High School shootings,
    28
Commerce Department, 12, 220
Committee system
    creation and role, 5–6
    legislative process. *See* House
        legislative process; Senate legisla-
        tive process
    reorganization, 95
    Senate assignments, 46
    *See also specific House and Senate
        committee names*

Concurrent resolutions
    budget resolutions as, 98
    definition, 11 n2
Conference committees, 76–89
    appointment of conferees, 76–79
    budget reconciliation process,
        100–101
    clean air legislation, 1, 3, 4
    conferees' power and its limits,
        86–89
    discharged committees'
        representation on, 15, 77–78
    energy legislation, 153–156
    incomplete knowledge of reports,
        280–281
    reaching agreement, 79–86
    use and purpose, 76
Confirmation process, 54–56, 69, 283
Congress
    budget process. *See* Budget process
    changes in legislative process. *See*
        Unorthodox lawmaking
    executive summits. *See* Summits
    legislative process. *See* House
        legislative process; Senate legisla-
        tive process; specific legislation
    omnibus bills. *See* Omnibus
        legislation
    public opinion of, 8
    reconciling House-Senate
        differences. *See* Reconciliation
        procedures
    tax policy. *See* Tax legislation
Congressional Black Caucus, 30, 199,
    200, 207
Congressional Budget and
    Impoundment Control Act of 1974.
    See Budget Act
Congressional Budget Office, 97, 98,
    146, 198–199, 217
Congressional Quarterly Weekly Report, 8
Congressional Record, 29, 39, 62
Constitutional amendments, 11 n2
    balanced budget, 18, 50–51
    flag desecration, 54
    gay marriage, 19
    legislative outcomes, 41, 71, 272 n1
    legislative procedures, 10, 51
    term limits, 33
Consultation process, 52–54, 72

Consumer interests, 279
Consumer price index, 130, 236
Continuing resolutions (CRs)
  1995 budget politics, 222, 224–228
  role in budget process, 95–96
  2000 budget politics, 245
Contract with America, 20, 29, 133,
  196, 216, 278
Corporate tax legislation, 50
CQ Weekly, 8
Craig, Larry E., 56, 65, 152
Crime legislation, 127
Crop insurance, 84
Cuba, 54, 69, 85
Culberson, John, 171

Dairy farm legislation, 69
D'Amato, Alfonse, 69
Daniels, Mitch, 254
Daschle, Tom
  Bush tax plan, 250, 255–257
  legislative politics, 48, 50, 52, 61,
  74, 83
  medical malpractice caps, 191
  prescription drug legislation, 164,
  165, 168, 173–175, 179–180
Davis-Bacon Act, 220
Daylight savings time, 142
Debate
  House rules and practice, 6, 23, 25,
  27, 29, 35, 37–40
  Senate rules and practice, 6, 51, 57,
  58, 60–62, 66, 100
  See also Filibuster
Debt. *See* National debt
DeConcini, Dennis, 209
Defense authorizations/
  appropriations
  legislative politics, 22, 40, 49, 61,
  63, 64, 66, 70, 80, 224, 254
Deficit. *See* Budget deficit
DeLay, Tom, 177
  budget politics, 100, 101, 223–225,
  261, 263
  energy legislation, 140, 142
  legislative politics, 78, 79
  prescription drug legislation, 174
Deliberation, 279–280, 282, 287
Democratic Congressional Campaign
  Committee, 175

Democratic Forum on Malpractice,
  187
Democratic Party, 114
Detainees, treatment of, 64
Dingell, John, 2, 29
  energy legislation, 142, 145, 146,
  154, 155
  medical malpractice caps, 188, 189
  prescription drug legislation, 167,
  171, 174
Dingell amendment, 28–29
Discharged committees, 14–15,
  17–18, 77–78, 121
Discretionary spending, 98
Dividends taxation, 261–263
Dole, Bob
  Clinton budget politics, 201, 206,
  217, 218, 221, 222, 224–227
  legislative politics, 54, 63, 64, 77,
  135
  line-item-veto bill, 50, 81–82
Domenici, Pete
  Bush tax plan, 83, 253, 254
  Clinton budget politics, 207–208,
  218, 225, 236, 243, 244
  energy legislation, 139, 147–149,
  151–154
Do-not-call list, 19, 74
Dorgan, Byron L., 169, 225
Dove, Robert B., 83
Drugs (illegal)
  anti-drug legislation, 48, 75, 92
Drugs (pharmaceuticals). *See*
  Medicare/prescription drug
  legislation
Durbin, Richard, 168, 190, 191

Earmarks, 87
Earned Income Tax Credit, 257
Economic Growth and Tax Relief Act,
  250–252
Economic policies. *See* Budget process
Education
  Bush budget politics, 88, 254, 257,
  285
  Clinton budget politics, 105, 127,
  221, 224, 228, 235, 236, 242, 244,
  245
  funding mechanism, 95
Eisenhower, Dwight, 248

Electricity market reform, 147, 148, 155
Electronic mail, 75
Electronic voting system, 39
Emergency procedures, 18–19
Emerson, Jo Ann, 172
Employment discrimination, 71
Energy legislation, 139–160
  complexity of, 92
  conference negotiations, 79, 82–84, 153–156
  failed bills, 139–140
  House action, 23, 27, 141–147
  as orthodox process, 7, 139–140, 156–157
  Senate action, 48, 65, 70, 147–153
  2005 chronology (table), 158–160
Energy Policy Act of 2003, 27
Energy tax, 198, 200, 201, 203
Ensign, John, 168, 190
Entitlement programs
  budget process and, 99
  funding mechanism, 96–97
  1993 budget politics, 203, 204, 208–209
  pay-as-you-go provisions, 129 n8
  share of federal spending, 98
  2003 tax cuts, 259–260
  2005 budget politics, 23
  See also Medicaid; Medicare entries; Social Security; Welfare reform
Environmental groups, 278, 279
Environmental legislation, 40, 41, 74, 116, 220, 221, 224, 228, 235
Environmental Protection Agency, 1, 40, 56, 222
Estate tax, 239, 242, 249, 256, 258, 259, 285
Estrada, Miguel, 68, 69
Ethanol, 149, 153, 155, 239, 240
Ethics reform legislation, 35, 70
Executive branch
  legislative politics, 84–86
  See also Summits
Exon, Jim, 225
Extended debate. See Filibuster
Extraction procedure, 18 n7

Faith-based initiatives, 30
Family and medical leave legislation, 63
Farm credit system, 21

Farm programs
  Bush budget politics, 50, 79, 87, 254
  Clinton budget politics, 69, 84, 135, 216, 218–220, 224
  funding mechanism, 96
Federal Communications Commission (FCC), 30–31, 85
Federal crop insurance, 84
Federal Election Commission, 56
Federal Energy Regulatory Commission, 142
Federal government shutdowns, 222–227, 235, 244
Federal Housing Finance Reform Act of 2005, 31
Federal pension legislation, 45, 218, 220
Federal Trade Commission, 19
Feingold, Russell D., 209
Feinstein, Dianne, 61, 64, 151, 190
Fetal protection legislation, 14–15, 73
Filibuster (extended debate)
  budget bills, 100, 101, 125, 206, 249
  decision making affected by, 281–282
  increased use, 110, 126–127
  legislative outcomes affected by, 275–276
  nomination politics, 54–55, 69
  prescription drug legislation, 179, 182
  Senate rules and practice, 5, 6, 43, 51, 53–54, 60, 67–72, 135, 137
Firearms
  gun control legislation, 28–29, 64, 65, 127
  industry liability legislation, 64–65, 72
Flag burning, 31
Flag desecration amendment, 54
"Flagship" legislation, 50
Floor procedures
  changes in, 6
  House rules and practice, 23, 25, 35–42
  Senate rules and practice, 43, 51, 61–72
Florida, 150
Foley, Tom, 2, 3, 79, 210
Food and Drug Administration, 56, 187
Food stamps, 84, 96–97, 218

Foreign aid, 12, 13, 94
Foster, Henry, 55, 69
Frank, Barney, 204
Franks, Trent, 179
Freedom to Farm bill, 135
Frist, Bill
  budget politics, 88, 260, 261
  energy legislation, 65, 140, 148, 151
  legislative politics, 48, 50, 52, 53,
    61, 68, 70, 71, 83–84
  medical malpractice caps, 190–193
  prescription drug legislation, 82,
    164–165, 169, 174–176, 179, 180

Ganske, Greg, 77
Gasoline additives, 140
Gasoline for America's Security Act,
  22, 34, 41
Gasoline tax, 205–207, 211
Gay rights. *See* Homosexual rights
General Agreement on Tariffs and
  Trade, 45, 102
Gephardt, Richard A., 203, 207, 250,
  252
Gilchrest, Wayne, 144
Gingrich, Newt
  Clinton budget politics, 100, 209,
    217, 219, 220, 222–227, 236, 237,
    239, 241, 242, 244
  legislative politics, 20, 77, 78, 82,
    114, 133
  prescription drug legislation, 177
Global HIV/AID bill, 61
Global warming, 150–151, 154
Goals 2000 program, 228
Gore, Al, 207, 210, 226, 248
Government Reform and Savings Act
  of 1993, 12
Government shutdowns, 222–227,
  235, 244
Graham, Bob, 166
Graham, Lindsay, 191, 192
Gramm, Phil, 48, 70, 206, 217, 241,
  257, 259
Gramm-Rudman balanced budget
  amendment, 48, 79, 103, 129, 130
Grassley, Charles, 56, 225
  Bush tax plan, 255–257, 261–263
  energy legislation, 148, 153
  legislative politics, 50, 53
  prescription drug legislation,
    163–165, 169, 174

"Great Society" Congress, 9 *n*3
Green, Gene, 142
Greenwood, James C., 187
Gregg, Judd, 168
Gulf Coast, 19, 74
Gun control legislation, 28–29, 64,
  65, 127

Hagel, Chuck, 150, 168
Harkin, Tom, 50, 254
Hastert, Dennis
  Bush tax plan, 252
  campaign finance reform, 18, 32
  Clinton budget politics, 100, 244,
    245
  energy legislation, 140
  legislative politics, 22, 23, 28, 78,
    79, 81, 85–86, 93, 134
  managed care legislation, 20, 77
  medical malpractice caps, 187
  prescription drug legislation, 82,
    163, 164, 166, 170–172, 175–178
Hatch, Orrin, 56, 61, 153, 174, 238,
  257
Hate crime laws, 63
Head Start, 22, 218
Health and Human Service
  Department (HHS), 88, 95, 105,
  176, 244, 245
Health care
  Clinton budget politics, 238–242
  legislative politics, 12, 18, 20, 64,
    77, 88–89, 165
  malpractice caps, 7, 186–195
  patients' bill of rights, 82, 135
  See also Medicaid; Medicare entries
Helms, Jesse, 54, 63
Hilley, John, 236, 242
Hirschmann, Susan B., 177
HIV/AIDS legislation, 48, 61
Holbrooke, Richard, 56
Holds
  on legislation, 52–53, 57, 68
  on nominations, 54–56
Homeland Security Department, 61,
  70, 76, 92–93
Homosexual rights
  employment discrimination, 71
  gay marriage amendment, 19
  legislative politics, 31, 55
  military service, 63
Hoover Dam, 69

Hopper, 11
Hormel, James, 55
"Hostage taking," 54, 56
"Hot line," 52, 57
House Agriculture Committee, 14,
  21, 79, 121, 220, 224
House Appropriations Committee,
  94–98, 219, 228, 243
House Armed Services Committee,
  15, 22
House Banking Committee, 21
House Budget Committee, 78
  budget process, 32, 97–101
  Bush tax plan, 252, 255, 259–260,
    264
  Clinton budget politics, 198–199,
    202, 207, 216, 218, 220, 223–225,
    236, 237, 240–241
  energy legislation, 141
  2005 reconciliation bill, 23, 34
House Commerce Committee, 19, 21,
  240
House Committee of the Whole,
  37–40, 111, 146, 189
House Democratic Caucus, 25
House Economic and Educational
  Opportunities Committee, 14
House Education and Labor
  Committee, 15, 16
House Education and the Workforce
  Committee, 45, 78, 79, 240
House Energy and Commerce
  Committee, 253
  clean air legislation, 2
  energy legislation, 27, 141, 142,
    146, 153, 154, 157
  jurisdictional changes, 132
  medical malpractice caps, 187–189
  prescription drug legislation, 164,
    166, 167, 172, 174, 177
House Financial Services Committee,
  14, 31
House Foreign Affairs Committee, 13
House Government Reform and
  Oversight Committee, 20, 78, 142,
  220
House Health Subcommittee, 187,
  188
House Homeland Security
  Committee, 78
House Immigration Subcommittee, 20

House Interstate and Foreign
  Commerce Committee, 1, 2
House Judiciary Committee
  legislative process, 14, 15, 18, 20,
    23, 35, 78, 121
  medical malpractice caps, 187–189
House legislative process, 1–7, 10–42
  bill introduction, 11
  bill referral, 11–20, 268–269
  budget politics. *See* Budget process
  bypassing committees, 17–20,
    120–121, 134, 269
  clean air legislation as example,
    1–4
  committee decision making, 16–17
  committee system, 5–6, 111
  current procedures, 5, 10–11,
    268–271
  early procedures, 5–6
  executive summits. *See* Summits
  floor procedure, 6, 35–42
  legislative outcomes, 271–276
  multiple referral, 12–16, 116–118
  new parliamentary devices, 32–35
  omnibus bills. *See* Omnibus
    legislation
  postcommittee adjustments,
    20–23, 119–120, 134
  reasons for changes, 6–7, 108
  reconciling House-Senate
    differences. *See* Reconciliation
    procedures
  reorganization of committees, 95,
    132
  rules suspension, 5, 23–25, 56
  selection of committee chairs, 136
  Senate compared, 43, 140–141
  special rules, 25–35, 60, 122–125
  tax policy. *See* Tax legislation
  unorthodox procedures effect on,
    42, 276–281, 283–287
  use of special procedures and
    practices, 105–107
  See also specific legislation
House Progressive Caucus, 253
House Resources Committee, 78, 141,
  143
House Rules Committee
  budget politics, 102, 220, 241, 245,
    251, 258
  clean air legislation, 2

energy legislation, 144, 147
legislative politics, 20, 31, 33, 35,
36, 78, 136, 280
medical malpractice caps, 188–189
prescription drug legislation, 171
rules process, 6, 18 *n*7, 23, 25–27,
29, 35, 39, 124, 270
selection of members, 111, 122,
132
House Science Committee, 78, 141
House Subcommittee on Oversight
and Investigations, 187
House Transportation and
Infrastructure Committee, 237
House Transportation Committee,
17, 78
House Ways and Means Committee
budget process, 99
Bush tax plan, 250–253, 261
Clinton budget politics, 201–202,
239, 240
earlier procedures, 122
energy legislation, 141, 143, 155
jurisdiction, and multiple referral,
13–16, 45, 117 *n*4
legislative politics, 17, 22, 78
prescription drug legislation, 163,
166–167, 172, 174, 177
Hoyer, Steny, 178, 189
"Hundred Hours" agenda, 138, 286
Hungary, 12, 13
Hurricane Katrina, 19, 22, 24, 31, 96
Hurricane Rita, 22, 24
Hyde amendment, 80
Hydroelectric dams, 152

Idaho, 56
Immigrants, welfare benefits for, 84
Immigration legislation, 12, 20
Impeachment, of Clinton, 52
Impoundment of funds, 112
Inheritance (estate) tax, 239, 242,
249, 256, 258, 259, 285
Inhofe, James, 151
Insurance, 77, 85, 238
Intelligence operations legislation,
12, 53, 66, 92, 93
Interest groups, 11, 278, 279
Interior Department, 36
Interior Secretary, 24
Internet tax legislation, 70, 74

Iraq war, 31, 59, 64, 66, 87, 96, 260,
286
Istook, Ernest, 179

Jeffords, Jim
budget politics, 254, 257, 260
energy legislation, 150, 156
party affiliation change, 122, 257
prescription drug legislation, 169,
175, 179
Job training legislation, 30
Johnson, Lyndon B., 225
Johnson, Nancy, 167, 174
Joint referral, 13, 14
Joint resolutions, 11 *n*2
Junk e-mail bill, 75
Juvenile justice legislation, 28–29

Kasich, John R., 199, 204, 218, 220,
225, 236, 241
Katrina (hurricane), 19, 22, 24, 31, 96
Kendrick Project, Wyoming (HR1046),
24
Kennedy, Edward (Ted)
Clinton budget politics, 200, 238
legislative politics, 61, 64, 66, 77
prescription drug legislation, 164,
165, 168, 173, 179, 180
Kennedy-Kassebaum bill, 77
Kerrey, Bob, 209
Kerry, John, 165
"Killer" amendments, 64–65, 72
King-of-the-hill procedure, 32–33
Kyl, Jon, 61, 63, 174

Labor Department, 88, 95, 105, 244,
245
Labor laws, 127
Landrieu, Mary, 150
Lautenberg, Frank R., 236
Layover rules, 280, 281
Leahy, Patrick, 61, 64, 66
Legislative amendments
clean air legislation, 1–3
effect on legislative outcomes,
274–275
House practice, 21, 111–112,
122–123. *See also* House legislative
process
motions to recommit with
instructions, 203

Legislative amendments *(cont.)*
  in reconciliation process, 74–75
  "relevance" and "germaneness"
    standards, 57 *n*3, 63
  Senate practice, 5, 43, 48–49,
    62–67, 109, 125–126, 135, 270,
    282
  tabling of, 66
Legislative-executive summits. *See*
  Summits
Legislative outcomes, 271–276
Legislative process
  budget process. *See* Budget process
  changes in. *See* Unorthodox
    lawmaking
  executive summits. *See* Summits
  in general. *See* House legislative
    process; Senate legislative process;
    specific legislation
  omnibus bills. *See* Omnibus
    legislation
  public opinion of, 8
  reconciling House-Senate
    differences. *See* Reconciliation
    procedures
Legislative success, term defined, 272
  *n*1
Levin, Sander M., 172
Lew, Jack, 244
Lieberman, Joe, 150
Lincoln, Blanche, 262
Linda White-Epps Post Office
  Designation Act, 24
Line-item veto legislation, 50, 70, 78,
  80, 81, 228
Liquefied natural gas (LNG)
  facilities, 142, 145, 147, 151, 155
Lobbying reform legislation, 31, 35,
  127, 222
Long, Huey, 68
Lott, Trent
  Bush tax plan, 249, 254, 255
  Clinton budget politics, 225, 237,
    238, 240, 242
  energy legislation, 157
  legislative politics, 48, 52, 64, 71,
    77, 81, 135
  nomination politics, 55, 56
  prescription drug legislation, 166
Louisiana, 150

Low Income Home Energy Assistance
  Program, 142
Lugar, Richard, 48

Malpractice law, 7, 70, 186–195
Manager's amendment, 21, 22, 31, 34,
  66
Margolies-Mezvinsky, Marjorie, 210
Markey, Ed, 145, 155
Marriage penalty, 249, 256, 258, 259
McCain, John
  Bush tax plan, 259, 261–263
  energy legislation, 150–152
  legislative politics, 48, 49, 64, 65,
    67, 80
McCain-Feingold bill, 74
McCarthy amendment, 28, 29
McClellan, Scott, 163
McCollum amendment, 28
McConnell, Mitch, 56, 57, 82, 190, 191
McCurry, Mike, 238
McGovern, James, 146, 172
Measure, term explained, 11 *n*2
Medicaid, 167
  Bush budget politics, 102, 259
  Clinton budget politics, 8, 216–221,
    224, 229, 240, 241, 245
  enactment, 225
  funding mechanism, 96
  legislative politics, 70
Medical malpractice caps, 7, 186–195
Medical savings accounts, 77, 171–173
Medicare
  Bush budget politics, 250, 253, 257,
    259
  Clinton budget politics, 8, 202, 205,
    216–221, 224, 229, 235, 238,
    240–242, 245
  enactment, 9 *n*3, 225
  funding mechanism, 96
  legislative politics, 17, 20, 70
Medicare/prescription drug legislation, 7, 161–185
  assessment, 285
  chronology (table), 183–185
  conference negotiations, 78, 79, 82,
    83, 173–180
  House action, 31, 41, 166–167,
    170–173

policy change created by, 161–164,
180–182, 253
Senate action, 65, 164–170
Methyl tertiary butyl ether (MTBE),
140, 142–144, 146, 147, 153, 155, 156
Metropolitan Washington Airports
Transfer Act, 69
Michel, Bob, 209
Mikulski, Barbara, 169–170
Military base closings, 85
Military prisons, 64
Military service, 22, 63
Miller, George, 30
Miller, Zell, 252–254, 261–263
Million Man March, 24
Minimum wage legislation, 48, 64, 70,
135
Mitchell, George, 2, 3, 50, 63, 205, 206
Modified closed rules, 26, 123*n*, 124,
136
Modified open rules, 26, 123*n*, 124
Motion on previous question, 35–36
Motion to approve nomination, 54
Motion to instruct, 87
Motion to proceed, 51–54, 60–61,
68, 70
Motion to recommit with/without
instructions, 40–41, 203
Motion to reconsider, 42
Motion to suspend rules, 23–24
"Motor voter" bill, 68, 127
Moynihan, Daniel Patrick, 205, 207
Multiple referral
conference committees, 78
House, 12–16, 21, 116–118, 134,
268–269
Senate, 42–45, 116–118, 269
Murkowski, Frank, 257
Murray, Patty, 56

National Association of
Manufacturers, 201
National Climate Change Strategy, 145
National debt, 22
debt limit legislation, 19, 47, 48, 61,
217, 218, 222, 225, 227–228
interest expenditures, 98
National defense spending. *See*
Defense authorizations/
appropriations

National Institutes of Health, 254
National Law Enforcement Officers
Memorial Maintenance Fund Act of
2005, 24
National Rifle Association (NRA), 28,
65
National service legislation, 51, 127,
228
Nelson, Ben, 262, 263
Neumann, Mark W., 226
New Hampshire, 153
Newlands Project Headquarters and
Maintenance Yard Facility Transfer
Act, 24
New Orleans, 19
New York, 69
New York Times, 22
Ney, Robert, 33
Nicaraguan contras, 41, 131
Nickles, Don
Bush tax plan, 257, 260, 262
Clinton budget politics, 225
prescription drug legislation, 165,
166, 174
Nixon, Richard, 1, 112
No Child Left Behind Act, 285
Nomination politics, 54–56, 69, 283
Nonconference reconciliation
procedures, 73–76
Nongermane amendments, 63–64
North American Free Trade
Agreement, 45
Northeast Dairy Compact, 69
Norwood, Charlie, 77
Norwood-Dingell bill, 77
"Nuclear option," 55, 283
Nunn, Sam, 51
Nussle, Jim, 141, 143, 239, 259

Obama, Barack, 56
Oberstar, James L., 237
Office of Management and Budget
(OMB), 85, 97, 104, 113
Oil drilling
in ANWR, 23, 48, 139–141, 143,
145, 147, 153, 260
Gulf Coast, 74
inventory of resources, 150, 155
Oil industry, 201, 202

Omnibus legislation
    amending activity, 65
    appropriations bills, 65, 82, 87
    budget process, 93–102, 128–129
    conference negotiations, 75, 82, 87
    disadvantages, 280
    drug bill, 48, 75, 92
    purpose and use, 5, 91–93,
        127–128, 136, 270
    reconciliation bills, 99–100
    scope and coverage, 22–23, 92
O'Neill, Paul, 250
O'Neill, Thomas P., Jr., 122, 130
Open rules, 1, 25, 39, 122–124, 270
"Organic food" definition, 87
Ornstein, Norman, 281
Otter, C. L. (Butch), 173
Outer Continental Shelf, 150, 154, 155
Outsourcing, 85
Overtime pay rules, 48, 64, 85

Packwood, Bob, 63
Panetta, Leon, 222, 225, 228
Parliamentarian, 12
"Partial-birth" abortion bill, 48, 89
Partisanship
    House dynamics, 16–17, 38
    party unity score, 114
    party voting scores, 114–115
    Senate dynamics, 43, 45–46
    trends and consequences, 110
        (table), 135–136
Patients' bill of rights, 82, 135
Pay-as-you-go (PAYGO) provisions, 88,
    129 n8, 286
Peace Officers Memorial Day, 24
Pelosi, Nancy, 143, 146, 178
Penny, Timothy J., 203
Pension legislation, 45
Permanent committees
    creation and role, 5–6
    See also specific House and Senate
        committee names
Perot, Ross, 198
Persian Gulf War, 62
Peterson, Lacy J., 73
Pharmaceuticals. *See* Medicare/
    prescription drug legislation
Pickering, Charles W. (Chip), Jr., 142
Pocket veto, 89
Poland, 12, 13

Pombo, Richard, 141, 143
Postcommittee adjustments
    House practice, 20–23
    increased use, 119–121, 134, 135
    reasons for, and effect on decision
        making, 269–270, 277
    Senate practice, 49–51
Potash Royalty Reduction Act of 2005,
    24
Prescription drugs. *See* Medicare/
    prescription drug legislation
President
    bill introduction, 11
    budget politics, 101
    conference negotiations, 84–86
    signing or vetoing of bills, 89–90
    See also specific presidents
President of the Senate, 49 n2
Previous question motion, 35–36
Product liability legislation, 135
    firearms, 64–65, 72
    MTBE fuel additive, 140, 142–144,
        146, 147, 153, 155, 156
Property rights legislation, 135
Proxy votes, 132
Pryce, Deborah, 171, 179
Public opinion
    on Bush tax cuts, 250
    of Congress, 8
Public Utilities Holding Company
    Act, 148, 155

Queen-of-the-hill procedure, 33
Quie, Albert H., 92
Quorum calls, 62

Radio Marti, 69
Rahall, Nick, 143
Raines, Fredrick, 236
Rangel, Charlie
    Bush tax plan, 251, 256, 258, 261
    prescription drug legislation, 171,
        174
Reagan, Ronald
    appointment politics, 55
    budget politics, 36, 92, 99, 103,
        113, 128, 130
    legislative politics, 41, 47, 114
Recess appointments, 55
Reconciliation bills. *See* Budget
    reconciliation bills

Reconciliation procedures, 73–90
  appointment of conferees, 76–79
  changes, 90
  conferees' power and its limits, 86–89
  conference committees, 76–89
  final step, 89–90
  nonconference procedures, 73–76
  reaching agreement, 79–86
Recorded votes, 36, 39, 41, 66, 111
Reed, Jack, 65
Referral of bills
  conference committees, 78
  House, 11–20, 116–118
  Senate, 44–49, 116–118
Regulatory reform legislation, 45, 47, 135
Reid, Harry, 52, 70, 83
Reinventing government legislation, 12, 13
Republican Conference, 132
Republican Party, 114
Republican Study Committee, 30
Resolutions
  "sense of the Senate" resolutions, 200
  term explained, 11 *n*2, 25
  See also Budget resolutions
Responsiveness and responsibility criteria, 283–285
Restrictive rules, 5, 25–26, 29, 87, 123–125, 134, 136–137, 270
Riders, 222, 228
Riggs, Frank, 227
Rita (hurricane), 22, 24
Rivlin, Alice, 225
Robert M. La Follette, Sr. Post Office Building Designation Act, 24
Rockefeller, John D. (Jay), IV, 166, 174, 241, 257
Roll call, 62
Roll call votes, 36, 65
Rostenkowski, Dan, 202, 207
Roth, William, 48, 241
Rother, John C., 177
Rubin, Robert, 223, 225, 227, 242
Rule X (House), 12
Rule 14 (Senate), 47, 48
Rule 22 (Senate), 67, 282
Rural Housing Hurricane Relief Act of 2005, 24

Sabo, Martin, 225
Santorum, Rick, 168, 192, 261
Sasser, James, 205
Satellite TV, 69
Savings and loan bailout, 49
School vouchers, 41
Schumer, Charles E., 64, 168
Second-degree amendments, 38
Select committees, 5
Self-executing rules, 33–35, 204, 220, 240, 280
Senate
  advise and consent power, 54
  presiding officer, 49
Senate Agriculture Committee, 50, 219, 224
Senate Appropriations Committee
  authority and tasks, 94–95
  budget process, 96, 98, 219, 228, 243
Senate Banking Committee, 45, 49
Senate Budget Committee, 48
  budget process, 97–101
  Bush tax plan, 253, 260
  Clinton budget politics, 199, 205, 207, 218–219, 224–225, 236–238, 241
Senate Commerce Committee, 49
Senate Energy and Natural Resources Committee, 45, 48
  energy legislation, 147, 149, 153, 154, 156
Senate Environment and Public Works Committee, 45, 68, 151
Senate Finance Committee
  budget process, 99
  Bush tax plan, 255–257, 261–262
  Clinton budget politics, 201, 203, 205, 219, 239, 240, 241
  energy legislation, 147, 148, 150, 153, 155, 156
  legislative politics, 45, 48, 50
  prescription drug legislation, 163–165, 167, 169, 174
Senate Foreign Relations Committee, 48
Senate Governmental Affairs Committee, 45, 93
Senate Health, Education, Labor and Pensions Committee, 45
Senate Judiciary Committee, 45, 50, 121, 190

Senate Labor Committee, 50, 190
Senate legislative process, 1–7, 43–72
  amendment rules and
    consequences, 62–67
  bill introduction, 43–44
  bill referral, 44–49, 269
  budget politics. *See* Budget process
  bypassing committees, 47–49,
    121–122, 135, 269
  clean air legislation as example,
    1–4
  committee decision making, 45–46
  committee jurisdictions, 45
  committee system, 5–6
  consultation process, 52–54
  current procedures, 5, 10–11,
    268–271
  early procedures, 5–6
  executive summits. *See* Summits
  extended debate and cloture,
    67–72
  floor procedure, 6, 61–72
  House compared, 43, 140–141
  legislative outcomes, 271–276
  multiple referral, 44–45, 116–118
  omnibus bills. *See* Omnibus
    legislation
  postcommittee adjustments,
    49–51, 121, 135
  reasons for changes, 6–7, 108
  reconciling House-Senate
    differences. *See* Reconciliation
    procedures
  reorganization of committees, 95
  scheduling legislation, 51–61
  "sense of the Senate" resolutions,
    200
  tax policy. *See* Tax legislation
  unanimous consent agreements, 2,
    43, 57–61
  unorthodox procedures effect on,
    72, 281–287
  use of special procedures and
    practices 106–107
  See also specific legislation
Senate Public Works and
  Environment Committee, 2
Senate Public Works Committee, 1
"Sense of the Senate" resolutions, 200
September 11, 2001, terrorist attacks,
  18–19, 23, 47, 85

Sequential referral, 13, 14, 21
Sequestration process, 103
Sessions, Jeff, 53
Shays, Chris, 218
Shays-Meehan bill, 32, 33, 74
Shelby, Richard, 53, 192
Shuster, Bud, 237
Slaughter, Louise, 171–172
Smith, Nick, 179
Snowe, Olympia
  Bush tax plan, 258, 260–263
  prescription drug legislation, 164,
    175
Social programs funding, 257
Social Security
  Bush budget politics, 250, 259
  Clinton budget politics, 203, 209
  funding mechanism, 95, 96
  legislative politics, 48, 51, 67, 69,
    130
Solomon, Gerald B. H., 33, 199, 200
Souder, Mark, 228
Speaker of the House
  appointment of conferees, 76, 77
  bill referral, 12–16, 268–269
  power and authority, 37, 40, 111
  rules suspension, 24
Special rules, 23, 25–35, 60, 122–125,
  134, 270
Specter, Arlen, 254
Sperling, Gene, 236
Split referral, 13, 14
Spratt, John, 236, 241, 255
Stabenow, Debbie, 163, 164, 168
Staff increases, 278
Standing committees
  creation and role, 5–6
  *See also specific House and Senate
    committee names*
Stark, Pete, 167
START II, 54
State Department, 54, 56, 57
Stenholm, Charles W., 203, 225, 251,
  252
Stockman, David, 113
Structured rules, 26, 124, 136
Subcommittees
  appointment of chairs, 111
  reorganization of, 95
Subconferences, 81
Substitute bills, 21

Summits, 41
  Clinton budget politics, 136,
    221–229, 243
  disadvantages, 280
  purpose and use, 102–105,
    130–131, 229, 271
  as standard practice, 5, 91–92
Sunset provisions, 94
Sunshine rules, 79, 111, 132
Superfund, 127
Supplemental appropriations bills,
  96, 97
Suspension of rules, 23–25, 56, 281

Task forces, 20, 134, 276, 277
Tauzin, Bill
  energy legislation, 139
  medical malpractice caps, 188
  prescription drug legislation, 164,
    166, 167, 170, 174, 177
Tax legislation, 248–267
  budget politics, 99, 104, 128
  Clinton program, 198
  conference negotiations, 78, 79
  energy policy and, 143
  House politics, 10, 22, 23, 34, 35,
    74, 122
  pay-as-you-go requirement, 129 *n*8
  Senate politics, 10, 50, 63–65, 69,
    70
  2001 tax cuts, 248–259, 265–267
  2003 tax cuts, 259–263
  unorthodox practices, 263–264,
    285
Telecommunications legislation, 54,
  127, 135
Ten Commandments display, 28
Term limits
  committee chairs, 132, 136
  constitutional amendment, 33
Terrorism insurance bill, 77, 85
Terrorist attacks, 18–19, 23, 47, 85
Thomas, Bill
  Bush tax plan, 258, 261, 263
  energy legislation, 141, 143
  prescription drug legislation, 166,
    170, 174, 176
Thompson, Tommy G., 163, 175,
  178–179
Thurmond, Strom, 68
Tie votes, 40

Tobacco litigation, 63
Tobacco taxes, 64, 135, 240
Torture (of prisoners) legislation,
  48–49, 80, 85, 87
Trade legislation, 12, 13, 41, 44–45,
  53, 78, 92, 102
Transportation legislation, 34, 45, 78,
  79, 83, 85, 86, 237
Transportation Secretary, 24
Treasury Secretary, 104
Trial lawyers, 186
"2–1" rule, 78

Unanimous consent agreements
  (UCAs)
  amendment requirements, 63
  clean air legislation, 2
  Senate practice, 5, 43, 44, 51–52,
    56–61, 72, 270
Unfunded mandates legislation, 39
Union Calendar, 23
United Seniors Association, 174
Unorthodox lawmaking, 105–138,
  268–288
  assessment, 8, 42, 72, 90, 283–287
  budget process changes, 112–113
  current procedures, 268–271
  decision making affected by, 91,
    276–283
  evolution of altered practices,
    116–131
  frequency of use of special
    procedures, 105–107
  hostile political climate as impetus,
    91–92, 113–116
  House reforms, 110–112
  legislative outcomes, 271–276
  reasons for changes, 108
  in Republican Congress after 1994,
    131–138
  Senate changes, 108–110
Upper Housatonic Valley National
  Heritage Area Act, 24
Urban aid, 69
USA PATRIOT Act, 23, 75, 85
U.S. Chamber of Commerce, 201
Utah, 57

Vessel Hull Design Protection
  Amendments of 2005, 57
Veterans Administration, 167

Veterans legislation, 85, 224, 254
Vetoes
    overriding of, 89–90
    pocket veto, 89
    veto bargaining, 84–86, 103
Vice president, 49 *n*2
Victims' Rights bill, 61
Voice vote, 39, 57
Voinovich, George, 260, 261
Voter registration legislation, 68,
    127
Voting Rights Act, 9 *n*3

Walker, Robert, 225, 226
Warner, John, 64
Waxman, Henry, 2, 155
Welfare reauthorization legislation,
    22, 70

Welfare reform, 97 *n*5
    Clinton budget politics, 8, 216, 218,
        220, 221, 224, 229, 235, 236,
        239–242
    legislative politics, 14, 21, 30, 33,
        84, 102
Whistleblowers, 47, 56
Wilson, Charles, 203
Wolfensberger, Don, 34, 35
Women, military service, 22
Workforce Investment Act, 30
"Wrap up," 5, 57
Wright, Jim, 79
Wu, David, 178
Wyden, Ron, 53, 54

Young, Bill, 229
Y2K legislation, 49, 51, 67, 69